kullu tamām!

تمام

تمام

Manfred Woidich
Rabha Heinen-Nasr

kullu tamām!

An Introduction to Egyptian Colloquial Arabic

The American University in Cairo Press
Cairo New York

The American University in Cairo Press
113 Sharia Kasr el Aini, Cairo, Egypt
420 Fifth Avenue, New York, NY 10018
www.aucpress.com

Dar el Kutub No. 16153/03
ISBN 977 424 842 2

Cover design by Andrea El-Akshar / AUC Press Design Center
Printed in Egypt

CONTENTS

Preface

The linguistic situation in the Arab world is characterized by what is often called diglossia, which means that there are two varieties of the Arabic language in use side by side. There is a 'high' variety, called Modern Standard Arabic (MSA), and there are 'low' varieties, mostly referred to as local dialects or colloquials. Whereas MSA does not vary significantly from place to place, the dialects offer a different picture: they differ considerably from region to region and are sometimes mutually incomprehensible. MSA is nobody's mother tongue, has to be learned at school, and is used mainly by the educated for writing purposes and for public speaking. The local dialect, on the other hand, is the speaker's first language for the Arab, and is used for all purposes in daily life.

In our view, there can be no doubt that those who want to have a real command of the Arabic language in all situations and settings need to master both varieties. At Western universities, Arabic was traditionally taught as a classical language, just as Classical Greek or Latin, aiming at the comprehension of classical texts. Nowadays, with the study of Arabic somewhat modernized, students still start with MSA in order to learn how to read and write, and perhaps at a later stage take a course in one of the colloquials to become more familiar with the spoken language. However, attitudes are now changing, and many students want to acquire Arabic as a second language, that is as a spoken language as well that can be used for any purpose, just like any other language in the world. The current argument for beginning with MSA is – apart from some more ideological arguments that we do not want to elaborate on here – that having a good command of MSA would facilitate the acquisition of any colloquial variety whatever. The idea behind this argument is apparently that the colloquials can somehow be derived from MSA and that the latter forms their common base, an idea that is certainly erroneous.

Some now argue that it is better to do things the other way around and begin with a colloquial. Experience teaches us, for example, that it is not easy to abandon established linguistic habits, such as the use of the semantically redundant case and mood endings in MSA (which were probably acquired in an arduous struggle), and switch over to one of the colloquial varieties, which do not have these. Apart from this pedagogical aspect, we believe that a command of any variety of Arabic will in some respects facilitate the acquisition of another one, while in other respects hampering it, and that the more natural way – that is, starting like an Arab with the colloquial as a first variety and learning MSA at a later stage — is at least as promising as the traditional way. It is a well established didactical principle that it is better to start with simple things and add more difficult items gradually. And this principle should be applied to the teaching of

Arabic too: the linguistic structures of the colloquials are simpler to learn than those of MSA and therefore form a good starting point for studying the Arabic language in both varieties.

This is true in particular when we decide not to introduce the Arabic script immediately, but to do this only at a later stage when students have mastered the main phonetic and structural problems Arabic offers. By postponing the Arabic script, we avoid introducing two problems at the same time: a new language and a new writing system. Another reason for using transcription rather than the Arabic script in the beginning is that we did not want to introduce secondary orthographic problems, which inevitably arise out of the fact that there is no established orthography for writing colloquial Arabic in Arabic letters, since the Arabic script is designed for MSA. Moreover, the Arabic writing system offers only limited means for linguistic description – it has, for example, no straightforward way to show and explain elisions and insertions of vowels, so important in the phonology and morphology of the colloquials. Thus, in our mind, there are sufficient grounds to start with a generally accepted phonological transcription for teaching the colloquial, and reserve the introduction of Arabic writing to a later stage.

Starting with the colloquial offers another advantage when it comes to classroom teaching. The student can be confronted with the new language in situations taken from real life, which makes teaching and learning much more attractive.

This is why this elementary course book of Egyptian Colloquial Arabic has been designed in this way: a general phonological introduction that may be used side by side with the first two lessons, the first lessons with dialogues only, then (starting from Lesson V), descriptive texts as well. From Lesson XI onward, the Arabic script as described in Lesson XVII may be introduced. The last four lessons contain more sophisticated texts, with vocabulary taken from newspapers. There are ample pattern drills and other materials for exercise, some of which can easily be done orally in the classroom, others being more suited for homework. The vocabularies, the key the exercises, and the texts on audio CD should help those who want to use this book for self-study.

kullu tamām! has now been used successfully for twelve years in the Department of Arabic Studies at the University of Amsterdam in the Netherlands, in introducing university students to Arabic. After having completed this introductory course, students should not only have a reasonable practical command and a good insight into the structure of an Arabic colloquial but should also be prepared to switch over to Modern Standard Arabic, since they will have become acquainted with quite a few words common in both the colloquial and the Modern Standard language as it is used in the press and other media. Moreover, they will have acquired an elementary knowledge of the Arabic script. Both these facts will, we are sure, facilitate the later acquisition of Modern Standard Arabic.

We wish to express our sincere thanks to several people who helped us greatly in preparing the English version of this book. In first instance, we thank Mrs. Kate McRay, who translated the Dutch text into English with tremendous patience and aptitude, pointing out from time to time errors and careless omissions. We are grateful to Neil Hewison of the AUC press for many corrections and useful hints. And, finally, we thank Robbert Woltering and Sabine Arndt for their assistance with preparing the manuscript. Needless to say, any remaining mistakes and shortcomings, which both learner and teacher inevitably will come across, are entirely our own fault.

INTRODUCTION

A. Writing and pronunciation

The transcription system used in this book adheres to the phonological principle of "one sign equals one sound."

I. Consonants

The following table shows the letters which represent the consonants of the dialect spoken in Cairo. They have been arranged according to the place in the mouth in which they are articulated.

1. Table

Place:[1]	1	2	3	4	5	6	7	8
Manner:								
Plosives								
unvoiced			*t*		*k*	*q*		ʾ
emphatic			*ṭ*					
voiced	*b*		*d*		*g*			
emphatic	*ḅ*		*ḍ*					
Fricatives								
unvoiced		*f*	*s*	*š*	*x*		*ḥ*	*h*
emphatic			*ṣ*					
voiced		*v*	*z*	*ž*	*ġ*		*ɛ*	
emphatic			*ẓ*					
the R-sound			*r*					
emphatic			*ṛ*					
the L-sound			*l*					
emphatic			*ḷ*					
Nasals	*m*		*n*					
emphatic	*ṃ*							
Semi-vowels	*w*			*y*				

---

1 Place of articulation: 1 = with both lips (bilabial), 2 = with the lower lip against the upper teeth (labio-dental), 3 = with the tip of the tongue against the back of the teeth (dento-alveolar), 4 = with the back of the tongue against the hard palate (palato-alveolar and palatal), 5 = with the back of the tongue against the soft palate (velar), 6 = with the back of the tongue against the uvula, 7 = in the pharynx (pharyngeal), 8 = in the glottis (glottal).

2. Pronunciation of consonants

(a) The consonants *b, d, f, k, l, m, n, s, t, v, w, y, z* sound very similar to the corresponding letters in English.

(b) The following consonants are pronounced somewhat differently:

g [g] is a hard *g* as in "game" and "get," e.g., *gamal* "camel," *ṛāgil* "man," *banafsigi* "violet."

ġ [ɣ] is a velar fricative, a voiced version of the *x*, e.g. *Baġdād* "Baghdad," *baġbaġān* "parrot," *ġani* "rich."

h [h] is pronounced *h* at the end of the syllable, and is never silent as in "Brahms," nor guttural as in "loch," e.g. *ʾahwa* "coffee," *ilʾahṛām* "the pyramids."

ḥ [ħ] is an unvoiced fricative which is produced in the pharynx. It occurs automatically if you try to whisper a word beginning with *h* to someone who is standing some distance away from you: "Harry hates history homework," e.g. *Muḥammad* "Muhammed," *Aḥmad* "Ahmed," *Ḥilwān* "Helwan."

q [q] is pronounced like *k* but the sound is post-velar or uvular, meaning that it is produced much farther back in the throat, e.g. *ilQāhira* "Cairo," *ilqurʾān* "the Koran," *qarya* "village."
The *q* only occurs in words which have been borrowed from standard Arabic.

r [r] is dental-alveolar. It is clearly articulated with the tip of the tongue, e.g. *rigl* "foot," *bīra* "beer," *nūr* "light," *Luʾṣur* "Luxor," *Maṣr* "Egypt" or "Cairo."

š [ʃ] is pronounced like *sh* in "ship" and "shoe."

x [x] is an unvoiced velar fricative which sounds like the Scots *ch* in "loch," e.g. *xōx* "peach," *tixīn* "thick," "fat."

ž [ʒ] sounds like the English *s* in "leisure," "pleasure." In Arabic *ž* only occurs in words of foreign origin, e.g. *žakitta* "jacket," *garāž* "garage."

ɛ [ʕ] is a voiced fricative which is pronounced in the pharynx, e.g. *ɛaṛabi* "Arabic," *Bur Saɛīd* "Port Said," *isSaɛudiyya* "Saudi Arabia."

It's important to make a clear distinction between *ḥ*, *x* and *h*:

wāḥid	:	*wāxid*	"one"	:	"taken"
naḥla	:	*naxla*	"bee"	:	"date palm"
ḥall	:	*xall*	"solution"	:	"vinegar"
nahla	:	*naxla*	a woman's name	:	"date palm"
fahm	:	*faḥm*	"understanding"	:	"charcoal"

The sign ʾ is known as a *hamza*. It is actually a glottal stop [ʔ] which occurs in English in words beginning with a vowel, e.g. (ʾ)arm, (ʾ)other. In Arabic the *hamza* can occur at the beginning, middle or end of a word. It is treated as a full consonant in its own right and must therefore be carefully enunciated, e.g. *ʾarḍ* "earth," *ʾōḍa* "room," *suʾāl* "question," *maʾli* "fried," *laʾ* "no!"

However, the pronunciation of the *hamza* can be omitted under the influence of the preceding word. For instance the *hamza* is clearly pronounced in *ʾibni* "my son," but one says *bēt ibni* "my son's house." Words of this type are listed in the vocabulary without a *hamza*, e.g. *ism* "noun," "name," *uxt* "sister," *umm* "mother."

It is also important to make a clear distinction between ع and ʾ:

عamal	:	*ʾamal*	"work"	:	"hope"
عāl	:	*ʾāl*	"excellent"	:	"to say"
عīd	:	*ʾīd*	"feast"	:	"hand"
suʾāl	:	*suعāl*	"question"	:	"cough"

(c) A dot written under a letter indicates **emphasis** or **velarization**. In other words, the sound is pronounced with the back of the tongue raised and the middle of the tongue lowered. The tip of the tongue becomes somewhat wider and thicker and touches the back of the teeth and the alveolum. This gives a duller sound to the consonant, which affects the neighboring vowels. This emphasis occurs principally with *ṭ, ḍ, ṣ, ẓ*, but other consonants such as *ḷ, ṛ, ḅ* and *ṃ* can also be velarized, e.g. *ṛāgil* "man," *Aḷḷāh* "God," *ḅāḅa* "papa," *ṃāṃa* "mama," *ṃayya* "water." Here below are some examples of minimal pairs:

ṭifl	:	*tifl*	"child"	: "dregs of tea"
bāṭ	:	*bāt*	"armpit"	: "to spend the night"
ṣāb	:	*sāb*	"to hit"	: "to allow"
iḍḍāni	:	*iddāni*	"lamb (meat)"	: "he gave me"
gāṛi	:	*gāri*	"my neighbor"	: "current"
ṛāyiḫ	:	*rāgiع*	"going"	: "returning"
baṣṣ	:	*bass*	"to look"	: "only"
ḍall	:	*dall*	"to lose the way"	: "to point at"

(d) All consonants can be either short or long. In this book, the long consonants are written as double consonants, and when correctly pronounced the doubling can clearly be heard:

mudarris	"teacher"	*izzayyak*	"how are you?"
isSadāt	"Sadat"	*Muḫammad*	"Muḫammad"
iddinya	"the world"	*igginēna*	"the garden"

II. Vowels

1. Table

a	*e*	*i*	*o*	*u*
ā	*ē*	*ī*	*ō*	*ū*

All vowels can either be short or long. Long vowels are written with a dash above them.

Moreover, in some words the emphatic *ạ* [ɑ] and *ạ̄* [ɑː] also occur.

2. Pronunciation of vowels

a tends to be pronounced as è [æ], but is more centralized and less open, closer to [ɐ], except when it occurs before or after emphatic consonants (→ I.2.c). In such cases, *a* is pronounced farther back in the mouth as [ɑ], e.g. *baṣṣ* [bɑs̴s̴] "to look," *ṣabr* [s̴ɑbr] "patience." When it occurs before or after ع or ḥ, it is pronounced more open as [a], e.g. [muħammɐd] "Muhammed."

ā tends to be pronounced as èè [æː], but is more centralized and less open, closer to [ɐː], except when it occurs before or after emphatic consonants (→ I.2.c). In such cases, *ā* is pronounced farther back in the mouth as [ɑː], e.g. *fāṛ* [fɑːr] "mouse," *ṭāṣa* [t̴ɑːsɑ] "frying pan"

e is pronounced like the short *i* and derives from a shortened *ē*, e.g. *betna* [bɪtna] "our house" (→ III.IV.3)

i is similar to the *i* in English as in "bid" [ɪ] , e.g. *dinya* "world"

o is pronounced like the short *u* and derives from a shortened *ō*, e.g. *lonha* [lʊnha] "her color" (→ III.IV.3)

u is similar to the *u* [ʊ] in English as in "put," e.g. *kullu tamām* "everything's okay"

ə is a short vowel which lies between *e* and *i* [ə] (schwa-sound). Native speakers of Egyptian Arabic insert it automatically after the second consonant when three consonants follow one another (→ III.I), e.g. *bintᵊ tanya* "another girl," *ibnᵊ ʿammi* "my cousin."

III. Other signs

‿ indicates that a vowel has been elided (→ I. I and II. I).

\- between two words indicates that they are linked as in the case of the negative *ma-truḥš* "don't go" or with the prepositions *bi-*, *li-*, *fi-* and the following noun, e.g. *fi-Maṣr* "in Egypt," *li-Ḥasan* "for Ḥasan." If elision of the vowels *-i-* or *-u-* occurs in the noun following the preposition, the sign - is retained, e.g. *li-Mḥammad* "for Muḥammad."

[ ] The International Phonetic Alphabet is presented between square bracket as in [æ].

B. Alphabetical order

The alphabetical order used in this book is as follows:

a	*ɔ*	*b*	*d*	*ḍ*	*f*	*g*	*ġ*	*h*
ḫ	*i*	*k*	*l*	*m*	*n*	*q*	*r*	*s*
ṣ	*š*	*t*	*ṭ*	*u*	*v*	*w*	*x*	*y*
z	*ẓ*	*ž*	*ɛ*					

In the case of the vowels, each short vowel occurs first, followed by the corresponding long vowel:

a ā e ē i ī o ō u ū

C. Abbreviations and references

adv.	adverb
adj.	adjective
c.	collective
fem./ f.	feminine
imperf.	imperfect
inf.	infinitive
masc./ m.	masculine
n.u.	nomen unitatis
pl.	plural
perf.	perfect
sing.	single
w	*wāḫid* "someone" s/o
ḫ	*ḫāga* "something" s/th

The lessons are referred to in Roman numerals and the Grammar sections in smaller Roman numerals: III.V means Lesson III, section V.

D. Some formal expressions

Many of the expressions in (A) are usually replied to as shown in (B):

Greetings:

A: *ṣabāḫ ilxēr!*	"good morning!"
B: *ṣabāḫ innūr!*	"good morning!"
A: *masāɔ ilxēr!*	"good evening!"
B: *masāɔ innūr!*	"good evening!"
A: *issalāmu ɛalēkum!*	"peace be upon you!"
B: *wi ɛalēkum issalām wi ṛaḫmatu‿ḷḷāh wi baṛakātu!*	"peace be upon you, and God's compassion and his blessings!"

A: *nahāṛak* (m.) *saɛīd* *nahāṛik* (f.) *saɛīd*	"may your day be happy!"
B: *nahāṛak* (m.) *saɛīd mubāṛak* *nahāṛik* (f.) *saɛīd mubāṛak*	"may your day be happy and blessed (too)!"

Eating and drinking:

A: *haniyyan!* (drinking)	"I hope you enjoyed it!"
A: *bi‿lhana wi‿ššifa!* (eating)	"I hope you enjoyed your meal!"
B: *Aḷḷa‿yhannīk* (m.)! *Aḷḷa‿yhannīki* (f.)!	"It was lovely, thank you!"
A: *sufṛa dayma!*	"May there always be food upon your table!"
B: *dāmit ḫayātak* (m.)! *dāmit ḫayātik* (f.)!	"Long may you live!"

Saying "goodbye":

A: *maɛa‿ssalāma!*	"Farewell!" (said by the person staying behind)
B: *Aḷḷa‿ysallimak* (m.)! *Aḷḷa‿ysallimik* (f.)!	"May God be with you!"

Congratulating:

A: *mabrūk!*	"Congratulations!"
B: *Aḷḷa‿ybārik fīk* (m.)! *Aḷḷa‿ybārik fīki*(f.)!	"God bless you!"

Thanking:

A: *šukṛan!*	"Thank you"
B: *ɛafwan!*	"Not at all!"

Wishing people well on special occasions:

A: *kullᵊ sana w‿inta ṭayyib* (m.)! *kullᵊ sana w‿nti ṭayyiba* (f.)!	"May every year find you in good health!"
B: w‿*inta ṭayyib* (m.)! w‿*inti ṭayyiba* (f.)!	"And you too!"

E. Other useful expressions

	masc.	fem.	pl.
come!	*taع̨āla!*	*taع̨āli!*	*taع̨ālu!*
go away!	*imši!*	*imši!*	*imšu!*
ask!	*isʾal!*	*isʾali!*	*isʾalu!*
take!	*xud!*	*xudi!*	*xudu!*
give (to me)!	*hāt!*	*hāti!*	*hātu!*
bring!	*hāt!*	*hāti!*	*hātu!*
take care!	*xalli bālak!*	*xalli bālik!*	*xallu balku!*
look out!	*ḥāsib!*	*ḥasbi!*	*ḥasbu!*
look!	*buṣṣ!*	*buṣṣi!*	*buṣṣu!*
shut up!	*iskut!*	*iskuti!*	*iskutu!*
I don't know	*miš ع̨ārif*	*miš ع̨arfa*	*miš ع̨arfīn*
I don't understand	*miš fāhim*	*miš fahma*	*miš fahmīn*
what did you say?	*afandim?*	*afandim?*	*afandim?*
sorry!	*ʾāsif!*	*ʾasfa!*	*ʾasfīn!*
excuse me!	*la muʾaxza!*	*la muʾaxza!*	*la muʾaxza!*
	ma-tʾaxiznīš!	*ma-tʾaxzinīš!*	*ma-tʾaxzunīš!*
	ma-ع̨lešš!	*ma-ع̨lešš!*	*ma-ع̨lešš!*
come on!	*yaḷḷa!*	*yaḷḷa!*	*yaḷḷa!*
don't worry!	*ma-txafš!*	*ma-txafīš!*	*ma-txafūš!*
no problem!	*miš muškila!*	*miš muškila!*	*miš muškila!*
it doesn't matter!	*ma-ع̨lešš!*	*ma-ع̨lešš!*	*ma-ع̨lešš!*
shame on you!	*ixṣᵊ ع̨alēk!*	*ixṣᵊ ع̨alēki!*	*ixṣᵊ ع̨alēku!*

LESSON I

DIALOGUES

ismak ᵓē?

A: *ḥiwāṛ bēn Sāmi, wi Ḥasan, wi Maha, wi Samya*

Sāmi: *ana‿smi Sāmi. w‿inta, ismak ᵓē ?*
Ḥasan: *ana‿smi Ḥasan. w‿inti, ismik ᵓē ?*
Maha: *ana‿smi Maha.*
Sāmi: *w‿inti kamān ismik Maha ?*
Samya: *lā, ana‿smi Samya.*

B: *ḥiwāṛ bēn Sāmi wi Maha*

Sāmi: *da mīn ya Maha ?*
Maha: *da ṭālib.*
Sāmi: *ismu ᵓē ?*
Maha: *ismu Ḥasan.*
Sāmi: *wi di mīn ya Maha ?*
Maha: *di ṭālíba.*
Sāmi: *ismaha ᵓē ?*
Maha: *ismaha Samya.*

inta ᵓē?

C: *ḥiwāṛ bēn Maha wi Samya*

Maha: *huwwa Sāmi da ṭālib, ya Samya ?*
Samya: *lā, da mudarris.*
Maha: *wi di, hiyya di ṭālíba ?*
Samya: *aywa, di ṭālíba.*
Maha: *huwwa Ḥasan kamān mudarris ?*
Samya: *lā, da miš mudarris. da ṭālib.*

huwwa mawgūd?

D: *ḥiwāṛ bēn Sāmi wi Samya*

Sāmi: *da mīn ya Samya ?*
Samya: *da‿bni Samīr.*
Sāmi: *wi di mīn ?*
Samya: *di binti Mirvat.*
Sāmi: *Aḥmad gōzik mawgūd?*
Samya: *lā, da miš mawgūd, da‿msāfir Iskindiriyya.*

VOCABULARY

ʾē	what?
ana	I
aywa	yes
bint	daughter; girl
bēn	between
da	that (masc.)
di	that (fem.)
fēn	where?
fi	in
gidd	grandfather
gōz	husband
hiyya	she
huwwa	he
ḥiwāṛ	dialogue
ibn	son
ibni	my son
inta	you (masc.)
inti	you (fem.)
Iskindiriyya	Alexandria
ism	name
ismaha	her name
ismak	your (masc.) name
ismi	my name
ismik	your (fem.) name
ismu	his name
kamān	also
lā ~ laʾ ~ laʾʾa	no!
lākin	but
mawgūd	present, here
misāfir	(gone) on a journey
miš	not
mudarris	teacher
muhandis	engineer
mīn	who?
sitt	woman, lady; grandmother
ṣuġayyar	little, small
ṭabʿan	naturally, of course
ṭālib	student (masc.)
ṭāliba	student (fem.)
umm	mother
uxt	sister
wi	and
ya ...	vocative particle (used when calling someone)
ʿamm	uncle (paternal)
ʿammik	your (fem.) uncle

GRAMMAR

I. Vowels

The sign ‿ means that the vowel with which the first word ends and the vowel with which the second word begins should be joined together so that the two words sound like one word. This process is known as "elision" and it usually occurs when the second word begins with the vowel *i-*.

wi + inta	> *w‿inta* (pronounced: *winta*)	and you
huwwa + ismu ʾē?	> *huwwá‿smu ʾē?*	what's his name?

Elision usually occurs when one is speaking at normal speed without pausing between words. It does not occur in slow speech.

To show that elision should **not** take place a *hamza* is placed before the second word, for example, *da ʾibni* "this is my son."

II. Personal pronouns

1. Independent personal pronouns

In Arabic there are two kinds of personal pronoun: dependent and independent.

Independent personal pronouns (singular)

huwwa	he	*inta*	you (masc.)	*ana*	I
hiyya	she	*inti*	you (fem.)		

The independent pronouns (I, you, he, and she) can stand alone, for example as the subject of a sentence:

ana ṭālib "I student" = "I (am) a student"

The second person singular "you" has two forms in Arabic depending on the gender of the person being addressed: *inta* (masc.), *inti* (fem.)

2. Dependent personal pronouns

The dependent form of a personal pronoun consists of a suffix which is added to nouns, prepositions, and verbs. When added to nouns, the suffix can be compared in function to a possessive adjective in English (my, your, his, her) and is therefore known as a possessive suffix.

Possessive suffixes following -CC

huwwa	*-u*	*ism-u*	his name
hiyya	*-aha*	*ism-aha*	her name
inta	*-ak*	*ism-ak*	your (masc.) name
inti	*-ik*	*ism-ik*	your (fem.) name
ana	*-i*	*ism-i*	my name

These endings are used if the noun ends in two consonants (-CC), for example: *ism* "name," *bint* "daughter," *ɛamm* "uncle," *uxt* "sister," *umm* "mother," *gidd* "grandfather," *ibn* "son."

For extra emphasis the appropriate independent personal pronoun can be used after the possessive suffix:

hiyya di bintik ? – aywa, di binti ***ʔana!***	"is that your daughter?" – "yes, that's **my** daughter!"
da giddaha ***hiyya****, miš giddak* ***inta***	"this is **her** grandfather, not **your** grandfather"

III. Sentence structure: nominal sentences

1. Word order

Subject and predicate are placed next to each other without a copula. In other words, unlike in English, the verb "to be" is omitted. In constructions of this type the predicate can be a noun, a participle, or an adjective:

di + *ṭālíba*	→	*di ṭālíba*
that + student	→	"that is a (female) student"

This only happens in the present tense. In the past and future, a copula is required (→ V.V and X.IV).

2. Negation
To form a negative sentence, the word *miš* is used in front of the predicate:

huwwa mudarris →	*huwwa miš mudarris*
"he's a teacher"	"he's not a teacher"

To make a contrast, *lākin* "but" is used:

di miš uxti lākin binti "this is not my sister, but my daughter"

3. Questions
(a) Unlike in English, interrogatives are frequently placed at the end of a sentence: *ismak ʾē* "what is your name?" [lit. "your name [is] what?"]. However, *mīn da?* "who's that?" is used just as frequently as *da mīn*, [lit. "that [is] who?"].

(b) The third person pronouns *huwwa* and *hiyya* can also be used to introduce a question:

huwwa‿nta ṭālib? "are you a student?" *hiyya di ʾuxtak?* "is that your sister?"

IV. Vocatives

When someone is being called or addressed, the word *ya* is used before the person's name or title. It is similar to the word "o" in English; but whereas "O Sir" or "O my father" are no longer used in modern English, *ya* is regularly used in Arabic:

ya Ḥasan! ya Maḥmūd! ya Samya! ya duktūr!

V. Feminine endings

The feminine ending is shown by the suffix *-a* which is added to nouns and adjectives. It can also be added to participles (→ VI. III).

ṣuġáyyar	+	*a*	→	*ṣuġayyára*	small, little (fem.)
mudárris	+	*a*	→	*mudarrísa*	female teacher
muhándis	+	*a*	→	*muhandísa*	woman engineer
ṭālib	+	*a*	→	*ṭālíba*	female student

Pay special attention to the way the stress shifts: *mudárris*, but *mudarrísa* (→ IV.I and II).

Useful Expressions

enough, leave it!	*balāš*
that's enough!	*kifāya kida*
everything's fine!	*kullu tamām*
good!	*kuwayyis*
sorry!	*la muʾaxza*
don't worry!	*ma-ɛalešš ~ ma-ɛlešš*
it doesn't matter!	*ma-ɛalešš ~ ma-ɛlešš*
that's excellent!	*tamām kida*
okay	*ṭayyib ~ ṭab*
come on, hurry up!	*ṭab yaḷḷa*
it doesn't matter!	*zayyᵊ baɛḍu*
slowly, take your time!	*ɛala mahlak* (masc.), *ɛala mahlik* (fem.)

Egyptian Place Names

Abbasiyya	*ilɛAbbasiyya*	Luxor	*Luʾṣur*
Agami	*ilɛAgami*	Maadi	*ilMaɛādi*
Ain Shams	*ɛĒn Šams*	Mar Girgis	*Mari Girgis*
Ain Sukhna	*ilɛĒn isSuxna*	Minya	*ilMinya*
Alexandria	*Iskindiriyya*	Mogamma	*ilMugammaɛ*
Aswan	*ʾAswān*	Mohandiseen	*ilMuhandisīn*
Asyut	*ʾAsyūṭ*	Moqattam	*ilMuʾaṭṭam*
Azhar	*ilʾAzhaṛ*	Mount Sinai	*Gabal Mūsa*
Bahariyya	*ilBaḥariyya*	Munira	*ilMunīra*
Basata	*Baṣāṭa*	Nag Hammadi	*Nagɛᵊ Ḥammādi*
Beni Suef	*Bani‿Swēf*	the Nile	*inNīl*
Bulaq	*Bulāʾ*	Nuweiba	*Nuwēbaɛ*
Cairo	*ilQāhíra; Maṣr*	Port Said	*Bur Saɛīd*
Corniche	*ikKurnīš*	Qasr al-Ainy	*ilʾAṣr ilɛĒni*
Dakhla	*idDaxla*	Qena	*ʾIna*
Damietta	*Dumyāṭ*	Ras Mohammed	*Rāṣ Muḥammad*
Doqqi	*idDuʾʾi*	Rhoda	*irRōḍa*
Edfu	*Idfu*	Saqqara	*iṣṢaʾʾāra*
El-Alamein	*ilɛAlamēn*	Ramses Street	*šāriɛ Ramsīs*
El-Arish	*ilɛArīš*	Sharm el-Sheikh	*Šarm išŠēx*
Esna	*Isna*	Shubra	*Šubṛa*
Farafra	*ilFaṛafra*	Sinai	*Sīna*
Fayoum	*ilFayyūm*	Siwa	*Sīwa*
Garden City	*Gardin Siti*	Sohag	*Suhāg*
Giza	*igGīza*	Suez	*isSuwēs*
Heliopolis	*Maṣr igGidīda*	Taba	*Ṭāba*
Helwan	*Ḥilwān*	Tahrir	*itTaḥrīr*
Hurghada	*ilĠardaʾa*	Talaat Harb	*Ṭalɛat Ḥarb*
Imbaba	*Imbāba*	Tanta	*Ṭanṭa*
Ismailia	*ilIsmaɛiliyya*	Tell al-Amarna	*Tall ilɛAmarna*
Karnak	*ilKarnak*	Wadi Natrun	*Wādi‿nNaṭrūn*
Kharga	*ilXarga*	Zagazig	*izZaʾazīʾ*
Kom Ombo	*Komumbu*	Zamalek	*izZamālik*

EXERCISES

I. Add suitable possessive suffixes to the nouns in the table below.

	bint	*ibn*	*gidd*	*ꜥamm*	*umm*	*uxt*
inta						
huwwa						
hiyya						
inti						
ana						

II. Having added suffixes to the nouns, write them into the table in their usual order: his, her, your (masc.), your (fem.), my.

	bint	*ibn*	*gidd*	*ꜥamm*	*umm*	*uxt*

III. Answer the questions below, using the words from Exercise I.

huwwa da ꜥammik? - *aywa, da ꜥammi* ~ *lā, da miš ꜥammi*

1. *huwwa da giddak?* - *lā,* ____________________
2. *hiyya di ʾummu?* - *aywa,* ____________________
3. *hiyya di ʾuxtaha?* - *lā,* ____________________
4. *hiyya di bintik?* - *aywa,* ____________________

5. *huwwa da‿bnaha?* - *lā,* ______________________________

6. *hiyya di ᵓummi?* - *aywa,* ____________________________

IV. That's not **my** daughter, that's **your** daughter! Answer the questions below.

hiyya di bintak? - *lā, di miš binti* ***ᵓana****, di bint****ak inta****!*

1. *hiyya di ᵓuxtak?* - *lā,* ______________________________

2. *huwwa da ᵓibnik?* - *lā,* ______________________________

3. *huwwa da ع̣ammik?* - *lā,* ______________________________

4. *hiyya di ᵓummak?* - *lā,* ______________________________

5. *huwwa da giddak?* - *lā,* ______________________________

6. *huwwa da ᵓismak?* - *lā,* ______________________________

V. Confusion over who's who! Give the correct reply.

huwwa da giddaha? - *lā, da ع̣amm-****aha***

1. *hiyya di ᵓuxtaha?* - *lā, di bint*_______

2. *hiyya di bintaha?* - *lā, di ᵓumm*______

3. *huwwa da ع̣ammaha?* - *lā, da‿bn*_______

4. *hiyya di ᵓummaha?* - *lā, di sitt*________

VI. Where is your ...? Fill in the blanks.

1. *ya‿Mḥammad, ibn*____ *fēn?*
2. *ya Samya, umm*_____ *fēn?*
3. *ya Fawzi, gidd*______ *fēn?*
4. *ya Maha, ibn*________ *fēn?*
5. *ya ع̣Ali, ع̣amm*_____ *fēn?*
6. *ya Ḥasan, uxt*_____ *fēn?*
7. *ya Muna, bint*_____ *fēn?*
8. *ya ع̣Abdu, sitt*_____ *fēn?*

VII. Their relatives are in different towns. Fill in the blanks.

1. *Ḫasan, ع̧amm____ f‿Iskindiriyya.*
2. *Maḫmūd, umm______ fi‿gGīza.*
3. *Aḫmad, ع̧amm______ fi-Luʔṣur.*
4. *ana, ع̧amm_________ fi-ʔAswān.*
5. *Maha, bint___ fi-Bur Saع̧īd.*
6. *Samya, ibn____ fi‿sSuwēs.*
7. *Mirvat, uxt___ fi‿lFayyūm.*
8. *Aḫmad, bint_____ fi Sīwa.*

VIII. Answer the questions using *kamān* "as well."

Sāmi mudarris, wi Samya? - *Samya mudarrisa kamān*

1. *Sāmi muhandis, wi Samya?* - ____________________
2. *gōzi mudarris, wi ʔuxtak?* - ____________________
3. *Ḫasan ṭālib, wi Samya?* - ____________________
4. *ع̧ammik mawgūd, wi ʔuxtik?* - ____________________
5. *ibnik ṭālib, wi bintik?* - ____________________
6. *giddi mudarris, wi ʔummik?* - ____________________

IX. He isn't a ... and she isn't one either! Complete the sentences.

Sāmi miš ṭālib, wi Randa kamān miš ṭālíba.

1. *huwwa miš mawgūd, wi ʔuxtu* ____________________
2. *hiyya miš mudarrisa, wi bintaha* ____________________
3. *ana miš muhandisa, wi ʔibni* ____________________
4. *Samya miš mawgūda, wi ع̧ammaha* ____________________
5. *inti miš ṭālíba, wi Ḫasan* ____________________
6. *inta miš mudarris, wi hiyya* ____________________

LESSON II

DIALOGUES

minēn?

A. *ḫiwāṛ maɛa Sāmi*

Sāmi: *inta‿mnēn?*
John: *ana min Kanada.*
Sāmi: *yaɛni‿nta kanadi?*
John: *aywa, ana kanadi.*
Sāmi: *w‿inti‿mnēn?*
Kate: *ana min ʔAmrīka.*
Sāmi: *yaɛni‿nti ʔamrikiyya?*
Kate: *aywa ṣaḫḫ, ana ʔamrikiyya.*

B. *ḫiwāṛ bēn Samya, wi Maha, wi Sāmi*

Sāmi: *inti‿mnēn, ya Samya?*
Samya: *ana min Maṣr.*
Sāmi: *w‿inti kamān min Maṣr, ya Maha?*
Maha: *aywa, ana kamān min Maṣr.*
Sāmi: *yaɛni‿ntu litnēn min Maṣr?*
Samya: *aywa ṣaḫḫ, iḫna litnēn min Maṣr, iḫna maṣriyyīn.*

C. *ḫiwāṛ bēn Mirvat wi Sāmi*

Mirvat: *dōl minēn ya Sāmi?*
Sāmi: *dōl ṭalaba ʔingilīz.*
Mirvat: *ismuhum ʔē ?*
Sāmi: *da‿smu Mike, wi di‿smaha Janet.*
Mirvat: *ya-taṛa humma‿mnēn?*
Sāmi: *min Durham wi min Manchester.*

afandim?

D. *ḫiwāṛ bēn Samya‿w Sāmi*

Samya: *afandim? ma-fhimtiš! humma‿mnēn?*
Sāmi: *humma litnēn min Maṣr.*
Samya: *wi dōl? dōl minēn?*
Sāmi: *dōl miš min Maṣr, dōl ʔagānib.*
Samya: *ya-taṛa humma‿kwayyisīn fi‿lɛaṛabi?*
Sāmi: *kuwayyisīn wi šaṭrīn ʔawi.*

VOCABULARY

afandim	pardon
ʾagnabi	foreigner; foreign
ʾagānib	foreigners
ʾahwa	coffee
ʾAmrīka	America
ʾamrīki	American
ʾawi	very
bakkallim	I speak
biyikkallim	he speaks
dōl	these, those
gamīl	pretty, beautiful
gibna	cheese
humma	they
iḫna	we
ingilīz	English people
intu	you (pl.)
Kanada	Canada
kanadi	Canadian
kuwayyis	good
litnēn	both
luġa	language
ma-fhimtiš	I didn't understand
Maṣr	Egypt; Cairo
maṣri	Egyptian
maɛa	with
min	from
minēn	where from?
ṣaḫḫ	right
šāṭir	clever
ṭarabēẓa, -āt	table
tilifōn, -āt	telephone
ṭalaba	students
ya-ṭara	I wonder
yaɛni	that means
ɛaṛabi	Arabic

GRAMMAR

I. The Vowels *-i-* and *-u-*

If a word ends with a vowel, an *-i-* or an *-u-* can be omitted from the first syllable of the following word. This is called elision of the *-i-* or *-u-*, and it is shown by the sign ‿ :

inta + *minēn*	→	*inta‿mnēn*	pronounced	*in-tam-nēn*
da + *misāfir*	→	*da‿msāfir*	pronounced	*dam-sā-fir*
di + *kuwayyisa*	→	*di‿kwayyisa*	pronounced	*dik-way-yisa*

For further examples of elision see lessons IV. II and V. IV.

II. Personal pronouns

1. The plural **independent personal pronouns** are as follows:

humma	they	*intu* ~ *intum*	you (pl.)	*iḫna*	we

The following table shows all forms of the independent personal pronoun, singular and plural:

huwwa	he	*inta*	you (masc.)	*ana*	I
hiyya	she	*inti*	you (fem.)		
humma	they	*intu* ~ *intum*	you (pl.)	*iḫna*	we

2. The **plural possessive suffixes** after a word ending in two consonants (-CC) are:

humma	***-uhum***	*umm-**uhum***	their mother
intu	***-uku***	*umm-**uku***	your (pl.) mother
iḫna	***-ina***	*umm-**ina***	our mother

Note that *-ukum* can be used instead of *-uku*, e.g., *ʕammukum* "your (pl.) uncle," but the ending *-uhum* never changes. Pay attention to the shifting stress (→ IV. I and II):

úmmi	but	*ummína*
bíntak	but	*bintúku* ~ *bintúkum*
gíddu	but	*giddáha*

The following table shows all forms of suffix: singular and plural:

3rd person		2nd person		1st person	
-u	his	***-ak***	your (masc.)	***-i***	my
-aha	her	***-ik***	your (fem.)		
-uhum	their	***-uku***	your (pl.)	***-ina***	our
		-ukum			

Here is an example of a noun followed by the various forms of the possessive suffix:

*bint**u***	*bint**ak***	*bint**i***
*bint**aha***	*bint**ik***	
*bint**uhum***	*bint**ukum***	*bint**ina***

III. Demonstrative pronouns

The following are **demonstrative pronouns**:

masc.	fem.	pl.
da this, that	***di*** this, that	***dōl*** these, those

Using these pronouns you can produce sentences which in English would start with the words "that's ..." "those are ...":

da Ḫasan	"that's Ḫasan"
di Samya	"that's Samya"
dōl ṭalaba	"those are students"

IV. Names of countries and *nisba*-adjectives

1. Names of countries can be combined with the so-called *nisba*- ending to form adjectives which show where someone or something comes from or belongs to. The masculine *nisba* ends in *-i*, the feminine in *-iyya* and the plural in *-iyyīn*. Amongst other things, the *nisba* can be used to denote language and nationality, e.g., *maṣri* "Egyptian."

Maṣr	→	*maṣri, maṣriyya, maṣriyyīn*	Egyptian
Lubnān	→	*lubnāni, lubnaniyya, lubnaniyyīn*	Lebanese
ilYunān	→	*yunāni, yunaniyya, yunaniyyīn*	Greek
isSudān	→	*sudāni, sudaniyya, sudaniyyīn*	Sudanese
Surya	→	*sūri, suriyya, suriyyīn*	Syrian
ʾIṭalya	→	*ʾiṭāli, ʾiṭaliyya, ʾiṭaliyyīn*	Italian
Kanada	→	*kanadi, kanadiyya, kanadiyyīn*	Canadian
ʾAmrīka	→	*ʾamrīki, ʾamrikiyya, ʾamrikiyyīn*	American
ilMaġrib	→	*maġribi, maġribiyya, maġarba*	Moroccan
Turkiya	→	*turki, turkiyya, atṛāk ~ taṛakwa*	Turkish
ʾIṭalya	→	*ṭalyāni, ṭalyaniyya, ṭalayna*	Italian

Note that the last three examples have an irregular plural.

2. A number of *nisba*-adjectives are derived from a collective noun.

ingilīz	English people	→	*ingilīzi, ingiliziyya*	English
ʾamrikān	Americans	→	*ʾamrikāni, ʾamrikaniyya*	American
ʾalmān	Germans	→	*ʾalmāni, ʾalmaniyya*	German
rūs	Russians	→	*rūsi, rusiyya*	Russian
ʿaṛab	Arabs	→	*ʿaṛabi, ʿaṛabiyya*	Arab

The names of these countries are *Ingiltiṛa*, *ʾAmrīka*, *ʾAlmanya*, and *Rusya*.

3. In the case of certain countries whose names end in an *-a*, the suffix *-āwi* is used to form the corresponding *nisba*-adjective:

inNimsa	→	*nimsāwi, nimsawiyya, nimsawiyyīn*	Austrian
Faṛansa	→	*faṛansāwi, faṛansawiyya, faṛansawiyyīn*	French

4. When referring to **individuals** the words *wāḥid* (masc.) or *waḥda* (fem.) are usually used with the *nisba* :

wāḥid ingilīzi	"an Englishman"
waḥda maġribiyya	"a Moroccan woman"

If the *nisba*-adjective occurs in the feminine singular or in the plural, it almost always relates to **persons**:

ṭāliba Kanadiyya	"a Canadian female student"
ṭalaba kanadiyyīn	"Canadian students"

When referring to **inanimate objects** (non-humans) of whatever gender and number, the *nisba*-adjective is always in the masculine singular:

ʾahwa faransāwi	"French coffee"
sagāyir ʾamrikāni	"American cigarettes"
saʿāt suwisri	"Swiss watches"
gibna hulandi	"Dutch cheese"

Languages are referred to by using the masculine singular of the *nisba*-adjective, defined or undefined:

bakkallim ʿarabi	"I speak Arabic."
ilʿarabi luġa gamīla	"Arabic is a beautiful language"

V. Plural endings

In Arabic the plural is often formed by means of endings. The masculine plural ending is *-īn*, the feminine plural ending is *-āt*.

1. The **plural ending** ***-īn*** is only used with nouns which refer to people, not to inanimate objects. Many of these begin with *mu-* or *mi-*:

mudarris + īn	→	*mudarrisīn*	"teachers"
muhandis + īn	→	*muhandisīn*	"engineers"

This ending is also used with most adjectives (for participles → VI. III) when these qualify people in the plural:

humma‿kwayyisīn	"they are good (people)"
dōl miš ṣuġayyarīn	"those (people) are not young"

This table shows all possibilities:

huwwa‿ṣġayyar	*da‿kwayyis*
hiyya‿ṣġayyara	*di‿kwayyisa*
humma‿ṣġayyarīn	*dōl kuwayyisīn*

2. The **plural ending** ***-āt*** is used with nouns which denote female people. Usually the singular of these words ends in an *-a* :

mudarrisa + āt	→	*mudarrisāt*	"female teachers"
ṭāliba + āt	→	*ṭalibāt*	"female students"

This ending is not used with adjectives. In other words, even if the pronouns *humma* or *dōl* refer to females, the plural *-īn* of the adjective is required:

Samya‿w Maha, dōl miš ***ṣuġayyarīn***
"Samya and Maha, (they) are not young"

The plural ending *-āt* also appears with nouns of either gender which refer not to people but to inanimate objects:

mutūr + āt	→	*muturāt*	"engines"
sāʿa + āt	→	*saʿāt*	"hours"

VI. Shortening a long vowel

When suffixes and endings, such as *-āt, -īn, -úkum* etc. are added to words, they cause the stress to be moved. This shifting of the stress means that long vowels which were originally stressed now lose their stress. For instance, the stress in the word *mawgūd* falls on the *-ū-*, but by adding *-īn* to form the plural, the stress moves to the *-īn-*, and *-ū-* becomes now shortened (→ IV.I):

mawgūd	but	*mawgudīn*	*ingilīzi*	but	*ingilizíyya*
sāɛa	but	*saɛāt*	*lubnāni*	but	*lubnaniyyīn*
ṭarabēẓa	but	*ṭarabeẓāt*	*tilifōn*	but	*tilifonāt*

For the pronounciation of *e* and *o* see Introduction II.2, for the shortening of long vowels before two consonants see III.IV.3.

📖 📖 📖

INCREASE YOUR VOCABULARY

In the classroom: *fi‿lfaṣl*

masc.	fem.	pl.	
ʔūl waṛāya	*ʔūli waṛāya*	*ʔūlu waṛāya*	say after me!
ismaɛ	*ismaɛi*	*ismaɛu*	listen!
iktib	*iktibi*	*iktibu*	write!
taɛāla	*taɛāli*	*taɛālu*	come!
hāt	*hāti*	*hātu*	give, bring!
xud	*xudi*	*xudu*	take!
buṣṣ	*buṣṣi*	*buṣṣu*	look!
baṭṭal kalām	*baṭṭali kalām*	*baṭṭalu kalām*	shut up!

tāni	once more!	*kamān maṛṛa*	one more time!
balāš	leave it!	*kifāya*	enough!
šukṛan	thank you!	*ɛafwan*	it's nothing!
xalāṣ	stop, enough!	*bišwēš*	slowly!

Greetings:

A: *ʔahlan wa sahlan!* welcome!

B: *ʔahlan bīk!* (masc.)
ʔahlan bīki (fem.)
ʔahlan bīkum (pl.)

EXERCISES

I. Add the correct possessive suffix to the nouns.

	gidd	*umm*	*uxt*	*ibn*	*ʿamm*	*bint*
intu						
ana						
huwwa						
iḥna						
inti						
humma						
inta						

II. That's not **our** daughter, but **their** daughter!

hiyya di bintukum? - *lā, di miš bint**ina**, lākin bint**uhum**!*

1. *hiyya di ʾummukum?* - *lā,* ____________________
2. *huwwa da ʾibnukum?* - *lā,* ____________________
3. *huwwa da giddukum?* - *lā,* ____________________
4. *hiyya di ʾuxtukum?* - *lā,* ____________________
5. *huwwa da ʾismukum?* - *lā,* ____________________
6. *huwwa da ʿammukum?*- *lā,* ____________________

III. Confusion! That's not **our** grandfather, that's **our** uncle!

giddukum da? - *da miš gidd**ina**, da ʿamm**ina**!*

1. *uxtukum di?* - *di miš uxt*________, *di bint*________
2. *ummukum di?* - *di miš umm*________, *di ʾuxt*________
3. *ʿammukum da?* - *da miš ʿamm*________, *da gidd*________
4. *ibnukum da?* - *da miš ibn*________, *da ʿamm*________
5. *bintukum di?* - *di miš bint*________, *di ʾuxt*________

IV. He comes from Canada, which means he's Canadian!

da min Kanada, yaꜥni huwwa kanadi.

1. *di min inNimsa, yaꜥni hiyya* ______________________________
2. *di min Faṛansa, yaꜥni hiyya* ______________________________
3. *da min ʾIṭalya, yaꜥni huwwa* ______________________________
4. *di min ʾAmrīka, yaꜥni hiyya* ______________________________
5. *da min Ingiltiṛṛa, yaꜥni huwwa* ______________________________
6. *di min ʾAlmanya, yaꜥni hiyya* ______________________________
7. *da min Maṣr, yaꜥni huwwa* ______________________________
8. *di min ilYunān, yaꜥni hiyya* ______________________________

V. They're from Australia, which means they're Australians!

dōl min Ustuṛalya, yaꜥni humma‿ustuṛaliyyīn.

1. *dōl min Maṣr, yaꜥni humma* ______________________________
2. *dōl min Lubnān, yaꜥni humma* ______________________________
3. *dōl min ʾIṭalya, yaꜥni humma* ______________________________
4. *dōl min Surya, yaꜥni humma* ______________________________
5. *dōl min Faṛansa, yaꜥni humma* ______________________________
6. *dōl min ʾAmrīka, yaꜥni humma* ______________________________
7. *dōl min Ingiltiṛṛa, yaꜥni humma* ______________________________
8. *dōl min ʾAlmanya, yaꜥni humma* ______________________________
9. *dōl min Rusya, yaꜥni humma* ______________________________

VI. He's an Egyptian and she's also an Egyptian!

huwwa maṣri, wi hiyya kamān maṣriyya

1. *huwwa yunāni, wi hiyya kamān* ______________________________
2. *ana ʾalmāni, w‿inti kamān* ______________________________
3. *ana ʾamrīki, w‿inti kamān* ______________________________

4. *di nimsawiyya, wi da kamān* ____________________

5. *di suriyya, wi da kamān* ____________________

6. *hiyya fạransawiyya, wi huwwa kamān* ____________________

7. *huwwa mudarris, wi hiyya kamān* ____________________

8. *inti ṭalíba, w‿inta kamān* ____________________

9. *ana muhandis, w‿inti kamān* ____________________

VII. Which language do you speak?

ana min ʾAlmanya‿w bakkallim (I speak) *ʾalmāni*

1. *ana min Hulanda‿w bakkallim* ____________________
2. *ana min Fạransa‿w bakkallim* ____________________
3. *ana min ilYunān wi bakkallim* ____________________
4. *ana min ʾAmrīka‿w bakkallim* ____________________
5. *ana min ʾIṭalya‿w bakkallim* ____________________
6. *ana min inNimsa‿w bakkallim* ____________________
7. *ana min Suwisra‿w bakkallim* ____________________

VIII. Put the following sentences into the plural.

ana ʿạrabi. - *iḥna ʿạrab.*

1. *ana ʾingilīzi* - ____________________
2. *hiyya‿kwayyisa fi‿lʿạrabi.* - ____________________
3. *inta mạsri?* - ____________________
4. *da fạransāwi.* - ____________________
5. *huwwa muhandis.* - ____________________
6. *ana ʾamrīki.* - ____________________
7. *inti ṭālíba?* - ____________________
8. *hiyya miš mawgūda.* - ____________________

9. *ana lubnāni.* - ____________

10. *di nimsawiyya.* - ____________

IX. And so is Samya! Put the following into the plural.

Sāmi‿kwayyis. - *Sāmi‿w Samya‿kwayyisīn.*

1. *Sāmi maṣri.* - *Sāmi‿w Samya* ____________
2. *Jane‿kwayyisa fi‿lɛarabi.* - *Jane wi Mike* ____________
3. *Janet ʔamrikiyya.* - *John wi Kate* ____________
4. *Mirvat miš ʔagnabiyya.* - *Mirvat wi Samya miš* ____________
5. *Sāmi mudarris.* - *Sāmi‿w Mark* ____________
6. *Samya ṭalíba.* - *Samya‿w Janet* ____________
7. *Mirvat muhandisa.* - *Mirvat wi Michael* ____________
8. *Janet miš mawgūda.* - *Janet wi Samya miš* ____________
9. *John ingilīzi.* - *John wi Jane* ____________
10. *Ann usturaliyya.* - *Ann wi Kevin* ____________

X. I'm a Canadian, not an American!

ana kanadi, miš ʔamrīki! *(Kanada, ʔAmrīka)*

1. *ana* ____________ , *miš* ____________ ! *(Lubnān, Maṣr)*
2. *uxti* ____________ , *miš* ____________ ! *(muhandis, mudarris)*
3. *humma* ____________ , *miš* ____________ ! *(ʔAlmanya, Suwisra)*
4. *da* ____________ , *miš* ____________ ! *(Rusya, Hulanda)*
5. *ummina* ____________ , *miš* ____________ ! *(Lubnān, Maṣr)*
6. *dōl* ____________ , *miš* ____________ ! *(ṭālib, mudarris)*
7. *John wi Jane* ____________ , *miš* ____________ ! *(ʔAmrīka, Faṛansa)*
8. *Mary wi Jane* ____________ , *miš* ____________ ! *(mudarris, muhandis)*

LESSON III

DIALOGUES

izzayyak?

A: *Maḫmūd wi Aḫmad*

Maḫmūd: *ᵓahlan wa sahlan ya Aḫmad!*
Aḫmad: *ᵓahlan bīk ya Maḫmūd!*
Maḫmūd: *izzayy ilḫāl?*
Aḫmad: *aho māši, w‿inta‿zzayyak?*
Maḫmūd: *kullᵊ ḫāga tamām, w‿ilḫamdu li‿llāh.*

B: *Mirvat wi Samya*

Mirvat: *ᵓahlan wa sahlan, ya Samya!*
Samya: *ᵓahlan bīki, ya Mirvat!*
Mirvat: *izzayyik? izzayyᵊ ḫālik?*
Samya: *ana‿kwayyisa‿lḫamdu li‿llāh!*
w‿inti‿zzayyik?
Mirvat: *wallāhi miš ᵓawi. taɛbāna‿šwayya kida,*
wi waxda bard.
Samya: *salamtik, bukṛa‿n šāᵓ Aḷḷāh tibᵓi ᵓaḫsan.*
ya-taṛa, izzayy abūki?
Mirvat: *aḫsan bi-ktīr, ilḫamdu li‿llāh.*
Samya: *huwwa lissa fi‿lmustašfa?*
Mirvat: *lā, ḅāḅa rigiɛ ilbēt min mudda.*

ikkilma di maɛnāha ᵓē?

Sāmi: *ya William!*
William: *aywa!*
Sāmi: *taɛāla ᵓawām!*
William: *xēr? gaṛa ᵓē?*
Sāmi: *fī mukalma ɛašānak.*
William: *mukalma? ikkilma di, maɛnāha ᵓē?*
Sāmi: *yaɛni, fī tilifōn ɛašānak.*
William: *ṭab ana gayyᵊ ḫālan.*

VOCABULARY

ᵓawām	quickly	*bard*	cold
abb ~ abu	father	*bi*	with
áho ~ ahó	there he is ~ there it is	*bi-ktīr*	much (adv.)
		bukṛa	tomorrow
aḫsan	better	*bēt*	house, home
ạxx ~ axu	brother	*fi‿lbēt*	at home
ᵓahlan	welcome	*dilwaᵓti*	now

filūs (pl.)	money
fī	there is ~ are
gamb	beside, next to
gaṛa ʾē	what's happened
gayy	coming
ana gayy	I'm coming (masc.)
ḥāga	thing
ḥāl	situation
ḥālan	immediately
ilḥamdu li‿llāh	praise be to God
in šaʾ Aḷḷāh	if God so wishes
izzayy	how
izzayyak ~ ik	how are you
kilma	word
kitīr	much, a lot
kull	all; every; whole
lissa	still (adv)
makān	place
maɛna	meaning
miš ʾawi	not so good ~ so much

mukalma	phone call
mustašfa	hospital
māši	it's going fine, okay
min mudda	some time ago
rigiɛ	he's back
salamtak	get better (masc.) (when someone's ill)
sahl	easy
ṣaɛb	difficult
šuwayya	a bit, a little
tamām	okay
taɛbān	tired
tibʾa (m.) ~ *tibʾi* (fem.)	you'll be
ṭab ~ ṭayyib	okay
wa ~ wi	and
waḷḷāhi	by God
wāxid	taking; got
ya-taṛa	I wonder by the way
xēr	good (wishes)
ɛašān	for, because

GRAMMAR

I. Consonant clusters

If more than two consonants are clustered next to each other in a word group, a schwa ^{ə} is placed between the second and the third consonant.

baɛd	+ *bukṛa*	→	*baɛd*^{ə} *bukṛa*
ana gayy	+ *bukṛa*	→	*gayy*^{ə} *bukṛa*
bint	+ *waḥda*	→	*bint*^{ə} *waḥda*
zayy	+ *baɛḍu*	→	*zayy*^{ə} *baɛḍu*

II. Definite article

1. In Arabic there is only one article, the definite article *il-*, which is used in front of both masculine and feminine words. It is put directly in front of a noun or adjective and attached to it to form one word:

mudarris	→	*ilmudarris*	the teacher
bint	→	*ilbint*	the girl
mudarrisīn	→	*ilmudarrisīn*	the teachers

2. If a word begins with a dental consonant *t, d, ṭ, ḍ, l, r, n* or with a sibilant *s, z, ṣ, ẓ, š, ž*, the *-l-* of the article is assimilated into the consonant which follows. These initial consonants are called "sun-

letters" after the word *šams* "sun" which occurs as the first word in the following table. Note that although the sounds *k* and *g* are not "sun-letters" in the strict sense of the word (no dentals, no sibilants) they behave in the same way:

šams	→	*iššams*	the sun	*tīn*	→	*ittīn*	the figs
dīn	→	*iddīn*	the religion	*ṭifl*	→	*iṭṭifl*	the child
ḍuhr	→	*iḍḍuhr*	the noon	*lōn*	→	*illōn*	the color
rayyis	→	*irrayyis*	the boss	*nās*	→	*innās*	the people
sinima	→	*issinima*	the cinema	*zēt*	→	*izzēt*	the oil
ṣabūn	→	*iṣṣabūn*	the soap	*ẓābiṭ*	→	*iẓẓābiṭ*	the officer
žakitta	→	*ižžakitta*	the jacket	*kursi*	→	*ikkursi*	the chair
gaṛas	→	*iggaṛas*	the bell	*kilma*	→	*ikkilma*	the word

3. If a word begins with a vowel, the *i*- of the definite article can be omitted (→ introduction A. I. 2c)

itnēn → *litnēn* "both" [the two]   *abyaḍ* → *labyaḍ* "the white one"

III. Demonstrative adjectives: *da, di, dōl* and *áho ~ ahó*

1. *da, di* and *dōl*

When *da, di,* "this," "that" and *dōl* "these," "those" are used as demonstrative adjectives (not as prounouns → II.III), they must be placed after the noun, and the noun must be defined:

iṛṛāgil da	"this man"	*ikkilma di*	"this word"
ilmudarrisīn dōl	"these teachers"	*ilbintᵊ di*	"this girl"

Note that as far as agreement is concerned, the plural of inanimate objects is followed by an adjective in the feminine singular (→ IV.IV.2c):

ilmuturāt di‿kwayyisa	"these engines are good"
issaʕāt di gamīla	"these watches are nice"

2. *áho ~ ahó*

The words *áho ~ ahó* (masc. sing.), *áhe ~ ahé* (fem. sing.) and *áhum ~ahúm* (pl.) are used to point at something with a certain degree of emphasis. When *aho, ahe,* or *ahum* are placed in front of a word, the accent is placed on the first vowel. When they are placed after the word, the final vowel is stressed:

áho gayy there he comes	*áhe gayya* there she comes	*áhum gayyīn* there they come
ilmudarris ahó the teacher (m.) is over there	*ilmudarrisa ahé* the teacher (f.) is over there	*ilmudarrisīn ahúm* the teachers are over there

áho māši "it's okay" is a possible answer to *izzayy ilḫāl* "how are you?"

IV. Possessive suffixes

1. After a vowel -V

The words *abb* "father" and *ạxx* "brother" take the form *abu* and *axu* when they are used with possessive suffixes, and the final *-u* is lengthened: *abu* + *ha* → *abūha* "her father." The same rule applies to other words which end in a vowel such as *waṛa* "behind," but it does not apply to feminine words ending in *-a* :

	3rd pers.	2nd pers.	1st pers.
abu- father	*abū-(h)* *abū-ha* *abū-hum*	*abū-k* *abū-ki* *abū-kum*	*abū-ya* *abū-na*
waṛa behind	*waṛā-(h)* *waṛā-ha* *waṛā-hum*	*waṛā-k* *waṛā-ki* *waṛā-kum*	*waṛā-ya* *waṛā-na*

2. After a single consonant -C

The following paradigms show the suffixes as they occur after a single consonant (-C), after a vowel (-V) and after two consonants (-CC):

	3rd pers.	2nd pers.	1st pers.
-C	*ʾalam-u* *ʾalam-ha* *ʾalam-hum*	*ʾalam-ak* *ʾalam-ik* *ʾalam-kum*	*ʾalam-i* *ʾalam-na*
-V	*axū-(h)* *axū-ha* *axū-hum*	*axū-k* *axū-ki* *axū-kum*	*axū-ya* *axū-na*
-CC	*gidd-u* *gidd-aha* *gidd-uhum*	*gidd-ak* *gidd-ik* *gidd-ukum*	*gidd-i* *gidd-ina*

When suffixes are added, they cause the stress to move, for instance *mudárris*, but *mudarrísu* and *mudarríshum* (→ IV.II).

3. As a rule, there are no long vowels before two consonants in Egyptian Arabic. Therefore, when a consonantal suffix is added to a noun or a verb, a long vowel is shortened:

makān	+ *ha*	> *makānha*	>	*makanha*		"her place"
filūs	+ *na*	> *filūsna*	>	*filusna*		"our money"
bēt	+ *kum*	> *bētkum*	>	*betkum*		"your (pl.) house"
lōn	+ *ha*	> *lōnha*	>	*lonha*		"her color"

For the pronounciation of *e* and *o* see Introduction II.1.

V. *gayy* and *wāxid*

In Arabic *gayy* "coming" and *wāxid* "having got" are both active participles and are given the same feminine or plural endings as adjectives and nouns (→ I.V and II.V):

ana gayy (masc.)	*ana gayya* (fem.)	*iḫna gayyīn* (pl.)
ana wāxid (masc.)	*ana waxda* (fem.)	*iḫna waxdīn* (pl.)

Therefore a female person would say: *ana gayya ḫālan* "I'm coming straightaway," while several persons would say: *iḫna waxdīn bard* "we've got a cold."

N.B. *waxdīn* comes from *wāxid + īn*, where the *-i-* has been elided and the *-ā-* has been shortened before two consonants: *wāxid+īn > wāxd+īn > waxd+īn > waxdīn* (→ above IV.3 and IV.II).

VI. Fronting of a topic

In spoken Arabic the most important idea in the sentence is usually put first. In the place where it would otherwise have been located, you will find a possessive suffix referring to it.

maꜥna‿kkilma di ʾē?	→	*ikkilma di, maꜥnā**ha** ʾē?*
		[lit: "this word, the meaning of it (is) what?"]
ism iṛṛāgil da ʾē?	→	*iṛṛāgil da, ism**u** ʾē?*
		[lit: "this man, the name of him (is) what?"]

VII. The adverbs *šuwayya, ʾawi, giddan,* and *xāliṣ*

šuwayya "a little" "a bit" "somewhat," *ʾawi, giddan, xāliṣ* "very" "completely" and *bi-ktīr* "much more" are placed after the adjectives or adverbs to which they refer:

aḫsan šuwayya	"a bit better"	*kuwayyis ʾawi*	"very good"
aḫsan bi-ktīr	"much better"	*kitīr xāliṣ*	"a lot"

INCREASE YOUR VOCABULARY

ilfaṣl "the classroom"

ashtray	*ṭaʔṭūʔa, ṭaʔaṭīʔ*	handtowel, cloth	*fūṭa, fuwaṭ*
	ṭaffāya, -āt	ink	*ḫibr*
bag	*šanṭa, šunaṭ*	lamp	*lamḅa, lumaḍ*
ballpoint pen	*ʔalam gāff*	light	*nūr, anwāṛ*
blackboard	*ṣabbura*	paper	*waraʔ*
book	*kitāb, kutub*	paper (sheet of)	*waraʔa, -āt*
carpet	*siggāda, sagagīd*	pen	*ʔalam, iʔlām ~ʔilíma*
chair	*kursi, karāsi*	pencil	*ʔalam ruṣāṣ*
chalk	*ṭabašīr*	photo, poster	*ṣūra, ṣuwar*
door	*bāb, abwāb*	room	*ʔōḍa, ʔuwaḍ*
eraser	*ʔastīka*	table	*ṭarabēẓa, -āt*
exercise book	*kuṛṛāsa, kaṛaṛīs*	wall	*ḫēṭa, ḫiṭān*
fountain pen	*ʔalam ḫibr*	window	*šibbāk, šababīk*

Saying goodbye

When leaving you can begin with one of the following sentences:

lāzim amši dilwaʔti "I've got to go now"
lāzim astaʔzin dilwaʔti "you'll have to excuse me"
baɛdᵊ ʔiznukum ~ *ɛan ʔiznukum* "with your permission"

The host or hostess could respond to this by saying:

lissa badri "but it's still early!"

Your answer to this is:

badri min ɛumrak (m.) ~ *ɛumrik* (f.) "may it be early in your life!" (may you live a long life!)

The person staying behind says:

maɛa‿ssalāma "go in peace," "have a safe journey!"

To which the answer is:

Aḷḷa‿ysallimak (m.) ~ *yisallimik* (f.) "may God protect you!"

When someone is introduced to you, you could say:

furṣa saɛīda "pleased to meet you"

And the answer to this is:

ana‿lʔasɛad "the pleasure is all mine"

If you want to say "goodnight," you should say:

tiṣbaḫ (m.) ~ *tiṣbaḫi* (f.) *ɛala xēr* "wake up healthy!"

And the answer to this is:

w‿inta (m.) ~ *w‿inti* (f.) *min ʔahlu* "may you be healthy too!"

EXERCISES

I. Add possessive suffixes to the following words.

	waṛa	*axu*	*bint*	*ḅāḅa*	*abu*
inta					
huwwa					
inti					
iḥna					
ana					
humma					
intu					

II. Fill in the blanks. *da ʾax**ūha**, miš ḅaḅāha.*

1. *da ʾabu____ , miš axūha.*
2. *da ʾaxu____ , miš ʕammi.*
3. *da ʾaxu____ , miš ʕammik*
4. *da ḅāḅa___ , miš giddi.*
5. *di bint_____ , miš uxtaha.*
6. *da gidd____ , miš abū(h).*
7. *da ʕamm____ , miš abūha.*
8. *ḅāḅa____ fēn, ya Samya?*

III. There he is! There they are! Use *ahó, ahé, ahúm!*

1. *ilmudarris fēn?* _______
2. *ilmudarrisa fēn?* _______
3. *ḅāḅa fēn?* _______
4. *ilmudarrisīn fēn?* _______
5. *uxtak fēn?* _______
6. *iṭṭalibāt fēn?* _______
7. *ilmustašfa fēn?* _______
8. *ilfūṭa fēn?* _______
9. *iẓẓābiṭ fēn?* _______
10. *innās fēn?* _______

IV. Read aloud and add ᵊ when necessary.

baɛd___ bukṛa	*bint___ waḥda*	*kitāb___ wāḥid*
ana gayy___ ḥālan	*bēt___ wāḥid*	*ɛamm___ɛAli*
bi-kull___ surūr	*gamb___ Maḥmūd*	*ma-ɛandakš___ waʔt*
intu saknīn___ fēn?	*ma-ɛandakš___ filūs*	*zayy___ baɛḍu*

V. Arrange the following words into sentences. Be careful to add the correct endings.

1. *taɛbān, šuwayya, ana* ____________________
2. *ʔawi, da, miš, kitīr* ____________________
3. *bi-ktīr, aḥsan, da* ____________________
4. *kuwayyis, dōl, ʔawi* ____________________
5. *šuwayya, taɛbān, inti* ____________________
6. *ʔawi, sahl, di* ____________________
7. *ɛayyān, giddan, hiyya* ____________________
8. *fi, lissa, humma, issinima* ____________________

VI. Using the example to help you, ask about each person's name.

ṛāgil - *iṛṛāgil da‿smu ʔē?*

1. *bint* - ____________________
2. *ṭifl* - ____________________
3. *ṭālib* - ____________________
4. *nās* - ____________________
5. *ẓābiṭ* - ____________________
6. *sitt* - ____________________
7. *ṭālíba* - ____________________
8. *ṭalaba* - ____________________

VII. Using the example to help you, ask where things are.

ṣūra - *iṣṣūra di, makanha fēn?*

1. *waraʾ* - ______
2. *fūṭa* - ______
3. *ṭaʾṭūʾa* - ______
4. *kutub* - ______
5. *lamḅa* - ______
6. *iʾlām* - ______
7. *ḫagāt* - ______
8. *siggāda* - ______
9. *kursi* - ______

VIII. Using the example to help you, make sentences with *šīl* "take away!"

lamḅa - *šīl illamḅa di, ya Ḫasan!*

1. *ṣūra* - ______
2. *fūṭa* - ______
3. *kitāb* - ______
4. *šanṭa* - ______
5. *kuṛṛāsa* - ______
6. *ṭarabēẓa* - ______
7. *ṣabūn* - ______
8. *zēt* - ______

IX. Translate the following sentences.

1. This is much better. ______
2. This hospital is very good. ______

3. I (fem.) have got a bit of a cold. ______________________________

4. The students (fem.) are coming right now. ____________________

5. Is she still in hospital? ______________________________________

6. This phone call is for you (m.). _______________________________

7. He's a bit better. ____

8. That's an awful lot. ____

9. This girl, what's her name? ___________________________________

10. *ʿAli* is at the cinema. _______________________________________

11. He's coming now! ____

12. You'll be better tomorrow! ____________________________________

13. *Sāmi*'s coming the day after tomorrow. _______________________

14. Where is your (pl.) classroom? _________________________________

15. Your (pl.) grandfather, what's his name? ______________________

LESSON IV

DIALOGUES

ilmaḥaṭṭa fēn?

William: *law samaḥt, ilmaḥaṭṭa fēn?*
iṛṛāgil: *maḥaṭṭit issikka‿lḥadīd?*
William: *aywa, di‿bɛīda min hina?*
iṛṛāgil: *miš biɛīda ʾawi, imši duġri kida,*
wi‿f-ʾāxir iššāriɛ da‿txušš^{ə}‿šmāl.
baɛd^{ə} kida ḥatšufha‿f-wiššak ɛala ṭūl.
William: *mutašakkir giddan.*
iṛṛāgil: *ilɛafw.*

ilmaṭɛam

William: *ya-taṛa fī maṭɛam kuwayyis hina?*
iṛṛāgil: *fī maṭāɛim kuwayyisa‿ktīr, miš wāḥid bass.*
William: *ɛawzīn min faḍlak maṭɛam rixīṣ, miš ġāli.*
iṛṛāgil: *fī‿hnāk ɛa‿nnaṣya maṭɛam miš baṭṭāl,*
ismu Kilubaṭra.
William: *wi da fātiḥ dilwaʾti?*
iṛṛāgil: *dilwaʾti‿ssāɛa talāta, ġāliban yikūn fātiḥ.*

humma miš mawgudīn

Sayyid: *humma mawgudīn?*
Samya: *mīn?*
Sayyid: *Ḥasan wi Yusri*
Samya: *lā, miš mawgudīn.*
Sayyid: *ya-taṛa humma fēn?*
Samya: *miš ɛarfa, yimkin fi‿nnādi.*
Sayyid: *wi‿nnādi‿bɛīd ɛan hina?*
Samya: *lā, da miš biɛīd, da‿ʾrayyib.*
Sayyid: *fēn bi‿ẓẓabṭ?*
Samya: *hināk, gamb iggāmiɛ ɛala ṭūl.*

inta‿mnēn bi‿ẓẓabṭ?

Maḥmūd: *inta ʾaṣlan minēn? min ilQāhira?*
Aḥmad: *lā, ana ʾaṣlan mi‿zZaʾazīʾ.*
Maḥmūd: *yaɛni‿nta mawlūd fi‿zZaʾazīʾ?*
Aḥmad: *ā̤, ana mawlūd wi mitṛabbi‿hnāk.*
Maḥmūd: *wi‿zZaʾazīʾ di fēn bi‿ẓẓabṭ?*
Aḥmad: *miš biɛīd ɛan Maṣr, fi‿šŠarʾiyya.*
Maḥmūd: *wi ya-taṛa di balad kibīra?*
Aḥmad: *miš ʾawi, lākin di balad rīfi gamīla.*

VOCABULARY

ā ~ aywa	yes	*mabṣūṭ*	happy, pleased
ʾaṣlan	originally	*maḫaṭṭa, -āt*	station; (bus) stop
ʾāxir	last; end	*maṭʿam, maṭāʿim*	restaurant
ʾurayyib min	near, close to	*mawlūd*	born
balad (fem.), *bilād*	country, town, village	*miš baṭṭāl*	not bad
		mitṛabbi	raised
bass	but, only, rather	*mīn*	who (inter.)
bi‿ẓẓabṭ	precisely, exactly	*naṣya, nawāṣi*	street corner
biʿīd min ~ ʿan	far from	*nādi, nawādi*	club
duġri	straight (on)	*nihāya, -āt*	end
fātiḫ	open	*rixīṣ, ruxāṣ*	cheap
film, aflām	film	*rīfi*	rural
fiṭār	breakfast	*sikka, sikak*	road, way
gabal, gibāl	mountain, hill	*issikka‿lḫadīd*	railway
gaʿān	hungry	*šāriʿ, šawāriʿ*	street
gāhiz	ready	*šimāl*	left
gāmiʿ, gawāmiʿ	mosque	*tixušš*	turn, turn into
giddan	very	*wiḫiš*	bad, ugly
ġāli, ġalyīn	expensive	*wišš, wušūš*	face
ġāliban	probably	*fi -wiššak*	in front of you
hina	here	*yafandim!*	sir! madam!
hināk	there	*yikūn*	is, be
ḫadīd	iron	*yimkin*	perhaps, maybe
ḫatšufha	you'll see it	*ilʿafw*	you're welcome
imši	walk; go (away)	*ʿala ṭūl*	straight on; right now
kibīr, kubāṛ	big		
kitīr, kutāṛ	many	*ʿaṭšān*	thirsty
law samaḫt	if you please if you don't mind	*ʿārif*	knowing (masc.)
		ʿāwiz	wanting (masc.)

GRAMMAR

I. Stress

As we have already seen in lessons I.V, II.VI and II.IV, there are many occasions where the principal stress shifts as suffixes and endings are added to a word. This shifting stress occurs when several consonants cluster together, or when vowels are lengthened, thereby causing the structure of the syllables to change, which means that new heavy clusters arise.

Heavy clusters are groups of letters with the form -**v̄C**- (long vowel + consonant) as in *bil-**ād**, **ṭāl**-ib*, or with the form -**vCC**- (short vowel + two consonants) as in *mitṛ**abb**-i, b-**ukṛ**-a*. These clusters determine where the stress falls. The rules for the placement of the accent are as follows:

1. The accent falls on the heavy cluster which is nearest to the end of the word:

mustašfa	→	*must**ášf**a*	*mustašfayāt*	→	*mustašfay**āt***
matɛam	→	*m**áṭɛ**am*	*šāriɛ*	→	***šār**iɛ*

2. If the heavy cluster is followed by more than one vowel, then the accent falls on the vowel which follows immediately after the cluster:

madrasa	→	*madr**á**sa*	*ɛandaha*	→	*ɛand**á**ha*
ġāliban	→	*ġālíban*	*ᵓurayyiba*	→	*ᵓurayyíba*

3. If a word contains no heavy cluster, then the accent falls on the first vowel:

balad	→	*b**á**lad*	*ġada*	→	*ġ**á**da*
baladi	→	*b**á**ladi*	*waraᵓa*	→	*w**á**raᵓa*

For exceptions to this, see lesson IX.IV.1.

II. Elision of the vowel *-i-*

If the vowel *-i* - occurs in an unstressed open syllable which is not the last syllable in the word, it is elided. An open syllable is one which ends in a vowel:

ɛā-rif + a	→	*ɛā-ri-fa*	→	*ɛārfa*	>	*ɛarfa*
wi-ḫiš + īn	→	*wi-ḫi-šīn*	→	*wiḫšīn*		
ma-dā-ris + u	→	*ma-dā-ri-su*	→	*madārsu*	>	*madarsu*

If the vowel *-i-* occurs in a protected position - that is, before or after two consonants (-**CC**-) - it is not elided. The *-i-* is accentuated if it occurs after two consonants, see the I.2 above:

mudárris → *mudarrísa*   *muhándis* → *muhandísa.*

The elision of the *-i-* can also occur within a phrase such as the genitive construction (→ V.III): *madrasit ilbanāt* → *madrast‿ilbanāt* "the girls' school," but to a certain extent it depends on the rhythm of the utterance.

If a syllable containing the vowel *-i-* follows another syllable also containing an *-i-*, and both are suitable for elision, it is usually the second one which is elided: *da fi nihāyit ilfilm* → *da fi‿nhayt‿ilfilm* "that's at the end of the film."

III. Prepositions of place

The most important prepositions of place are:

taḫt	under	*fōʾ*	above	*gamb*	next to
bēn	between	*ʿala*	on	*fi*	in
ʿand	with	*waṛa*	behind	*ʾuddām*	in front of
ʾuṣād	facing				

Prepositions are placed in front of the noun:

taḫt iṭṭarabēẓa	"under the table"
gamb innādi	"near the club"
ʾuṣād iggāmiʿ	"facing the mosque"

IV. The plural

1. Noun plurals

(a) As has already been mentioned (→ II.V), plurals can be formed by adding the endings *-īn* or *-āt* to the singular. These are known as **sound plurals**. Plural endings are frequently found attached to words which begin with *mu-* or *mi-*, and which usually refer to masculine and feminine persons respectively.

In addition, many feminine nouns ending in *-a* which refer to inanimate objects also form their plurals in *-āt* :

muhandis + īn	→	*muhandisīn*	engineers
mudarrisa + āt	→	*mudarrisāt*	female teachers
tarabēẓa + āt	→	*tarabeẓāt*	tables
waraʾa + āt	→	*waraʾāt*	sheets of paper
ḥāga + āt	→	*ḥagāt*	things
maḥaṭṭa + āt	→	*maḥaṭṭāt*	stations

Note that a small number of nouns ending in *-a* receive the addition of a *-y-* before the plural ending *-āt* :

mustašfa + āt → *mustašfayāt* "hospitals"

(b) However, a large group of nouns have what are called **broken plurals**. This means that when the noun is put into the plural, its structure changes. Broken plurals can be formed according to various patterns; but it is not always obvious for beginners why a particular pattern is given preference. It is therefore better to learn the plural of a word at the same time as you learn the singular.

A word consists of consonants and vowels which follow a certain pattern. The first, second, third - and if necessary fourth - consonants are allocated the letters **K**, **T**, **B**, and **L**. Thus ***ṭālib*** has the pattern

KāTiB in the singular; its broken plural *ṭalaba* "students" has the pattern **KaTaBa**.

Examples of broken plurals:

aKTāB	*awlād*	children	KiTūB	*biyūt ~ buyūt*	houses
~ iKTāB	*aṭfāl*	children	KuTuB	*kutub*	books
	alwān	colors		*mudun*	towns
	abnāʾ	sons	KuTūB	*wušūš*	faces
	asɛāṛ	prices		*nuṣūṣ*	texts
	abwāb	doors	KaTāBiL	*madāris*	schools
	iʾlām	pens		*maṭāɛim*	restaurants
KaTāB	*banāt*	girls	KaTaBīL	*mafatīḥ*	keys
KiTāB	*kilāb*	dogs		*šababīk*	windows
	gibāl	mountains		*sagagīd*	carpets
KuTaB	*ṣuwar*	photos	KawāTiB	*gawāmiɛ*	mosques
~ KiTaB	*šunaṭ*	bags		*šawāriɛ*	streets
	fuwaṭ	cloths	KaTāyiB	*kanāyis*	churches
	sikak	roads		*ɛaṛāyis*	brides

2. Adjective plurals

(a) When adjectives apply to people, they usually form their plural by adding *-īn* (→ II.V):

humma kuwayyisīn	*mawgudīn*	*taɛbanīn*	*mabṣuṭīn*
they are good	present	tired	happy

Note that words with the pattern **KāTi** such as *ġāli* "expensive" and *nāsi* "forgetting" have a feminine form **KaTya** and a plural form **KaTyīn**:

ġāli	*ġalya*	*ġalyīn*	"expensive"
nāsi	*nasya*	*nasyīn*	"forgetting"

Other adjectives and participles ending in *-i* which don't have the pattern **KāTi** are treated in the same way as *nisba*-adjectives, adding *-yy-* before the feminine suffix *-a* and the plural suffix *-īn* :

mistanni	*mistanniyya*	*mistanniyyīn*	"waiting"
mitṛabbi	*mitṛabbiyya*	*mitṛabbiyyīn*	"raised"

(b) Some of the most commonly used adjectives have a broken plural form which follows the pattern **KuTāB**:

(kibīr) ***kubāṛ***	"big"	*(biɛīd)* ***buɛād***	"far"
(ṭawīl) ***ṭuwāl***	"long"	*(laṭīf)* ***luṭāf***	"friendly" "nice"
(gamīl) ***gumāl***	"pretty"	*(ẓarīf)* ***ẓuṛāf***	"kind" "friendly"

Other patterns of adjective plurals are also to be found:

(faʾīr)	*fuʾaṛa*	"poor"	*(šāṭir)*	*šuṭṭār*	"well-behaved"
(ġani)	*aġniya*	"rich"	also:	*šaṭrīn*	"diligent"
also:	*ġunāy*				

V. Agreement

In Arabic there are three classes of numbers: singular, plural, and dual (for the dual → VIII.I) and two genders: masculine and feminine. Adjectives, pronouns, and verbs agree in gender and in number with the nouns with which they are connected or to which they refer.

1. In the singular, masculine and feminine nouns are connected with masculine or feminine adjectives, pronouns, and verbs, depending on their own gender (→ above IV):

walad šāṭir a diligent boy	*bintᵊ šaṭra* a diligent girl

2. In the plural, there is a significant difference between the treatment of people and inanimate objects. Grammatically speaking, the plural of inanimate objects is treated like a feminine singular, along with its adjectives, pronouns, and verbs. (For exceptions to this rule → II.IV and VII.I):

maṭāɛim gidīda new restaurants	*ilmaṭāɛim di* these restaurants
hiyya‿lmaṭāɛim gidīda ? are these restaurants new?	*ilmaṭāɛim ʾasɛarha ġalya* he restaurant prices are high

In other words, the plural form of adjectives, demonstratives, and pronouns only occurs (a) when referring to people, (b) when listing several items or (c) in combination with numbers (→ VI.V):

(a)	*ṭālibāt hulandiyyīn*	"Dutch female students"
	ilʾawlād dōl luṭāf	"these children are nice"
	ilbanāt dōl abūhum ġani	"the father of these girls is rich"
(b)	*ilkitāb wi‿lkuṛṛāsa ġalyīn*	"the book and notebook are expensive"
	ikkursi wi‿ttaṛabēẓa gudād	"the chair and the table are (both) new"
(c)	*talāta‿kbāṛ*	"three adults ~ big ones"
	talat kutub gudād	"three new books"
	ittalat kutub dōl	"these three books"

3. Adjectives which end in *-i*, the so-called *nisba*-ending, remain uninflected (→ II.IV.4):

balad rīfi gamīla	"a nice rural town"
sagāyir ʾamrikāni	"American cigarettes"

In the case of **people**, however, the plural form of the *nisba* is used:

ṭalaba maṣriyyīn	"Egyptian students"

4. *aḫsan* "better" has no feminine ending in *-a* (→ X.III), and no plural form. *kitīr* "many" "much" is also not usually inflected, but in more formal style *kitīra* (fem.) and *kutāṛ* (pl.) may be found:

dōl kitīr "those are a lot" *di ʾaḫsan* "this one (fem.) is better."

VI. "Please" and "Thank you"

1. The English word "please" is expressed in Arabic by two different words. *itfaḍḍal* is used when you offer something to someone, and *min faḍlak* is used when asking for a favor or making a request:

offer	*itfaḍḍal*	(m.)	**request**	*min faḍlak*	(m.)
	itfaḍḍali	(f.)		*min faḍlik*	(f.)
	itfaḍḍalu	(pl.)		*min faḍlukum*	(pl.)

law samaḫt (masc.), *law samaḫti* (fem.), *law samaḫtu* (pl.) "if you please" can be used instead of *min faḍlak* etc.

2. Below you will find expressions which are used when thanking someone, together with suitable replies:

Thanks		**Reply**	
šukṛan	"thank you"	*ʿafwan*	"not at all"
ʾalfᵉ šukr	"a thousand thanks"	*iššukrᵉ li‿llāh*	"don't thank me, thank God"
aškurak! aškurik! aškurkum!		*ʿala ʾē?*	"whatever for?"
mutšakkir! mutšakkira! mutšakkirīn! *mutašakkir! mutašakkira! mutašakkirīn!*		*ilʿafw*	"my pleasure"
kattaṛ xērak! kattaṛ xērik! kattaṛ xerku!		*xērak sābiʾ*	"it's you who should be thanked" (lit: your goodness preceded mine)

mutšakkir and *mutašakkir* actually mean "grateful" and are given a feminine or a plural ending as necessary.

kattaṛ xērak [lit: "May God increase your good fortune!"] and *aškurak* "I thank you" change according to the gender or number of the person being addressed: *kattaṛ xērik* (fem.), *kattaṛ xerkum* (pl.) and *aškurik*, (fem.), *aškurku* (pl.).

PROVERBS

ilḫaṛaka baṛaka	"a rolling stone gathers no moss" [lit. movement is a blessing]
ilɛagala min iššiṭān	"fools rush in where angels fear to tread" [lit. hurry belongs to the devil]
iṣṣabr^{ə} ṭayyib	"patiencc is a virtue"

baṛaka	blessing	*ṣabr*	patience
ḫaṛaka	movement	*ṭayyib*	good
šiṭān, šayaṭīn	devil	*ɛagala*	hurry

INCREASE YOUR VOCABULARY

mabāni "buildings"

airport	*maṭār, maṭarāt*	museum	*matḫaf, matāḫif*
block of flats	*ɛimāṛa, -āt*	National Public Library	*dāṛ ilkutub*
building	*mabna, mabāni*	police station	*ʾism, aʾsām*
church	*kinīsa, kanāyis*	office	*maktab, makātib*
club	*nādi, nawādi*	shop	*dukkān, dakakīn*
first aid post	*ʾisɛāf*	store, shop	*maḫall, -āt*
hotel	*funduʾ, fanādiʾ* / *lukạnda, -āt*	supermarket	*subarmarkit*
institute	*maɛhad, maɛāhid*	tower	*burg, abṛāg*
library	*maktaba, -āt*	university	*gamɛa, gāmiɛāt*
minaret	*madna, midan*	zoo	*ginent‿ilḫayawanāt*
mosque	*gāmiɛ, gawāmiɛ*		

EXERCISES

I. Show where the stress falls e.g., *waraʾa* → *wá̱raʾa*

mudarris	*mudarrisa*	*ṭalaba*	*ibnaha*	*baladu*
baladha	*baladik*	*siggāda*	*maṛṛa*	*maṛṛitēn*
šawāriɛ	*šawariɛna*	*waraʾāt*	*waraʾ*	*ismi*
ismaha	*šāriɛ*	*šariɛna*	*maṭɛam*	*šibbāk*
daʾāyiʾ	*ɛarfīn*	*ɛārif*	*muhandis*	*muhandisīn*
muhandisa	*ɛaṛabiyyiti*	*šanṭa*	*šanṭiti*	*xidmitak*

II. Where are you from? From Egypt? Yes, we are Egyptians.

intu‿mnēn? min Maṣr? - *aywa, iḫna maṣriyyīn.*

1. *dōl minēn? min inNimsa?* - *aywa,* ______________________
2. *humma‿mnēn? min Lubnān?* - *aywa,* ______________________
3. *intu‿mnēn? min ʾAmrīka?* - *aywa,* ______________________
4. *intu‿mnēn? min Surya?* - *aywa,* ______________________
5. *dōl minēn? min isSudān?* - *aywa,* ______________________
6. *dōl minēn? min ilYunān?* - *aywa,* ______________________
7. *dōl minēn? min Faṛansa?* - *aywa,* ______________________
8. *humma‿mnēn? min ʾIṭalya?* - *aywa,* ______________________
9. *intu‿mnēn? min ilMaġrib?* - *aywa,* ______________________
10. *dōl minēn? min Rusya?* - *aywa,* ______________________

III. How are you *Maḫmūd*? *izayy-**ak** ya Maḫmūd?*

1. *izzayy______ ya Sāmi?*
2. *izzayy______ ya banāt?*
3. *izzayy______ ya Maha?*
4. *izzayy______ ya ʾawlād?*
5. *izzayy______ ya ḅāḅa?*
6. *izzayy______ ya Samya?*
7. *izzayy______ ya Sayyid?*
8. *izzayy______ ya Ḫasan?*
9. *izzayy______ ya Mirvat?*
10. *izzayy______ ya ʾaṭfāl?*

IV. Where is your daughter, *Ḫasan*? *bint-***ak** *fēn ya Ḫasan?*

1. *bint_______ fēn ya Maha?*
2. *ɛamm______ fēn ya bint?*
3. *gidd _______ fēn ya Sāmi?*
4. *umm______ fēn ya banāt?*
5. *ḅāḅa________fēn ya ʔawlād?*
6. *abu________ fēn ya Salwa?*
7. *uxt______ fēn ya Maḫmūd?*
8. *awlād_____ fēn ya Mirvat?*

V. Tell me, how is your brother *Ḫasan*?

*ʔulli, axūk Ḫasan izzayy-***u***?*

1. *ʔulli, uxtak Samya, izzayy* ______________________________?
2. *ʔulli, ḅāḅa‿w ṃāṃa, izzay* ______________________________?
3. *ʔulli, bintak Mirvat, izzayy* ______________________________?
4. *ʔulli, ɛAyda, izzayy* ____________________________________?
5. *ʔulli, ibnak, izzayy* ____________________________________?
6. *ʔulli, awlādak, izzayy* __________________________________?
7. *ʔulli, ɛammak Aḫmad, izzayy* _____________________________?
8. *ʔulli, iṭṭalaba, izzayy* ___________________________________?

VI. He's not, but she is.

1. *huwwa miš wāxid bard, lākin hiyya* _______________________.
2. *huwwa miš mitṛabbi‿f-Ṭanṭa, lākin hiyya* ________________.
3. *Ḫasan miš šāṭir, lākin Samīḫa* ________________________.
4. *ana miš ɛārif, lākin hiyya* ____________________________.
5. *huwwa miš ɛāwiz, lākin hiyya* _________________________.
6. *iggāmiɛ miš ʔuṛayyib, lākin ikkinīsa* ___________________.
7. *iṭṭālib miš wiḫiš, lākin ilmadrasa* ______________________.
8. *abūya miš misāfir, lākin ummi* ________________________.
9. *Aḫmad miš mawgūd, lākin uxtu* ________________________.
10. *innādi miš biɛīd, lākin ilmaḫaṭṭa* ________________________.

VII. He's not ..., but they are ...

1. *Aḫmad miš misāfir, lākin Sāmi‿w Maha* ________________.
2. *huwwa miš laṭīf lākin Sāmi‿w Maha* ________________.
3. *ana miš šāṭir, lākin Sāmi‿w Maha* ________________.
4. *huwwa miš ṭawīl, lākin Sāmi‿w Maha* ________________.
5. *inta miš ġani, lākin Sāmi‿w Maha* ________________.
6. *inti miš kibīra, lākin Sāmi‿w Maha* ________________.
7. *inta miš ʕārif, lākin Sāmi‿w Maha* ________________.
8. *huwwa miš ʕāwiz, lākin humma* ________________.
9. *inti miš faʔīra, lākin humma* ________________.
10. *iṭṭālib da miš gidīd, lākin intu ṭalaba* ________________.

VIII. Take one word from each of the columns (a), (b), (c), and combine them into logical sentences. Make the necessary changes.

(a)	(b)	(c)
nādi	*fi*	*ṭarabēẓa*
šanṭa	*ʕala*	*iddōr ilʔawwal*
kitāb	*gamb*	*kursi*
ʔalam	*taḫt*	*mustašfa*
bint	*ʕand*	*šanṭa*
gāmiʕ	*ʔuṣād*	*naṣya*
šaʔʔa	*fi*	*maṭʕam*
iddōr ittāni	*fōʔ*	*ummaha*

1. ________________
2. ________________
3. ________________
4. ________________
5. ________________
6. ________________
7. ________________
8. ________________

IX. Give the singular form of the following plurals.

gawāmiʕ	________	*kanāyis*	________
kubāṛ	________	*kararīs*	________
kutub	________	*madāris*	________
banāt	________	*ṣuwar*	________
bilād	________	*biyūt*	________
šunaṭ	________	*aṭfāl*	________
gudūd	________	*abwāb*	________
lumaḍ	________	*asmāʾ*	________
alwān	________	*maḥaṭṭāt*	________
maṭāʕim	________	*gudād*	________
šuṭṭār	________	*gumāl*	________
nawāṣi	________	*šawāriʕ*	________
fuʾaṛa	________	*iʾlām*	________

X. Put the following sentences in the plural.

1. *ilmuhandis miš mawgūd.* ________________
2. *ilmustašfa‿kwayyisa.* ________________
3. *iṭṭālib laṭīf giddan.* ________________
4. *iggāmiʕ biʕīd ʕan hina.* ________________
5. *ilmaṭʕam fātiḥ.* ________________
6. *ilbintᵊ gamīla.* ________________
7. *ilbintᵊ di mawlūda fi‿gGīza.* ________________
8. *iṭṭiflᵊ gaʕān.* ________________
9. *ilbēt kibīr.* ________________
10. *iṭṭarabēẓa‿ṣġayyara.* ________________

XI. Arrange the following words into logical sentences.

1. *iḥna, ʾawi, gaʕanīn* ________________
2. *ʾawi, kitīr, dōl, miš* ________________
3. *innādi, yimkin, humma, fi* ________________
4. *hina, ʾuṛayyiba, min, ilmadrasa* ________________
5. *biʕīda, xāliṣ, ilbalad, di* ________________

6. *mawludīn, mitrabbiyyīn, wi, humma, hina* ________________

7. *ʕala ṭūl, waṛa, iggāmiʕ, ilmadrasa* ________________

8. *wiḫša, iṣṣuwar, di, miš* ________________

9. *ġāli, da, ʔawi, ilmaṭʕam* ________________

10. *balad, Ṭanṭa, gamīla, rīfi* ________________

11. *fēn, law, ilmaḫaṭṭa, samaḫti* ________________

12. *ismu, da, ʔē, iššāriʕ* ________________

XII. Translate the following sentences.

1. These girls are pretty.

____

2. The female students are at the club.

____

3. Breakfast isn't ready.

____

4. Where exactly were you born?

____

5. The restaurant is on the street corner.

____

6. My daughter and your (sing.) daughter aren't present today.

____

7. This restaurant is a bit better.

____

8. I am originally from Alexandria.

____

9. This telephone call is not for you.

____

10. These mosques aren't far from the club.

____

11. Are the schools far from here?

____

12. These restaurants are not bad.

____

13. Is *Aḫmad* still in the hospital?

____

14. We want these keys!

15. It's now three o'clock.

16. These carpets are very dear.

17. *Rašīd* is a pretty town in the countryside.

18. *Ḥasan* and *Samya* are nice children.

19. Where is your home?

20. *Salma*'s father is not a teacher.

LESSON V

DIALOGUES

¿andik awlād?

Salwa:	*¿andik awlād?*
Maha:	*¿andi‿tnēn, bintᵊ‿w walad.*
Salwa:	*wi ¿Ayda? ¿andaha ʾawlād kamān?*
Maha:	*aywa, lākin ¿andaha bintᵊ waḫda bass.*
Salwa:	*w‿axūki ma-¿andūš awlād?*
Maha:	*lā, ma-¿andūš, da lissa‿ṣġayyaṛ wi miš miggawwiz.*

ma¿āk walla ma-m¿akš?

Sāmi:	*ma¿āk kabrīt?*
Ḫasan:	*li‿lʾasaf ma-m¿ayīš kabrīt.*
Sāmi:	*ma¿āk wallā¿a?*
Ḫasan:	*aywa‿m¿āya, ahé!*
Sāmi:	*ma¿āk sagāyir?*
Ḫasan:	*ʾāsif, barḍu ma-m¿ayīš, yimkin Mike ma¿ā(h) sagāyir.*
Sāmi:	*Mike fēn?*
Ḫasan:	*miš ¿ārif, kān hina‿w miši.*

iššuġl

Samya:	*bitištaġal ʾē?*
Sāmi:	*ana muhandis.*
Samya:	*wi mabsūṭ min šuġlak?*
Sāmi:	*ya¿ni, miš baṭṭāl, ilḫamdu li‿llāh. w‿inti‿btištaġali fēn?*
Samya:	*ana mudarrisit sanawi.*
Sāmi:	*ana kamān kuntᵊ zamān mudarris, lākin dilwaʾti baštaġal fi-maṣna¿ fi-Ḫilwān.*

fi‿lmaṭ¿am

Sāmi:	*ya rayyis!*
iṣṣufragi:	*ana gayyᵊ ḫālan! ...... ʾayyᵊ xidma?*
Sāmi:	*hāt itnēn ʾahwa wi talāta šāy, min faḍlak!*
iṣṣufragi:	*ʾahwa turki walla niskafē?*
Sāmi:	*turki, min faḍlak, wāḫid maẓbūṭ wi wāḫid ¿a‿rrīḫa. wi hāt ilḫisāb bi‿lmaṛṛa, iḫna mista¿gilīn šuwayya.*
iṣṣufragi:	*ḫāḍir, ya Bē!*

VOCABULARY

ʾahwa	coffee
ʾasaf	regret
li‿lʾasaf	unfortunately
ʾāsif (m.), *ʾasfa* (f.)	I'm sorry
barḍu	also, too
barīza, barāyiz	10 piaster piece
baštaġal	I work
Bē	Bey (title)
bitištaġal/i	you work (sing.)
bi‿lmaṛṛa	also
fakka	small change
gidīd lang	brand new
ḫāḍir	right away, certainly
ḫālan	immediately
ḫisāb	check, bill
ḫēṭa, ḫiṭān	wall
kabrīt	matches
kunt	I was
kān	he was
mabsūṭ	happy, pleased
maṣnaʿ, maṣāniʿ	factory
maẓbūṭ	right; normally sweet (applied to sugar in coffee)
maʿa	with, by
miggawwiz	married
min faḍlak	please (when requesting)
mistaʿgil	in a hurry
miši	he's gone
nāʾiṣ	minus
niskafē	Nescafé
rayyis	waiter
rīḫa	smell, scent
ʿa‿rrīḫa	with a bit of sugar
sanawi	secondary (school)
mudarrisit sanawi	secondary (school) teacher
sigāṛa, sagāyir	cigarette
ṣufragi, -yya	waiter
šuġl, ašġāl	work
šāy	tea
talāta	three
turki	Turkish
ṭabbāx	cook
wala	nor
walla	or
wallāʿa, -āt	lighter (cigarettes)
widn, widān	ear
xidma	service
ʾayyᵊ xidma	how can I help you
yibʾa	is, becomes
yisāwi	is equal to, is
zamān	previously
ʿand	with; to have
ʿa‿rrīḫa	with a bit of sugar (lit. scented)

GRAMMAR

I. Prepositional sentences: "to have"

1. In Arabic, "to have" meaning "to possess" is expressed by means of prepositions such as *ʿand, maʿa* or *li*, in combination with a possessive suffix which refers to the "possessor." Preposition + suffix come first, and what is "possessed" comes afterwards. Instead of saying "I have a car," we say "with me is a car." Sentences of this type are known as prepositional sentences and their structure is always **predicate + subject**:

ʿandi bint	"I've got a daughter"
maʿāya‿flūs	"I've got (some) money (on me)"
lu(h)ʾuxt	"he's got a sister"

The subject of the prepositional sentence is generally undefined, but sentences with a defined subject are possible as well.

ʿandak ilkitāb da kamān? "do you have this book too?"

2. *ɛand*, *maɛa* and *li* are the most important prepositions used to express the word "to have." When combined with suffixes, they appear as follows:

ɛand			
	ɛandi	*ɛandak*	*ɛandu*
		ɛandik	*ɛandaha*
	ɛandina	*ɛanduku(m)*	*ɛanduhum*
maɛa			
	maɛāya	*maɛāk*	*maɛā(h)*
		maɛāki	*maɛāha*
	maɛāna	*maɛāku(m)*	*maɛāhum*
li			
	liyya	*lik ~ līk*	*lu(h) ~ lī(h)*
		liki ~ līki	*laha ~ līha*
	lina ~ līna	*luku(m) ~ līku(m)*	*luhum ~ līhum*

(a) *ɛand* means "having" in the sense of "owning" or "possessing":

ɛandina ɛaṛabiyya‿kbīra "we've got a big car"

(b) *maɛa* is used for "having on one's person" or "with one":

maɛāya ɛišrīn ginēh "I've got 20 pounds with me"

(c) *li* expresses "having got" in the sense of "s/th is intended for s/o":

līk gawāb fi‿lbusṭa "you've got a letter in the mail"
luh talāta‿gnēh ɛandi "I owe him three pounds"
[lit: there are for him three pounds with me]

li is also used to refer to parts of the body:

kān luh šanab zamān "he used to have a moustache "

Both *ɛand* and *li* are used when referring to some of the members of one's family:

liyya ɛamm^{ə} *wāḫid bass* "I have only one uncle"

If the "possessor" is an inanimate object, *li* is usually used:

ilʔōḍa līha bāb wi šibbakēn "the room has a door and two windows"

3. In a prepositional sentence, the preposition cannot be followed by a noun. For this reason, when the "possessor" is a noun, the sentence starts with this noun and a suffix referring to it is attached to the preposition. In other words, one cannot say: ***ɛand iṭṭālib kutub*** but ***iṭṭālib ɛandu kutub*** "the student has (some) books" nor ***li‿lḫiṭān widān*** but ***ilḫiṭān līha‿wdān*** "walls have ears."

4. The prepositions *fi*, *ɛala*, *waṛa* and *ʔuddām* can also be used in a prepositional sentence with the meaning of "to have":

issana fīha‿tnāšar šahr	"in a year there are twelve months" (lit: the year has twelve months)
iššaʾʾa fīha takyīf	"the flat's got airconditioning"
issagāyir ʿalēha ḍarība	"cigarettes have a tax (levied) on them"
warāya mišwār	"I've got an errand to run" (lit: behind me is an errand)
ʾuddāmak ḫallᵊ tāni ?	"do you have any other solution?"

Note: Something to be careful of is the type of sentence with the structure subject + predicate, where the suffix attached to the preposition does not refer to any "possessor" and the original meaning of the preposition e.g., "with" "at" "on" is retained: *ilʾawlād ʿandaha* "the children are with her," *kutubak lissa‿mʿāya* "I still have your books with me."

II. Negation of prepositional sentences

When prepositional sentences with the meaning "to have" are put in the negative, *ma-...-š* [not *miš*] is used. In this case, *ma-* is put in front of the preposition and *-š* is added after the possessive suffix. If the suffix ends in a vowel, this is lengthened (→ III.IV.1):

ʿandu ʾawlād →	*ma-ʿandūš ʾawlād*	"he's got no children."
maʿāya sagāyir →	*ma-mʿayīš sagāyir*	"I haven't got any cigarettes with me"

ʿand			
	ma-ʿandīš	*ma-ʿandakš*	*ma-ʿandūš*
		ma-ʿandikīš	*ma-ʿandahāš*
	ma-ʿandināš	*ma-ʿandukūš*	*ma-ʿanduhumš*
maʿa			
	ma-mʿīš	*ma-mʿakš*	*ma-mʿahūš*
		ma-mʿakīš	*ma-mʿahāš*
	ma-mʿanāš	*ma-mʿakūš*	*ma-mʿahumš*
li			
	ma-līš	*ma-lakš*	*ma-lūš*
		ma-lkīš	*ma-lhāš*
	ma-lnāš	*ma-lkūš*	*ma-lhumš*

When negated, the second person singular feminine ending *-ik* takes an extra *-i* and becomes *-iki*, and the third person singular masculine ending (*-h*) takes an extra *-u* and becomes *-hu*. Both lengthen their vowels before the final *-š*. This means that forms such as *ma-ʿandikīš*, *ma-lkīš* and *ma-mʿahūš* will arise.

As well as *ma-ʿandūš*, you will also find the form *ma-ʿanduhūš*. As well as *-ku*, there is also the variant *-kum* as found in *ma-lkumš* and *ma-ʿandukumš*. Instead of *ma-mʿayīš* you may also hear *ma-mʿīš*.

ma-ʿandīš waʾt	"I haven't got time"
ma-mʿahāš wallāʿa	"She hasn't got a lighter on her"
ma-līš ʾabbᵊ wala ʾumm	"I have got neither father nor mother"

Note that if the prepositional phrase does not carry a sense of "having" and the sentence has the form subject + predicate, as in *ilᵓawlād ɛandᵊ ḅaḅāhum* "the children are with their father," then it is negated by simply using *miš* (→ above I.4 note):

ilᵓawlād miš ɛandᵊ ḅaḅāhum	"the children are not with their father"
kutubak miš maɛāya	"I haven't got your books with me"

III. The genitive construction

1. Two nouns can be connected to each other by what is known as a genitive construction, thereby becoming one noun phrase:

ism ilwalad	"the boy's name"	(the name of the boy)
uxtᵊ Samīra	"Samīra's sister"	(the sister of Samīra)
bintᵊ ɛammi	"my cousin"	(the daughter of my uncle)

2. In such cases, if the first noun ends with the feminine ending *-a* this will change to *-it*:

maḫaṭṭa	+	*ilᵓutubīs*	→	*maḫaṭṭit ilᵓutubīs*	"the bus stop"
nimra	+	*ittilifōn*	→	*nimrit ittilifōn*	"the telephone number"

3. If the second noun, which is functioning as a genitive, is defined, then grammatically speaking the whole construction is defined. In the category "defined" we include proper nouns and nouns preceded by an article or followed by a possessive suffix. If the second noun is not defined, then the whole construction is treated as undefined.

awlād ɛamm	"first cousins"	(children of an uncle)
nimrit tilifōn	"a telephone number"	(a number of a telephone)
mudarrisit sanawi	"a secondary (school) teacher"	(a female teacher of a secondary school)

4. In the genitive construction, the first noun must **never** be given an article or a possessive suffix. What's more, no other word may be placed between the two nouns. If there is an adjective, it has to be placed after the entire construction.

di mudarrisit sanawi‿kwayyisa ᵓawi
"she is a very good secondary school teacher"

IV. Feminine nouns and their suffixes

If a possessive suffix has to be added to a feminine noun ending in *-a*, then the noun will change its ending to *-it* as it did in the genitive construction.

báʾaṛa "cow"	*šaʾʾa* "flat"	*ṣūra* "picture"
*baʾ**áṛti***	*šaʾʾ**íti***	***ṣurti***
*baʾ**áṛtak***	*šaʾʾ**ítak***	***ṣurtak***
*baʾ**áṛtik***	*šaʾʾ**ítik***	***ṣurtik***
*baʾ**áṛtu***	*šaʾʾ**ítu***	***ṣurtu***
*baʾaṛ**ítha***	*šaʾʾ**ítha***	*ṣur**ítha***
*baʾaṛ**ítna***	*šaʾʾ**ítna***	*ṣur**ítna***
*baʾaṛ**ítk**um*	*šaʾʾ**ítk**um*	*ṣur**ítk**um*
*baʾaṛ**íth**um*	*šaʾʾ**íth**um*	*ṣur**íth**um*

Note that when suffixes are added:
* new heavy clusters may arise (→ IV.I).
* the *-i-* of the feminine ending *-it* may find itself in an unprotected position which means that it must be elided and this will cause the stress to move (→ IV.II).

V. Past time: *kān*

In Arabic, the verb "to be" is omitted in the present tense, and the subject and predicate follow directly one after the other (→ I.III):

huwwa hina	*ana mudarris*
"he (is) here"	"I (am) a teacher"

When describing past time however, the verb *kān* "he was" is used.

(huwwa) kān hina	*(ana) kuntᵊ mudarris*
"(he) was here"	"(I) was a teacher"

The following table shows all the forms of *kān:*

3rd person	2nd person	1st person
(huwwa) kān hina	*(inta) kuntᵊ hina*	*(ana) kuntᵊ hina*
(hiyya) kānit hina	*(inti) kunti hina*	
(humma) kānu hina	*(intu) kuntu hina*	*(iḫna) kunna hina*

The endings of *kān* are the same as those which are used to form the perfect (→ IX.III). With endings that start with a consonant, *kān* becomes *kun-*. With endings that start with a vowel, *kān* remains unchanged.

Note that in Arabic:
* the 3rd person singular masculine is used to refer to a verb because it is the simplest form of the verb in question. In English the infinitive is used in such a case.
* personal pronouns are not normally used as subjects of verbs, though they may be used to add particular emphasis.

kān is also used in prepositional sentences which describe a past event. In this instance, there is no agreement and *kān* remains **unchanged**, whatever the subject:

kān ʿandaha waʾt	"she had time"	(there) was with her time
kān maʿāya ʿaṛabiyya	"I had a car with me"	(there) was with me a car

The negative of *kān* is formed by adding *ma-...-š*, just as is done with *ʿand* and *maʿa* meaning "to have."

ma-kanš "he wasn't"

3rd person	2nd person	1st person
ma-kanš *ma-kanitš* *ma-kanūš*	*ma-kuntiš* *ma-kuntīš* *ma-kuntūš*	*ma-kuntiš* *ma-kunnāš*

Note that after double consonants the negational suffix is *-iš* (→ III.I): *ma-kunt + iš > ma-kuntiš.*

Samya ma-kanitšᵊ‿mʿāna	"Samya wasn't with us"
Aḥmad ma-kanšᵊ mawgūd	"Aḥmad wasn't there"
ma-kuntiš ʿarfa	"I (fem.) didn't know"
ma-kanšᵊ ʿandi waʾt	"I had no time"
ma-kanšᵊ‿mʿāya‿flūs	"I had no money on me"

VI. The numbers 1 to 12

The numbers used for counting from one to twelve are as follows:

wāḥid	one	*sabʿa*	seven
itnēn	two	*tamanya*	eight
talāta	three	*tisʿa*	nine
aṛbaʿa	four	*ʿašaṛa*	ten
xamsa	five	*ḥidāšaṛ*	eleven
sitta	six	*itnāšaṛ*	twelve

1. *wāḥid* follows a noun only if the singular is being **emphasized** for some reason. It also has a feminine form *waḥda*:

walad wāḥid "(only) one boy" *bintᵊ waḥda* "(only) one girl"

wāḥid can sometimes be used as an indefinite article, but only when referring to people (→ II.IV)

wāḥid ingilīzi "an Englishman" *waḥda maṣriyya* "an Egyptian woman"

N.B. *wāḥid ~ waḥda* can also mean "someone":

fī wāḥid ~ waḥda ʿašānak "there's someone for you"

For examples of how to combine numbers with nouns, refer to lesson VI.V.

2. The numbers mentioned above can be used when ordering in a restaurant. In this case they are used uninflected in front of the singular of the item being ordered:

talāta ʾahwa	"three coffees!"	*xamsa šāy*	"five teas!"
wāḫid lamūn	"one lemonade!"	*wāḫid kōka*	"one coke!"

3. With the exception of *wāḫid,* numbers are used with the singular when combined with weights, measures, or units of money e.g., *mitr* "meter," *ṣanti* "centimeter," *milli* "millimeter," *kīlu* "kilogram" "kilometer," *sāġ* "piaster," *ginē(h)* "Egyptian pound," *ʾadam* "foot," *būṣa* "inch":

xamsa ‿gnē(h)	"five pounds"
tallāga xamsa ʾadam	"a five-cubic foot fridge"
tisʿa kīlu	"nine kilos"
talāta sāġ	"three piasters"

wāḫid and *waḫda* can only be used with the above words if the number "one" is to be emphasised. In this case they follow the noun and are treated as adjectives:

ginē(h) wāḫid	"(just) one pound"	*barīza waḫda bass*	"only 10 piasters"

4. When asking "how many?" *kām* is used, followed by a singular noun:

kām bint?	"how many girls?"	*kām ginē(h)?*	"how many pounds?"

5. Asking the time is done in the following way:

issāʿa kām?	*issāʿa waḫda*	"it's one o'clock"
	issāʿa xamsa	"it's five o'clock"

INCREASE YOUR KNOWLEDGE

More examples of prepositional sentences: "to have" "to have got"

ʿandi:	*ʾagāza*	"a day off"	*ʿandi:*	*ginēna*	"a garden"
	ʾuṭṭa	"a cat"		*kalb*	"a dog"
	bēt	"a house"		*maʿād*	"an appointment"
	dars	"a class"		*šuġl*	"a job" "work"
	fakka	"small change"		*waʾt*	"time"
	filūs	"money"		*ʿaṛabiyya*	"a car"

N.B. *ʿandu ḫaʾʾ* "he's right," *ʿandi šuġl* "I'm busy."

Coffee *ʾahwa* or *bunn*?

* *ʾahwa* doesn't only mean the drink itself. It can also mean a coffeeshop. As such, it has the plural *ʾahāwi.*

* *bunn* means ground coffee, and *bunnᵊ ḫabb* means coffee beans.

The coffee beans are often mixed with spices such as *ḫabbahān* "cardamom" in which case it's called *bunnᵊ‿mḫawwig.*

* Turkish coffee is served with four different degrees of sweetness:

sāda	without sugar	*ɛa‿rrīḫa*	just a little sugar
maẓbūṭ	normally sweet	*ziyāda*	lots of sugar

A cup of tea with a little sugar is usually ordered by saying:

wāḫid šāy sukkaṛ xafīf min faḍlik! "one tea with a little sugar please!"

EXERCISES

I. wāɧid or waɧda?

ɛandi bintᵊ __________ bass. maɛāya kuṛṛāsa ________ bass.

ɛandaha kalb __________ bass. ɛandina‿ktāb __________ bass.

ɛandu šaᵓᵓa __________ bass. ɛandina villa __________ bass.

maɛāya ᵓalam __________ bass. maɛāha ṣūra __________ bass.

II. I haven't got ... ! Answer using ɛand or li .

humma dōl awlādak? - lā, ma-ɛandīš awlād.

1. hiyya di bintak? - lā, __________________ banāt.
2. hiyya di ᵓuxtuhum? - lā, __________________ ixwāt.
3. huwwa da ɛammu? - lā, __________________ ɛimām.
4. hiyya di kutubhum? - lā, __________________ kutub.
5. huwwa da ᵓabūkum? - lā, __________________ abb.
6. huwwa da ᵓalamak? - lā, __________________ ᵓilima.
7. hiyya di ɛaṛabiyyitik? - lā, ________________ ɛaṛabiyya.
8. hiyya di‿flūsak? - lā, __________________ filūs.

III. I've only got one! Answer using ɛand or li .

ɛandak kām bint? - ɛandi bintᵊ waɧda bass.

1. ɛandak kām walad? - ________ walad ________ bass.
2. ɛandukum kām ɛaṛabiyya? - _______ ɛaṛabiyya ______ bass.
3. ɛandaha kām šaᵓᵓa? - __________šaᵓᵓa________ bass.
4. lukum kām uxt? - __________ uxt_________ bass.
5. ɛandak kām wallāɛa? - ______ wallāɛa _________ bass.
6. ɛandu kām bint? - ________ bint ___________ bass.
7. līki kām ạxx? - ________ ᵓạxx __________bass.
8. ilbēt lī(h) kām bāb? - ilbēt ______ bāb ________ bass.
9. maɛāk kām ᵓalam? - ________ ᵓalam ________ bass.

10. *maɛāku kām šanṭa?* - ________ *šanṭa* ________ *bass.*

11. *ɛanduku kām bēt?* - ________ *bēt* ________ *bass.*

IV. Ask questions: Have you got a ... on you?

(inta) *maɛāk kabrīt?*

1. *(inta)* ______________ *wallāɛa?*
2. *(inti)* ______________ *filūs?*
3. *(humma)* ______________ *ɛaṛabiyya?*
4. *(intu)* ______________ *sagāyir?*
5. *(iḫna)* ______________ *fakka?*
6. *(huwwa)* ______________ *kām ginē(h)?*
7. *(hiyya)* ______________ *šanṭa?*

V. Answer the following questions in the negative.

ya Ḫasan, maɛāk fakka? - *laʾ,* *ma-mɛayīš*

1. *ya ʾawlād, ɛanduku ʾalam ruṣāṣ?* - *laʾ,* ______________.
2. *ilʾawlād ɛandᵊ Samya?* - *laʾ,* ______________.
3. *ya-taṛa‿ššaʾʾa di līha bāb tāni?* - *laʾ,* ______________.
4. *intu līkum ʾuxtᵊ‿ṣġayyaṛa?* - *laʾ,* ______________.
5. *aṣḫabku ɛanduhum šaʾʾa‿kbīra?* - *laʾ,* ______________.
6. *ya-taṛa saɛti‿mɛāki?* - *laʾ,* ______________.
7. *ya Samya, ɛandik bēt f‿Iskindiriyya?* - *laʾ,* ______________.

VI. They've got one, but they haven't got it with them! Use *maɛa.*

ɛanduhum ɛaṛabiyya, lākin miš maɛāhum.

1. *ɛandaha ɛaṛabiyya, lākin miš* ________________________.
2. *ɛandi wallāɛa, lākin miš* ________________________.
3. *ɛandina‿flūs, lākin miš* ________________________.
4. *ɛanduhum sagāyir, lākin miš* ________________________.
5. *ɛandu kabrīt, lākin miš* ________________________.

VII. Perhaps Ḫasan's got some matches on him?

ma-mɛayīš kabrīt, yimkin Ḫasan maɛā(h).

1. *ma-mɛayīš kabrīt, yimkin Samya* ____________________.
2. *ma-mɛayīš kabrīt, yimkin iṭṭalaba* ____________________.
3. *ma-mɛayīš kabrīt, yimkin inta* ____________________.
4. *ma-mɛayīš kabrīt, yimkin Maḥmūd* ____________________.
5. *ma-mɛayīš kabrīt, yimkin inti* ____________________.
6. *ma-mɛayīš kabrīt, yimkin intu* ____________________.
7. *ma-mɛahumšᵊ kabrīt, yimkin iḥna* ____________________.
8. *ma-mɛahūš kabrīt, yimkin ana* ____________________.

VIII. Who's that phonecall for?

ilmukalma di‿l-mīn? - ilmukalma di līna ʔiḥna!

1. *ilmukalma di‿l-mīn?* - ____________________ *huwwa!*
2. *ilmukalma di‿l-mīn?* - ____________________ *ana!*
3. *ilmukalma di‿l-mīn?* - ____________________ *iḥna!*
4. *ilmukalma di‿l-mīn?* - ____________________ *intu!*
5. *ilmukalma di‿l-mīn?* - ____________________ *hiyya!*
6. *ilmukalma di‿l-mīn?* - ____________________ *inti!*
7. *ilmukalma di‿l-mīn?* - ____________________ *humma!*

IX. Arithmetic! *nāʔiṣ* "minus," *yibʔu* ~ *yisāwi* "is" "equals."

talāta‿w xamsa yibʔu tamanya

1. *itnēn w‿arbaɛa yibʔu* ____________________.
2. *itnāšar nāʔiṣ tisɛa yisāwi* ____________________.
3. *tamanya nāʔiṣ wāḥid yisāwi* ____________________.
4. *xamsa‿w sitta yibʔu* ____________________.
5. *ɛašara w‿itnēn yibʔu* ____________________.
6. *ḥidāšar nāʔiṣ arbaɛa yibʔu* ____________________.

X. Ordering in a restaurant.

(4x)	*aṛbaɛa*	*ᵓahwa min faḍlak!*	(6x)	*sitta*	*burtuᵓān!*
(5x)	________	*šāy, min faḍlak!*	(4x)	________	*lamūn!*
(1x)	________	*ᵓahwa, min faḍlak!*	(9x)	________	*bibsi!*
(2x)	________	*kōka, min faḍlak!*	(3x)	________	*niskafē!*
(7x)	________	*ᵓahwa turki!*	(1x)	________	*bīra!*
(10x)	________	*šāy, min faḍlak!*	(12x)	________	*ᵓahwa!*

XI. Ten minus three is seven, so you owe me seven pounds.

ɛašaṛa nāᵓiṣ talāta yibᵓu sabɛa, yaɛni liyya ɛandak sabɛa‿gnēh.

1. *xamsa nāᵓiṣ talāta yibᵓu‿tnēn, yaɛni* ________________________.
2. *sabɛa nāᵓiṣ aṛbaɛa yibᵓu talāta, yaɛni* ________________________.
3. *tisɛa nāᵓiṣ tamanya yibᵓa wāḥid, yaɛni* ________________________.
4. *talāta nāᵓiṣ wāḥid yibᵓu‿tnēn, yaɛni* ________________________.
5. *ɛašaṛa nāᵓiṣ xamsa yibᵓu xamsa, yaɛni* ________________________.

XII. Put into the past tense using *kān* + *imbāriḥ* "yesterday" or *zamān* "previously."

ana taɛbāna. - *kuntᵊ taɛbāna‿mbāriḥ.*

1. *huwwa miš mawgūd.* - ________________ *imbāriḥ.*
2. *Ḥasan ɛandu maɛād.* - ________________ *imbāriḥ.*
3. *hiyya miš fi‿lmadrasa.* - ________________ *imbāriḥ.*
4. *baštaġal fi‿lmaṣnaɛ.* - ________________ *zamān.*
5. *Samya miggawwiza.* - ________________ *zamān.*
6. *iḥna fi‿lmustašfa.* - ________________ *imbāriḥ.*
7. *ana waxda bard.* - ________________ *imbāriḥ.*
8. *humma lissa miš ɛarfīn.* - ________________ *imbāriḥ.*
9. *inta fi‿nnādi?* - ________________ *imbāriḥ?*
10. *iṭṭalaba miš mawgudīn.* - ________________ *imbāriḥ.*

XIII. She wasn't here yesterday! Answer in the negative.

hiyya kānit hina‿mbāriḫ? - *lā, ma-kanitš^{ə} hina‿mbāriḫ.*

1. *huwwa Sāmi kān mudarrisak?* - *lā,* ______________________.
2. *kān ɛandaha waʾt?* - *lā,* ______________________.
3. *iṭṭalaba kānu‿mɛākum?* - *lā,* ______________________.
4. *ilmaṭɛam kān ġāli?* - *lā,* ______________________.
5. *inta kunt^{ə}‿f-ʾAlmanya?* - *lā,* ______________________.
6. *kuntu waxdīn bard imbāriḫ?* - *lā,* ______________________.
7. *intu kuntu taɛbanīn šuwayya?* - *lā,* ______________________.
8. *huwwa‿ḫna kunna ɛarfīn?* - *lā,* ______________________.
9. *hiyya kānit miggawwiza?* - *lā,* ______________________.
10. *kuntu fi‿lbēt?* - *lā,* ______________________.

XIV. Add possessive suffixes and complete the following table.

	ṣūra	*ʾōḍa*	*xidma*	*wallāɛa*	*šanṭa*
inta					
huwwa					
iḫna					
humma					
inti					
ana					
hiyya					

XV. Answer the following questions using a genitive construction.

awlād mīn dōl? - *dōl awlād Salwa!*

1. *banāt mīn dōl?* - ______________________
2. *bēt mīn da?* - ______________________
3. *šanṭit mīn di?* - ______________________

4. *wallāʿit mīn di?* - ______________________

5. *gidd^ə mīn da?* - ______________________

6. *abu mīn da?* - ______________________

7. *umm^ə mīn di?* - ______________________

8. *sāʿit mīn di?* - ______________________

9. *mudarrisit mīn di?* - ______________________

10. *mudarris mīn da?* - ______________________

XVI. Ḫasan's got a car - that's Ḫasan's car!

Ḫasan ʿandu ʿaṛabiyya. - *di ʿaṛabiyyit Ḫasan!*

1. *Samya ʿandaha sāʿa.* - ______________________

2. *Ḫasan ʿandu‿gnēna.* - ______________________

3. *humma ʿanduhum maṣnaʿ.* - ______________________

4. *Ḫasan ʿandu ʾawlād.* - ______________________

5. *aṣḫābi ʿanduhum šaʾʾa.* - ______________________

6. *Sāmi ʿandu maṭʿam.* - ______________________

7. *iḫna ʿandina bint.* - ______________________

8. *Samīr lu(h) ʾuxt.* - ______________________

9. *Ṭāriʾ ʿandu ʾuṭṭa.* - ______________________

10. *Mirvat laha gidda.* - ______________________

XVII. Translate the following sentences.

1. I've only got one daughter.

______________________________________.

2. He hasn't got a lighter on him.

______________________________________.

3. The children aren't with us.

______________________________________.

4. We don't have a car.

______________________________________.

5. Three cokes, please!

____________________________________.

6. One coffee, please!

____________________________________.

7. Have you got a pencil (on you)?

____________________________________.

8. Perhaps *Ḥasan*'s got some cigarettes on him?

____________________________________.

9. Perhaps *Samya* hasn't got time?

____________________________________.

10. I haven't got any change.

____________________________________.

11. Where is the bus stop?

____________________________________.

12. Whose children are those?

____________________________________.

13. That boy - what's his name?

____________________________________.

14. The girls are still young (little) and not married.

____________________________________.

15. She was a teacher - and he was a teacher in a secondary school.

____________________________________.

16. I'm now working in a school in Alexandria.

____________________________________.

17. Formerly I was a cook for an Englishman.

____________________________________.

18. I work as an engineer in a factory

____________________________________.

19. *Maḥmūd*'s children are at a French school.

____________________________________.

20. What *(kām)* is her telephone number, please?

____________________________________.

21. There is a gas station on the corner. (gas = *banzīn*)

____________________________________.

LESSON VI

DIALOGUES

ilwuṣūl fi-Maṣr

A. *fi‿lmaṭār*

izẓābiṭ: *ilbasbōr, law samaḫt!*
Jim: *itfaḍḍal, ahó!*
izẓābiṭ: *wi‿lvīza fēn?*
Jim: *ahé!*
izẓābiṭ: *siyadtak gayyᵊ‿syāḫa walla šuġl?*
Jim: *ana gayyᵊ‿syāḫa.*
izẓābiṭ: *ʾahlan wa sahlan!*
Jim: *ʾahlan bīk! ya-táṛa taslīm iššunaṭ fēn?*
izẓābiṭ: *iššunaṭ hinākk, guwwa!*
Jim: *wi fēn iggumruk?*
izẓābiṭ: *ahó, gambᵊ bāb ilxurūg.*

B. *iggumruk*

ilmuwaẓẓaf: *law samaḫt, itfaḍḍal hina!*
Jim: *afandim?*
ilmuw.: *maɛa ḫaḍritak šunaṭ?*
Jim: *aywa.*
ilmuw.: *kām šanṭa?*
Jim: *itnēn.*
ilmuw.: *iššanṭa di‿btāɛit ḫaḍritak?*
Jim: *aywa, di‿btaɛti.*
ilmuw.: *wi fīha ʾē?*
Jim: *fīha‿hdūm wi‿šwayyit hadāya.*

izziyāṛa

A. *ɛala fēn in šāʾ Aḷḷāh?*

Samya: *ɛala fēn ya Muna?*
Muna: *ana‿mrawwaḫa, ṛayḫa‿dDuʾʾi.*
Samya: *miš kuntu saknīn fi‿lMaɛādi?*
Muna: *kunna saknīn fi‿lMaɛādi zamān wi ɛazzilna.*
Samya: *yaɛni‿dDuʾʾi ʾaḫsan mi‿lMaɛādi?*
Muna: *lā ʾabadan! lākin ilmadrasa kānit biɛīda ʾawi ɛa‿lʾawlād.*
Samya: *intu waxdīn šaʾʾa fi‿dDuʾʾi?*
Muna: *aywa, ɛandina šaʾʾa miš baṭṭāla fi‿ɛmāṛa‿kbīra.*
Samya: *iššaʾʾa di fēn bi‿ẓẓabṭ?*
Muna: *fi šāriɛ Nādi‿ṣṢēd.*
Samya: *yaɛni gambina ɛala ṭūl. lāzim tīgi‿tzurīna maṛṛa.*
Muna: *bi-kullᵊ surūr!*

B. *inta gayy imta?*

Sāmi: *inta gayy^{ə} ʿandina ʾimta?*
Pete: *kunt^{ə} ʿāwiz āgi ya bukṛa ya baʿdu.*
Sāmi: *ʾāsif, iḫna ṛayḫīn ḫafla ʿand aṣḫabna bukṛa bi‿llēl. taʿāla baʿd^{ə} bukṛa ʾaḫsan!*
Pete: *ma-fīš māniʿ. baʿd^{ə} bukṛa‿ssāʿa kām?*
Sāmi: *zayy^{ə} ma‿nta ʿāwiz. issāʿa sitta‿kwayyis?*
Pete: *kuwayyis xāliṣ. ašūfak baʿd^{ə} bukṛa baʾa in šāʾ Aḷḷāh.*
Sāmi: *inta ʿārif ilbēt?*
Pete: *ṭabʿan ʿarfu, ma-txafš!*

VOCABULARY

ašūfak	I'll see you
ʾusbūʿ, ʾasabīʿ	week
ʾabadan	never
baʾa	then, in that case
basbōr, -āt	passport
baʿd^{ə} bukṛa	the day after tomorrow
bi-kull^{ə} surūr	with pleasure
bi‿llēl	in the evening
bitāʿ	belonging to
bukṛa	tomorrow
bulīs	police
fāḍi	empty; free
fēn	where?
fiṭār	breakfast
ginēna, ganāyin	garden
gumruk (sg.)	customs
guwwa	inside
hidiyya, hadāya	gift, present
hidūm (pl.)	clothing
ḫaḍritak ~ ḫaḍritik	you (polite)
ḫafla, ḫafalāt	party
imta	when?
in šāʾ Aḷḷāh	if God wills
lā ʾabadan	no, not at all
lāzim	(it's) necessary
ma-txafš ~ ma-txafīš	don't worry
maṛṛa, -āt	once
maṭār, -āt	airport
māniʿ	obstacle
miṛawwaḫ	going home
miṣammim	determined
mudda ṭawīla	a long period of time
mumkin	possibly
muwaẓẓaf	official
rāgiʿ	returning
ṛāyiḫ	going
sāʾiḫ, suwwāḫ	tourist
sākin	living
siyadtak ~ siyadtik	you (very polite)
siyāḫa	tourism
surūr	pleasure
sūʾ, aswāʾ	market
ṣāḫib, aṣḫāb	friend; owner
šaʾʾa, šuʾaʾ	flat
šanṭa, šunaṭ	bag, suitcase
taslīm	reclaim
taslīm iššunaṭ	baggage reclaim
tizurna	you (m.) visit us
tīgi	you (sg.) come
ṭabʿan	of course, naturally
vīza, -āt	visa
wuṣūl	arrival
xāliṣ	very, quite
xurūg	exit
ya ... ya ...	either ... or ...
ziyāṛa, -āt	visit
ʿala fēn	where to
ʿala ṭūl	straightaway straight on
ʿazzilna	we've moved (house)
ʿaskari, ʿasākir	policeman
ʿīd, aʿyād	celebration

GRAMMAR

I. *fī* "there is," "there are"

1. *fī* "there is" "there are" and *ma-fīš* "there isn't" "there aren't" are also used to form prepositional sentences (→ V.II). *fī* is always placed first in the sentence, the subject which follows is mostly not defined:

fī‿gnēna	"there is a garden"
ma-fīš takyīf	"there is no air-conditioning"

2. Past time can be expressed by adding *kān*, which itself always remains unchanged:

kān fī šuġlᵊ‿ktīr	"there was a lot of work"
kān fī nās kitīr	"there were many people"
ma-kanšᵊ fī furṣa	"there was no opportunity"

II. *fēn? ʕala fēn?* "where," "where to"

The question *fēn* "where" can be answered by using one of the following adverbs of place:

hina	here	*hināk*	there
fōʔ	above	*taḥt*	below, under
waṛa	behind	*ʔuddām*	opposite
yimīn	right	*šimāl*	left
min hina	along here	*ʕala ṭūl*	straight on
duġri	straight on	*fi-wiššak*	right in front of you

fēn in combination with *ṛāyiḥ* means "where to":

inta ṛāyiḥ fēn?	"where are you going?"
ana rāyiḥ ilʕAgami	"I'm going to Agami"

When inquiring about your destination, a taxi driver usually asks:

ʕala fēn	"where to?"

The passenger can give directions by saying: *xuššᵊ‿šmāl* "turn left," *xuššᵊ‿ymīn* "turn right" or *ʕa‿ššimāl* "on the left," *ʕa‿lyimīn* "on the right."

III. Verbs: active participles

1. Structure

(a) In the questions *inta sākin fēn* "where do you live?" and *inta ṛāyiḥ fēn* "where are you going?," the words *sākin* and *ṛāyiḥ* do not correspond to conjugated forms of the verbs "to live" and "to go." They are in fact masculine active participles which can also have a feminine ending in *-a* and a plural ending in *-īn*.

Both participles follow the pattern **KāTiB**. In the case of *sākin* **K** = *s* ; **T** = *k* and **B** = *n*, and in the case of *ṛāyiḫ* **K** = *ṛ* ; **T** = *y* and **B** = *ḫ*.

For all forms of the participle, see table below:

m.	(*huwwa*) *sākin*	(*inta*) *sākin*	(*ana*) *sākin*
f.	(*hiyya*) *sakna*	(*inti*) *sakna*	(*ana*) *sakna*
pl.	(*humma*) *saknīn*	(*intu*) *saknīn*	(*iḫna*) *saknīn*

An unprotected *-i-* is elided, and a long *-ā-* is shortened if an ending is added, according to the rules given in lesson IV.II: *sākin + a > sākina > sakna.*

Note that in the first person singular there is a masculine form of the participle (*sākin*) and a feminine form (*sakna*). Personal pronouns (*ana, inta, huwwa* etc.) are only used when it is not obvious what the subject is:

huwwa sākin fi Maṣrᵊ w‿ana sākin fi‿Iskindiriyya
"He lives in Cairo and I live in Alexandria"

(b) Not all active participles follow the pattern **KāTiB** as given above. Some of them begin with the prefix *mi-* and follow the pattern mi**KāTiB** (*misāfir* "going on a journey"), mi**KaTTiB** (*miṣammim* "determined") or mi**KaTTaB** (*miṛawwaḫ* "going home").

2. Use

With a number of commonly used verbs, present time is expressed by means of a participle:

ana gayy	I'm coming	*ana mistanni*	I'm waiting
ana ṛāyiḫ	I'm going	*ana fākir*	I remember
ana‿mṛawwaḫ	I'm going home	*ana ɛārif*	I know
ana‿msāfir	I'm going on a trip	*ana fāhim*	I understand
ana nāzil	I'm going down(stairs)	*ana ɛāwiz*	I want
ana nāyim	I'm sleeping	*ana sāmiɛ*	I hear
ana wāʔif	I'm standing	*ana šāyif*	I see
ana ʔāɛid	I'm sitting	*ana wāxid bard*	I've got a cold

The participle is negated by using *miš* :

Ḫasan ɛārif → *Ḫasan miš ɛārif* "Ḫasan doesn't know"

To refer to past time you simply put the appropriate form of *kān* in front of the participle. In such cases, it is *kān* which is negated and not the participle:

kānu waʔfīn hina → *ma-kanūš waʔfīn hina* "they weren't standing here"

IV. The numbers from 13 onwards

1. The numbers from 13 to 19 consist of an abbreviated form of the units plus the ending *-ṭāšaṛ*, which you can recognize as being derived from the word *ʿašaṛa* "ten":

talattāšaṛ	thirteen	*sabaʿṭāšaṛ*	seventeen
aṛbaʿṭāšaṛ	fourteen	*tamantāšaṛ*	eighteen
xamasṭāšaṛ	fifteen	*tisaʿṭāšaṛ*	nineteen
sitṭāšaṛ	sixteen		

2. Multiples of ten are formed from the numbers 3 to 9 with the addition of the ending *-īn*. An exception to this is *ʿišrīn* "twenty," which is not derived from the word "two" *itnēn*, but from *ʿašaṛa* "ten":

ʿišrīn	twenty	*sittīn*	sixty
talatīn	thirty	*sabʿīn*	seventy
arbiʿīn	forty	*tamanīn*	eighty
xamsīn	fifty	*tisʿīn*	ninety

3. Hundreds are formed by means of the word *miyya* "hundred." *mitēn* is the dual of *miyya*. From 300 onwards, *-miyya* is added to a special form of the unit numbers *tultu-*, *rubʿu-* etc:

miyya	100	*suttumiyya*	600
mitēn	200	*subʿumiyya*	700
tultumiyya	300	*tumnumiyya*	800
rubʿumiyya	400	*tusʿumiyya*	900
xumsumiyya	500		

4. Thousands consist of a shortened form of the number combined with the ending *t-alāf*, where it is possible to recognize *alāf* which is the plural of *ʾalf* "1000":

ʾalf	1000	*sit t-alāf*	6000
ʾalfēn	2000	*sabaʿ t-alāf*	7000
talat t-alāf	3000	*taman t-alāf*	8000
aṛbaʿ t-alāf	4000	*tisaʿ t-alāf*	9000
xamas t-alāf	5000	*ʿašaṛ t-alāf*	10 000

5. Numbers above 10 000 are formed as in English, with the numbers from *ḫidāšaṛ* "eleven" onwards plus the word *ʾalf* "thousand":

ḫidāšaṛ ʾalf	"11 000"	*itnāšaṛ ʾalf*	"12 000"
mīt ʾalf	"100 000"	*xumsumīt ʾalf*	"500 000"

For the "millions" one uses *milyōn*, *malayīn*:

milyōn	"1 000 000"	*nuṣṣᵊ milyōn*	"500 000"
itnēn milyōn	"2 000 000"	*talāta milyōn*	"3 000 000"

6. With number combinations containing tens and units, the units are placed first and the word *wi* "and" is added before the tens:

wāḫid wi ɛišrīn (21) 1 and 20	*talāta‿w xamsīn* (53) 3 and 50

If the number consists of more than two digits, the word *wi* is only used before the last digit:

miyya‿w xamastāšaṛ (115) 100 and 15	*suttumiyya‿tnēn wi talatīn* (632) 600 2 and 30
mitēn wāḫid wi ɛišrīn (221) 200 1 and 20	*ʾalfᵊ suttumiyya w‿itnāšaṛ* (1612) 1000 600 and 12

7. Years are not described as in English "nineteen ..." but rather by listing the digits in order "one thousand, nine hundred...":

ʾalfᵊ tusɛumiyya tisɛa‿w tamanīn	"1989"
ʾalfᵊ xumsumiyya‿w sabaɛtāšaṛ	"1517"

V. Combining numbers with nouns

1. weights and measurements combined with numbers are shown in lesson V.VI:

ɛašaṛa mitr	"10 meters"	*xamsa‿gnē (h)*	"5 pounds"
tisɛa ṣanti	"9 centimeters"	*sabɛa kīlu*	"7 kilos"
tamanya ʾadam	"8 feet"	*talāta litr*	"3 liters"

2. All numbers from eleven onwards are combined with a singular noun:

ḫidāšaṛ sana	"11 years"	*itnāšaṛ ṭālib*	"12 students"
ɛišrīn ḫitta	"20 pieces"	*xamsīn maṣri*	"50 Egyptians"
arbiɛīn yōm	"40 days"	*ʾalfᵊ lēla‿w lēla*	"1001 nights"

In these cases *miyya* "hundred" is changed to *mīt* :

mīt maṛṛa	"100 times"	*xumsumīt sana*	"500 years"
tultumīt giṛām	"300 grams"	*rubɛumīt ginē(h)*	"400 pounds"

3. Only the numbers 3 to 10 require a plural noun. In these instances, the shortened form of the number is used. This shortened form is the same as the one you already met with the numbers from 13 to 19, and when counting in thousands: *talat-tāšaṛ* "thirteen," *xamas-tāšaṛ* "fifteen," *tisaɛ t-alāf* "9000."

number	short form	example	
talāta	*talat*	*talat kutub*	3 books
aṛbaɛa	*aṛbaɛ*	*aṛbaɛ gawabāt*	4 letters
xamsa	*xamas*	*xamas sinīn*	5 years
sitta	*sitt*	*sittᵊ bawāki*	6 packets
sabɛa	*sabaɛ*	*sabaɛ kuruta*	7 cards
tamanya	*taman*	*taman ɛilab*	8 boxes
tisɛa	*tisaɛ*	*tisaɛ šuhūr*	9 months
ɛašaṛa	*ɛašaṛ*	*ɛašaṛ daʾāyiʾ*	10 minutes

When plurals of the form a**KT**āB (→ IV.IV) are combined with numbers, they usually change to i**KT**āB and are preceded by the letter *t-* : *ayyām* ~ *iyyām* ~ *xamas t-iyyām.*

An extra *t-* is also placed in front of the words *alāf* "thousands" and *ušhur* "months."

yōm, ayyām	*sabaɛ t-iyyām*	7 days
bāb, abwāb	*talat t-ibwāb*	3 doors
ʾalf, alāf	*xamas t-alāf*	5000
šahṛ, ušhur	*aṛbaɛ t-ušhur*	4 months

VI. *bitāɛ-, bitāɛit-, bitūɛ-* "belonging to ..."

1. **Structure**: as well as using a noun + a genitive or a possessive suffix to express ownership as in *bēt Faṭma* "Faṭma's house" or *betha* "her house," ownership can also be expressed by using the words *bitāɛ* (m.), *bitāɛit* (f.) and *bitūɛ* (pl.) "belonging to."

bitāɛ agrees in gender and number with its noun. It is followed by a noun or a suffix which refers to the "owner":

ilbēt bitāɛ Faṭma	"Faṭma's house"
ilɛaṛabiyya‿btāɛit Faṭma	"Faṭma's car"
ilmudarrisīn bitūɛ Faṭma	"Faṭma's teachers"

The following table shows all forms of *bitāɛ* with suffixes:

masc.	fem.	pl.
bitāɛi	*bitaɛti*	*bitūɛi*
bitāɛak	*bitaɛtak*	*bitūɛak*
bitāɛik	*bitaɛtik*	*bitūɛik*
bitāɛu	*bitaɛtu*	*bitūɛu*
bitaɛha	*bitaɛitha*	*bituɛha*
bitaɛna	*bitaɛitna*	*bituɛna*
bitaɛku(m)	*bitaɛitku(m)*	*bituɛku(m)*
bitaɛhum	*bitaɛithum*	*bituɛhum*

2. Use:

(a) In cases where the plural ends in *-īn*, the construction with *bitūʕ* is used exclusively, and not the construction with noun + suffix:

ilmudarrisīn bituʕna	"our teachers"

(b) With foreign borrowings, the construction with *bitāʕ* is usually preferred:

ilbanṭalōn bitāʕ Samīḫa	"Samīḫa's trousers"
ilbaṣbōr bitaʕha	"her passport"

(c) Most genitive constructions can be replaced by a construction using *bitāʕ*:

ilḫafla‿btāʕit bukṛa	"tomorrow's party"
ikkitāb bitāʕ ilhandasa	"the geometry book"

Body parts and the nouns denoting family members never take *bitāʕ*:

riglak	"your foot"	*ʕenayya*	"my eyes"
abūhum	"their father"	*agdādu*	"his grandparents"

Note the difference in meaning between *sitti* "my grandmother" and *issittᵊ‿btaʕti* "my wife."

(d) Furthermore, *bitāʕ* can be used to describe people's occupations:

bitāʕ ikkawitš	"the tire man"	*bitāʕ ilʔūṭa*	"the tomato seller"
bitāʕ illaban	"the milkman"	*bitāʕ iggaṛāyid*	"the newspaper seller"

VII. Adverbs and prepositions of time

1. *imta* "when?"

Here are some possible answers to the question *imta* "when?":

innahaṛda	today	*iṣṣubḫ*	in the morning
bukṛa	tomorrow	*iḍḍuhr*	at midday
imbāriḫ	yesterday	*bi‿llēl*	in the evening
baʕdᵊ bukṛa	the day after tomorrow		~at night
ʔawwil imbāriḫ	the day before yesterday	*baʕd iḍḍuhr*	in the afternoon

These adverbs of time can also be combined with each other:

imbāriḫ baʕd iḍḍuhr	yesterday afernoon	*ilʔusbūʕ iggayy*	next week
innahaṛda‿ṣṣubḫ	this morning	*ilʔusbūʕ illi fāt*	last week
bukṛa‿ṣṣubḫ	tomorrow morning	*zayy innahaṛda*	a week today
bukṛa bi‿llēl	tomorrow evening		
bukṛa walla baʕdu	tomorrow or the day after tomorrow		

2. *min, baᶜd* and *ᵓabl* can also be used in expressions of time:

min	"since" "for" "ago"	*John_fi Maṣrᵊ min sana* "John has been in Egypt for a year" *hiyya ᶜandina min ᵓawwil imbāriḫ* "she's been with us since the day before yesterday" *ilᶜaskari kān hina min nuṣṣᵊ sāᶜa* "the policeman was here half an hour ago"
baᶜd	"after" "in"	*Ḫasan gayy innādi baᶜdᵊ iššuġl* "Ḫasan's coming to the club after work" *Maha_mṛawwaḫa baᶜdᵊ rubᶜᵊ sāᶜa* "Maha's going home in a quarter of an hour"
ᵓabl	"before"	*kuntᵊ hina ᵓablak* "I was here before you" *Ḫasan miš misāfir ᵓabl issāᶜa sitta baᶜd iḍḍuhr* "Ḫasan won't be leaving before 6 p.m."

Be careful: the adverb of place "before" meaning "in front of" can only be expressed by *ᵓuddām* or *ᵓusāḍ* (→ IV.III):

kuntᵊ waᵓfa ᵓuddām ilᶜimāṛa	"I was standing in front of the building"

3. *baᵓāl-* with a suffix means "for" when it refers to an event which began in the past and is still continuing in the present. The suffix then refers to the subject:

*baᵓā**li** xamas sinīn fi-Maṣr*	"**I** have (already) been in Egypt for 5 years"
*baᵓā**lu** xamas t-iyyām fi_lmustašfa*	"**he**'s been in hospital for five days"
*baᵓal**ha** mudda ṭawīla hina*	"**she**'s been here for a long time"

4. *ᵓaddᵊ ᵓē* and *kām*

(a) *ᵓaddᵊ ᵓē* "how long?" "how much?" "to what extent?" is used to ask about the quantity, the length, the weight, or the extent of something:

iššanṭa_btaᶜtak ᵓaddᵊ ᵓē?	"how big is your suitcase?"
ᶜāwiz ᵓaddᵊ ᵓē ṛuzz?	"how much rice do you want?"
bitḫibbini ᵓaddᵊ ᵓē?	"how much do you love me?"

(b) *ᵓaddᵊ ᵓē* can also be used after *baᵓāl-* and a suffix to ask questions about the duration of a period of time:

baᵓālik ᵓaddᵊ ᵓē ᶜayyāna?	"how long have you (fem.) been ill?"
baᵓalha ᵓaddᵊ ᵓē sakna hina?	"how long has she been living here?"

Another way to ask how long something has lasted is to use *kām* "how many?" followed by the relevant word (hour, day, year, etc.).

Note that *kām* is followed in Arabic by the singular whereas in English it is followed by a plural:

kām sāᶜa?	"how many hours?"
baᵓālak kām sana_f maṣr?	"how many years have you been (living) in Egypt?"

5. *issāɛa kām?*

If you want to know the time, say:

issāɛa kām?	"what's the time?" [lit. "the hour (is) how many?"]

But *issāɛa kām?* can also mean "at what time?" "when?":

intu ragɛīn issāɛa kām?	"at what time are you (pl.) coming back?"

To refer to the hours by themselves, normal numbers are used (→ V.VI), except in the case of "one o'clock":

issāɛa kām?	*issāɛa waḥda*	"it's one o'clock" ~ "at one o'clock"
	issāɛa xamsa	"it's five o'clock" ~ "at five o'clock"

The hour is further divided into quarters *rubɛ*, thirds *tilt*, and halves *nuṣṣ*. *wi* "plus" and *illa* "minus" are used to express "past" and "to" the hour:

issāɛa kām?	*itnēn wi rubɛ*	2.15	*itnēn illa rubɛ*	1.45
	itnēn wi tilt	2.20	*itnēn illa tilt*	1.40
	itnēn wi nuṣṣ	2.30		

For more precise divisions of the hour into minutes *diʾīʾa, daʾāyiʾ* normal numbers are used:

issāɛa kām?	*issāɛa‿tnēn wi xamsa*	2.05
	issāɛa‿tnēn illa xamsa	1.55
	issāɛa‿tnēn wi nuṣṣ illa xamsa	2.25
	issāɛa‿ttnēn wi nuṣṣᵊ‿w xamsa	2.35

EXERCISES

I. Put the following participles

(a) in the feminine (b) in the plural.

	(a)	(b)
nāzil	________	________
ع̣ārif	________	________
šāyif	________	________
nāyim	________	________
misāfir	________	________
miṛawwaḫ	________	________
gayy	________	________
wāxid	________	________
ع̣āwiz	________	________
fākir	________	________

II. I don't live here, but she lives here!

ana miš sākin hina, lākin hiyya sakna hina.

1. *ana miš ع̣ārif ilbēt, lākin hiyya* ________ *ilbēt.*
2. *ana miš ع̣āwiz ʾahwa, lākin humma* ________ *ʾahwa.*
3. *iḫna ṛayḫīn iggāmiع̣, lākin hiyya miš* ________ *iggāmiع̣.*
4. *inta miš* ________ *ḫāga, lākin hiyya samع̣a ḫāga.*
5. *huwwa miš šāyif ḫāga, lākin hiyya* ________ *ḫāga.*
6. *ana sakna fi‿dDuʾʾi, w‿inta* ________ *fēn?*
7. *Sāmi ṛāyiḫ innādi, w‿inti* ________ *fēn?*
8. *Ḫasan gayyᵊ bukṛa, wi Maha* ________ *imta?*
9. *ilwalad nāyim, w‿ilbint* ________ *kamān.*
10. *inti fakra‿kwayyis, lākin ana li‿lʾasaf miš* ________.
11. *hiyya‿msafra innahaṛda, w‿iḫna* ________ *bukṛa.*

III. Work out these sums.

sabع̣a‿w tamanya - yibʾu xamastạšaṛ

1. *talāta‿w ع̣ašaṛa - yibʾu* ________
2. *xamsa‿w sabع̣a - yibʾu* ________
3. *itnēn wi tisaع̣tāšaṛ - yibʾu* ________

4. *tisɛa‿w tisɛa* - *yibʔu* ______________________
5. *sitta‿w xamsa* - *yibʔu* ______________________
6. *ɛašaṛa‿w sabɛa* - *yibʔu* ______________________
7. *sabɛa‿w sabɛa* - *yibʔu* ______________________
8. *xamsa wi‿ḫdāšaṛ* - *yibʔu* ______________________
9. *aṛbaɛa‿w tisɛa* - *yibʔu* ______________________
10. *tamanya‿w talāta* - *yibʔu* ______________________
11. *ɛašaṛa‿w tisɛa* - *yibʔu* ______________________

IV. Read aloud and work out the answers *wi* or *zāʔid* is "plus" in Arabic.

1. 14 + 7 - *yibʔu* ______________________ .
2. 57 +12 - *yibʔu* ______________________ .
3. 17 + 21 - *yibʔu* ______________________ .
4. 15 + 13 - *yibʔu* ______________________ .
5. 62 + 22 - *yibʔu* ______________________ .
6. 47 + 15 - *yibʔu* ______________________ .
7. 8 + 37 - *yibʔu* ______________________ .
8. 19 + 22 - *yibʔu* ______________________ .
9. 35 + 37 - *yibʔu* ______________________ .
10. 12 + 19 - *yibʔu* ______________________ .
11. 44 + 33 - *yibʔu* ______________________ .
12. 27 + 34 - *yibʔu* ______________________ .

V. Complete columns.

xamsa - *xamastāšaṛ* - *xamsīn* - *xumsumiyya* - *xamas t-alāf*

tisɛa - ____

talāta - ____

aṛbaɛa - ____

wāḫid - ____

sitta - ____

itnēn - ____

sabɛa - ____

tamanya - ____

VI. Add on another ten.

	talat kutub wi kamān ɛašaṛa	*yibˀu*	*talattāšaṛ kitāb .*
1.	*xamas maṛṛāt wi kamān ɛašaṛa*	*yibˀu*	________________
2.	*bintēn wi kamān ɛašaṛa*	*yibˀu*	________________
3.	*šanṭa waḫda‿w kamān ɛašaṛa*	*yibˀu*	________________
4.	*xamas šuˀaˀ wi kamān ɛašaṛa*	*yibˀu*	________________
5.	*aṛbaɛ madāris wi kamān ɛašaṛa*	*yibˀu*	________________
6.	*talat gawāmiɛ wi kamān ɛašaṛa*	*yibˀu*	________________
7.	*sabaɛ aṭfāl wi kamān ɛašaṛa*	*yibˀu*	________________
8.	*tisaɛ saɛāt wi kamān ɛašaṛa*	*yibˀu*	________________
9.	*sittᵊ kanāyis wi kamān ɛašaṛa*	*yibˀu*	________________
10.	*talat šababīk wi kamān ɛašaṛa*	*yibˀu*	________________
11.	*sabaɛ ṭalaba‿w kamān ɛašaṛa*	*yibˀu*	________________
12.	*tisaɛ sagāyir wi kamān ɛašaṛa*	*yibˀu*	________________
13.	*aṛbaɛ t-iyyām wi kamān ɛašaṛa*	*yibˀu*	________________
14.	*taman ɛimaṛāt wi kamān ɛašaṛa*	*yibˀu*	________________
15.	*talat ɛaˀilāt wi kamān ɛašaṛa*	*yibˀu*	________________
16.	*xamas t-ibwāb wi kamān ɛašaṛa*	*yibˀu*	________________

VII. Combine the following plurals with the given numbers and remember to put the noun in the singular if necessary.

(*ṭālibāt*)	20 ____________	(*abwāb*)	4 ____________
(*muwaẓẓafīn*)	14 ____________	(*šababīk*)	97 ____________
(*madāris*)	10 ____________	(*sagāyir*)	9 ____________
(*ayyām*)	7 ____________	(*šuˀaˀ*)	15 ____________
(*ɛanawīn*)	3 ____________	(*maṣāniɛ*)	11 ____________
(*ḫafalāt*)	6 ____________	(*ṣawāni*)	33 ____________
(*maṛṛāt*)	12 ____________	(*banāt*)	24 ____________
(*kalimāt*)	5 ____________	(*suwwāḫ*)	13 ____________

VIII. Answer the question: How long have you been in Egypt?

baˀālak ˀaddᵊ ˀē‿f-Maṣr? – baˀāli talat sinīn fi Maṣr (3, *sana*)

1. ____ (5, *yōm*)

2. ____ (4, *usbūɛ*)

3. ______________________________ (12, *sana*)
4. ______________________________ (5, *šahṛ*)
5. ______________________________ (17, *šahṛ*)
6. ______________________________ (3, *sā*ع*a*)
7. ______________________________ (15, *yōm*)

IX. Ask: How long have you been ..... ?

	ana ʕayyāna.	- *ya-taṛa baʔālik ʔaddᵊ ʔē ʕayyāna* ?
1.	*ana waxda bard.*	- ______________?
2.	*hiyya‿f-Maṣr.*	- ______________?
3.	*iḥna‿f-Aswān.*	- ______________?
4.	*iḥna miggawwizīn.*	- ______________?
5.	*humma mistanniyyīn.*	- ______________?
6.	*inta mašġūl.*	- ______________?
7.	*hiyya‿msafra.*	- ______________?
8.	*Sāmi sākin hina.*	- ______________?
9.	*ilawlād fi‿lmadrasa.*	- ______________?

X. With which word would you translate the following prepositions?

	after	before	in	since	ago
1. *hiyya ʕayyāna min imbāriḥ.*	☐	☐	☐	☐	☐
2. *Sāmi gayyᵊ baʕdᵊ sāʕa*	☐	☐	☐	☐	☐
3. *iḥna‿msafrīn baʕd ilʕīd.*	☐	☐	☐	☐	☐
4. *miš miṛawwaḥ ʔabl issāʕa waḥda.*	☐	☐	☐	☐	☐
5. *ilʕīd kān min ʔusbuʕēn.*	☐	☐	☐	☐	☐
6. *humma nazlīn ilbalad baʕd ilfiṭār.*	☐	☐	☐	☐	☐
7. *ana ʕarfu min mudda ṭawīla.*	☐	☐	☐	☐	☐
8. *kānit hina min diʔiʔtēn bass.*	☐	☐	☐	☐	☐
9. *ilḥafla baʕdᵊ ʔusbūʕ.*	☐	☐	☐	☐	☐
10. *kānu mawgudīn ʔabl issafaṛ*	☐	☐	☐	☐	☐
11. *hiyya nazla‿ssūʔ baʕdᵊ‿šwayya.*	☐	☐	☐	☐	☐

XI. Who does it belong to?

	ilbēt da‿btāɛ mīn?	*il bēt da‿btāɛ Ḥasan.*	*(Ḥasan)*
1.	*ilbaṣbōr da‿btāɛ mīn?*	________________	*(axūya)*
2.	*ilvilla di‿btāɛit mīn?*	________________	*(Farūˀ)*
3.	*ilɛaṛabiyya di‿btāɛit mīn?*	________________	*(Maha)*
4.	*iššunaṭ di‿btāɛit mīn?*	________________	*(issuwwāḫ)*
5.	*ilwallāɛa di‿btāɛit mīn?*	________________	*(Ḥasan)*
6.	*ilhidūm di‿btāɛit mīn?*	________________	*(Samya)*
7.	*ilhidiyya di‿btāɛit mīn?*	________________	*(uxti)*

XII. Fill in the blanks with *bitāɛ*, *bitāɛit* or *bitūɛ*.

1. *ilhadāya di* ____________________ *Ḥasan.*
2. *ikkitāb da* ____________________ *ilmudīr.*
3. *ikkalbᵊ da* ____________________ *ilbulīs.*
4. *ilbanāt dōl* ____________________ *Samya.*
5. *ilwallāɛa di* ____________________ *ilmudarris.*
6. *ilmudarrisīn dōl* ________________ *ilfaransāwi.*
7. *ilmaktab da* ____________________ *issikirtēra.*
8. *issuwwāḫ dōl* ________________ *maktab inNīl.*
9. *ilɛaṛabiyyāt di* ______________ *maṣnaɛ issukkaṛ.*

XIII. Use *bitāɛ* to replace the possessive suffixes.

	ɛaṛabiyyiti	-	*ilɛaṛabiyya‿btaɛti*
1.	*šanṭiti*	-	____________________
2.	*šawariɛha*	-	____________________
3.	*banathum*	-	____________________
4.	*ginenitha*	-	____________________
5.	*kitābik*	-	____________________
6.	*ḫaflitna*	-	____________________
7.	*betkum*	-	____________________
8.	*saɛtu*	-	____________________
9.	*ṭalabitna*	-	____________________

XIV. It doesn't belong to me, it belongs to him!

iššanṭa di‿btaɛtak? - *lā, di miš bitaɛti, lākin bitaɛtu huwwa!*

1. *iššanṭa di‿btaɛtik?* - *lā, di miš ______lākin ______huwwa!*
2. *išša*ᵓᵓ*a di‿btaɛitkum?* - *lā, di miš ______lākin ______humma!*
3. *igginēna di‿btaɛtak?* - *lā, di miš ______lākin ______ hiyya!*
4. *issāɛa di‿btaɛtu?* - *lā, di miš ______lākin ______ hiyya!*
5. *ilɛaṛabiyya di‿btaɛtak?* - *lā, di miš ______lākin ______humma!*
6. *ilbasbōr da‿btāɛak?* - *lā, da miš ______lākin ______huwwa!*
7. *iṭṭalaba dōl bituɛna?* - *lā, dōl miš ______lākin ______humma!*
8. *ilhidiyya di‿btaɛitha?* - *lā, di miš ______lākin ______huwwa!*
9. *innimra di‿btaɛitkum?* - *lā, di miš ______lākin ______ hiyya!*
10. *iṣṣūra di‿btaɛtak?* - *lā, di miš ______lākin ______humma!*

XV. Use *bitāɛ*, *bitāɛit* or *bitūɛ* with the correct suffix.

iššanṭa‿btaɛti‿gdīda. (ana)

1. *ilbaṣbōr* ________________ *fēn?* (inta)
2. *innādi* ________________ *fi‿lMuhandisīn.* (iḥna)
3. *ilmudarrisīn* ________________ *miš mawgudīn.* (iḥna)
4. *iššāriɛ* ________________ *fī(h) maṭɛam.* (intu)
5. *išša*ᵓᵓ*a* ________________ *kibīra* ᵓ*awi.* (humma)
6. *igginēna* ________________ *gamb innādi.* (inti)
7. *iṭṭalaba* ________________ *gayyīn bukṛa* (iḥna)
8. *ilbēt* ________________ *gamīl giddan.* (ana)

XVI. Reply to the following, using the example to help you.

hiyya di šanṭitak? - *aywa, iššanṭa di‿btaɛti* ᵓ*ana .*

1. *hiyya di ɛarabiyyitha?* - *aywa,* ____________________________.
2. *humma dōl awladhum?* - *aywa,* ____________________________.
3. *hiyya di‿gnentak?* - *aywa,* ____________________________.
4. *hiyya di ša*ᵓᵓ*itu?* - *aywa,* ____________________________.
5. *huwwa da bethum?* - *aywa,* ____________________________.
6. *hiyya di saɛtik?* - *aywa,* ____________________________.
7. *huwwa da‿ktabha?* - *aywa,* ____________________________.

8. *hiyya di nimritkum?* - *aywa,* ______________________.
9. *hiyya di maḫaṭṭitak?* - *aywa,* ______________________.

XVII. Organize the words into sentences.

1. *Maha, ṛayḫa, imbāriḫ, kānit, ilMuhandisīn*

____

2. *sakna, inti, hina, zamān, kunti?*

____

3. *dōl, minēn, kānu, gayyīn?*

____

4. *hiyya, ʾē, kānit, ʿawza?*

____

5. *ma-kuntūš, ʿarfīn, ḫāga, intu.*

____

6. *gayyīn, bukṛa, bi‿llēl, humma, hina.*

____

7. *kām, dilwaʾti, issāʿa?*

____

8. *hiyya, ḫāga, šayfa, ma-kānitš.*

____

9. *iṣṣubḫ, ʾāsif, ana, fāḍi, imbāriḫ, kunt, ma-...-š.*

____

10. *ilḫafla, laṭīfa, kānit, bitāʿit, imbāriḫ.*

____

11. *maʿāya , šunaṭ, talat, kān.*

____

XVIII. Translate the following sentences.

1. *Ḫasan*'s coming at three o'clock.

____

2. I was asleep yesterday afternoon.

____

3. Where are the students going to?

____

4. Where does *Maha* live?

____

5. Do you see anything?

6. Lunch isn't ready.

7. At nine o'clock we're going to the club.

8. Come here tomorrow!

9. I'm not free now.

10. Unfortunately I don't have time tomorrow.

11. Do you know *ʾAṣr inNīl*-street?

12. Where is the baggage reclaim?

13. Where is your (polite) visa?

14. *Ḥasan*'s got four daughters.

15. That phonecall wasn't for you.

16. Have you (polite) come as a tourist or on business?

17. I've been in Cairo for three days.

18. My wife was on a journey.

19. How long have you (fem.) been living in Alexandria?

20. Where is the customs official?

21. *Nadya* is either at school or at home now.

LESSON VII

DIALOGUES

tišṛab ʾē?

Craig: *izzayyak ya Sāmi?*
Sāmi: *Aḷḷāh yixallīk!*
Craig: *itfaḍḍal, istarayyaḥ!*
Sāmi: *mutšakkir.*
Craig: *tišṛab ʾē, ʾahwa walla šāy?*
Sāmi: *wala ḥāga!*
Craig: *laʾ, lāzim tišṛab ḥāga.*
Sāmi: *xalāṣ, ašṛab šāy, bassᵊ sukkaṛ xafīf, min faḍlak!*

arūḥ hināk izzāy?

Sayyid: *inta ʿārif ilMugammaʿ fēn?*
Ḥasan: *ṭabʿan, fi-Midān itTaḥrīr.*
Sayyid: *arūḥ hināk izzāy?*
Ḥasan: *timši min hina‿lġāyit Midān Silimān Bāša,*
wi baʿdᵊ kida‿txuššᵊ‿šmāl šāriʿ Ṭalʿat Ḥarb, wi timši
fī(h) ʿala ṭūl liġāyit Midān itTaḥrīr.
Sayyid: *yaʿni da‿bʿīd ʾawi?*
Ḥasan: *aywa, da mišwāṛ ṭawīl šuwayya. mumkin tāxud ilʾutubīs*
wi tinzil fi-Midān itTaḥrīr. lākin aḥsan ḥāga tirkab taks.

taʿāla ya‿Mḥammad!

Sāmi: *taʿāla hina ya‿Mḥammad!*
Muḥ.: *aywa fī ḥāga?*
Sāmi: *min faḍlak, iʾfil ilbāb w‿iftaḥ iššababīk, wi baʿdᵊ kida*
imsaḥ ittarabēẓa‿w ṭallaʿha hiyya wi‿lkarāsi fi‿lbalakōna!
Muḥ.: *ḥāḍir! aʿmil iššāy dilwaʾti?*
Sāmi: *laʾ, istanna‿šwayya ʿa‿ššāy!*

ittaks

Craig: *taks, taks! fāḍi, ya‿sṭa?*
issawwāʾ: *aywa! itfaḍḍal! ʿala fēn ʾin šāʾ Aḷḷāh?*
Craig: *waṣṣalni šāriʿ ʾAṣr inNīl, min faḍlak!*
issawwāʾ: *fēn bi‿ẓẓabṭ?*
Craig: *ʿandᵊ šāriʿ Širīf.*
Craig: *yāh, iddinya zaḥma ʾawi‿nnahaṛda.*
issawwāʾ: *áho kullᵊ yōm kida!*
Craig: *ya-taṛa šāriʿ ʾAṣr inNīl biʿīd?*
issawwāʾ: *miš ʾawi. ḥawāli tiltᵊ sāʿa.*
Craig: *ṭab, ʿaddi ʿala Midān itTaḥrīr!*

issawwāʾ:	*lē? da zaḫma ʾawi dilwaʾti!*
Craig:	*huwwa fī ṭarīʾ tāni?*
issawwāʾ:	*aywa, mumkin nāxud šāriɛ Silimān Bāša. da ʾashal bi-ktīr.*
Craig:	*xalāṣ, fūt ɛala šāriɛ Silimān!*

Craig:	*xuššᵊ‿ymīn, min faḍlak.*
issawwāʾ:	*hina? ɛa‿nnaṣya?*
Craig:	*laʾ, baɛdaha bi-šwayya.*
issawwāʾ:	*zayyᵉ ma‿tḫibb.*
Craig:	*bass, ɛandak hina‿hó!*

VOCABULARY

ʾadīm, ʾudām	old
ʾaṣr, ʾuṣūr	castle, palace
ʾawwil	first (adj.)
ilʾawwil	first (adv.)
ʾutubīs, -āt	bus
ashal	simpler, easier
balakōna, -āt	balcony
bawwāb	doorman janitor
baɛd	after
baɛdᵊ kida	thereafter after that
bāʾi	rest, remainder
Bāša	Pasha (title)
dinya ~ dunya	world
istanna	wait
istarayyaḫ	have a rest take a seat
itfaḍḍal	please
izzāy	how
ḫawāli	about
ḫāḍir	at your service
lē	why
lissa	not yet, still not
liġāyit	until, as far as up to
midān, mayadīn	square
miš ʾawi	nothing special
mišwāṛ, mašawīr	errand
ilMugammaɛ	administrative center in Cairo on *Taḫrīr* Square
raʾy, aṛāʾ	opinion
sawwāʾ, -īn	driver
sitt, -āt	woman, lady
sūʾ, aswāʾ	market
šimāl	left

taks, taksiyāt ~ tukúsa	taxi
taḫrīr	liberation
tāni	again, another
ṭabɛan	of course
ṭarīʾ, ṭuruʾ	road
ṭawīl, ṭuwāl	long
ṭayyib ~ ṭab	good, okay
usṭa, usṭawāt	way to address a workman
wala ḫāga	nothing
waṣṣalni	take me to ...
xafīf	light
xalāṣ	fine, leave it
yāh	o!
yāxud ḫ	he takes
yiʾfil ḫ	he shuts, he closes
yibʾa	he is, he becomes
yiftaḫ ḫ	he opens
yifūt ɛala w ~ ḫ	he drops in
yiḫibb w ~ ḫ	he likes he'd like to
yiḫuṭṭ ḫ	he puts
yimīn	right, on the right
yimsaḫ ḫ	he sweeps he brushes
yimši	he goes, he walks
yinaḍḍaf	he cleans
yinzil	he gets off
yirkab ḫ	he gets in ~ on he takes (a taxi)
yirūḫ ḫ	he goes to
yisʾal w ɛan ḫ	he asks s/o about s/th
yistarayyaḫ	he rests
yišṛab ḫ	he drinks
yišṛab sagāyir	he smokes

yiṭallaɛ ḥ	he takes s/th out	*zayyᵊ ma‿tḥibb*	whatever you want
yixušš ḥ	he goes into		as you like
yiwaṣṣal w	he accompanies	*ɛala*	on, towards
yiɛaddi ɛala ḥ	he drops in		in the direction of
	he drives through	*ɛandak!*	stop here!
yiɛmil ḥ	he makes	*ɛāyiz*	wanting, desiring
yōm, ayyām	day	~ *ɛāwiz*	
zaḥma	crowd; crowded		

GRAMMAR

I. Adjectives

1. (a) When used attributively, adjectives are placed after the noun which they modify. If this noun is definite, the adjective also receives a definite article:

bēt kibīr	→	*ilbēt ikkibīr*
"a big house"		"the big house"
walad šāṭir	→	*ilwalad iššāṭir*
"a clever boy"		"the clever boy"

Pay attention: *ilbēt kibīr* means "the house is big."

(b) After a feminine singular noun, the adjective receives the feminine ending *-a*:

šaʔʔa‿kbīra	"a large flat"
ilbint iššaṭra	"the clever girl"

A plural noun which refers to people is followed by an adjective in the plural:

ṭalaba kanadiyyīn	"Canadian students"	*banāt luṭāf*	"nice girls"
nās aġniya	"rich people"	*nās fuʔaṛa*	"poor people"

For examples of the plural of adjectives see lesson IV.IV.2b.

When the plural noun refers to inanimate objects or non-humans, the adjective which follows receives the feminine singular ending *-a*:

karāsi‿gdīda	"new chairs"	*ḥagāt tanya*	"other things"
šababīk maʔfūla	"closed windows"	*ɛimaṛāt ɛalya*	"tall blocks of flats"

2. When describing people, *nisba*-adjectives such as *maṣri, ingilīzi, ʔalmāni* etc, agree with the noun they modify:

ṭālíba ingiliziyya	"an English female student"
muhandisīn ɛaṛab	"Arab engineers"

But when describing inanimate objects, they stay in the masculine singular regardless of the gender or number of the noun:

gibna hulandi	"Dutch cheese"	*saɛāt suwisri*	"Swiss watches"
sagāyir ʾamrikāni	"American cigarettes"	*ʾahwa turki*	"Turkish coffee"

3. Adjectives and participles which contain the vowel *-ā-* and end in an *-i* are given a *-y-* before the feminine ending *-a* and the plural ending *-īn.*

hādi + y + a >	*hādiya* >	*hadya*	"quiet (fem.)"
ġāli + y + īn >	*ġāliyīn*>	*ġalyīn*	"expensive (pl.)"

You should also note *fāḍi, faḍya, faḍyīn* "empty" "free" "vacant" and *māši, mašya, mašyīn* "walking" (→ IV.IV.2 a).

Be careful! * This rule does not apply to the *nisba*-adjective *ɛādi, ɛadiyya, ɛadiyyīn* "usual" "ordinary."

The adjective *kitīr* "many" "a lot" usually remains unchanged:

kabāri‿ktīr "many bridges" *awlād kitīr* "a lot of children."

II. Verbs

1. The imperfect

(a) **Structure:** For the next few lessons the verbs in your vocabulary lists will be given in the 3rd person masculine singular of the imperfect. The imperfect consists of a prefix, a basis, and in some cases an ending: *yi-šṛab* "he drinks," *yi-waṣṣal* "he brings," *yi-waṣṣal-u* "they bring."

yi -	*šṛab*	*yi* -	*waṣṣal* -	*u*
⇓	⇓	⇓	⇓	⇓
prefix	**basis**	**prefix**	**basis**	**ending**

Prefixes and endings which relate to the subject of the verb can be found in the paradigm below. They occur with all verbs in the imperfect irresspective of what basis they have. The folloswing table shows the imperfect of *yiktib* "he writes":

3rd person	2nd person	1st person
(*huwwa*) *yi-ktib*	(*inta*) *ti-ktib*	(*ana*) *a-ktib*
(*hiyya*) *ti-ktib*	(*inti*) *ti-ktib-i*	
(*humma*) *yi-ktib-u*	(*intu*) *ti-ktib-u*	(*iḫna*) *ni-ktib*

If the basis of the imperfect ends in the vowels *-i* or *-a* as in *yimši* "he goes" or *yistanna* "he waits," and this is followed by the *-i* or *-u* of the imperfect ending, then the vowels will be elided, e.g., *tistanna + i > tistanni*, *yimši* + u > *yimšu*. The complete paradigm for *yistanna* is as follows:

3rd person	2nd person	1st person
(*huwwa*) *yistanna*	(*inta*) *tistanna*	(*ana*) *astanna*
(*hiyya*) *tistanna*	(*inti*) *tistanni*	
(*humma*) *yistannu*	(*intu*) *tistannu*	(*iḩna*) *nistanna*

(b) Use: The simple form of the imperfect is used to express something which has not yet taken place, but still can - or must - happen. Its function is therefore modal. *yiktib* does not mean "he's writing" but "he should ~ may ~ could write."

The simple form of the imperfect is often used in questions such as *tišṛab* *ʾē?* "what'll you have to drink?" (not "what are you drinking?"), *aʿmil ʾē bass?* "what can I do?." It can also be used when giving directions or making suggestions: *timši min hina‿lġāyit iggāmiʿ* "you could walk from here to the mosque."

2. The imperative

To form the imperative, the basis of the imperfect is used without prefix or ending. If the basis begins with two consonants, an *i-* is placed in front of them:

yi-msaḩ →	*-msaḩ* →	*i-msaḩ*	"sweep!"
yi-ftaḩ →	*-ftaḩ* →	*i-ftaḩ*	"open!"

Otherwise, the basis is used just as it is:

yisāfir →	*sāfir*	"go on a journey!"

To make a feminine singular imperative, *-i* is added to the end of the basis; to make a plural imperative, *-u* is added:

fūt	*fūti*	*fūtu*	"go past!"
xušš	*xušši*	*xuššu*	"get in!"
naḍḍaf	*naḍḍafi*	*naḍḍafu*	"clean!"

However, if the basis ends in a vowel, this vowel will disappear when followed by *-i* or *-u*:

i-mši	*imši*	*imšu*	"go away!"
i-stanna	*istanni*	*istannu*	"wait!"

Be careful! The imperatives *hāt* "give!" "bring!" and *taʿāla* "come!" are irregular. They are not directly derived from the imperfects of *yigīb* "he brings," *yiddi* "he gives" or *yīgi* "he comes."

III. *yāxud* and *yākul*

yāxud "he takes" and *yākul* "he eats" are irregular forms of the imperfect with the base form *-xud*, *-kul* and the prefixes *yā-*, *tā-*, *ā-* and *nā-* instead of *yi-*, *ti-* etc.

3rd person	2nd person	1st person
(*huwwa*) *yāxud* (*hiyya*) *tāxud* (*humma*) *yaxdu*	(*inta*) *tāxud* (*inti*) *taxdi* (*intu*) *taxdu*	(*ana*) *āxud* (*iḥna*) *nāxud*

When adding the endings of the 2nd person fem. sing. and the 2nd and 3rd persons plural, the *-u* in the base form becomes unprotected and will therefore disappear: *tāxud* + u > *tāxdu* > *taxdu* "you (pl.) take."

Their imperatives *xud* and *kul* follow the pattern given in II.2 above.

IV. Modal auxiliaries

1. In order to express the English verbs "must," "can," and "want to," the Arabic words *lāzim* "necessary," *mumkin* "possible" and *ʿāwiz* ~ *ʿāyiz* "wanting" are placed in front of the imperfect. *lāzim* and *mumkin* remain unchanged, but *ʿāwiz* changes in accordance with the rules given in lesson VI.III:

lāzim tišṛab ḥāga	"you (sg.) must drink something"
mumkin nirkab ilʾutubīs	"we could go by bus"
ʿawzīn ninzil fi‿lMaʿādi	"we want to get out at Maadi"
ʿawza tišṛabi šāy?	"do you (fem.) want to drink some tea?"

Be careful! To ask questions or make suggestions, a simple imperfect is usually used without a modal auxiliary (→ above II.1.b).

2. Negatives are formed by placing *miš* in front of the modal auxiliary:

miš mumkin arkab ilʾutubīs	"I can't take the bus"
miš ʿāwiz yistanna	"he doesn't want to wait"
miš lāzim tišṛab ʾahwa	"you (sing.) don't have to drink coffee"

V. Negation of the imperfect and the imperative

1. Imperfect: The negative of the imperf. is formed by using *ma-...-š*. This may cause a vowel at the end of the verb to be lengthened and the stress to be moved.

yirūḥ	→	*ma-yruḥš*	he musn't go
yiftaḥu	→	*ma-yiftaḥūš*	they shouldn't open
tišṛabi	→	*ma-tišṛabīš*	you (fem.) shouldn't drink

2. Imperative: The imperative cannot be linked directly to a negative particle. Instead, the second person of the imperfect is used, in combination with *ma-....-š*.

inzil (*tinzil*)	→	*ma-tinzilš*	don't get out!
inzili (*tinzili*)	→	*ma-tinzilīš*	
inzilu (*tinzilu*)	→	*ma-tinzilūš*	
rūḫ (*tirūḫ*)	→	*ma-truḫš*	don't go!
rūḫi (*tirūḫi*)	→	*ma-truḫīš*	
rūḫu (*tirūḫu*)	→	*ma-truḫūš*	
insa (*tinsa*)	→	*ma-tinsāš*	don't forget!
insi (*tinsi*)	→	*ma-tinsīš*	
insu (*tinsu*)	→	*ma-tinsūš*	
xušš (*tixušš*)	→	*ma-txuššiš*	don't enter!
xušši (*tixušši*)	→	*ma-txuššīš*	
xuššu (*tixuššu*)	→	*ma-txuššūš*	
xud (*tāxud*)	→	*ma-taxudš*	don't take!
xudi (*taxdi*)	→	*ma-taxdīš*	
xudu (*taxdu*)	→	*ma-taxdūš*	

N.B. The additional *-i* in *ma-txuššiš* is explained in lesson V.V.

3. The irregular imperatives *taɛāla* "come!" and *hāt* "give!" "bring!" are negated by using the negative form of the imperfect of *tīgi* "you come" and *tigīb* "you bring," or *tiddi* "you give."

taɛāla (*tīgi*)	→	*ma-tgīš, ma-tgīš, ma-tgūš*	don't come!
hāt (*tigīb*)	→	*ma-tgibš, ma-tgibīš, ma-tgibūš*	don't bring!
	or:	*ma-tiddīš, ma-tiddūš*	don't give!

INCREASE YOUR VOCABULARY

Eating and drinking

nišṛab ʾē? nākul ʾē?

beef	*laḥma kandūz*
beer	*bīra*
bread	*ʕēš*
bread (loaf)	*ʕēš baladi*
butter	*zibda*
cheese	*gibna*
chicken	*farxa, firāx*
cookies	*kaḥk ~ kaʕk*
cream	*šantiyī*
eggs	*bēḍ*
fish	*samak*
flour	*diʾīʾ*
fruit	*fakha, fawākih*
garlic	*tōm*
ham	*žambōn*
honey	*ʕasal*
jam	*miṛabba*
juice	*ʕaṣīr*
kebab	*kabāb*
lamb	*laḥma ḍāni*
lemon juice	*ʕaṣīr lamūn*
macaroni	*makarōna*
mango juice	*ʕaṣīr manga*
meat	*laḥma*
milk	*laban*
mineral water	*ṃayya maʕdaniyya*
oil	*zēt*
onions	*baṣal*
pepper	*filfil*
pickles	*ṭurši*
potatoes	*baṭāṭis*
prawns	*gambari*
rice	*ṛuzz*
roast beef	*laḥma rustu*
salad	*salaṭa*
soup	*šurba*
spices	*tawābil*
veal	*laḥma bitillu*
vegetables	*xuḍār*
vinegar	*xall*
water	*ṃayya*
wine	*nibīt*
yoghurt	*zabādi*

All cold, canned or bottled drinks such as coke are called *ḥāga saʾʕa* "something cold."

Starters *ṣalaṭāt* in an Egyptian restaurant are not only salads as in the English sense, but also:

ḅāḅa ġannūg	sesame paste with aubergine
bidingān mixallil	pickled aubergines
ṭiḥīna	sesame puree
buṣāra	bean paste with parsley
gibna ʾadīma	mature cheese
ṭurši	mixed pickled vegetables

EXERCISES

I. What should I do? Ask yourself questions, using the verbs that are given in brackets.

(*yiɛmil*) *aɛmil ʾē?*

1. (*yirkab*) ________________ *ilʾutubīs?*
2. (*yiʾfil*) ________________ *ilbāb?*
3. (*yiftaḩ*) ________________ *iššibbāk?*
4. (*yistanna*) ________________ *liġāyit imta?*
5. (*yiɛmil*) ________________ *ʾahwa?*
6. (*yirūḩ*) ________________ *fēn?*
7. (*yāxud*) ________________ *ḩāga saʾɛa?*
8. (*yixušš*) ________________ *dilwaʾti?*
9. (*yifūt ɛalēk*) ________________ *issāɛa kām?*
10. (*yinzil*) ________________ *fi-Midān itTaḩrīr?*
11. (*yiwaṣṣalak*) ________________ *šāriɛ ʾAṣr inNīl?*
12. (*yiɛaddi*) ________________ *ɛala Midān itTaḩrīr?*

II. Mark has to go to the *Mugammaɛ*. What should he do?
Make suggestions, combining one item from (a) with one from (b).

(a) *yirkab, yāxud, yisʾal, yimši, yinzil, yirūḩ*

(b) *liġāyit ilmidān, ilʾutubīs, taks, fi-Midān itTaḩrīr*
šāriɛ Ṭalɛat Ḩarb, ilɛaskari

1. *Mark lāzim* ________________
2. *Mark lāzim* ________________
3. *Mark lāzim* ________________
4. *Mark lāzim* ________________
5. *Mark lāzim* ________________
6. *Mark lāzim* ________________

III. *Fawziyya* is your housekeeper. What are the things she has to do today? Combine one item from (a) with one from (b).

(a) *yiḫuṭṭ, yiɛmil, yirūḫ, yiʔfil, yistanna, yinaḍḍaf, yiftaḫ*

(b) *issūʔ, ikkarāsi fi‿lbalakōna, ilbāb, ilʔahwa, šuwayya, iššababīk, ittaṛabēẓa*

1. *Fawziyya lāzim* ____________________
2. *Fawziyya lāzim* ____________________
3. *Fawziyya lāzim* ____________________
4. *Fawziyya lāzim* ____________________
5. *Fawziyya lāzim* ____________________
6. *Fawziyya lāzim* ____________________
7. *Fawziyya lāzim* ____________________

IV. *Fawziyya* and *Ḫusniyya* are your maids. What are all the things they have to do today?

1. *Fawziyya‿w Ḫusniyya lāzim* ____________________
2. *Fawziyya‿w Ḫusniyya lāzim* ____________________
3. *Fawziyya‿w Ḫusniyya lāzim* ____________________
4. *Fawziyya‿w Ḫusniyya lāzim* ____________________
5. *Fawziyya‿w Ḫusniyya lāzim* ____________________
6. *Fawziyya‿w Ḫusniyya lāzim* ____________________
7. *Fawziyya‿w Ḫusniyya lāzim* ____________________

V. Give the feminine singular and the plural forms of the following imperatives.

iṣ̌rab iššāy!	*iṣ̌rabi iššāy!*	*iṣ̌rabu iššāy!*
1. *iftaḫ ilbāb!*	____________	____________
2. *iʔfil iššibbāk!*	____________	____________

3. *iɛmil iššāy!* _______________ _______________

4. *istarayyaḫ!* _______________ _______________

5. *itfaḍḍal!* _______________ _______________

6. *naḍḍaf ikkursi!* _______________ _______________

7. *irkab taks!* _______________ _______________

8. *isʔal ilbawwāb!* _______________ _______________

9. *inzil issūʔ!* _______________ _______________

10. *xuššᵊ‿ymīn!* _______________ _______________

VI. Answer the following questions, using an imperative.

lāzim amši? - *aywa, imši ya Ḫasan!*

1. *lāzim aʔfil ilbāb?* - *aywa,* _______________ *ya Ḫasan!*

2. *lāzim aftaḫ iššibbāk?* - *aywa,* _______________ *ya Maha!*

3. *mumkin astarayyaḫ hina?* - *aywa,* ____________*hina, ya Samya!*

4. *mumkin nistanna hina?* - *aywa,* _______________ *ya ʔawlād!*

5. *lāzim aɛmil šāy?* - *aywa,* _______________ *ya Ḫasan!*

6. *mumkin asʔal suʔāl?* - *itfaḍḍal__ ya Ḫasan,*_____________*!*

7. *lāzim anzil hina?* - *itfaḍḍal___ ya Samya,*____________*!*

8. *mumkin āxud ilʔalam?* - *itfaḍḍal__ ya Ḫasan,*_______*ilʔalam!*

9. *lāzim nimši?* - *itfaḍḍal___ ya banāt,* __________*!*

10. *lāzim aʔṛa‿lkitāb?* - *aywa,* ______________ *min faḍlik!*

11. *mumkin nixušš?* - *ṭabɛan, itfaḍḍal*________________*!*

12. *mumkin aɛaddi min hina?* - *ṭabɛan, itfaḍḍal*________________*!*

VII. I don't want to! Say what you don't want to do.

imši ya Ḫasan! - *miš ¿āwiz amši.*

1. *inzil ya Muṣṭafa!* - ______________________
2. *inzili ya Fawziyya!* - ______________________
3. *inzilu ya ʾawlād!* - ______________________
4. *iṣ̌rab ya ¿Ali!* - ______________________
5. *irkab ya Sāmi!* - ______________________
6. *istarayyaḫi ya Maha!* - ______________________
7. *iftaḫu ya banāt!* - ______________________
8. *kulu ya ʾawlād!* - ______________________
9. *kuli ya Samya!* - ______________________
10. *istannu ya banāt!* - ______________________
11. *rūḫ ya‿bni!* - ______________________
12. *xudu ya ʾawlād!* - ______________________

VIII. Don't do it! Give negative commands.

arkab? - *lā ya Ḫasan,* *ma-tirkabš!*

1. *amši?* - *lā ya Ḫasan,* ______________________*!*
2. *aftaḫ?* - *lā ya Ḫasan,* ______________________*!*
3. *axušš* - *lā ya Ḫasan,* ______________________*!*
4. *a¿addi?* - *lā ya Ḫasan,* ______________________*!*
5. *asʾal?* - *lā ya Ḫasan,* ______________________*!*
6. *aštiri?* - *lā ya Ḫasan,* ______________________*!*
7. *anzil?* - *lā ya Samya,* ______________________*!*
8. *arūḫ?* - *lā ya Samya,* ______________________*!*

9. *āxud?* - *lā ya Samya,* ______________________________!

10. *ākul?* - *lā ya Samya,* ______________________________!

11. *astanna?* - *lā ya Samya,* ______________________________!

IX. Of course you've got to do it! Insist on it.

astanna? - *ṭabɛan, lāzim tistanni ya Samya!*

1. *anzil?* - *ṭabɛan,* ______________________________ *ya Ḥasan!*
2. *ašṛab?* - *ṭabɛan,* ______________________________ *ya Fawzi!*
3. *asˀal?* - *ṭabɛan,* ______________________________ *ya Fawziyya!*
4. *arūḥ?* - *ṭabɛan,* ______________________________ *ya‿bni!*
5. *nistanna?* - *ṭabɛan,* ______________________________ *ya banāt!*
6. *nimši?* - *ṭabɛan,* ______________________________ *ya ˀawlād!*
7. *nirkab?* - *ṭabɛan,* ______________________________ *ya ˀaṭfāl!*
8. *nākul?* - *ṭabɛan,* ______________________________ *ya banāt!*
9. *āxud taks?* - *ṭabɛan,* ______________________________ *ya binti!*
10. *aftaḥ?* - *ṭabɛan,* ______________________________ *ya Samya!*
11. *anaḍḍaf?* - *ṭabɛan,* ______________________________ *ya Fawziyya!*
12. *axušš?* - *ṭabɛan,* ______________________________ *ya Ḥasan!*

X. I don't want to do it; they'll have to do it! Write the correct form of the verb.

miš ɛawiz arūḥ, lāzim yirūḥu humma!

1. *miš ɛāwiz arkab,* ______________________________ *humma!*
2. *miš ɛāwiz astarayyaḥ,* ______________________________ *humma!*
3. *miš ɛawza astanna,* ______________________________ *humma!*
4. *miš ɛāwiz asˀal,* ______________________________ *humma!*
5. *miš ɛawza‿mši,* ______________________________ *humma!*

6. *miš ɛāwiz anaḍḍaf,* ______________________ *humma!*

7. *miš ɛawzīn ništaġal,* ______________________ *humma!*

8. *miš ɛawza‿nzil,* ______________________ *humma!*

XI. What uncertainty! Indicate this by using the negative form of the verb.

(*nisāfir*) - *ya-taṛa‿nsāfir walla ma-nsafirš innahaṛda?*

1. (*arkab*) - ______________________ *ilʾutubīs da?*

2. (*nistanna*) - ______________________ *ḅāḅa?*

3. (*taxdu*) - ______________________ *taks?*

4. (*tišṛabi*) - ______________________ *illaban da?*

5. (*aɛmil*) - ______________________ *ilʾahwa?*

6. (*axušš*) - ______________________ *šimāl?*

7. (*nigīb*) - ______________________ *ilʾawlād maɛāna?*

8. (*nākul*) - ______________________ *issamak da?*

9. (*addi*) - ______________________ *Sāmi‿lkutub?*

10. (*akallim*) - ______________________ *ilmudīr?*

11. (*ništiri*) - ______________________ *ilɛaṛabiyya di?*

12 (*tiwaṣṣalu*) - ______________________ *Randa‿lbēt?*

13. (*nibīɛ*) - ______________________ *iššaʾʾa?*

14. (*nirūḩ*) - ______________________ *ilḩafla?*

15. (*afukk*) - ______________________ *ilmīt ginēh dōl?*

XII. Complete, using the correct form of the adjective.

1. *inti ɛawza ʾahwa* ______________________ ? (*turki*)

2. *ɛawzīn nizūr ilmaṣāniɛ* ______________________ . (*gidīd*)

3. *Maṣrᵊ fīha maṭāᶓim* ________________________ . (*rixīṣ, kitīr*)

4. *issagāyir* ______________________ *di‿btāᶓit mīn ?* (*ingilīzi*)

5. *baḫibb iššawāriᶓ* ___________________________ . (*hādi*)

6. *fēn iṭṭalaba* ______________________________ ? (*gidīd*)

7. *āxud walla ma-xudš iššaᵓᵓa* ________________ *di?* (*ġāli*)

8. *huwwa miggawwiz waḫda* ________________ *xāliṣ.* (*ġani*)

9. *Samya ṭālíba* _________________________ *giddan.* (*zaki*)

10. *fī suwwāḫ* ______________________ *ᵓawi‿f-Maṣr.* (*kitīr*)

11. *miš ᶓāwiz ilhadāya* _____________________ *di.* (*ġāli*)

12. *iššanṭa* ______________________ *di‿btaᶓti ᵓana!* (*kibīr*)

13. *innās* ___________________ *ma-ᶓanduhumšᵊ‿flūs.* (*faᵓīr*)

14. *ilᵓawlād* _________________ *lāzim yināmu badri.* (*ṣuġayyar*)

15. *mumkin tiddīni nimritak* __________________ ? (*gidīd*)

16. *inta šāyif ilᶓimāṛa* _______________________ *di?* (*kibīr*)

17. *Samya ma-ᶓandahāš waᵓt, hiyya miš* _________ *dilwaᵓti.* (*fāḍi*)

XIII. Translate the following sentences.

1. *ᶓAzīza* doesn't want to wait, ___________________________

2. *Kawsaṛ* (fem.) doesn't have to go. ________________________

3. Whom should I ask? ____________________________________

4. *Samīra*, please make some coffee! _________________________

5. You (masc.sing.) don't have to wait. ______________________

6. The students (fem.) must wait for a while. __________________

7. Is the club far from here? _______________________________

8. What should I do? _____________________________________

9. How do I get there? ______________________

10. Shut the window please, *Fawziyya*! ______________________

11. We don't want to wait. ______________________

12. We're in a bit of a hurry. ______________________

13. *Muḩammad*, put the table on the balcony please!

____

14. You (fem.sing.) should walk as far as the new petrol station.

____

15. First, ask (sing.) the doorman!

____

16. You (masc.sing.) must get out by the old mosque.

____

17. Do you want to smoke a cigarette, *Samya*?

____

18. Until what time should I wait?

____

19. Don't take that taxi, *Samīra*!

____

20. Don't come before midday, *Ḩasan*!

____

21. Don't drive via *Taḩrīr* square today, *Samya*!

____

22. Don't wait (masc.sing.) till tomorrow!

____

23. Unfortunately I'm not free now.

____

24. It's really crowded today.

____

25. Please, bring (fem.sing.) *Samīra* home!

____

LESSON VIII

READING PASSAGES

ilbēt

ilʾustāz John sākin fi‿lMaɛādi‿w bētu‿ʾrayyib min innādi. iššāriɛ bitāɛu hādi ma-fhūš dawša.

bētu‿ṣġayyaṛ wi ḥawalē‿gnēna fīha ward aḥmaṛ w‿aṣfar wi ʾalwān tanya kamān wi fīha šagaṛ kitīr wi naxlitēn. ilbēt da fī(h) ʾoḍtēn nōm wi ṣāla‿w ṣalōn wi maṭbax wi kamān ḥammām.

John mistanni‿ṣḥābu fi‿lveranda. ɛandu ḥafla‿w kullᵊ ḥāga gahza‿ w maḥṭūṭa ɛa‿ṣṣufra: ʾakl, wi šurb, wi ḥilwᵊ‿w fakha kamān.

iššaʾʾa

Mark sākin fi‿lMuhandisīn. huwwa‿l-waḥdu wi‿mʾaggaṛ šaʾʾa‿ ṣġayyaṛa. iššaʾʾa di fi-ɛmāṛa‿kbīra fi‿ddōr ittālit. fī ʾaṣanṣēr lākin innahaṛda ilʾaṣanṣēr ɛaṭlān wi Mark lāzim yiṭlaɛ issalālim mašy.

iddinya ḥaṛṛᵊ ʾawi‿w ɛašān kida lāzim yiftaḥ ittakyīf. imbāriḥ kān iggaww aḥsan šuwayya. Mark kān ɛāwiz yirūḥ yinām ɛala ṭūl, lākin innahaṛda ʾawwil iššahṛ, wi lāzim yirūḥ yidfaɛ ilʾigāṛ li-ṣaḥb‿ilbēt ilʾawwil.

ʾigāṛ šaʾʾa

Maha:	*masāʾ ilxēr*
issimsāṛa:	*masāʾ innūr! ʾahlan wa sahlan!*
Maha:	*min faḍlik, fī waḥda sitt ingiliziyya gayya tištaġal kām sana hina‿f-Maṣrᵊ w‿ɛayza‿tʾaggaṛ šaʾʾa mafrūša.*
issimsāṛa:	*ana ɛandi šaʾʾa mafrūša fi‿lMuhandisīn, fi‿ddōr ilxāmis, wi faršaha‿gdīd lang.*
Maha:	*wi da ʾāxir dōr ya-taṛa?*
issimsāṛa:	*lā, fī foʾha dorēn kamān.*
Maha:	*bi‿nnisba li‿lṃayya, ya-taṛa fī ʾayyᵊ mašākil?*
issimsāṛa:	*lā, ma-fīš mašākil xāliṣ, ṣaḥb‿ilbēt ɛāmil mutūr wi xazzān kibīr fōʾ ilɛimāṛa.*
Maha:	*ṭayyib, mumkin ašūf iššaʾʾa?*
issimsāṛa:	*ṭabɛan, ya-taṛa bukṛa baɛd iḍḍuhr issāɛa sabɛa‿ynāsib ḥaḍritik?*
Maha:	*aywa, da maɛād munāsib.*
issimsāṛa:	*xalāṣ. ana muntaẓira ḥaḍritik bukṛa‿ssāɛa sabɛa‿f-maktabi.*
Maha:	*mutšakkira ʾawi.*
issimsāṛa:	*ilɛafwᵊ yafandim, maɛa‿ssalāma.*

VOCABULARY

ʾakl	food, eating
ʾaṣanṣēr, -āt	lift, elevator
ʾawwil iššahṛ	the first of the month
ʾayy	any
ʾāxir	last, latest
ʾigāṛ	rent
ʾustāz, ʾasatza	gentleman professor
baɛdēn	afterwards
bi‿nnisba li ḥ	with regard to; as for
bunni	brown
burtuʾāni	orange (color)
dars, durūs	lesson
dawša	noise
dāxil	entering
dōr, adwāṛ ~ idwāṛ	floor, story
dulāb, dawalīb	cupboard
farš	furniture
gallabiyya, galalīb	gallabiyya (garment)
gaww	weather
ġarīb	foreign(er); strange
hamdān	tired, weary
hādi	quiet, calm
ḥammām, -āt	bathroom
ḥaṛṛ	heat, warmth
ḥawalēn	round, around
ḥilw	sweet, nice ; dessert
ḥurr, aḥṛāṛ	free
iza	if
kanaba, -āt	sofa, bench
kuḥli	dark blue
kām sana	a couple of years
law	if
li-waḥdu	alone
lōn, alwān	color
mafrūš	furnished
maḥgūz	reserved
maḥṭūṭ	placed, put
mašy	walking, on foot
maṭbax, maṭābix	kitchen
māši	walking; it's fine
miʾaggaṛ	rented, hired
ilMuhandisīn	district in Gīza
muntaẓir	waiting
muškila, mašākil	problem

naṣṣ, nuṣūṣ	reading passage
naxla	date palm
nōm	sleep
qarn, qurūn	century
ṛaff, ṛufūf	shelf
rumādi	gray
sana, sinīn	year
sawṛa	revolution
sillim, salālim	stair, step
simsāṛ, samasra	house agent
ṣaff, ṣufūf	row (of seats)
ṣaḥb‿ilbēt	landlord
ṣalōn, -āt	drawing room
ṣāla, -āt	living room
ṣēf	summer
ṣufra	dining room table
šagaṛ (c.)	trees
šurb	drink (noun)
takyīf	air-conditioning
tālit	third
ward (c.)	flowers, roses
wāʾif	switched off, stopped; standing
xazzān, -āt	water tank
xāmis	fifth
yiʾaggaṛ ḥ	to rent, to hire
yidfaɛ ḥ	to pay
yilāʾi ḥ	to find
yinām	to sleep
yināsib w	to suit, to be convenient to
yirgaɛ	to return
yisīb ḥ	to leave
yištaġal	to work
yišūf ḥ	to see
yitfaṛṛag ɛala ḥ	to have a look at to watch
yiṭlaɛ ḥ	to climb
yiɛazzil	to move house
yiɛīš	to live
zatūni	olive-green
ɛalašān ~ ɛašān	because, so that; for
ɛasali	hazel (color)
ɛaṭlān	out of order broken down
ɛāmil	having made

GRAMMAR

I. The dual

1. Form: The dual is formed by adding the ending *-ēn* to a noun. In the case of feminine nouns, the feminine ending *-a* will change to *-it* before the dual ending:

waladēn	two boys	*bintēn*	two girls
kitabēn	two books	*ṣurtēn*	two pictures
šanṭitēn	two bags	*ʾoḍtēn*	two rooms
šaʾʾitēn	two flats	*baʾarṭēn*	two cows

If a word ends in an *-i*, the ending will be *-yyēn* :

kursi + ēn → *kursiyyēn* "two chairs"

2. Use: The dual is used for pairs of things. Two persons, however, are usually expressed by *itnēn* "two" in conjunction with the plural:

itnēn mudarrisīn "two teachers" *itnēn ṭalaba* "two students"

Exceptions to this occur, for instance when referring to some family members such as *axxēn* "two brothers," *uxtēn* "two sisters"

When a word is used in the dual, the demonstrative pronouns, verbs or adjectives which accompany it are put in the plural:

ikkitabēn dōl gudād "both these books are new"

By using *itnēn* with a dual noun, extra emphasis is placed on the dual:

šaʾʾitēn itnēn "**two** flats" *yomēn itnēn* "**two** days"

Occasionally the dual can be used to express a small quantity, as in English "a couple of days," "a pound or two":

ʾiršēn "some money" *yomēn* "a few days"

The dual cannot be combined with a possessive suffix. In such cases, the construction with *bitūɛ* must be used (→ VI.VI):

ilʾoḍtēn bitūɛi "my two rooms" "both my rooms"

II. Object suffixes

1. In Arabic object pronouns e.g., "me," "him," "her," are expressed by adding object suffixes to the verb. With the exception of the first person singular where *-i* changes to *-ni*, the object suffixes are identical with the possessive suffixes:

xudni‿mɛāk "take me with you!" *iddīha‿lkitāb* "give her the book"

The rules for changing the stress, eliding the letter *-i-* and shortening certain vowels are the same as for possessive suffixes:

3rd person	2nd person	1st person
(*bētu*) *yišūfu* (*betha*) *yišufha* (*bethum*) *yišufhum*	(*bētak*) *yišūfak* (*bētik*) *yišūfik* (*betkum*) *yišufkum*	(*bēti*) *yišufni* (*betna*) *yišufna*

2. Object suffixes are attached to participles in the same way:

ɛārif:	*ɛarfu* *ɛarifha* *ɛarifhum*	*ɛarfak* *ɛarfik* *ɛarifku(m)*	*ɛarifni* *ɛarifna*
ɛarfa:	*ɛarfā(h)* *ɛarfāha* *ɛarfāhum*	*ɛarfāk* *ɛarfāki* *ɛarfāku(m)*	*ɛarfāni* *ɛarfāna*
ɛarfīn:	*ɛarfīnu* *ɛarfinha* *ɛarfinhum*	*ɛarfīnak* *ɛarfīnik* *ɛarfinku(m)*	*ɛarfinni* *ɛarfinna*

N.B. The *-a* ending of a feminine participle is lengthend if an object suffix is attached to it:

hiyya šayfa	+ *ni*	>	*šayfāni*	"she sees me"
hiyya miš ɛarfa	+ *hum*	>	*ɛarfāhum*	"she doesn't know them"

III. Ordinal numbers

1. **Structure:** Ordinal numbers are derived from the cardinals and follow the pattern **KāTiB**. So, for example, *tālit* "third" comes from *talāta*, and *sābiɛ* "seventh" from *sabɛa*. This only applies to the numbers 2 to 10. The ordinal number derived from *wāḩid* "one" is *ʾawwil* (masc.), *ʾūla* (fem.), *ʾawāʾil* (pl.).

wāḩid	→	*ʾawwil*	*sitta*	→	*sādis ~ sātit*
itnēn	→	*tāni*	*sabɛa*	→	*sābiɛ*
talāta	→	*tālit*	*tamanya*	→	*tāmin*
aṛbaɛa	→	*ṛābiɛ*	*tisɛa*	→	*tāsiɛ*
xamsa	→	*xāmis*	*ɛašaṛa*	→	*ɛāšir*

From eleven onwards, the cardinal numbers are used.

2. Use:

(a) The ordinals 1 to 10 can be used as adjectives, which means that you have to pay attention to agreement (→ VII.I). In this case, *ʾawwal* is used instead of *ʾawwil*:

iddars ittāmin	"the eighth lesson"	*iṣṣūra‿ṛṛabɛa*	"the fourth picture"
ilyōm issābiɛ	"the seventh day"	*iṣṣaff ilʔawwal*	"the first row"
ilqarn issādis	"the sixth century"	*ilmaṛṛa‿lʔūla*	"the first time"

(b) The ordinals from 1 to 10 can also be used in a genitive construction. In this case, they remain in the masc. sing. and the noun which follows is not defined:

ilʔaṣanṣēr biyiṭlaɛ liġāyit xāmis dōr	"the lift goes to the fifth floor"
udxul ʔawwil šāriɛ yimīn	"enter the first street to the right"
huwwa‿f- sābiɛ sama	"he is in seventh heaven"

(c) From 11 onwards, cardinal numbers are used exclusively, and they are treated adjectivally:

ilqarn ilɛišrīn	"the 20th century"	*iddōr ilḥidāšar*	"the eleventh floor"

N.B. As well as *ʔawwal*, you will also find *ʔawwalāni* (masc.), *-iyya* (fem.), *-iyyīn* (pl.) meaning "first." They are exclusively used as adjectives.

IV. Colors and physical characteristics

Colors and adjectives which refer to certain physical characteristics have a special form a**KT**a**B** (masc.), **K**a**TB**a (fem.) and **K**u**TB** (pl.).

masc.	fem.	pl.	
aṣfar	*ṣafra*	*ṣufr*	yellow
asmaṛ	*samra*	*sumr*	dark (skin)
azraʔ	*zarʔa*	*zurʔ*	blue
aḥmaṛ	*ḥamra*	*ḥumr*	red
axḍar	*xaḍra*	*xuḍr*	green
ašʔaṛ	*šaʔṛa*	*šuʔṛ*	blond
aṭraš	*ṭarša*	*ṭurš*	deaf
aɛṛag	*ɛarga*	*ɛurg*	lame
aɛma	*ɛamya*	*ɛumy*	blind
abyaḍ	*bēḍa*	*bīḍ*	white
iswid	*sōda*	*sūd*	black
ašwal	*šōla*	*šūl*	left-handed
aḥwal	*ḥōla*	*ḥūl*	cross-eyed

However, you unexpectedly find *bēḍa* not **bayḍa* and *sōda* not **sawda*; *bīḍ* not **buyḍ* and *sūd* not **suwd*. Similarly you will find:

huwwa aḥwal	"he squints"	*hiyya ḥōla*	"she squints"
huwwa ašwal	"he is left-handed"	*humma šūl*	"they are left-handed

V. Prepositions *ɛala, min,* and *ɛan*

1. The prepositions *ɛala* "on" and *min* "from" can be shortened when followed by the definite article:

ɛala‿ṣṣufra	~ *ɛa‿ṣṣufra*	"on the dining table"
min ilbēt	~ *mi‿lbēt*	"from ~ out of the house"

2. When combined with a suffix beginning with a vowel, the *-n-* of the words *min* and *ɛan* "away from" is doubled: *minni, minnak, minnik, minnu* and *ɛanni, ɛannak, ɛannik, ɛannu.*

In the case of suffixes beginning with a consonant, the *-n-* may or may not be doubled: *minha ~ minnaha, minna ~ minnina* etc.

3. In the case of *ɛala*, the final *-a* changes to *-ē-* in front of all suffixes: *ɛalēk, ɛalēki, ɛalēha* etc., except the suffix of the first person singular. The form of *ɛala* with the suffix of the first person singular is *ɛalayya.*

VI. *ṛāyiḫ* with the imperfect

When *ṛāyiḫ* "he's going" and *yirūḫ* "he has to go" are followed by the imperfect, they give a sense of purpose:

lāzim tirūḫ tidfaɛ ilʔigāṛ	"you've got to go and pay the rent"
ana ṛāyiḫ aštiri sagāyir	"I'm going to buy some cigarettes"
ṛayḫīn nitɛašša fi‿lHilton	"we're going to have dinner in the Hilton"

VII. Polite forms of address

To address someone politely, instead of saying "you," one uses *ḫaḍritak* (masc.), *ḫaḍritik* (fem.) and *ḫaḍaratkum* (pl.) with the verb in the second person. To be even more formal, one can use *siyadtak, siyadtik* (fem.):

ḫaḍritak taɛāla‿ymīn	"(kindly) turn to the right!"
ḫaḍritik ɛawza ʔē?	"what would madam like?"
siyadtak lāzim tistanna‿šwayya	"(be so good as to) wait a bit."

The polite forms are also used as objects of a sentence:

ɛawza asʔal ḫaḍritak suʔāl	"I'd like to ask you (m.) a question"

VIII. The use of *gaww* and *dinya*

The word *gaww* "weather" is used when you are making a judgment about the weather:

iggawwᵊ gamīl fi-Maṣrᵊ fi‿ššita	"in winter the weather in Egypt is lovely"
iggawwᵊ wiḫiš giddan innahaṛda	"the weather's terrible today"

But if you're making a factual statement, you use the word *dinya* "world" to express the English "it's":

iddinya ḫaṛṛ	"it's hot"	*iddinya bard*	"it's cold"
iddinya bitmaṭṭar	"it's raining"	*iddinya_mġayyima*	"it's cloudy"
iddinya ḍalma	"it's dark"	*iddinya šams*	"it's sunny"

iddinya is also used in many other common expressions as:

iddinya zaḫma	"it's crowded"
iddinya wiḫša	"the world's a bad place"
iddinya kida	"that's life" "that's how things are!" (condolence)

PROVERBS

ḫumarti_lɛarga wala suʾāl illaʾīm	Better the devil you know than the devil you don't know [lit. better my lame donkey than asking someone untrustworthy]
ilʾirš ilʾabyaḍ yinfaɛ fi_lyōm ilʾiswid	Save your money for a rainy day [lit. white coins are useful for black days]
ilġarīb aɛma walaw baṣīr	The outsider is blind even with his eyes open.
ittalta tabta	Third time lucky
ya_nhāṛ abyaḍ!	Oh lackaday! [lit. what a white day].
ya xabaṛ iswid!	What a sad story! [lit. what black news!]

ʾirš, ʾurūš	piaster, coin	*nahāṛ*	daytime
baṣīr	clear-sighted	*tābit*	constant, stable (only in proverbs)
ġarīb	foreigner, outsider	*walaw*	even if
ḫumāṛa	female donkey	*yinfaɛ*	to be useful
laʾīm	untrustworthy		

INCREASE YOUR VOCABULARY

iggism "the body" (→ X.I)

arm	*dirāɛ, -āt*	hair	*šaɛr* (c.)
cheek	*xadd, xudūd*	hand	*ʾīd* (f.), *ʾidēn*
ear	*widn* (f.), *widān*	head	*ṛās* (f.), *rūs*
eye	*ɛēn* (f.), *ɛenēn*	knee	*rukba, rukab*
face	*wišš, wušūš*	mouth	*buʾʾ*
finger	*ṣubāɛ, ṣawābiɛ*	neck	*raʾaba, riʾāb*
foot	*rigl* (f.), *riglēn*	nose	*manaxīr* (f.)
forehead	*ʾūṛa*	stomach	*baṭn* (f.)

ilmalābis "clothes"

belt	*ḫizām, ḫizíma*	sandal	*ṣandal, ṣanādil*
blouse	*bilūza, -āt*	shirt, blouse	*ʾamīṣ, ʾumṣān*
cap	*ṭaʾiyya, ṭawāʾi*	shoes (a pair)	*gazma, gizam*
clothes	*hidūm; malābis*	a shoe	*fardit gazma*
coat	*balṭu, balāṭi*	slipper	*šibšib, šabāšib*
dress	*fustān, fasatīn*	socks	*šaṛāb, -āt*
fez	*ṭarbūš, ṭarabīš*	a sock	*fardit šaṛāb*
glasses	*naḍḍāra, -āt*	suit	*badla, bidal*
hat	*burnēṭa, baranīṭ*	tie	*karafatta, -āt*
handkerchief	*mandīl, manadīl*	trousers	*banṭalōn, -āt*
jacket	*žakitta, -āt*	turban	*ɛimma, ɛimam*
jellabah (cloak)	*gallabiyya, galalīb*	vest ~ undershirt	*fanilla, -āt*
pullover	*bulōfaṛ, -āt*		

EXERCISES

I. Use the ordinal number in brackets adjectivally.

1. Ḫasan ᵓāɛid fi‿ṣṣaff________________. (7)

2. Samya sakna fi‿ddōr ________________. (5)

3. sana ________________ ṣaɛbᵊ ᵓawi. (1)

4. iṣṣaff ________________ miš maḫgūz. (9)

5. Madīḫa sakna fi‿ddōr ________________. (11)

6. lāzim yiṭlaɛu li‿ddōr ________________ ? (8)

7. sīb iššāriɛ ______________ wi ________________. (1, 2)

   wi xuššᵊ fi‿ššāriɛ ________________. (3)

8. issawṛa‿f-Maṣrᵊ kānit fi‿lqarn ________________. (20)

9. ɛUmaṛ fi-sana ________________ fi‿ggamɛa. (3)

10. miš ɛāwiz yirūḫ wi yirgaɛ maṛṛa ________________. (2)

II. Use the ordinal number in brackets in a genitive construction.

1. ɛAmrᵊ sākin fi-________________ dōr. (8)

2. ilᵓasansēr wāᵓif fi-________________ dōr. (6)

3. __________ wi __________ ṣaffᵊ maḫguzīn li‿lmudīr. (4, 5)

4. ________________ darsᵊ ṣaɛbᵊ ᵓawi. (10)

5. di ________________ maṛṛa ᵓaɛazzil fīha. (9)

6. ya‿ṣṭa, xuššᵊ min faḍlak fi- __________ šāriɛ yimīn. (4)

7. di ________________ šaᵓᵓa ᵓašufha‿nnahaṛda. (3)

8. Samīḫa daxla ________________ ɛimāṛa ɛa‿lyimīn. (2)

9. di ________________ ḫāga yiɛmilha‿nnahaṛda. (1)

10. ṣaḫbiti ɛAzza ᵓaɛda‿f-________________ ṣaff. (7)

III. Who pays the bill?

ilḫisāb ɛala mīn? - *ɛalēk inta.*

1. *ilḫisāb ɛala mīn?* - ____________________ *huwwa.*
2. *ilḫisāb ɛala mīn?* - ____________________ *ana.*
3. *ilḫisāb ɛala mīn?* - ____________________ *inti.*
4. *ilḫisāb ɛala mīn?* - ____________________ *humma.*
5. *ilḫisāb ɛala mīn?* - ____________________ *hiyya.*
6. *ilḫisāb ɛala mīn?* - ____________________ *intu.*
7. *ilḫisāb ɛala mīn?* - ____________________ *iḫna.*

IV. You look really....

ana ɛayyān. *aywa‿nta bāyin ɛalēk fiɛlan ɛayyān.*

1. *iḫna ɛayyanīn.* - ______________________________.
2. *huwwa taɛbān.* - ______________________________.
3. *hiyya miš mabṣūṭa.* - ______________________________.
4. *di taɛbāna.* - ______________________________.
5. *dōl kuwayyisīn.* - ______________________________.
6. *ilfarš^{ə}‿gdīd lang.* - ______________________________.
7. *ilʾaṣansēr ɛaṭlān.* - ______________________________.

V. Whatʾs he going to do? Answer the following.

ɛala fēn ya Sāmi? - *ana ṛāyiḫ adfaɛ ilʾigāṛ.* (*yidfaɛ*)

1. *ɛala fēn ya ʾawlād?* - *iḫna* ________________ (*yinām*)
2. *ɛala fēn ya Ḫasan?* - *ana* ________________ *sagāyir.* (*yištiri*)
3. *ɛala fēn ya Samya?* - *ana* ____________ *šuwayya.* (*yitmašša*)
4. *ɛala fēn ya banāt?* - *iḫna* _________ *iššaʾʾa‿ggidīda.* (*yišūf*)

5. *humma ṛayḫīn fēn?* - _______________ *fi‿lmaṭɛam.* (*yitɛašša*)

6. *ɛala fēn ya ṃāṃa?* - *ana* _______________ *uxti.* (*yizūr*)

VI. Not one but two! Use the dual.

miš kitāb wāḫid, ___________. *miš bēt wāḫid,* ___________.

miš sāɛa waḫda, ___________. *miš šaᵓᵓa waḫda,* ___________.

miš ḫāga waḫda, ___________. *miš ṣūra waḫda,* ___________.

miš ɛaṛabiyya waḫda, ___________. *miš dōr wāḫid,* ___________.

miš ᵓōḍa waḫda, ___________. *miš dulāb wāḫid,* ___________.

miš baᵓara waḫda, ___________. *miš šanṭa waḫda,* ___________.

miš kursi wāḫid, ___________. *miš hidiyya waḫda,* ___________.

miš ṣāla waḫda, ___________. *miš ɛimāṛa waḫda,* ___________.

VII. Answer in the affirmative.

aftaḫ iššibbāk? - *aywa, iftaḫu.*

1. *adfaɛ ilᵓigāṛ?* - *aywa,* ___________________________.
2. *aᵓfil ilbāb?* - *aywa,* ___________________________.
3. *aftaḫ ittakyīf?* - *aywa,* ___________________________.
4. *ašṛab iššāy?* - *aywa,* ___________________________.
5. *ākul illaḫma?* - *aywa,* ___________________________.
6. *anaḍḍaf ilmaṭbax?* - *aywa,* ___________________________.
7. *asᵓal ilbawwāb?* - *aywa,* ___________________________.
8. *āxud ilᵓutubīs?* - *aywa,* ___________________________.

VIII. Answer in the affirmative.

aftaḫ iššababīk? - *aywa, iftaḫha.*

1. *arkab ittaks?* - *aywa,* ______________________.
2. *aḫuṭṭ ilwardᵊ hina?* - *aywa,* ______________________.
3. *aʔfil ilʔabwāb?* - *aywa,* ______________________.
4. *aṣ̌rab ilʔahwa?* - *aywa,* ______________________.
5. *aftaḫ ilbalakōna?* - *aywa,* ______________________.
6. *anaḍḍaf ilʔuwaḍ?* - *aywa,* ______________________.
7. *asʔal ilmudarrisa?* - *aywa,* ______________________.
8. *awaṣṣal uxtak?* - *aywa,* ______________________.

IX. What do I have to clean?

ikkarāsi di, lāzim anaḍḍafha?

1. *ilbalakōna di, lāzim*______________________?
2. *ikkursi wi‿ttaṛabēẓa dōl, lāzim*______________________?
3. *ʔoḍt‿innōm di, lāzim* ______________________?
4. *ilbēt da, lāzim* ______________________?
5. *iššababīk di, lāzim* ______________________?
6. *iššawāriɛ di, lāzim* ______________________?
7. *ilmaṭbax wi‿lḫammām dōl, lāzim* ______________________?
8. *ilʔuwaḍ di, lāzim*______________________?

X. What does *Ḫusniyya* have to clean?

ikkarāsi, lāzim tinaḍḍafīha, ya Ḫusniyya!

1. *ilmaṭbax wi‿lḫammām, lāzim* ______________________, *ya Ḫusniyya!*
2. *ikkursi, lāzim* ______________________, *ya Ḫusniyya!*
3. *ʔoḍt‿innōm, lāzim*______________________, *ya Ḫusniyya!*

4. *išša^{\circ\circ}a, lāzim* ____________________, *ya Ḫusniyya!*

5. *iššababīk, lāzim* ____________________, *ya Ḫusniyya!*

6. *iddawalīb wi‿rrufūf, lāzim* ____________________, *ya Ḫusniyya!*

7. *ilmaṭbax, lāzim* ____________________, *ya Ḫusniyya!*

8. *ilʾuwaḍ, lāzim* ____________________, *ya Ḫusniyya!*

XI. I do, but she doesn't!

ana šayifha, lākin hiyya miš šayfāni.

1. *ana ʿarifhum, lākin humma miš* ____________________.
2. *hiyya fakrāni, lākin huwwa miš* ____________________.
3. *iḫna ʿarfīnak, lākin inta miš* ____________________.
4. *intu šayfinni, lākin ana miš* ____________________.
5. *ana ʿarfākum, lākin intu miš* ____________________.
6. *inta fakirha, lākin hiyya miš* ____________________.
7. *huwwa ʿarfak, lākin inta miš* ____________________.
8. *hiyya samʿāki, lākin inti miš* ____________________.
9. *ana šayfik, lākin inti miš* ____________________.
10. *humma samʿinha, lākin hiyya miš* ____________________.

XII. What did the man in the photo look like? Fill in each blank with a suitable word from the list below.

aḫmaṛ, aṣfar, azraʾ, axḍar, abyaḍ, iswid, asmaṛ,
bunni, kuḫli, ʿasali, zatūni, burtuʾāni, ruṃādi

kān fī fi‿lktāb bitāʿi ṣūra‿l-wāḫid ṛāgil ġarīb ʾawi

wiššu kān abyaḍ. *šaʿṛu* _______________.

ʿenē (pl.) _______________. *widānu* (pl.) _______________.

ʾidē (pl.) _______________. *manaxīru* _______________.

*iggallabiyyitu*________________.	*ṭarbūšu* ________________.
ilfanilla‿btaɛtu _____________.	*ilbulōfaṛ bitāɛu* _____________.
ʾamīṣu ___________________.	*iggazma‿btaɛtu* ___________.
šaṛābu ___________________.	*ilkaṛafatta‿btaɛtu* __________.
ižžakitta‿btaɛtu ____________.	*innaḍḍāra‿btaɛtu* __________.

XIII. Choose a different color, using the words below.

aḫmaṛ, aṣfar, azraʾ, axḍar, abyaḍ, iswid

ana miš ɛawza‿ṣṣabūna‿ṣṣafra di, iddīni iṣṣabūna‿lbēḍa.

1. *ana miš ɛawza‿lbulōfaṛ ilʾaṣfar da, iddīni*__________________.
2. *ana miš ɛāwiz ikkuṛṛāsa‿lḫamra di, iddīni*__________________.
3. *ana miš ɛawza‿ššanṭa‿lbēḍa di, iddīni* ____________________.
4. *iḫna miš ɛayzīn issiggāda‿zzarʾa di, iḫna ɛawzīn*_____________.
5. *ana miš ɛāwiz ittaṛabēẓa‿ssōda di, ana ɛāwiz* ________________.
6. *iḫna miš ɛawzīn ilʾalam ilʾaḫmaṛ da, hāt*__________________.
7. *ana miš ɛawza‿lward ilʾaṣfar da, iddīni*___________________.

XIV. Form sentences with the words below.

1. *ṛābiɛ, saknīn, dōr, iḫna, fi.*

____

2. *fīha, iššaʾʾa, ma-...-š, takyīf, iggidīda.*

____

3. *iggaww, kān, imbāriḫ, šuwayya, aḫsan.*

____

4. *ilawlād, ɛala ṭūl, ɛawzīn, yināmu, yirūḫu.*

____

5. *yitṣallaḫ* (to be repaired), *ilʾaṣansēr, lāzim, wi, ɛaṭlān.*

____

6. *ḫaṛṛ, iṣṣēf, iddinya, ʾawi, fi, kānit.*

---

7. *nās, kān, fī, ilḫafla, kitīr, imbāriḫ, fi.*

---

8. *mumkin, Nabīl, tidfaع, ilḫisāb, ya, innahaṛda!*

---

9. *bitāعit, di, issōda, iẓẓakitta, mīn?*

---

10. *di, bitaعti, ana, iššunaṭ, izzarʾa.*

XV. Translate the following sentences.

1. My flat is small.

---

2. I used to live in Alexandria.

---

3. My father has gone to pay the rent.

---

4. Where is your mother?

---

5. Your (sg.) new photo is very pretty (*ḫilw*).

---

6. The flat had no air-conditioning.

---

7. The block of flats hasn't got a lift.

---

8. *عAmr* knows me very well.

---

9. There are two long dresses in the shop window.

---

10. She had rented a small flat.

---

11. *Samya* is going to buy some bread.

____

12. My flat is on the fifth floor.

____

13. It was very hot yesterday.

____

14. *Ḩasan*'s got two (pairs of) trousers, a red one and a green one.

____

15. Please (could you) turn off (*yiˀfil*) the air-conditioning?

____

16. They are waiting for their friends.

____

17. I'd like two black bags, please.

____

18. The yellow pens are for you.

____

19. We can either eat at home or go and have dinner at the restaurant.

____

LESSON IX

READING PASSAGES

qiṣṣit ḫayāti

1. *ismi Samīra Muṣṭafa Gōhaṛ. itwaladtᵊ fi‿zZaᵓazīᵓ sanat wāḫid wi xamsīn.*

2. *izZaᵓazīᵓ balad ṣuġayyaṛa fi‿mḫafẓit išŠarᵓiyya wi miš biɛīda ɛan Maṣr. abūya, Aḷḷā yirḫamu, kān muwaẓẓaf ḫukūma. ɛandi ᵓaxxēn wi ᵓuxt.*

3. *lamma kān ɛandi xamas sinīn abūya‿tnaᵓal Maṣr, fa biɛna‿ ššaᵓᵓa‿btaɛitna wi ᵓaggaṛna šaᵓᵓa tanya‿f-Bulāᵓ. ɛazzilna‿w daxalt ilmadrasa‿libtidāᵓi, wi baɛdᵊ kida‿ssanawi, wi xadt issanawiyya‿ lɛāmma sanat tamanya‿w sittīn.*

4. *baɛdᵊ ma xallaṣt ilmadrasa, daxaltᵊ kulliyyit iṭṭibb. xallaṣt iddiṛāsa wi xadt ilmažistēr b-imtiyāz.*

5. *baɛd ilmagistēr iggamɛa baɛatitni ᵓAmrīka ɛašān atābiɛ dirasti, w‿āxud idduktuṛā.*

6. *baɛdᵊ ma‿rgiɛtᵊ min ᵓAmrīka, ištaġaltᵊ kām sana fi-mustašfa‿ lɛAgūza wi fataḫtᵊ‿ɛyāda.*

7. *iggawwiztᵊ min aṛbaɛ sinīn. gōzi ṭabīb barḍu wi ɛandina walad wi bint.*

tagdīd ilᵓiqāma

Craig:	*ilᵓiqāma‿btaɛti ɛawza tagdīd.*
ilmuwaẓẓaf:	*warrīni‿lbaṣbōr bitāɛak, min faḍlak. aywa, ṣaḫḫ.* *rūḫ ištiri‿stimāṛa mi‿lxazna wi ma-tinsāš iddamġa.* *di muhimma giddan.*
Craig:	*wi baɛdᵊ kida aɛmil ᵓē?*
ilmuwaẓẓaf:	*hāt maɛāk ṣuwar baṣbōr.*
Craig:	*kām ṣūra?*
ilmuwaẓẓaf:	*ṣurtēn bass. imla‿listimāṛa wi gīb iṣṣuwar* *w‿irgaɛ hina tāni.*
Craig:	*kida‿kwayyis?*
ilmuwaẓẓaf:	*aywa, bassᵊ fī ḫāga naᵓṣa, ilᵓimḍa wi‿ttarīx. imḍi hina* *w‿iktib ittarīx gamb ilᵓimḍa, min faḍlak.*
Craig:	*ya-taṛa mumkin astilim ilbaṣbōr bitāɛi ᵓimta ?*
ilmuwaẓẓaf:	*taɛāla baɛd issāɛa‿tnēn ᵓaw bukṛa‿ṣṣubḫ.*

VOCABULARY

ʾaggaṛ, yiʾaggaṛ ḫ	to rent, to hire
ʾimḍa, -āt	signature
ʾiqāma, -āt	residence permit
basīṭ	simple
baɛat, yibɛat ḫ ~ w	to send
baɛdᵊ ma	after
bāɛ, yibīɛ ḫ	to sell
b‿imtiyāz	with honors
damġa, -āt	revenue stamp
diṛāsa, -āt	study
dukturā	doctorate
fa	then, thereupon
ḫayā	life
ḫukūma, -āt	government
ibtidāʾi	primary (school)
iggawwiz, yiggawwiz w	to marry
illi	who, which
ilmafrūḍ	it's necessary
istalam, yistilim ḫ	to receive
istimāṛa, -āt	form (to fill in)
itnaʾal, yitniʾil	to be transferred
itwalad, yitwilid	to be born
kubri, kabāri	bridge
kulliyya, -āt	faculty (univ.)
maḍa, yimḍi ḫ	to sign
lamma	when
mala, yimla ḫ	to fill, to fill in
maraḍ, amrāḍ	sickness
mažistēr	master's degree
muhimm	important
muḫafẓa, -āt	governorate
nāʾiṣ	missing, lacking; minus
nisi, yinsa ḫ ~w	to forget
nizil, yinzil	to get out to go down
qiṣṣa, qiṣaṣ	story
ṛaḫam, yiṛḫam w	to take pity on
rigiɛ, yirgaɛ	to come back
sanawiyya ɛāmma	final school exam
sillim, salālim	steps, stairs
ṣaḫḫ!	that's right!
tagdīd	extension; renewal
tarīx	date; history
tābiɛ, yitābiɛ ḫ	to continue
tāni	second; again, a second time
ṭabīb, aṭibbāʾ	medical doctor
ṭibb	medical studies
warra, yiwarri w	to show, to let someone see
wādi, widyān	valley
xallaṣ, yixallaṣ ḫ	to complete, to finish
xazna, xizan	till, cashdesk
ɛamal, yiɛmil ḫ	to do, to make
ɛaṛabiyya, -āt	car
ɛaskari, ɛasākir	policeman
ɛirif, yiɛraf ḫ	to know; to be able to
ɛiyāda, -āt	practice (medical)

In your vocabulary lists from now on the perfect will be written before the imperfect.

NB: *sanawiyya ɛāmma* is a borrowing from Standard Arabic which allows here a long vowel before two consonants.

GRAMMAR

I. *kām* "how many?"

When enquiring about the number of something, one should use *kām* after the noun in question:

nimritak kām?	"what is your number?"
iššaʾʾa‿btaɛtak nimra kām?	"what number's your flat?"

When asking about amounts or totals *kām* is followed by an undefined noun in the singular:

kām ṣūra? "how many photos?" *kām ṭālib?* "how many students?"

One can also use *kām* to ask the date:

innahaṛda kām fi‿ššahṛ?	"what date is it today?" [lit. today is what day of the month?]

The answer could be, for example:

innahaṛda xamsa yulyu ~ xamsa sabɛa
"today is the fifth of July ~ the fifth of the seventh (month)"

II. *illi* "who" or "which"

The relative pronoun is expressed by the word *illi*. It is uninflected and is only used after nouns which have been defined either by the definite article or by a possessive suffix. In Arabic, unlike in English, adjectival phrases which refer to a definite noun have to be written out as a relative clause:

"the policeman (who is) at the door"	→	*ilɛaskari illi ɛa‿lbāb*
"the door (which is) on the right"	→	*ilbāb illi ɛa‿lyimīn*
"the people (who are) upstairs"	→	*innās illi fō'*

Be careful: If the above phrases are written without the relative pronoun *illi*, they have a completely different meaning in Arabic:

ilɛaskari ɛa‿lbāb	"the policeman is at the door"
ilbāb ɛa‿lyimīn	"the door is on the right" (→ XII.III)

III. The perfect (past time)

Instead of using *kān* to express past time (→ V.V), it is also possible to use a form of the verb itself: the perfect. The perfect can be derived from the basis of the imperfect (→ VII.II).

A. Roots and verbal stems

1. Roots: The basis of the verb follows different patterns which can be classified systematically by using the consonants **K, T, B** and **L**. These consonants, also known as "radicals," form the root of the verb. A root can have three or four radicals:

yirgaɛ	"he comes back"	follows the pattern	yi-**KT**a**B**
yixallaṣ	"he finishes"	follows the pattern	yi-**K**a**TT**a**B**
yirmi	"he throws"	follows the pattern	yi-**KT**i
yidardiš	"he chatters"	follows the pattern	yi-**K**a**TB**i**L**

There are, moreover, both strong and weak roots:

(a) **Strong roots** consist of three different consonants or radicals as in *yi-nzil* {nzl} "he goes down," *yi-fham* {fhm} "he understands." These verbs are called three-radical verbs. Sometimes the root consists of four radicals as in *yi-laxbaṭ* {lxbṭ} "he mixes (up)," *yidardiš* {drdš} "he chatters." These are called four-radical verbs.

(b) **Weak roots** consist of only two consonants, or of three consonants where the second and the third consonants are the same.

* Bases with only two different consonants and a long vowel between them are known as **mediae infirmae** (med. inf.) because the middle radical, which is in fact *-w-* or *-y-* , is not visible in this form of the verb: *yi-šūf* {šwf} "he sees," *yi-šīl* {šyl} "he carries," *yi-xāf* {xwf} "he fears."

* Bases with two different consonants and a vowel at the end are called **tertiae infirmae** (tert. inf.). The final radical, which is always *-y-*, is not visible in this form of the verb: *yi-nsa* {nsy} "he forgets," *yi-rmi* {rmy} "he throws," *yi-mši* {mšy} "he walks."

* Bases whose second and third radicals are the same are called **mediae geminatae** (med. gem.): *yi-fukk* {fkk} "he unties," *yi-murr* {mrr} "he passes by," *yi-ḩill* {ḩll} "he solves."

If the root of a verb is strong, it is called a "strong verb"; similarly, if the root is weak, the verb is known as a "weak verb."

Verbs such as *yā-xud* {xd} "he takes" and *yā-kul* {kl} "he eats" whose bases consist of only two consonants, are exceptions.

2. Stems: different stems can be derived from the root of a verb. The first three stems (I, II, III) are shown below.

(a) **Stem I** or **base stem**: in the case of this stem the basis of the imperfect follows the pattern -**KTaB**, -**KTiB** or -**KTuB**, having thus an *a*-imperfect, an *i*-imperfect, or a *u*-imperfect: *yifham* "he understands," *yiktib* "he writes," *yidxul* "he goes inside."

The basis of the perfect is different from the basis of the imperfect. It follows the pattern **KaTaB**, **KiTiB** or **KuTuB**, having an *a*-perfect, an *i*-perfect, or a *u*-perfect: *samaḩ* "he allowed," *ɛirif* "he knew," *xuluṣ* "he's run out."

As a general rule you could say that an *a*-perfect usually has an *i*- or *u*-imperfect, and that contrariwise, an *i*-perfect usually has an *a*-imperfect. But in fact there are so many exceptions that it is advisable to learn the perfects and imperfects together at the same time, starting with the perfect: *katab, yiktib; fihim, yifham,* etc. (see list at the end of this lesson).

(b) **Stem II**: the basis of this stem has the pattern **KaTTaB** or **KaTTiB** and is easily recognized by the doubling of the middle consonant or radical: *xallaṣ, yixallaṣ* "to finish," *fahhim, yifahhim* "to explain."

(c) **Stem III**: the basis of this stem has the pattern **KāTiB** and is recognized by the long *-ā-* after the first radical: *sāfir, yisāfir* "to go on a journey," *ḩāwil, yiḩāwil* "to try."

Unlike stem I, which shows a difference between the basis of the perfect and that of the imperfect, stems II and III have the same basis in the perfect and imperfect. This basis is also identical to the imperative (→ VII.II.2).
Taking the base stem as a starting point, it is possible to form other stems by applying the pattern of the desired stem to the root: *fihim* {fhm} "to understand" + **KaTTiB** → *fahhim* "to make s.o. understand," *ɛamal* {ɛml} "to do," "to make" + **KāTiB** → *ɛāmil* "to treat" (→ XI).

3. Weak verbs: as far as weak verbs (med.inf., med.gem., tert.inf.) are concerned, stem I verbs form their perfects using the basis of the imperfect as a starting point.

(a) **med. inf**: the long vowel *-ā-*, *-ī-* or *-ū-* in the middle of the basis of the imperfect is replaced by *-ā-* :

yi-šūf	{šwf}	→	*šāf*	"to see"
yi-šīl	{šyl}	→	*šāl*	"to carry"
yi-xāf	{xwf}	→	*xāf*	"to fear"

(b) **med. gem**: the vowel which follows the first radical of the basis of the imperfect is replaced by a short *-a-*. The verbs med. gem. always end in a double consonant:

yi-fukk	{fkk}	→	*fakk*	"to untie"
yi-ḫill	{ḫll}	→	*ḫall*	"to solve"

(c) **tert. inf**: these verbs always end in a vowel. They can have an *a*-perfect or an *i*-perfect in the same way as a strong verb.

yi-nsa	{nsy}	→	*nisi*	"to forget"
yi-rmi	{rmy}	→	*rama*	"to throw"

verbs and stems

	strong verbs	weak verbs		
		med.inf.	**tert.inf.**	**med.gem.**
I.	*ɛamal, yiɛmil* *niḍif, yinḍaf* *nizil, yinzil* *xuluṣ, yixlaṣ*	*šāf, yišūf* *šāl, yišīl* *xāf, yixāf* *ṛāḫ, yirūḫ*	*rama, yirmi* *nisi, yinsa* *mala, yimla* *miši, yimši*	*fakk, yifukk* *ḫall, yiḫill* *xaff, yixiff* *ḫabb, yiḫibb*
II.	*naḍḍaf, yinaḍḍaf* *nazzil, yinazzil*			
III.	*ɛāmil, yiɛāmil* *sāfir, yisāfir*			

For the II and III stems of the weak verbs see lesson XI.I.

B. Endings of the perfect

Perfect bases can end in a vowel (tert.inf.), a consonant (strong verbs, med.inf.) or two consonants (med.gem.). They can contain an unprotected *-i-* or *-u-*, or a long vowel. However, in the perfect they all have exactly the same endings as *kān* (→V.v). Some of these endings begin with a vowel (*-it, -u*), others with a consonant (*-t, -ti, -tu, -na*). When endings are connected to bases, differences arise which are dependent on the ending and the basis in question.

1. Stem I or base stem of strong verbs

Stem I can have an *a*-perfect basis or an *i*-perfect basis:

3rd person	2nd person	1st person
***a*-perfect**		
(*huwwa*) *katab*	(*inta*) *katab-t*	(*ana*) *katab-t*
(*hiyya*) *katab-it*	(*inti*) *katab-ti*	
(*humma*) *katab-u*	(*intu*) *katab-tu*	(*iḫna*) *katab-na*
***i*-perfect**		
(*huwwa*) *misik*	(*inta*) *misik-t*	(*ana*) *misik-t*
(*hiyya*) *misk-it*	(*inti*) *misik-ti*	
(*humma*) *misk-u*	(*intu*) *misik-tu*	(*iḫna*) *misik-na*

When endings are added to the basis of an *a*-perfect, nothing changes. However in the case of an *i*-perfect, when the *-i-* finds itself in an unprotected position after the addition of endings which begin with a vowel such as *-it* and *-u* , the *-i-* will be dropped. (→ IV.II):

misik + it > *miskit* *misik + u* > *misku*

fihim, fihmit, fihmu "to understand" is another example of an *i*-perfect, and *xuluṣ, xulṣit, xulṣu* "to run out" is an example of a *u*-perfect.

2. Stem I or base stem of weak verbs

(a) **med. inf**: the characteristic of verbs of this type is a long vowel between the first and the last consonant of the basis. In the perfect this vowel is always an *-ā-* . In the imperfect it can be a *-ū-*, *-ī-* or *-ā-*:

sāb, yisīb "to leave" *šāf, yišūf* "to see"
xāf, yixāf "to fear" *nām, yinām* "to sleep"

At this point, if an ending which begins with a consonant is added to the basis of the perfect, then the *-ā-* in the basis is replaced by a short vowel:

* by an *-i-* if the relevant imperfect has an *-ī-* (med. y):

sāb, yisīb → *sibt* "I have left"

* by a *-u-* if the relevant imperfect has a *-ū-* (med. w). Compare the conjugation of *kān* in V.v:

šāf, yišūf → *šuft* "I have seen"

verbs med. inf: *sāb* "to leave" – *šāf* "to see"

	3rd p.	2nd p.	1st p.		3rd p.	2nd p.	1st p.
(*yisīb*)	*sāb*	*sibt*	*sibt*	(*yišūf*)	*šāf*	*šuft*	*šuft*
	sābit	*sibti*			*šāfit*	*šufti*	
	sābu	*sibtu*	*sibna*		*šāfu*	*šuftu*	*šufna*

Be careful: * In the case of *xāf, yixāf* "to be afraid" one says *xuft* "I was afraid," and in the case of *nām, yinām* "to sleep" one says *nimt* "I was asleep."

* The long vowel *-ā-* of the perfect does not change after the addition of an object suffix. It is simply shortened if necessary:

šāf + ha > *šafha* "he saw her"
sāb + ni > *sabni* "he left me"

(b) **tert. inf:** the basis of verbs of this type ends in a vowel, which can be either *-a* or *-i*, while the third consonant, which is usually a *-y* is not visible in this form of the verb:

mala, yimla "to fill" *maḍa, yimḍi* "to sign"
nisi, yinsa "to forget" *miši, yimši* "to walk (away)"

Depending on whether the basis of the verb in the perfect ends in *-a* or *-i*, the way of adding the endings will be different.

(α) Verbs ending in *-a*: when adding endings which begin with a consonant, the *-a* of the basis will be replaced by *-ē-*. When adding endings which begin with a vowel, the *-a* of the basis will be dropped.

verbs tert. inf. with a-perfect: *mala* "to fill" – *maḍa* "to sign"

3rd p.	2nd p.	1st p.	3rd p.	2nd p.	1st p.
mala	*malēt*	*malēt*	*maḍa*	*maḍēt*	*maḍēt*
malit	*malēti*		*maḍit*	*maḍēti*	
malu	*malētu*	*malēna*	*maḍu*	*maḍētu*	*maḍēna*

baʾa, yibʾa "to become" and *ʾaṛa, yiʾṛa* "to read" are also conjugated this way.

(β) Verbs ending in *-i*: if the basis of the perfect ends in an *-i*, this will be replaced by the long vowel *-ī-*, in the case of endings which begin with a consonant: *nisi + t > nisīt* "I have forgotten."

But in the case of endings which begin with a vowel, the *-y-* of the original basis will reappear: *nisi + it > nisiyit → nisyit* "she has forgotten."

verbs tert. inf. with i-perfect: *nisi* "to forget" – *miši* "to go"

3rd p.	2nd p.	1st p.	3rd p.	2nd p.	1st p.
nisi	*nisīt*	*nisīt*	*miši*	*mišīt*	*mišīt*
nisyit	*nisīti*		*mišyit*	*mišīti*	
nisyu	*nisītu*	*nisīna*	*mišyu*	*mišītu*	*mišīna*

ġili, yiġli "to boil" and *giri, yigri* "to run" are treated in a similar fashion.

Be careful! When combined with object suffixes, the last vowel is lengthened:

mala + ha	>	*malāha*	"he filled it in"
nisi + ki	>	*nisīki*	"he has forgotten you"
nisyu + ha	>	*nisyūha*	"they've forgotten her"

(c) **med. gem**: these are the verbs which end in a doubled consonant: *fakk, yifukk* "to untie," *baṣṣ, yibuṣṣ* "to look," *ḫaṭṭ, yiḫuṭṭ* "to put." They are conjugated the same way as the verbs med. inf. with an *a*-perfect, which means that when followed by endings which begin with a consonant, they receive an additional *-ē-*.

verbs med. gem: *baṣṣ* "to look"– *ḫaṭṭ* "to put"

3rd p.	2nd p.	1st p.	3rd p.	2nd p.	1st p.
baṣṣ	*baṣṣēt*	*baṣṣēt*	*ḫaṭṭ*	*ḫaṭṭēt*	*ḫaṭṭēt*
baṣṣit	*baṣṣēti*		*ḫaṭṭit*	*ḫaṭṭēti*	
baṣṣu	*baṣṣētu*	*baṣṣēna*	*ḫaṭṭu*	*ḫaṭṭētu*	*ḫaṭṭēna*

C. Meaning of the perfect

The perfect in Arabic refers to completed past action. When translating into English, we would use the simple past tense: *katab* "he wrote," *ʾāl* "he said."

On the other hand *kān* + *bi*-imperfect refers to an action which took place in the past but lasted for some time. When translating we would use the past continuous or "used to" (→ X.V):

kān biyiktib	"he was (busy) writing"
kān biyišṛab kitīr	"he used to drink a lot"

The negative of the perfect is formed in the same way as in the case of *kān*, that is by using *ma- ... -š*:

širbu‿llaban	→	*ma-širbūš illaban*	"they didn't drink the milk"
fihimna‿ddars	→	*ma-fhimnāš iddars*	"we didn't understand the lesson"

IV. Object suffixes: peculiarities

1. The ending *-it* of the 3rd person fem. sing. perfect

When suffixes are affixed to it, the third person feminine singular ending of the perfect *-it* is always stressed, which means that the *-i-* is never dropped:

ɛamalit	+ *u*	>	*ɛamalítu*	"she did it"
naḍḍafit	+ *u*	>	*naḍḍafítu*	"she cleaned it"
ramit	+ *u*	>	*ramítu*	"she threw it"
šāfit	+ *ik*	>	*šafítik*	"she saw you (fem.)"

Even when stress is changed by the negational suffix *-š* and falls on the last syllable, the *-i-* remains:

naḍḍafítu	→	*ma-naḍḍafitūš*	"she didn't clean it"
sabítu	→	*ma-sabitūš*	"she didn't leave him"

2. Object suffixes *-ik* and *-(h)*

If the second person singular feminine object suffix *-ik*, or the third person singular masculine object suffix *-(h)* is followed by another suffix, then the *-ik* will change to *-iki* and the *-(h)* will change to *-hu*. This is the case with the negative suffix *...-š* and the suffix *-li-* which introduces an indirect object (→ X.VI):

-iki + *š* > *-ikīš*	*šuftik*	→ *ma-šuftikīš*	I didn't see you
	šāfik	→ *ma-šafkīš*	he didn't see you
-āhu + *š* > *-ahūš*	*insā(h)*	→ *ma-tinsahūš*	
-īhu + *š* > *-ihūš*	*insī(h)*	→ *ma-tinsihūš*	don't forget him
-ūhu + *š* > *-uhūš*	*insū(h)*	→ *ma-tinsuhūš*	

VERBS IN THE PERFECT

yākul → *kal*
yāxud → *xad*
yiᵓaggaṛ → *ᵓaggaṛ*
yiᵓūl → *ᵓāl*
yiᵓūm → *ᵓām*
yiᵓfil → *ᵓafal*
yibᵓa → *baᵓa*
yibaṭṭal → *baṭṭal*
yibīɛ → *bāɛ*
yibuṣṣ → *baṣṣ*
yibārik → *bārik*
yibɛat → *baɛat*
yidardiš → *dardiš*
yiddāyiᵓ → *iddāyiᵓ*
yidfaɛ → *dafaɛ*
yidxul → *daxal*
yidūr → *dāṛ*
yiḍrab → *ḍarab*
yifawwil → *fawwil*
yiftaḥ → *fataḥ*
yifukk → *fakk*
yigahhiz → *gahhiz*
yigīb → *gāb*
yiġayyaṛ → *ġayyaṛ*
yiḥawwid → *ḥawwid*
yiḥibb → *ḥabb*
yiḥill → *ḥall*

yiḥuṭṭ → *ḥaṭṭ*
yiḥāwil → *ḥāwil*
yiksaṛ → *kasaṛ*
yiktib → *katab*
yikšif → *kašaf*
yikūn → *kān*
yilāᵓi → *laᵓa* (!)
yilbis → *libis*
yilɛab → *liɛib*
yimla → *mala*
yimši → *miši*
yinaᵓᵓaṭ → *naᵓᵓaṭ*
yinarfis → *narfis*
yinaḍḍaf → *naḍḍaf*
yindah → *nadah*
yinazzil → *nazzil*
yinsa → *nisi*
yinzil → *nizil*
yinām → *nām*
yināsib → *nāsib*
yirgaɛ → *rigiɛ*
yirkab → *rikib*
yirūḥ → *ṛāḥ*
yirḥam → *raḥam*
yisᵓal → *saᵓal*
yismaḥ → *samaḥ*
yisīb → *sāb*

yisāfir → *sāfir*
yiṣallaḥ → *ṣallaḥ*
yišṛab → *širib*
yišūf → *šāf*
yiṭallaɛ → *ṭallaɛ*
yiṭlaɛ → *ṭiliɛ*
yiwarri → *warra*
yiwaṣṣal → *waṣṣal*
yiwgaɛ → *wagaɛ*
yiwṣal → *waṣal*
yixṣar → *xiṣir*
yixallaṣ → *xallaṣ*
yixalli → *xalla*
yixiff → *xaff*
yixlaṣ → *xuluṣ* ~ *xiliṣ*
yixušš → *xašš*
yizūr → *zāṛ*
yiɛaddi → *ɛadda*
yiɛdil → *ɛadal*
yiɛmil → *ɛamal*
yiɛazzil → *ɛazzil*
yiɛṛaf → *ɛirif*
yiɛīš → *ɛāš*
yuᵓmur → *ᵓamaṛ*
yuẓbuṭ → *ẓabaṭ*

Look up the meaning of these words in your glossary!

EXERCISES

I. How many exactly?

dōl banāt kitīr ʾawi! - *kām bintᵊ bi‿ẓẓabṭ ?*

1. *dōl ṭalaba‿ktīr ʾawi!* - *kām* ________________________?
2. *di kutub kitīr ʾawi!* - *kām* ________________________?
3. *dōl suwwāḫ kitīr ʾawi!* - *kām* ________________________?
4. *dōl ɛasākir kitīr ʾawi!* - *kām* ________________________?
5. *di‿stimaṛāt kitīr ʾawi!* - *kām* ________________________?
6. *di damġāt kitīr ʾawi!* - *kām* ________________________?
7. *di ʾuwaḍ kitīr ʾawi!* - *kām* ________________________?
8. *di šuʾaʾ kitīr ʾawi!* - *kām* ________________________?

II. I was the one who ...! Answer the questions.

mīn illi daxal? - *ana‿lli daxalt.*

1. *mīn illi saʾal?* - *ana‿lli* ______________________________.
2. *mīn illi ṭiliɛ?* - *ana‿lli* ______________________________.
3. *mīn illi nizil?* - *ana‿lli* ______________________________.
4. *mīn illi ɛazzil?* - *ana‿lli* ______________________________.
5. *mīn illi sāfir?* - *ana‿lli* ______________________________.
6. *mīn illi ɛirif?* - *ana‿lli* ______________________________.
7. *mīn illi rigiɛ?* - *ana‿lli* ______________________________.
8. *mīn illi kal?* - *ana‿lli* ______________________________

Repeat this exercise using different personal pronouns.

hiyya‿lli ________________ *humma‿lli* ____________________

III. I was the one who ...! Answer the questions.

mīn illi ṛāḫ? - *ana‿lli ṛuḫt.*

1. *mīn illi fāt?* - *ana‿lli* ________________
2. *mīn illi ʾāl?* - *ana‿lli* ________________
3. *mīn illi šāf?* - *ana‿lli* ________________
4. *mīn illi nām?* - *ana‿lli* ________________
5. *mīn illi ʾām?* - *ana‿lli* ________________
6. *mīn illi xāf?* - *ana‿lli* ________________
7. *mīn illi gāb?* - *ana‿lli* ________________
8. *mīn illi bāɛ?* - *ana‿lli* ________________

Repeat this exercise using different personal pronouns.

hiyya‿lli ____________ *iḫna‿lli* ____________ etc.

IV. I was the one who ...! Answer the questions.

mīn illi maḍa? - *ana‿lli maḍēt.*

1. *mīn illi mala?* - *ana‿lli* ________________
2. *mīn illi laʾa?* - *ana‿lli* ________________
3. *mīn illi nisi?* - *ana‿lli* ________________
4. *mīn illi miši?* - *ana‿lli* ________________
5. *mīn illi ɛadda?* - *ana‿lli* ________________
6. *mīn illi ṣalla?* - *ana‿lli* ________________
7. *mīn illi ṭaffa?* - *ana‿lli* ________________

Repeat this exercise using different personal pronouns.

hiyya‿lli ____________ *iḫna‿lli* ____________ etc.

V. I was the one who ....! Answer the questions.

mīn illi baṣṣ? - *ana‿lli baṣṣēt.*

1. *mīn illi xaff?* - *ana‿lli* ______________________________
2. *mīn illi fakk?* - *ana‿lli* ______________________________
3. *mīn illi xašš?* - *ana‿lli* ______________________________
4. *mīn illi ḫaṭṭ?* - *ana‿lli* ______________________________
5. *mīn illi laff?* - *ana‿lli* ______________________________
6. *mīn illi ṛadd?* - *ana‿lli* ______________________________

Repeat this exercise using different personal pronouns.

iḫna‿lli _______________ *intu‿lli* ____________________ etc.

VI. No, she was the one who ...! Answer the questions.

inti‿lli daxalti? - *laʾ, hiyya‿lli daxalit.*

1. *inti‿lli fataḫti?* - *laʾ, hiyya‿lli* ________________________
2. *inti‿lli saʾalti?* - *laʾ, hiyya‿lli* ________________________
3. *inti‿lli‿šribti?* - *laʾ, hiyya‿lli* ________________________
4. *inti‿lli safirti?* - *laʾ, hiyya‿lli* ________________________
5. *inti‿lli naḍḍafti?* - *laʾ, hiyya‿lli* ________________________
6. *inti‿lli ṭabaxti?* - *laʾ, hiyya‿lli* ________________________
7. *inti‿lli ḫawilti?* - *laʾ, hiyya‿lli* ________________________
8. *inti‿lli ʿazzilti?* - *laʾ, hiyya‿lli* ________________________
9. *inti‿lli‿nzilti?* - *laʾ, hiyya‿lli* ________________________

VII. They were the ones who... ! Answer the questions.

intu‿lli ruḫtu? - *laʾ, humma‿lli ṛāḫu.*

1. *intu‿lli biʿtu?* - *laʾ, humma‿lli* ______________________
2. *intu‿lli ʾumtu?* - *laʾ, humma‿lli* ______________________

3. *intu‿lli ʾultu?* - *laʾ, humma‿lli* ________________

4. *intu‿lli nimtu?* - *laʾ, humma‿lli* ________________

5. *intu‿lli xuftu?* - *laʾ, humma‿lli* ________________

6. *intu‿lli gibtu?* - *laʾ, humma‿lli* ________________

7. *intu‿lli šuftu?* - *laʾ, humma‿lli* ________________

VIII. They were the ones who ... ! Answer the questions.

intu‿lli maḍētu? - *laʾ, humma‿lli maḍu.*

1. *intu‿lli malētu?* - *laʾ, humma‿lli* ________________

2. *intu‿lli laʾētu?* - *laʾ, humma‿lli* ________________

3. *intu‿lli ṣallētu?* - *laʾ', humma‿lli* ________________

4. *intu‿lli naʾʾētu?* - *laʾ, humma‿lli* ________________

5. *intu‿lli‿nsītu?* - *laʾ, humma‿lli* ________________

6. *intu‿lli ɛaddētu?* - *laʾ, humma‿lli* ________________

7. *intu‿lli‿mšītu?* - *laʾ, humma‿lli* ________________

IX. I've already done it!

ibɛat Ḥasan. - *xalāṣ, baɛattu.*

1. *ṭallaɛ ikkarāsi baṛṛa.* - *xalāṣ,* ________________.

2. *idfaɛ ilḥiṣāb.* - *xalāṣ,* ________________.

3. *iɛmil ilʾahwa.* - *xalāṣ,* ________________.

4. *iftaḥi‿ššanṭa di.* - *xalāṣ,* ________________.

5. *ḥuṭṭ ikkursi fi‿lbalakōna.* - *xalāṣ,* ________________.

6. *iʾfil ilbāb.* - *xalāṣ,* ________________.

7. *ibɛat Samya ʾAmrīka.* - *xalāṣ,* ________________.

8. *ḥuṭṭ ittaṛabēẓa fi‿lbalakōna.* - *xalāṣ,* ________________.

9. *sīb iggamɛa.* - *xalāṣ,* ____________________.

10. *nazzil iṛṛāgil hināk.* - *xalāṣ,* ____________________.

11. *waṣṣal Samya‿lbēt.* - *xalāṣ,* ____________________.

X. I did it ages ago! *min zamān*

lāzim yištiru‿stimāṛa. - *ištaṛūha min zamān.*

1. *lāzim yištiru damġa.* - ________________ *min zamān.*

2. *lāzim yigaddidu‿lᵓiqāma.* - ________________ *min zamān.*

3. *lāzim yimlu‿listimāṛa.* - ________________ *min zamān.*

4. *lāzim yimḍu‿listimāṛa.* - ________________ *min zamān.*

5. *lāzim yiktibu ᵓasamīhum.* - ________________ *min zamān.*

6. *lāzim yaxdu‿lbasbortāt.* - ________________ *min zamān.*

7. *lāzim yiɛmilu‿lvīza.* - ________________ *min zamān.*

8. *lāzim yiᵓaggaṛu‿ššaᵓᵓa di.* - ________________ *min zamān.*

9. *lāzim yaxdu‿ssanawiyya* - ________________ *min zamān.*

10. *lāzim yixallaṣu‿lmadrasa.* - ________________ *min zamān.*

XI. I told her to ... and she actually (*fiɛlan*) did it!

ᵓultilha‿tgaddid ilᵓiqāma wi *gaddiditha* *fiɛlan.*

1. *ᵓultilha tisᵓal issikirtēra wi* ________________________ *fiɛlan.*

2. *ᵓultilu yištiri‿listimāṛa wi* ________________________ *fiɛlan.*

3. *ᵓultilha timḍi taḥt ittarīx wi* ________________________ *fiɛlan.*

4. *ᵓultilhum yigību‿ddamġa wi* ________________________ *fiɛlan.*

5. *ᵓultilha tibɛat axūha wi* ________________________ *fiɛlan.*

6. *ᵓultilhum yidxulu mi‿lbāb da wi* ________________________ *fiɛlan.*

7. *ᵓultilha‿tɛaddi ɛa‿kkubri wi* ________________________ *fiɛlan.*

8. *ʾultilu‿ysīb iggamʿa wi* ______________________________ *fiʿlan.*

9. *ʾultilha tinsa‿ṛṛāgil da wi* ______________________________ *fiʿlan.*

10. *ʾultilu yidfaʿ ilḥisāb wi* ______________________________ *fiʿlan.*

11. *ʾultilhum yixallaṣu‿ššuġl wi* ______________________________ *fiʿlan.*

12. *ʾultilha tiftaḥ ilʿiyāda wi* ______________________________ *fiʿlan.*

XII. She's done it.

ṛāḥit li‿lbāb wi *fataḥítu.* (*fataḥ*)

1. *ṛāḥit li‿lʿaskari wi* ______________________________. (*saʾal*)
2. *xadit iggawāb wi* ______________________________. (*ʾaṛa*)
3. *ṭallaʿit ilmuftāḥ wi* ______________________ *li‿lbawwāb.* (*idda*)
4. *katabit iggawāb wi* ______________________ *fi‿ssandūʾ.* (*rama*)
5. *ṛāḥit li‿ššibbāk wi* ______________________________. (*ʾafal*)
6. *naḍḍafit ilxuḍār wi* ______________________________. (*ġasal*)
7. *xadit issamak kullu wi* ______________________________. (*kal*)
8. *šāfit Ḥasan maṛṛa waḥda bass, wi* ________________ *ʿala ṭūl.* (*ḥabb*)

XIII. Rearrange the following words into logical sentences.

1. *tagdīd, ilʾiqāma, ʿayza, bitaʿitha.*

____

2. *šāriʿ Lubnān, ḥawwid, šimāl, fi!*

____

3. *ya, isʾal, ilʿaskari, ʿala, Munīr, ilbāb, illi!*

____

4. *šāyif, kibīr, ana, ʾawi, mabna*

____

5. *tinsa, maʿāk, basbōr, ma-...š, ṣuwar, tigīb!*

____

6. *ilbasbōr, faḍlak, bitāʿak, warrīni, min!*

____

7. *bukṛa, madām, taʿāli, hina, ya!*

---

8. *wi, ittarīx, ilʾimḍa, naʾṣīn.*

---

9. *illi, xuššu, ʿa‿lyimīn, ilbāb, min.*

---

10. *ḥukūma, abūya, muwaẓẓaf, kān.*

---

11. *yištiri, nizil, issūʾ, ʿēš, ʿašān, ʿAli.*

XIV. Translate the following sentences.

1. We wanted to go to the zoo (*ginent‿ilḥayawanāt*).

---

2. The cash desk at the *Mugammaʿ* was shut (*ʾāfil*).

---

3. The fish market isn't far from here.

---

4. My upstairs neighbors (*iggirān*) are quiet.

---

5. She left Egypt and went to work in Lebanon for two years.

---

6. *Randa*, where were you yesterday evening?

---

7. I have to work in order to live (*ʿāš, yiʿīš*).

---

8. Go (fem.) and buy two revenue stamps.

---

9. Don't leave your passport at home!

---

10. Let me see your passport and your residence permit.

---

11. Could you fill in the form?

---

12. Your passport needs renewing.

---

13. My residence permit needs to be extended.

14. I didn't see you (fem.) in school yesterday.

15. I wanted to learn Arabic, that's why the University sent me to Egypt.

16. They sold their old car and bought a new car.

17. I was born in a little town in the United States.

XV. *iktib qiṣṣit ḫayātak fi ḫawāli* (approximately) *ʿašaṛ gumal.*

LESSON X

READING PASSAGES

biyiʕmil ʔē kullᵊ yōm iṣṣubḥ?

1. *kullᵊ yōm iṣṣubḥ, Ibṛahīm biyʔūm mi‿nnōm issāʕa sabʕa. biyāxud dušṣᵊ‿w yiġsil sinānu. baʕdᵊ kida‿byilbis hidūmu wi‿ysaṛṛaḥ šaʕru.*

2. *wi baʕdēn biyrūḥ ilmaṭbax. miṛātu bitkūn miḥaḍḍarālu‿lfiṭār: šāy wi ʕēš wi‿fūl midammis. biyišṛab iššāy wi yākul ilʕēš w‿ilfūl.*

3. *issāʕa tamanya‿byinzil mi‿lbēt wi yirkab ʕaṛabiyyitu wi‿yṛūḥ iššuġl.*

4. *lamma‿byiwṣal ilmaktab biyiṭlaʕ issalālim wi yiftaḥ ilbāb wi‿yṣabbaḥ ʕala zumalāʔu.*

iggawwᵊ‿f-Maṣr

1. *ilxarīf min ʔagmal ilmawāsim ʕandina‿f-Maṣr. iggawwᵊ fī(h) mustaqirrᵊ‿w dāfi‿w laṭīf, la ḥaṛṛᵊ wala bard.*

2. *iššawāṭiʔ bitkūn niḍīfa wi‿lbaḥrᵊ hādi. fī nās kitīr bitāxud ʔagazitha fi‿lxarīf wi‿trūḥ ilBaḥṛ ilʔAḥmaṛ wi Sīna, ʔaw ʔayyᵊ šāṭiʔ min iš-šawāṭiʔ.*

3. *fi‿lxarīf innās bitilbis hidūm xafīfa, illa ʔinnaha‿btiḥtāg ʔaḥyānan li‿blōfaṛ ʔaw žakitta ṣūf bi‿llēl.*

4. *amma‿ššita fa da ʔaʔṣar mūsim. iddinya bitbaṛṛad šuwayya lākin daṛagit ilḥaṛāṛa ma-bitkunš aʔallᵊ min xamsa fōʔ iṣṣifr. biyinzil šuwayyit maṭar fi‿ššita‿w ʔaḥyānan bitʔūm zawābiʕ.*

5. *fi‿ṛṛabīʕ iggawwᵊ biykūn ġēr mustaqirr, yōm ḥarrᵊ‿w yōm bard, yōm šamsᵊ‿w yōm miġayyim, yōm tuṛāb wi yōm min agmal ilʔayyām.*

6. *iṣṣēf fi‿lQāhíra šēʔ lā yuṭāq. fi‿nnahāṛ iddinya bitkūn ḥaṛṛᵊ‿w katma. amma bi‿llēl fa‿nnās bitḥibbᵊ tuxrug fi‿ṭṭarāwa, wi‿trūḥ titfassaḥ fi‿gganāyin wi tuʔʕud ʕa‿lʔahāwi. iššawāriʕ bitibʔa kullaha ḥayawiyya‿w našāṭ liġāyit wišš iṣṣubḥ.*

ʔidāṛit iggawazāt

Michael: *fēn ʔidaṛt‿iggawazāt, min faḍlak?*
Sāmi: *di fi‿lMugammaʕ fi‿tTaḥrīr.*
Michael: *ṭab, awṣal hināk izzāy?*
Sāmi: *basīṭa ʔawi: xud taks, ḥaywaṣṣalak liġāyit Midān itTaḥrīr. inzil ʕa‿lyimīn, ḥatlāʔi mabna‿kbīr ʔawi. idxul mi‿lbāb illi ʕa‿lyimīn, iṭlaʕ issalālim wi fi‿ddōr ilʔawwalāni ḥatlāʔi ʔidaṛt‿iggawazāt. isʔal ilʕaskari‿lli ʕa‿lbāb ḥayʔullak tirūḥ li-mīn.*
Michael: *mutšakkirīn giddan ʕa‿lmaʕlumāt di.*

VOCABULARY

aʾṣar	shorter ~ shortest
agmal	more ~ most beautiful
amma... fa...	as regards ... concerning ...
ʾagāza, -āt	holiday
ʾahwa, ʾahāwi	café
ʾaḫyānan	sometimes
ʾaɛad, yuʾɛud	to sit, to stay
ʾām, yiʾūm	to get up
ʾidāṛit iggawazāt	passport office
ʾihmāl	negligence
ʾuṣayyar	short
baḫr	sea
ilBaḫr ilʾAḫmaṛ	the Red Sea
baṛṛad, yibaṛṛad	to cool down
basīṭ	simple
burg, abṛāg	tower
daṛaga, -āt	degree (of heat)
dayman	always
dāfi	warm
dušš	shower
fa	then
faṣl, fuṣūl	season
fūl midammis	beans (boiled)
gahl	ignorance
gawāb, -āt	letter
ġasal, yiġsil ḫ	to wash
ġēr	not
ḫaʾīʾa	truth
ḫaḍḍaṛ, yiḫaḍḍaṛ ḫ	to prepare
ḫaṛāṛa	temperature
ḫayawiyya	liveliness
ḫikāya, -āt	story, happening
ḫitta, ḫitat	part, piece; place, district
iḫtāg, yiḫtāg li ḫ	to need
illa ʾinn	but, rather
irtifāɛ	height
itfassaḫ, yitfassaḫ	to go for a walk
katma	oppressive weather
kitir, yiktar	to increase
lamma	when
la ... wala ...	neither ... nor ...
libis, yilbis ḫ	to put on (clothing)
mabna (m.), *mabāni*	building
maṭar	rain
maɛlumāt (pl.)	information particulars
miṛātu	his wife
muʾaddab	polite
mustaqirr	stable
mūsim, mawāsim	season
nahṛ, anhār	river
našāṭ	activity, bustle
niḍīf	clean
nizil, yinzil ḫ	to go down
nizil, yinzil min ḫ	to get out of
ṛabīɛ	spring (season)
saṛṛaḫ, yisaṛṛaḫ ḫ	to comb
sinn(a), sinān	tooth
Sīna	Sinai
ṣabbaḫ, yiṣabbaḫ ɛala w	to say good-morning to ...
ṣifr	zero
ṣiḫḫa	health
ṣūf	wool
šahr, šuhūr ~ušhur	month
šāṭiʾ, šawāṭiʾ	coast, beach
šita	winter
tiʾīl, tuʾāl	heavy
tuṛāb	dust
ṭarāwa	coolness
ṭūl	length
xafīf, xufāf	light
xaṛag, yuxrug	to go out(side)
xarīf	autumn
wazn	weight
wāgib, -āt	duty; homework
wišš iṣṣubḫ	early morning (metaphor)
zaki, azkiya	clever
zawbaɛa, zawābiɛ	storm
zimīl, zumala ~ zumalāʾ	colleague
ɛala riglē(h)	on foot
ɛālam	world

GRAMMAR

I. Gender of nouns

Most feminine nouns end in *-a*. However a group of words such as *bint* "daughter," *umm* "mother" do not end in *-a* but are inherently feminine. There is also another group of nouns which are not obviously feminine, but are still treated as such:

ʾarḍ	earth, ground	*daʾn*	beard, chin	*rigl*	foot, leg
ʾīd	hand	*filūs*	money	*šams*	sun
balad	town, village	*manaxīr*	nose	*ṭamāṭim*	tomatoes
baṭāṭiṣ	potatoes	*markib*	ship, boat	*widn*	ear
baṭn	stomach	*ṛās*	head	*ʿēn*	eye

In such cases, adjectives which relate to these nouns are given the feminine ending *-a*: *riglu maksūṛa* "his leg is broken," *ilmarkib di‿kbīra* "this boat is large," *ʾīdu ṭawīla* "he's a thief" (lit. his hand is long).

Note that the word *nās* "people" can be treated as either feminine singular *nās tanya*, or as plural *nās tanyīn* "other people."

II. *kull* "each", "every"; "the whole", "all"

The quantifiers "each" "every" and "the whole" can be expressed by using the word *kull* "whole." The meaning is determined by whatever *kull* is connected to in a genitive construction:

1. *kull* + an undefined genitive singular means "every" "each":

kullᵉ sana	"each year"	*kullᵉ wāḥid*	"everyone (masc.)"
kullᵉ yōm	"every day"	*kullᵉ waḥda*	"everyone (fem.)"

2. *kull* + a defined genitive singular means "the whole":

kull ilbalad or *ilbalad kullaha* "the whole village"
kull ilḥikāya or *ilḥikāya kullaha* "the whole story"

3. *kull* + a defined genitive plural means "all":

kull ilmašākil or *ilmašākil kullaha* "all the problems"
kull innās or *innās kulluhum* "all the people"
kull ilʿaṛabiyyāt "all the cars"
kull ilʾuwaḍ "all the rooms"

When *kull* is connected to a possessive suffix in the singular it has the same meaning as in (2) above: *kullak luṭf* "you are really nice" [lit. the whole of you is friendliness ~ you're allover friendly]. When it is connected to a plural suffix, it has the same meaning as (3) above: *kullina* "all of us," *kullukum* "all of you," *kulluhum* "all of them."

III. Comparisons: the elative

1. To make comparisons one can simply use an adjective or participle followed by the preposition *ɛan* : *inta‿kbīr ɛanni fi‿ssinn* "you are older than me," *iggaww*ᵊ *ḫaṛṛ*ᵊ *ɛan imbāriḫ* "the weather is warmer than yesterday."

2. Degrees of comparison can also be expressed by means of the so-called elative, which is derived from the adjectives in question.

(a) Form of the elative

The pattern of the elative is a**KT**a**B** and it is uninflected. In other words, it does not differentiate between masculine and feminine. Using this pattern, one can make *agmal* "prettier" "prettiest" from the adjective *gamīl* "pretty."

kitīr	many	→	*aktaṛ*	more
ḫadīs	modern	→	*aḫdas*	more modern
kibīr	great	→	*akbaṛ*	greater
rixīṣ	cheap	→	*arxaṣ*	cheaper
wiḫiš	bad	→	*awḫaš*	worse
sahl	simple	→	*ashal*	simpler

In roots of the type med. inf, a *-w-* or a *-y-* appears in the elative.

ṭawīl	long	→	*aṭwal*	longer
ṭayyib	good	→	*aṭyab*	better
šīk	elegant	→	*ašyak*	more elegant

In roots of the type tert. inf, the elative is formed from the pattern a**KT**a.

ḫilw	nice	→	*aḫla*	nicer
zaki	intelligent	→	*azka*	more intelligent
ġāli	expensive	→	*aġla*	more expensive

And in the case of the med. gem, the pattern is a**K**a**TT**:

xafīf	light	→	*axaff*	lighter
ʾulayyil	few	→	*aʾall*	fewer, less
lazīz	tasty	→	*alazz*	tastier

Note that the elative of *muhimm* "important" is *ahamm* "more ~ most important," and the elative of *kuwayyis* "good" is *aḫsan* "better" "best." The word "than" which is used in the comparative is expressed by the preposition *min*:

ɛAli ʾazka min Maḫmūd	"ɛAli is more intelligent than Maḫmūd"
Samīra ʾaṭwal minni	"Samīra is taller than me"

(b) Use of the elative

* **attributively**: just like an adjective, the elative can be placed after a noun. It is then translated as a comparative:

ʕāwiz bēt akbaṛ	"I want a bigger house"
iddīni šanṭa ʔaṣġar min di	"give me a smaller bag than this one"

If the elative is preceded by an article, it can be translated as a comparative or a superlative, depending on the context:

ḫāxud maʕāya‿ššanṭa‿lʔaṣġar "I'll take the smaller ~ smallest bag"

* **predicatively**: the elative can also form the predicate of a sentence. For more emphasis one can use *bi-ktīr* "much," "a lot":

ilʔūṭa di ʔaḫsan	"these tomatoes are better"
iṭṭarīʔ da ʔaʔṛab	"this way is shorter"
da ʔaḫsan bi-ktīr	"that's much better"

* **In the genitive construction**: The elative can be followed by a noun. In this case the combination elative + noun forms a genitive construction.

i. When combined with an undefined noun, the elative is used as an (absolute) superlative:

aḫdas mudēl	"the latest model"
da ʔaʔallᵊ wāgib	"it was the least I could do" (as a reply to being thanked)
aḫsan talat talamza	"the three best pupils"

The elative can also be used with the words *ḫāga, šēʔ* "thing" "matter" or *wāḫid ~ waḫda* "one" "someone":

aḫammᵊ šēʔ	"the most important"	*aḫsan ḫāga*	"the best"
aṣġar waḫda	"the smallest (fem.)"	*awḫaš wāḫid*	"the worst"

Note the phrases formed with *aḫsan wāḫid* "the best one to ...": *inti ʔaḫsan waḫda‿btilʕab tinnis fi‿nnādi* "you are the best tennis player in the club."

ii. When combined with a defined noun in the plural the elative is used to single out one item from a group:

di min asṛaʕ ilʕaṛabiyyāt illi fi‿ssūʔ	"this is one of the fastest cars on the market"
da min aḫdas ilmudelāt illi ʕandina	"this is one of the most modern models we've got"
aktaṛ innās	"most of the people"

Finally, a possessive suffix can also be added to the elative:

aktaṛhum	"most of them"
aṭwalkum	"the tallest of you"

(c) In the case of most participles beginning with *mi-* or *mu-*, or of words having the pattern **KaTB**ān or a**KT**a**B**, and of *nisba*-adjectives, it is not possible to form an elative. Comparison will then be made by means of the so-called adjective or participle preceded by words such as *aktaṛ* "more," *aḫsan* "better" or *aʾall* "less":

hiyya mitnarfisa ʾaktaṛ minnak	"she's more irritated than you are"
ana gaɛān aktaṛ min imbāriḫ	"I'm more hungry than yesterday"
da ṭabīɛi ʾaktaṛ	"that's more natural"

IV. *ḫa*-imperfect

To refer to future time, you simply put *ḫa-* in front of the imperfect. The *-i-* from the prefixes *yi-*, *ti-*, *ni-* will be dropped if it is in an unprotected position, e.g. *ḫa* + *tikūn* > *ḫatkūn*:

ḫa-imperfect

	3rd person	2nd person	1st person
(*yiktib*)	*ḫayiktib*	*ḫatiktib*	*ḫaktib*
	ḫatiktib	*ḫatiktibi*	
	ḫayiktibu	*ḫatiktibu*	*ḫaniktib*
(*yikūn*)	*ḫaykūn*	*ḫatkūn*	*ḫakūn*
	ḫatkūn	*ḫatkūni*	
	ḫaykūnu	*ḫatkūnu*	*ḫankūn*

iššuġlāna di ḫatāxud waʾt	"this job will take a while"
fi‿ddōr ittāni ḫatlāʾi ʾidaṛt‿iggawazāt	"you'll find the passport office on the second floor"

Be careful: * the participles *ṛāyiḫ*, *gayy*, *māši*, *rāgiɛ*, *nāzil*, *ṭāliɛ* and *misāfir* among others, may, depending on the context, refer to the present or future time (→ VI.III):

iḫna ṛayḫīn li-Mḫammad bukṛa	"we're going to Muḫammad tomorrow"

* To negate the *ḫa*-imperfect one uses *miš*:

miš ḫaxdak maɛāya	"I shall not be taking you with me"
ḫatiɛmilu ʾē bukṛa?	"what are you doing tomorrow?"

V. *bi*-imperfect

1. In the case of most verbs which are describing an action, present time is not expressed by means of a participle (→ VI.III), but by the *bi*-imperfect. The expression "present time" means that the action is taking place at the moment of speaking. The answer to the question *biyiɛmil ʾē?* "what's he doing?" is therefore:

biyiktib gawāb	"he's writing a letter"
biyištaġal	"he's working"

biyiṣ̌rab šāy	"he's drinking tea"
biyiʾṛa‿ktāb	"he's reading a book"

The *-i-* of the prefixes *yi-*, *ti-*, *ni-* is elided if it is not protected: *bi* + *tirūḥ* > *bitrūḥ* "she goes." As for the *-i-* of *bi-*, it is elided before the *-a-* of the 1st pers. sg. and the prefix becomes *ba-*: *bi* + *aṣ̌rab* > *baṣ̌rab* "I'm drinking":

bi-imperfect

	3rd person	2nd person	1st person
(*yištaġal*)	*biyištaġal* *bitištaġal* *biyištaġalu*	*bitištaġal* *bitištaġali* *bitištaġalu*	*baštaġal* *biništaġal*
(*yiḫaḍḍar*)	*biyḫaḍḍar* *bitḫaḍḍar* *biyḫaḍḍaru*	*bitḫaḍḍar* *bitḫaḍḍari* *bitḫaḍḍaru*	*baḫaḍḍar* *binḫaḍḍar*

2. The *bi*-imperfect is also used to express general statements or facts, habitual actions or events and states. *William biyitkallim ɛaṛabi* can thus have the meaning: "William speaks the Arabic language" as well as "William is speaking Arabic" (at this moment).

biyiṣ̌rab sagāyir	"he smokes"
biyḫibb ilʾakl	"he loves eating"
bitinsa‿ktīr	"she's forgetful"
binitɛašša‿ssāɛa tamanya	"we usually have dinner at eight"

3. In the case of verbs which express present time by means of their participles (→ VI.III), the *bi*-imperfect only has the meaning given in (2) above.

bašūf kuwayyis "I see well" (my sight is good)	but: *ana šayfu‿kwayyis* "I can see him clearly"
bašūfu kullᵊ yōm "I see him every day"	but: *ana miš šāyif ḥāga* "I can't see anything"
biyismaɛ kuwayyis "he hears well" (he has good ears)	but: *inta samiɛni‿kwayyis?* "can you hear me okay?"
biyīgi issāɛa‿tnēn "he (usually) comes at 2 o'clock"	but: *aho gayy!* "there he comes!"
biyrūḥ ilmadṛasa "he goes to school"	but: *huwwa ṛāyiḥ ilmadrasa* "he is going to school"
banzil ilbalad kullᵊ yōm "I go to town every day"	but: *ana nāzil ilbalad dilwaʾti* "I'm going to town now"
banām badri "I (usually) go to bed early"	but: *huwwa nāyim fi‿lbalakōna* "he is sleeping on the balcony"

4. In principle, the negative is formed with *ma-...-š*. But, more recently, *miš* may be heard in this case as well:

ma-biyruddiš ~ miš biyrudd	"he doesn't answer."
ma-btifhamnīš ~ miš bitifhamni	"she doesn't understand me"

VI. *-li-* as a suffix after the verb

1. *-li-* can be added to a verb as a suffix. This is usually translated into English as an indirect object:

baktiblu gawāb	"I'm writing (to) him a letter"
biyibɛatlaha ward	"he's sending (to) her flowers"
mumkin tidfaɛlu mīt ginē(h)	"can you pay (to) him a hundred pounds?"

2. When *-li-* is combined with another suffix and added to a verb, it will appear somewhat different from the independent form of *li-* plus possessive suffix (→ V.I):

3rd person	2nd person	1st person
(*yiktib*) *yiktíblu* *yiktibláha* *yiktiblúhum*	*yiktíblak* *yiktíblik* *yiktiblúku*	*yiktíbli* *yiktiblína*
(*yifukk*) *yifukkílu* *yifukkílha* *yifukkílhum*	*yifukkílak* *yifukkílik* *yifukkílku*	*yifukkíli* *yifukkílna*

3. *-li-* can also follow another suffix and it can be followed by the *-š* of the negative which is then placed at the end. This can generate quite complicated verb forms:

bitʾaggaṛuhāli	< *bi-tiʾaggaṛu-ha-li*	"you are renting it (fem.) to me"
ma-byibɛatuhalnāš	< *ma-bi-yibɛatu-ha-lina-š*	"they're not sending her to us"
ma-biywarrihalūš	< *ma-bi-yiwarri-ha-lu-š*	"he's not showing it (fem.) to him"

In these cases the third pers. masc. sg. suffix *-(h)* changes to *-hu* in exactly the same way as it does when forming the negative (→ lesson IX.IV).

-ī(h) + *lu* > *-īhu* + *lu* > *-ihūlu*	*iddihūlu* give it to him!

When people speak more formally, *-u-* is usually also changed to *-hu-* :

-u + *-lu* > *-ūlu* ~ *-hūlu*	*ibɛatūlu* ~ *ibɛathūlu* send it to him *bingibulku* ~ *bingibhulku* we're bringing him to you

INCREASE YOUR VOCABULARY

The time *ilwaʾt, izzaman*

The date *ittarīx*

For how to ask about the date see lesson IX.I.

innahaṛda kām fi‿ššahṛ?	*innahaṛda xamsa yunyu*
"what's the date today?"	"it's the fifth of June"

The days of the week *ayyām ilʾusbūɛ*

The week begins on Saturday and ends on Friday, which is a holiday for most people. Many people enjoy a two-day weekend, with either Thursday or Saturday off in addition to Friday.

Saturday	*yōm issabt*	Wednesday	*yōm ilʾaṛbaɛ ~ laṛbaɛ*
Sunday	*yōm ilḥadd*	Thursday	*yōm ilxamīs*
Monday	*yōm illitnēn ~ litnēn*	Friday	*yōm iggumɛa*
Tuesday	*yōm ittalāt*		

The months *šahṛ, šuhūr ~ ušhur*

The European names for the months are often used.

yanāyir	*fabṛāyir*	*māris*	*ʾabrīl*	*māyu*	*yunyu*
yulyu	*ʾaġusṭus*	*sibtimbir*	*ʾuktōbaṛ*	*nufimbir*	*disimbir*

But most commonly the months are referred to by their number: *šahṛᵉ wāḥid, šahṛ itnēn* etc. In addition, Islamic and Coptic calendars are in use.

The four seasons *fuṣūl issana‿laṛbaɛa*

spring	*iṛrabīɛ*	autumn	*ilxarīf*
summer	*iṣṣēf*	winter	*iššita*

More useful words:

day	*yōm, ayyām ~ iyyām*
week	*ʾusbūɛ, ʾasabīɛ*
month	*šahṛ, šuhūr ~ ušhur*
year	*sana, sinīn ~ sanawāt*
century	*qarn, qurūn*

EXERCISES

I. Yes, I'll do it today.

ḫatinzil issūˀ innahaṛda? - *aywa, ḫanzil innahaṛda.*

ḫatġayyaṛ ilfilūs dilwaˀti? - *aywa, ḫaġayyaṛha dilwaˀti.*

1. *ḫatrūḫ innādi‿nnahaṛda?* - aywa, ____________________
2. *ḫatištiri‿ššaˀˀa di ꜥala ṭūl?* - aywa, ____________________
3. *ḫatnāmi badri‿nnahaṛda?* - aywa, ____________________
4. *ḫataklu‿llaḫma di‿nnahaṛda?* - aywa, ____________________
5. *ḫatiꜥmili‿lˀahwa dilwaˀti?* - aywa, ____________________
6. *ḫatšūfu Aḫmad innahaṛda?* - aywa, ____________________
7. *ḫatilbis ilbadla di‿nnahaṛda?* - aywa, ____________________
8. *ḫatīgi‿nnahaṛda?* - aywa, ____________________
9. *ḫatnaḍḍaf ilˀuwaḍ dilwaˀti?* - aywa, ____________________
10. *ḫatisˀalu‿lmudarris baꜥd iddars?* - aywa, ____________________

II. Don't worry, I won't forget it!

ma-tinsāš iddamġa! - *ma-txafš, miš ḫansāha.*

1. *ma-tinsāš ittarīx!* - *ma-txafš,* ____________________
2. *ma-tinsāš ittarīx wi‿lˀimḍa!* - *ma-txafš,* ____________________
3. *ma-txuššīš ilˀōḍa di!* - *ma-txafš,* ____________________
4. *ma-tilbisīš innaḍḍāra di!* - *ma-txafš,* ____________________
5. *ma-tišṛabš ilṃayya di!* - *ma-txafš,* ____________________
6. *ma-tˀaggaṛūš iššaˀˀa di!* - *ma-txafš,* ____________________
7. *ma-tištirīš ilkutub di!* - *ma-txafš,* ____________________
8. *ma-timḍīš ilistimāṛa di!* - *ma-txafš,* ____________________
9. *ma-tbiꜥšᵊ kutubak di!* - *ma-txafš,* ____________________

10. *ma-tinsāš ilʔawlād!* - *ma-txafš,* ____________________

11. *ma-takulš ilʕēš da!* - *ma-txafš,* ____________________

III. I'll do it for you.

miš ʕarfa amla‿listimāṛa. - *ana ḫamlahālik.*

1. *miš ʔadra aftaḫ iššibbāk.* - *ana* ____________________
2. *miš ʕārif aʔṛa‿nnaṣṣ.* - *ana* ____________________
3. *miš ʕāyiz aštiri‿lkutub di.* - *ana* ____________________
4. *ma-ʕandīš waʔt agīb ilxuḍār.* - *ana* ____________________
5. *ma-ʕandināš waʔtᵊ niʕmil ilʔahwa.* - *ana* ____________________
6. *ma-līš nifs anaḍḍaf ilʔōḍa.* - *ana* ____________________
7. *miš ʕarfa aktib ikkilma di.* - *ana* ____________________
8. *miš ʕarfīn nimla‿listimāṛa di.* - *ana* ____________________
9. *miš ʕarfīn niftaḫ ilbāb.* - *ana* ____________________
10. *miš ʕāyiz yibʕatli‿kkutub.* - *ana* ____________________
11. *miš ʕawzīn yifukkulna‿lfilūs di.* - *ana* ____________________

IV. He did it for me.

mīn illi fataḫlak ilbāb? - *huwwa‿lli fataḫhūli.*

1. *mīn illi katablak iggawāb?* - *huwwa‿lli*____________________
2. *mīn illi ṭallaʕlak ilḫagāt di?* - *hiyya‿lli* ____________________.
3. *mīn illi ḫaḍḍarlak ilfiṭār?* - *huwwa‿lli*____________________
4. *mīn illi naḍḍaflik ilʔōḍa di?* - *hiyya‿lli* ____________________
5. *mīn illi gablak ilxuḍār?* - *humma‿lli*____________________
6. *mīn illi malalhum ilistimaṛa?*- *iḫna‿lli* ____________________
7. *mīn illi ḫakālik ilḫikāya?* - *humma‿lli*____________________

8. *mīn illi ʿamallukum ilʾahwa?* - *hiyya‿lli* ________________

9. *mīn illi ṣallaḥluku‿lmutūṛ?* - *iḥna‿lli* ________________

10. *mīn illi baʿatlina‿lḥagāt di?* - *hiyya‿lli* ________________

11. *mīn illi fakkilik ilxamsa‿gnē(h) dōl?* - *huwwa‿lli* ________________

V. Of course there is a ... ! Answer the questions.

huwwa fī ʾasansēr fi‿lbēt da? - *ṭabʿan, kullᵊ bēt fī ʾasansēr.*

1. *huwwa fī nās fi‿lbalad di?* - *ṭabʿan,* ________________

2. *huwwa fī takyīf fi‿lʾōḍa di?* - *ṭabʿan,* ________________

3. *huwwa fī duššᵊ fi‿lbēt da?* - *ṭabʿan,* ________________

4. *huwwa fī faršᵊ fi‿ššaʾʾa di?* - *ṭabʿan,* ________________

5. *huwwa fī duktūr fi‿lmustašfa di?* - *ṭabʿan,* ________________

6. *huwwa fī madrasa fi‿lbalad di?* - *ṭabʿan,* ________________

7. *huwwa fī maṭʿam fi‿ššāriʿ da?* - *ṭabʿan,* ________________

8. *huwwa‿ntu ḥatsafru‿ssana di?* - *ṭabʿan,* ________________

9. *huwwa fī wardᵊ fi‿gginēna di?* - *ṭabʿan,* ________________

10. *huwwa fī kutub fi‿lmaktaba di?* - *ṭabʿan,* ________________

11. *huwwa fī tilifōn fi‿ššaʾʾa di?* - *ṭabʿan,* ________________

12. *huwwa‿ntu ḥatrūḥu iššuġl ilʾusbūʿ da?* - *ṭabʿan,* ________________

VI. Where possible, change each sentence in the same way as in the example below.

kull innās misafrīn. - *innās kulluhum misafrīn.*

1. *kull ilmaṭāʿim fatḥa.* - ________________

2. *kull ilmudarrisīn mawgudīn.* - ________________

3. *kull ilʾuwaḍ faḍya.* - ________________

4. *kull ilʿimāṛa‿nḍīfa.* - ________________

5. *kullᵊ ḫāga gahza.* - ____________________

6. *kull iṭṭalaba šaṭrīn.* - ____________________

7. *kull iššuˀaˀ mafrūša.* - ____________________

8. *kullᵊ‿sana w‿inti ṭayyiba!* - ____________________

9. *kull ilmuwaẓẓafīn taɛbanīn.* - ____________________

10. *kull issaɛāt maẓbūṭa.* - ____________________

VII. "The whole of" "all" or "every" "each"? Put a cross to show what *kull* means in each sentence.

	whole (of)	all	every
1. *kullᵊ sana w‿inta ṭayyib.*	☐	☐	☐
2. *kull iṣḫabna f‿Iskindiriyya.*	☐	☐	☐
3. *iššuˀaˀ kullaha mafrūša.*	☐	☐	☐
4. *ana ɛārif ilQāhíra kullaha.*	☐	☐	☐
5. *innās kulluhum biyaxdu ˀagāza.*	☐	☐	☐
6. *ḫatgībi‿lfaršᵊ kullu‿mɛāki?*	☐	☐	☐
7. *miš lāzim tīgi kullᵊ yōm.*	☐	☐	☐
8. *fī takyīf fi-kull ilˀuwaḍ.*	☐	☐	☐
9. *biyīgi kullᵊ ˀusbūɛ yizurna.*	☐	☐	☐
10. *lāzim timla kull ilistimaṛāt.*	☐	☐	☐
11. *ḫakenālu kull ilḫikāya.*	☐	☐	☐
12. *iššawāṭiˀ kullaha‿nḍīfa.*	☐	☐	☐
13. *ana ɛāwiz afham kullᵊ kilma.*	☐	☐	☐

VIII. Contradict the speaker, but be careful to make sense.

ilˀōḍa di ma-fihāš takyīf. - *miš mumkin, kull ilˀuwaḍ fīha takyīf.*

1. *ilmadrasa di ma-lhāš mudīr.* - *miš mumkin,* ____________ *mudirīn.*
2. *ilbiyūt di ma-fihāš ṃayya.* - *miš mumkin,* ____________ *ṃayya.*
3. *fī hina mudarrisīn miš luṭāf.* - *miš mumkin,* ____________ *luṭāf.*
4. *fī ṭalaba miš kuwayyisīn.* - *miš mumkin,* ____________ *kuwayyisīn.*

5. *fī kutub naʾṣa.* - *miš mumkin,* ____________ *mawgūda.*
6. *ana ʿāyiz aʾābil ilmudarrisīn.* - *miš mumkin,* ____________ *fi-ʾagāza.*
7. *iššuʾaʾ di‿ṣġayyaṛa ʾawi.* - *miš mumkin,* ____________ *kibīra.*
8. *ma-fīš ʾaṣansēr fi‿lmustašfa.* - *miš mumkin,* ____________ *fīha ʾaṣanseṛāt.*

IX. Make comparisons.

1. *innādi ʾurayyib, lākin ilbēt* ____________.
2. *ilbulōfaṛ tiʾīl, lākin iżżakitta* ____________.
3. *ilbēt da ġāli, lākin ilbēt bitāʿak* ____________.
4. *ilbintᵊ di ḥilwa, lākin uxtaha* ____________.
5. *ilbintᵊ ṭawīla‿w axūha* ____________ *minha.*
6. *iṭṭālib šāṭir, lākin iṭṭālíba* ____________.
7. *ilʿēš muhimm, lākin ilṃayya* ____________.
8. *Ḥasan mitʿallim, lākin Maḥmūd* ____________ *minnu.*
9. *bēti ʿāli, lākin bēt Muna* ____________.
10. *Ḥasan mitnarfis, lākin Faṭma* ____________.
11. *iššanṭa di ṣaḥīḥ xafīfa, lākin šanṭiti* ____________ *minha.*
12. *Ramaḍān karīm! - Aḷḷāhu* ____________.

X. Make comparisons and work out the difference using *bi-*.

Ḥasan ʿandu 15 sana wi ʿAli ʿandu 22 sana,
yaʿni ʿAli akbaṛ min Ḥasan bi-sabaʿ sinīn .

1. *ilfakha di b‿ʿašaṛa‿gnēh wi‿lxuḍār bi-sabʿa‿gnēh,*
   yaʿni‿lfakha ____________.
2. *ilBurg irtifāʿu tamanīn mitrᵊ wi‿lMuʾaṭṭam irtifāʿu 200 mitr,*
   yaʿni‿lMuʾaṭṭam ____________.
3. *Faṭma ṭulha 169 santi‿w Samya ṭulha 165 santi,*
   yaʿni Faṭma ____________.

4. *Fatḫi waznu 70 kīlu‿w Fawziyya waznaha 50 kīlu, yaɛni Fatḫi* ______________________.
5. *bēn Maṣrᵊ‿w Ṭanṭa mīt kīlumitrᵊ‿w bēn Maṣrᵊ w‿Iskindiriyya 230 kīlumitr, yaɛn‿Iskindiriyya* ______________________.
6. *ilʔaṭrᵊ‿byiɛmil mīt kīlu fi‿ssāɛa wi‿lɛaṛabiyya‿btiɛmil tamanīn kīlu fi‿ssāɛa, yaɛni‿lʔaṭr* ______________________.

XI. That's the biggest we have! Use a contrasting adjective.

iššanṭa di‿ṣġayyara xāliṣ.- di ʔakbaṛ šanṭa ɛandina.

1. *ilmudēl da ʔadīm.* - *da* ______________ *ɛandina.*
2. *iṣṣūra di wiḫša xāliṣ.* - *di* ______________ *ɛandina.*
3. *issāɛa di ġalya giddan.* - *di* ______________ *ɛandina.*
4. *ilbēt da‿bɛīd ʔawi.* - *da* ______________ *min ilbalad.*
5. *ilbulōfar da‿tʔīl xāliṣ.* - *da* ______________ *ɛandina.*
6. *ilbantalōn ʔuṣayyaṛ ʔawi.* - *da* ______________ *fi‿lmaḫall.*
7. *ittamrīn da ṣaɛbᵊ ʔawi.* - *da* ______________ *fi‿kkitāb.*
8. *da‿ktīr ʔawi!* - *da* ______________ *wāgib!*

XII. Give me one which is a little bigger - lighter - more modern!

ilmudēl da ʔadīm ʔawi, hāt mudēl aḫdas šuwayya.

1. *iggazma di‿ṣġayyara ɛalayya, hāt gazma* ______________ *šuwayya.*
2. *issiggāda di wiḫša, hāt siggāda* ______________ *minha.*
3. *iššanṭa di‿tʔīla ɛalayya, ɛawza šanṭa* ______________ *šuwayya.*
4. *ittamrīn da sahl, iddīna tamrīn* ______________ *šuwayya.*
5. *ilfustān da ṭawīl ɛalayya, šufli fustān* ______________ *šuwayya.*
6. *ilʔamīṣ da‿ʔṣayyaṛ ʔawi, šufli ʔamīṣ* ______________ *šuwayya.*
7. *innaḍḍāra di‿kbīra ʔawi, ɛawza naḍḍāra* ______________ *šuwayya.*
8. *iššʔʔa di ġalya ʔawi, ɛāwiz šaʔʔa* ______________ *šuwayya.*

XIII. That's not the very best! There's an even better one!

irrabīɛ ṣaḫīḫ mūsim gamīl, lākin agmal mūsim huwwa‿lxarīf.

1. *ilfilūs ṣaḫīḫ šēᵓ muhimm, lākin* ______________ *huwwa‿ṣṣiḫḫa.*
2. *ilmudēl da ṣaḫīḫ ḫadīs, lākin* ____________ *lissa ma-nzilš issūᵓ.*
3. *ilmudarris da‿kwayyis, lākin Sāmi* ______________ *fi‿lmadrasa.*
4. *iggahlᵊ ṣaḫīḫ ḫāga wiḫša, lākin* ______________ *hiyya‿lᵓihmāl.*
5. *ilfustān da šīk, lākin* __________________ *huwwa‿btāɛ Faṭma.*
6. *ilxuḍār rixīṣ ᵓawi hina, lākin* ___________ *ḫatlaᵓī‿f-sūᵓ ilɛAtaba.*
7. *ilfakha ġalya‿šwayya hina, lākin* __________ *ḫatlaᵓīha fi‿lMaɛādi.*
8. *Ḫasan fiɛlan ṭālib zaki, lākin* _______________ *huwwa Sāmi.*
9. *ilᵓaklᵊ da lazīz, lākin* ______________________ *bitāɛ ṃaṃti.*
10. *madrasti‿kwayyisa, lākin* ________________ *mawgūda fi‿gGīza.*

XIV. The prettiest - most modern - most important!

	gamīla?	*di miš gamīla‿w bass, di ᵓagmal ḫāga*	*šuftaha.*
1.	*ḫilwa?*	*di miš ḫilwa‿w bass, di* ______________	*šuftaha.*
2.	*ḫadīsa?*	*di miš ḫadīsa‿w bass, di* ______________	*šuftaha.*
3.	*xafīfa?*	*di miš xafīfa‿w bass, di* ______________	*šuftaha.*
4.	*laṭīfa?*	*di miš laṭīfa‿w bass, di* ______________	*šuftaha.*
5.	*muhimma?*	*di miš muhimma‿w bass, di* ____________	*šuftaha.*
6.	*ɛalya?*	*di miš ɛalya w‿bass, di* ______________	*šuftaha.*
7.	*šīk?*	*di miš šīk wi bass, di* ______________	*šuftaha.*
8.	*kuwayyisa?*	*di miš kuwayyisa‿w bass, di* ____________	*šuftaha.*
9.	*sarīɛa?*	*di miš sarīɛa‿w bass, di* ______________	*šuftaha.*
10.	*ġalya?*	*di miš ġalya‿w bass, di* ______________	*šuftaha.*

XV. He's one of the best - fastest - cleverest!

Ḫasan walad šāṭir giddan, da min ašṭar ilʾawlād illi fi‿lmadrasa.

1. *ʿAli sawwāʾ kuwayyis giddan, da min* ____________________ *illi fi‿lbalad.*

2. *ilʿaṛabiyya di sarīʿa giddan, di min* ____________________ *illi fi‿ggarāž.*

3. *Faṭma ṭalíba zakiyya ʾawi, di fiʿlan min* ____________________ *illi fi‿lfaṣl.*

4. *Sanāʾ bintᵊ laṭīfa giddan, di min* ____________________ *illi‿ʿrifnāhum.*

5. *Ḫasan ṛāgil karīm giddan, da min* ____________________ *illi‿f-baladna.*

6. *ilbalad di gamīla giddan, di min* ____________________ *illi šufnāha.*

7. *innuṣūṣ di muhimma giddan, di min* ____________________ *illi fi‿kkitāb*

8. *ilmaḫallᵊ da ġāli giddan, da min* ____________________ *illi fi‿lQāhíra.*

XVI. They don't know. Use *-li-* in your answer, with the correct suffix.

ḫatrūḫ li‿dduktūr imta? - *miš ʿārif* *aruḫlu imta.*

1. *ḫatʾūl li-Samya ʾē?* - *miš ʿārif* ____________________

2. *ḫatiḫku ʾē li‿lawlād?* - *miš ʿarfīn* ____________________

3. *ḫatāxud ʾē li‿lʾawlād?* - *miš ʿārif* ____________________

4. *ḫatiddi ʾē‿l-Samīr?* - *miš ʿārif* ____________________

5. *ḫatʾūlu ʾē li‿ṭṭalaba?* - *miš ʿarfīn* ____________________

6. *ḫatiktibi‿l-Ḫasan ʾē?* - *miš ʿarfa* ____________________

7. *ḫatiddu ʾē‿l-Faṭma?* - *miš ʿarfīn* ____________________

8. *ḫatibʿatu‿l-ʾabūkum ʾē?* - *miš ʿarfa* ____________________

9. *ḫatgībi‿l-ʾummik ʾē?* - *miš ʿarfa* ____________________

10. *ḫatiʿmili‿l-ʾaxūki ʾē?* - *miš ʿarfa* ____________________

XVII. Agree with the suggestions.

abɛatlak kīlu? - *aywa, min faḍlak ibɛatli kīlu!*

1. *aɛmillak šāy?* - aywa, ______________________
2. *aktiblaha gawāb?* - aywa, ______________________
3. *aftaḫlukum?* - aywa, ______________________
4. *aʾfillik ilbāb?* - aywa, ______________________
5. *anaḍḍaflak iššibbāk?* - aywa, ______________________
6. *afukkilak?* - aywa, ______________________
7. *aʾṛalku‿ktāb?* - aywa, ______________________
8. *aɛmillukum ʾahwa?* - aywa, ______________________
9. *abɛatlik ilʾawlād?* - aywa, ______________________
10. *agaddidlak ilʾiqāma?* - aywa, ______________________

XVIII. That's too difficult - too dear - too heavy for us!

intu ɛawzīn aṣɛab min kida? - *lā, da ṣaɛbᵊ ʾawi ɛalēna.*

1. *intu ɛawzīn aktaṛ min kida?* - *lā, da*______________________
2. *ɛawzīn ḫāga aġla kamān?* - *lā, di* ______________________
3. *agiblak banṭalōn akbaṛ?* - *lā, da*______________________
4. *agiblik fustān aʾṣar?* - *lā, da*______________________
5. *ɛayzīn ʾōḍa ʾaṣġaṛ?* - *lā, di* ______________________
6. *agiblik žakitta ʾaṭwal?* - *lā, di* ______________________
7. *awarrīkum šaʾʾa ʾakbaṛ?* - *lā, di* ______________________
8. *agiblak šanṭa ʾatʾal?* - *lā, di* ______________________
9. *addīku‿ktāb ashal?* - *lā, da*______________________
10. *agiblik naḍḍāra ʾaṣġaṛ?* - *lā, di* ______________________

XIX. Arrange the following words into logical sentences.

1. *bitāɛit, iššanṭa, idduktūṛa, iswid, lonha.*

2. *mūsim, ʔuṣayyaṛ, Maṣr, fi, ʔawi, iššita.*

3. *kuwayyis, muhandis, iḫna, ɛarfīn.*

4. *ɛand, šahṛ, aḫla, Ramaḍān, ilmuslimīn.*

5. *miš, ya-taṛa, intu, miwafʔīn?*

6. *ʔawi, di, baṣīṭa, ḫāga!*

7. *ilbalad, iggāmiɛ, mabna, aɛla, fi.*

8. *dōl, ḫilwīn, ilbintēn, ʔawi.*

9. *ṭūl innahāṛ, iḫna, biništaġal.*

10. *bukṛa, Iskindiriyya, Ḫasan, misāfir.*

11. *ilʔamrikāni, ġalya, ilɛaṛabiyyāt, xāliṣ.*

12. *naxlitēn, igginēna, bitaɛti, fīha, ɛalyīn.*

13. *biyištaġalu, iṭṭalaba, kuwayyis, iggudād.*

14. *kullaha, ḫayawiyya, našāṭ, ilbalad, wi.*

15. *ilfiṭār, kānit, miṛātu, miḫaḍḍara.*

XX. Translate the following sentences.

1. In summer we wear light summer clothing.

2. People (*ilwāḫid*) need (to wear) a pullover in winter.

3. It cools down in the evening.

4. Everybody strolls around the gardens until the early morning.

5. Probably, the lift in the block of flats is out of order.

6. My grandmother doesn't see well with those glasses.

7. What are you writing?

8. I didn't know what to write.

9. Next week we're going to Sinai by bus.

10. *Ḥasan*'s got the fastest car in the whole town!

11. Those are the American cars.

12. The bus always arrives at twelve oʾclock.

13. We go to school every day.

14. *ʿAli* takes a shower every morning.

15. He's coming to fetch the rent for the flat.

16. She washed her face (*wišš*) and brushed her teeth.

17. Lots of people go to the Red Sea in winter.

18. My country is the most beautiful country in the world.

19. We'll all be (present) at the club tomorrow.

LESSON XI

DIALOGUE

taṣlīḥ ilḥanafiyya

issitt: *ya Ṣalāḥ, ilḥanafiyya‿btaɛt‿ilmaṭbax xasṛāna. ṭūl illēl wi hiyya bitnaʔʔaṭ ṃayya, wi miš mixalliyya ḥaddᵊ‿ynām. di ḥāga‿tnarfis.*

Ṣalāḥ: *ana ɛārif sabbāk kuwayyis wi‿bnᵊ ḥalāl, tiḥibbi ʔarūḥ agību dilwaʔti ɛala ṭūl?*

issitt: *mistanni ʔē, ya Ṣalāḥ? ma-trūḥ tindahlu!*

========================

issabbāk: *ṣabāḥ ilxēr! fēn ilḥanafiyya‿lbayẓa?*

Ṣalāḥ: *xušš ilmaṭbax. ḥatlāʔi ḥanafiyyitēn, ilbayẓa ɛa‿lyimīn.*

issabbāk: *ạ̄, ṣaḥīḥ, di lāzim titfakk wi yitrakkiblaha gilda‿gdīda*

Ṣalāḥ: *ma-fīš māniɛ, bassᵊ law samaḥt, tikūn gilda min nōɛ kuwayyis, miš ʔayyᵊ kalām ɛašān miš kullᵊ yōm wi‿ttāni tixsaṛ ilḥanafiyya wi‿ssittᵊ tiddāyiʔ.*

issitt: *bassᵊ nittifiʔ ɛa‿lʔugṛa ya‿sṭa, ɛašān ma-ykunšᵊ fī sūʔ tafāhum. w‿illi ʔawwilu šarṭ, ʔaxru nūr, miš kida walla ʔē?*

issabbāk: *intu ṭabɛan ɛawzīn ḥāga‿kwayyisa wi tistaḥmil, wi ɛarfīn inn ilġāli tamanu fī(h), yaɛni‿ššuġlāna di ḥatkallifkum talatīn ginē(h) bass.*

issitt: *ḥaṛām ɛalēk ya‿sṭa! da‿ktīr ʔawi ʔawi! ana šayfa innᵊ xamsa‿w ɛišrīn ginē(h) maɛʔūl xāliṣ. ʔē ṛaʔyak? miwāfiʔ?*

issabbāk: *ana‿mwāfiʔ ya sitti, bassᵊ ɛašān tibʔu ɛandi zabāyin.*

VOCABULARY

ʔayyᵊ kalām	nonsense; just any old thing; poor quality
ʔāwim, yiʔāwim ḥ	to resist
ʔugṛa	wages, pay
baʔa, yibʔa	to become
bāyiẓ	broken, out of order
ḍarūri	necessary
gilda	washer (leather)
ḥadd	someone
ḥalāl	permitted, allowed
ḥanafiyya, -āt	faucet; tap
ḥaṛām ɛalēk!	have pity! shame on you!
ibnᵊ ḥalāl	an honest fellow
iddāyiʔ, yiddāyiʔ	to be annoyed
istaḥmil, yistaḥmil (ḥ)	to bear, to last
itfakk, yitfakk	to be taken apart
itkallif, yitkallif	to cost
itrakkib, yitrakkib	to be put together
ittafaʔ, yittifiʔ ɛala ḥ	to agree on
ma-fīš māniɛ	there is no problem
maɛʔūl	understandable reasonable
miwāfiʔ : ana ~	I agree
naʔʔaṭ, yinaʔʔaṭ	to drip
nadah, yindah li w	to call s/o
narfis, yinarfis w	to annoy, to irritate

nōʿ, anwāʿ	kind, type, sort	*taṣlīḥ*	repair
nūr, anwāṛ	light	*ṭabʿan*	naturally
ṛaʾy, ʾaṛāʾ	opinion	*ṭūl illēl*	the whole night
sabbāk	plumber	*wāfiʾ, yiwāfiʾ*	to agree
sāʿid, yisāʿid w	to help	*xalla, yixalli w*	to let
sūʾ tafāhum	misunderstanding	*xaṣrān*	broken
ṣaḥīḥ ~ ṣaḥḥ	right, true	*xaṭṭ*	writing
ṣallaḥ, yiṣallaḥ ḥ	to repair, to fix	*xisir, yixsaṛ*	to break down
šarṭ, šurūṭ	condition	*zibūn, zabāyin*	client
šuġlāna ~ šuġl	job		

See Lesson XVII for the introduction of the Arabic script.

GRAMMAR

I. Verb stems II and III

1. Verb stem II

(a) Stem II of strong verbs can be derived from stem I, or from nouns or adjectives, according to the pattern **KaTTaB** or **KaTTiB** (→ IX.III). Whether the final syllable contains an *-a-* or an *-i-* depends on the surrounding consonants. The consonants *ṭ, ḍ, ṣ, ẓ, ṛ, ġ, x, ʿ, ḥ, ʾ* will give rise to the vowel *-a-*, other consonants will give rise to an *-i-*:

ʾaggaṛ	"to rent"	*ʿazzil*	"to move house"
saxxan	"to heat up"	*kallim*	"to speak to s/o"
sarraḥ	"to comb"	*gahhiz*	"to prepare"
ballaġ	"to warn"	*rakkib*	"to assemble"

The same distribution of vowels applies to 4-radical verbs such as *dardiš* "to chatter" and *laxbaṭ* "to confuse" or "to mix up."

(b) Verbs with med. inf. will form their stem II in the same way as strong verbs do, the second radical being a *-w-* or a *-y-*. As for the verbs with med. gem., they form their stem II in exactly the same way as strong verbs:

{rwḥ}	*ṛāḥ, yirūḥ*	"to go"	→	*ṛawwaḥ*	"to go home"
{syḥ}	*sāḥ, yisīḥ*	"to melt"	→	*sayyaḥ*	"to melt s/th"
{nwm}	*nām, yinām*	"to sleep"	→	*nawwim*	"to put s/o to sleep"
{šmm}	*šamm, yišimm*	"to smell"	→	*šammim*	"to let s/o smell s/th"

The *-i-* is protected, due to the doubled consonant which is characteristic of stem II, and therefore always remains unaltered, e.g. *kallimt, kallimit, kallimna, kallimu* etc.

In the case of stem II the base form of the perfect and the imperfect is the same: *saxxan, yisaxxan* "to warm up," *fakkaṛ, yifakkaṛ* "to think."

(c) Verbs with tert.inf. have two different bases, one with *-a* for the perfect, and another with *-i* for the imperfect: *warra, yiwarri* "to show," *ɛadda, yiɛaddi* "to cross," "to pass."

(d) Stem II changes the meaning of verbs in their base form, giving them usually the sense of making or letting someone do something:

waṣal	"to arrive"	→	*waṣṣal*	"to bring"
rigiɛ	"to return"	→	*raggaɛ*	"to bring back"
fihim	"to understand"	→	*fahhim*	"to explain"
nizil	"to go downstairs"	→	*nazzil*	"to bring downstairs"

Nouns and adjectives can also be transformed into stem II verbs:

nimra	"number"	→	*nammaṛ*	"to number"
bard	"cold"	→	*baṛṛad*	"to cool down"
ṣūra	"photo"	→	*ṣawwaṛ*	"to photograph"
lēl	"night"	→	*layyil*	"to become night"

2. Verb stem III

(a) Stem III always shows an *-ā-* after the first radical, and an *-i-* before the last radical, regardless of the surrounding consonants. With strong verbs the pattern is therefore **KāTiB** (→ lesson IX.III):

sāfir, yisāfir	"to travel"	*ʾābil, yiʾābil*	"to meet"
sāɛid, yisāɛid	"to help"	*sāmiḫ, yisāmiḫ*	"to forgive"

If it is followed by a suffix which begins with a vowel, the *-i-* will become unprotected and will be dropped (→ lesson IV.II):

sāfir + u > sāfiru > safru *sāfir + it > sāfirit > safrit.*

The base forms of the perfect and the imperfect are the same in stem III: *rāsil, yirāsil* "to correspond," *ɛāmil, yiɛāmil* "to treat."

(b) Verbs with med.inf. usually have *-w-* as their second radical in stem II: *ʾām, yiʾūm* → *ʾāwim, yiʾāwim* "to resist," but sometimes they have a *-y-* : *dāyiʾ, yidāyiʾ* "to disturb," "to annoy."

(c) Verbs with tert.inf. behave in the same way as they did in stem II, with *-a-* in the perfect and *-i-* in the imperfect: *dāra, yidāri* "to conceal," *gāra, yigāri* "to indulge," *ɛāda, yiɛādi* "to make enemies" "to be hostile."

(d) Unlike stem II, it is practically impossible to allocate a basic meaning to stem III.

II. Verb stems V, VI and VII: the *t*-stems

1. By using the base stem and stems II and III as a starting point it is possible to form other stems, the so-called *t*-stems, through the addition of the prefix *it-* . Stem VII (*it-* + base stem) and stem V (*it-* + stem II) have a **passive** or sometimes **reflexive** meaning. Stem VI (*it-* + stem III) is however usually **reciprocal** in meaning, in other words it

expresses a certain degree of interchange of action where in English one might say "each other" "one another."

perfect of *t*-stems (strong verbs)

it+walad	I	>	*itwalad*	VII	to be born
it+misik	I	>	*itmasak*	VII	to be caught
it+rakkib	II	>	*itrakkib*	V	to be put together
it+ṣallaḫ	II	>	*itṣallaḫ*	V	to be repaired
it+ʾābil	III	>	*itʾābil*	VI	to meet each other
it+ṣāliḫ	III	>	*itṣāliḫ*	VI	to make peace with each other

Other examples are: *itkatab* (VII) "to be written," *itnasa* (VII) "to be forgotten," *itġasal* (VII) "to be washed," *itġayyaṛ* (V) "to be changed," *itṣawwar* "to be photographed" "to imagine," *itxāniʾ* (VI) "to quarrel with one another," *itḫāsib* (VI) "to settle up with one another."

2. Total assimilation of the *-t-* of the prefix *it-* usually occurs if followed by a dental consonant; it also occurs with sibilants, and with *-k-* and *-g-*.

itṭabax	>	*iṭṭabax*	"to be cooked"
itdāyiʾ	>	*iddāyiʾ*	"to be annoyed"
itḍarab	>	*iḍḍarab*	"to be beaten"
itsaraʾ	>	*issaraʾ*	"to be stolen"
itṣallaḫ	>	*iṣṣallaḫ*	"to be repaired"
itẓabaṭ	>	*iẓẓabaṭ* ~ *idẓabaṭ*	"to be fixed" (engines)
itšaṛṛaf	>	*iššaṛṛaf*	"to be honored"
itkallim	>	*ikkallim*	"to speak"
itgaddid	>	*idgaddid* ~ *iggaddid*	"to be renewed"

Assimilation may be partial as in *idẓabaṭ* "to be fixed," *idgaddid* "to be renewed" above.

3. The perfect: whenever *it-* is added to the base stem in order to form stem VII, the *-i-* of the *i*-perfect will change to *-a-*: *it* + *misik* > *itmasak* "to be caught," *it* + *širib* > *itšarab* "to be drunk."

4. The imperfect: in stems V and VI the vowels of the imperfect are the same as in the perfect. In stem VII, however, the *-a-* of the perfect will change to *-i-* in the imperfect:

perfect and imperfect of *t*-stems: strong verbs

ṣallaḫ	→	*iṣṣallaḫ*	→	*yiṣṣallaḫ*	V	to be repaired
gaddid	→	*itgaddid*	→	*yitgaddid*	V	to be renewed
dāyiʾ	→	*iddāyiʾ*	→	*yiddāyiʾ*	VI	to be annoyed
ġasal	→	***itġasal***	→	***yitġisil***	VII	to be washed
misik	→	***itmasak***	→	***yitmisik***	VII	to be caught
širib	→	***itšarab***	→	***yitširib***	VII	to be drunk

5. In the case of weak verbs, some irregularities occur when forming the *t*-stems:

(a) With verbs that are med.inf. or med.gem., the vowels *-ā-* or *-a-* remain unchanged in the imperfect: *itšāl* → *yitšāl* "to be carried away," *itḫall* → *yitḫall* "to be solved."

(b) With verbs that are med.inf., if the *-ā-* of the perfect is followed by two consonants, it will be shortened: *itšāl* → *itšalt* "I was carried away."

(c) With verbs that are tert.inf., both vowels change to *-i-* in the imperfect, just as in the case of strong verbs: *itmala* → *yitmili* "to be filled," *itrama, yitrimi* "to be thrown away."

(d) With verbs that are tert.inf., in stems V and VI both the perfect and the imperfect will have the vowel *-a-*, in contrast to stems II and III: *itrabba, yitrabba* "to be bred," *itmašša, yitmašša* "to go for a walk"; *iddāra, yiddāra* "to take shelter."

perfect and imperfect of *t*-stems: weak verbs

med.gem.							
lamm	→	*itlamm*	→	*yitlamm*	**VII**	to come together
laff	→	*itlaff*	→	*yitlaff*	**VII**	to be wrapped
med.inf.							
bāɛ	→	*itbāɛ*	→	*yitbāɛ*	**VII**	to be sold
šāl	→	*itšāl*	→	*yitšāl*	**VII**	to be carried (away)
tert.inf.							
mala	→	*itmala*	→	*yitmili*	**VII**	to be filled
nisi	→	*itnasa*	→	*yitnisi*	**VII**	to be forgotten
mašša	→	*itmašša*	→	*yitmašša*	**V**	to go for a walk
dāra	→	*iddāra*	→	*yiddāra*	**VI**	to be found

III. Verb stem VIII

In the case of certain verbs, the *-t-* of the *t*-stem is not placed in front of the first radical of the base stem, but as an infix after it. This stem is called stem VIII. The vowels are the same as those in stem VII:

iftakaṛ, yiftikir	"to remember"	*ištara, yištiri*	"to buy"
ištaka, yištiki	"to complain"	*iḫtāg, yiḫtāg*	"to need"
iḫtall, yiḫtall	"to occupy"		

Exceptions are: *ištaġal, yištaġal* "to work," which keeps its *-a-* in the imperfect; *ittākil, yittākil* "to be eaten" "to be worn out" from *kal, yākul* "to eat"; and similarly *ittāxid, yittāxid* "to be taken" from *xad, yāxud* "to take."

IV. Basic form of the imperfect

1. Used by itself without *bi-* or *ḫa-* the imperfect has a modal function: *tikūn min nōɛ kuwayyis* "it must be a good quality one."

2. The basic form of the imperfect is also used after various words expressing need, preference, possibility, capacity, capability (the so called modal auxiliaries):

ʾidir, yiʾdaṛ, ʾādir	*miš ʾādir amši*	"I can't walk"
	tiʾdar tīgi bukṛa?	"can you come tomorrow?"
ɛirif, yiɛṛaf, ɛārif	*tiɛrafi tiʾri?*	"can you (f.) read?" "do you know how to read?"
ḍarūri	*ḍarūri tīgi*	"you (absolutely) must come"
ḫabb, yiḫibb	*tiḫibbᵊ tišṛab ʾē?*	"what would you like to drink?"
liḫiʾ, yilḫaʾ, lāḫiʾ	*miš ḫalḫaʾ agahhiz ilɛaša*	"I shan't manage to get supper ready"
nifs +suffix	*nifsu yitfaṛṛag ɛa‿kkōṛa*	"he feels like watching football"

For *mumkin, lāzim* and *ɛāwiz* → VII.IV.

3. Clauses of purpose
(a) After verbs which indicate movement in a particular direction such as *ṛāḫ,yirūḫ - gih,yīgi - nizil,yinzil - ṭiliɛ,yiṭlaɛ* the basic form of the imperfect gives a sense of purpose:

huwwa ṛāyiḫ yizūr uxtu	"he's going to visit his sister"
ana gayy asʾal siyadtak suʾāl	"I've come to ask you a question"

(b) The basic form of the imperfect can also express purpose when used after *ɛašān ~ ɛalašān* "in order to" "so that":

ɛalašān afham kalāmik	"so that I may understand your point"
ɛašān tiḫaḍḍar ilfiṭār	"so that she prepares breakfast"
ɛašān astafīd minnu	"so that I may benefit from it"

Be careful: if *ɛašān ~ ɛalašān* is not followed by the basic form of the imperfect, then it means "because" and has the same meaning as *liʾann*:

ɛašān ma-ɛandīš filūs	"because I don't have any money"
ɛalašān iddinya lēl	"because it is dark (night)"
ɛalašān biyikkallim ɛaṛabi *~ liʾannu‿byikkallim ɛaṛabi*	"because he speaks Arabic"

EXERCISES

I. Make a counter-suggestion.

miš ʿāwiz arūḥ innaharda. - *ma-trūḥ bukṛa !*

1. *miš ʿāwiz asāfir innaharda.* - ________________ *bukṛa!*
2. *miš ʿāwiz ašṛab šāy.* - ______________ *ḥāga saʾʿa!*
3. *miš ʿāwiz arkab ilʾutubīs.* - ____________________ *taks!*
4. *miš ʿāwiz ākul dilwaʾti.* - _________________ *baʿdēn!*
5. *miš ʿawzīn ninzil dilwaʾti.* - __________________ *bukṛa!*
6. *miš ʿawzīn nisʾal ilmudīr.* - ________________ *issikirtēra!*
7. *miš ʿawzīn niʾaggaṛha dilwaʾti.* - _________________ *baʿdēn!*
8. *miš ʿawza‿ktiblaha gawāb.* - ___________________ *kart!*

II. List all the things you can't do.

yiʾūm badri, yinām bi‿llēl, yištaġal hina, yākul ḥāga, yišṛab ḥāga, yiṣallaḥ ilmutūr, yixallaṣ šuġlu, yistanna‿ktīr, yimla‿listimāṛa‿btaʿtu, yigīb ṣaḥbu‿mʿā, yiʾṛa‿lʿaṛabi

miš ʾādir aštaġal *miš ʿarfīn niʾṛa‿lxaṭṭᵊ da*

1. ____
2. ____
3. ____
4. ____
5. ____
6. ____
7. ____
8. ____
9. ____

III. Explain why you have come.

yisʾal siyadtak suʾāl	*yiṣallaḫ ilḫanafiyya*
yišūf ittakyīf	*yigaddid ilʾiqāma*
yāxud ilʾugṛa‿btaʿtu	*yištiri damġa*
yidfaʿ ilʾigāṛ bitāʿ iššaʾʾa	*yimḍi‿listimāṛa*
yištaġal maʿāhum	*yizūrak fi-bētak*

1. *ana gayy* ______________________________
2. *huwwa gayy* ______________________________
3. *intu gayyīn* ______________________________
4. *hiyya gayya* ______________________________
5. *iḫna gayyīn* ______________________________
6. *ana gayya* ______________________________
7. *humma gayyīn* ______________________________
8. *inta gayy* ______________________________
9. *inti gayya* ______________________________
10. *humma gayyīn* ______________________________

IV. They've all got to go to the doctor! Make the same suggestion to everyone, using the words in the example.

(inta) *ma-trūḫ li‿dduktūr yišūf ʿandak ʾē!*

1. *(inti)* ______________________________
2. *(intu)* ______________________________
3. *(hiyya)* ______________________________
4. *(humma)* ______________________________
5. *(huwwa)* ______________________________
6. *(iḫna)* ______________________________
7. *(ana)* ______________________________

V. What goes with what? Match each phrase in (b) with a phrase from (a).

	(a)	(b)
1.	*humma nazlīn issūᵓ*	*¿ašān asarraḫ ša¿ri*
2.	*ḫafukk ilḫanafiyya*	*¿ašān nirūḫ iggam¿a*
3.	*bitikkallim ma¿a‿ssabbāk*	*¿ašān tit¿allim ingilīzi*
4.	*biyindahu‿ssabbāk*	*¿ašān nitfassaḫ šuwayya*
5.	*lāzim yištaġal kuwayyis*	*¿ašān yištiru gilda‿gdīda*
6.	*ana gayy*	*¿ašān arakkib ḫanafiyya‿gdīda*
7.	*iḫna ¿awzīn ḫāga‿kwayyisa*	*¿ašān tittifiᵓ ma¿ā ¿a‿lᵓugṛa*
8.	*xadna ᵓagāza*	*¿ašān yiġayyaṛ iggilda*
9.	*safrit ᵓAmrīka*	*¿ašān tidrisu il¿aṛabi*
10.	*intu ṛayḫīn Maṣr*	*¿ašān nibᵓa ¿andu zabāyin*
11.	*daxalt ilḫammām*	*¿ašān aṣallaḫ ilḫanafiyya*
12.	*nizilna mi‿lbēt*	*¿ašān tistaḫmil wi ma-tixsaṛš*

1a + ______________________________

2a + ______________________________

3a + ______________________________

4a + ______________________________

5a + ______________________________

6a + ______________________________

7a + ______________________________

8a + ______________________________

9a + ______________________________

10a + ______________________________

11a + ______________________________

12a + ______________________________

VI. It's already been done! Use the t-stems!

ṣallaḫt ilḫanafiyya? - *ā̦, ilḫanafiyya‿ṣṣallaḫit xalāṣ!*

1. *ᵓaddimt ilᵓawṛāᵓ?* - *ā̦, ______________ xalāṣ!*

2. *fakkēt ilḫanafiyya?* - *ā̦, ______________ xalāṣ!*

3. *rakkibt iggilda?* - *ā̩,* ________________ *xalāṣ!*

4. *ġasalt ilɛaṛabiyya?* - *ā̩,* ________________ *xalāṣ!*

5. *ɛamalti‿lʔahwa?* - *ā̩,* ________________ *xalāṣ!*

6. *huwwa‿nta dafaɛt ilḫisāb?* - *ā̩,* ________________ *xalāṣ!*

7. *humma naʔalu‿lmuwaẓẓaf Maṣr?* - *ā̩,* ________________ *xalāṣ!*

VII. It doesn't need to be done! It can't be done!

malēti‿listimāṛa? - *ilistimāṛa miš lāzim titmili!*

1. *ṣallaḫt ittakyīf?* - *ittakyīf miš lāzim* ____________!
2. *naḍḍaft ilmaṭbax?* - *ilmaṭbax miš lāzim* ___________!
3. *ġayyaṛt iggilda?* - *iggilda miš lāzim* ____________!
4. *fakkēt ilḫanafiyya?* - *ilḫanafiyya miš lāzim* __________!
5. *biɛt ilɛaṛabiyya?* - *ilɛaṛabiyya miš mumkin* ________!
6. *nisīt Salwa?* - *Salwa miš mumkin* ___________!
7. *ġasalt ilɛaṛabiyya?* - *ilɛaṛabiyya miš lāzim* __________!
8. *širibt ilṃayya?* - *ilṃayya di miš mumkin* ________!
9. *fataḫt iššibbāk?* - *iššibbāk miš mumkin* __________!
10. *ḫatinsāni?* - *inti miš mumkin* ______________!
11. *dafaɛt ilḫisāb?* - *ilḫisāb da miš lāzim* ___________!
12. *ma-ʔafaltiš iššibbāk lē?* - *da miš mumkin* ______________!
13. *ma-kaltūš issamak lē?* - *da miš mumkin* _____________!
14. *ʔafalt ilbāb?* - *ilbāb da miš mumkin* __________!
15. *šilt ikkarāsi?* - *ikkarāsi miš mumkin* __________!
16. *lāzim nibīɛ ilbēt!* - *Ilbēt miš lāzim* ___________!
17. *ma-tnarfisnīš!* - *inta miš mumkin* _____________!

18. *gaddit ilbasbōr walla lissa?* - *ilbasbōr miš lāzim* ____________!

19. *ḥallu‿lmuškila?* - *ilmuškila miš mumkin* ________!

20. *lāzim tiʾullu‿kkalām da!* - *ikkalām da miš mumkin* _______!

VIII. We want to do it! We really ought to do it!

ɛawzīn tirgaɛu ʾimta? - *ɛawzīn nirgaɛ innahaṛda bi‿llēl.*

1. *ɛawzīn yirgaɛu ʾimta?* - *ɛawzīn* _______________ *issāɛa‿tnēn.*
2. *tiḥibbu tišṛabu ʾē?* - *niḥibb* ____________________ *ṃayya.*
3. *ɛawzīn timḍu fēn?* - *ɛawzīn* ____________________ *hina.*
4. *ilmafrūḍ tisʾalu mīn?* - *ilmafrūḍ* ________________ *ilɛaskari.*
5. *ilmafrūḍ tiɛaddu‿mnēn?* - *ilmafrūḍ* ________________ *min hina.*
6. *ɛawzīn tixuššu fēn?* - *ɛawzīn* ___________________ *šimāl.*
7. *ilmafrūḍ timlu ʾē?* - *ilmafrūḍ* ________________ *ilistimāṛa.*
8. *ilmafrūḍ taxdu ʾē?* - *ilmafrūḍ* ________________ *ilʾutubīs.*
9. *tiḥibbu‿tṛawwaḥu ʾimta?* - *niḥibb* __________________ *dilwaʾti.*
10. *ḍarūri tiwṣalu‿ssāɛa kām?* - *ḍarūri* _______________ *bukṛa‿ṣṣubḥ.*

IX. The policeman will tell you where to get off!

anzil fēn? - *ilɛaskari ḥayʾullak tinzil fēn.*

1. *amḍi fēn?* - *ilɛaskari ḥayʾullak* __________________.
2. *aštiri damġa‿mnēn?* - *ilɛaskari ḥayʾullak* __________________.
3. *adxul fēn?* - *ilɛaskari ḥayʾullak* __________________.
4. *asʾal mīn?* - *ilɛaskari ḥayʾullak* __________________.
5. *amla ʾē?* - *ilɛaskari ḥayʾullak* __________________.
6. *aktib ʾē?* - *ilɛaskari ḥayʾullak* __________________.
7. *arūḥ fēn?* - *ilɛaskari ḥayʾullak* __________________.

8. *aʾūl ʾē?* - *ilʿaskari ḥayʾullak* ________________.

9. *āxud ʾē?* - *ilʿaskari ḥayʾullak* ________________.

10. *aʿmil ʾē?* - *ilʿaskari ḥayʾullak* ________________.

X. Rewrite the sentences below, replacing *mumkin* with one of the following words: *yiḥibb, yiʿraf, yiʾdar, lāzim, nifs, ḍarūri.* Be sure to make all the necessary changes.

mumkin tilbisu‿lhidūm di? *nifsuku tilbisu‿lhidūm di?*

1. *mumkin ašṛab ilmayya di?* ________________

2. *mumkin ninzil hina.* ________________

3. *mumkin tiġayyaṛu‿lfilūs?* ________________

4. *mumkin tiwarrīna‿lbalad?* ________________

5. *mumkin aštaġal ṭabbāx.* ________________

6. *mumkin tisʾali suʾāl?* ________________

7. *mumkin ništiri ʿaṛabiyya.* ________________

8. *mumkin aggawwiz Randa.* ________________

9. *mumkin asīb iggamʿa.* ________________

10. *mumkin aʿīš fi-Maṣr.* ________________

XI. Fill each blank with a suitable word and be careful of agreement.

tāni, kibīr, xiliṣ, ṭawīl, ʿāli, da, wagaʿ, ṭiliʿ, bārid, mablūl, maksūr

1. *iššams^{ə} lissa ma-* ________________*-š.*

2. *baṭni* ________________*-ni*

3. *ilmarkib* ____________ *rikibnā*______ *imbāriḥ.*

4. *inti šayfa‿lmabna* ________________*da?*

5. *iṛṛāgil da ʾīdu* ________________.

6. *ilḥarb^{ə} lissa ma-* ________________*-š.*

7. *issitt*ᵊ *di manaxirha* ____________________ *ʔawi.*

8. *ilʔarḍ* ____________________.

9. *ɛēni ɛalēk* ____________________.

10. *ikkilma di laha maɛna* ____________________.

11. *riglu* ____________________.

XII. Arrange the following words into logical sentences.

1. *bitlayyil, iššita, iddinya, badri, fi.*

____

2. *midammis, binākul, fūl, yōm, kull.*

____

3. *tarīx, fākir, miš, innahaṛda, ana, ʔē.*

____

4. *kām, bukṛa, ḫaykūn, fi, ya-taṛa, iššahṛ?*

____

5. *titṣallaḫ, ilḫanafiyya, miš, di, lāzim.*

____

6. *ilMaġrib, Miryam, ɛašān, ṛāḫit, ilɛaṛabi, titɛallim.*

____

7. *wišš, itmaššēna, ilbalad, liġāyit, iṣṣubḫ, fi.*

____

8. *ḫaykūn, bukṛa, ya-taṛa, iggaww, kuwayyis?*

____

9. *issabbāk, baʔit, ɛand, issitt, zibūna.*

____

XIII. Translate the following sentences.

1. The car must be washed.

____

2. The children don't want to go to sleep

____

3. We met (each other) at the station yesterday.

4. There is a hospital in every large town.

5. We're all waiting for you.

6. My big sister works in this factory.

7. Thank God, our old car has been sold.

8. I'll write to her so that she can come and have a look at the flat.

9. I expect her tomorrow morning at ten.

10. That girl is unforgettable (cannot be forgotten).

11. The new meter (*ʿaddād*) is broken and must be repaired.

12. I love going to the cinema (*sinima*).

13. Would you (pl.) like to go to the party with us?

14. The beaches are beautiful and quiet in autumn

15. Many people like to go to Sinai in summer.

16. I've come to tell you something important

17. She saw a nice dress in the shop and she bought it.

18. At the university she got to know (*itʿaṛṛaf ʿala*) two Egyptian students.

LESSON XII

READING PASSAGES

ilwuṣūl fi-Maṣr

lamma wiṣil William maṭār ilQāhíra‿ddawli kānit iddinya layyilit. xallaṣ kullᵊ ʾigṛaʾāt iggumruk bi-surɛa wi rikib taks. idda‿ssawwāʾ ɛinwān ilfunduʾ illi kān ḥāgiz fī(h). wi lamma wiṣil ilfunduʾ, nizil mi‿ttaks, wi daxal ilistiʾbāl wi sallim ɛala‿lmuwaẓẓafa.

fi‿listiʾbāl

ilmuwaẓẓafa:	*masāʾ ilxēr.*
William:	*masāʾ innūr, min faḍlik ana ḥāgiz ġurfa hina.*
ilmuwaẓẓafa:	*ismᵊ‿syadtak ʾē?*
William:	*ismi William Knight.*
ilmuwaẓẓafa:	*aywa, ismᵊ‿syadtak mawgūd ɛandi.*
William:	*kuwayyis, wi‿lġurfa‿btaɛti nimra kām ya-taṛa?*
ilmuwaẓẓafa:	*ġurfit ḥaḍritak nimra mitēn wi tisɛa.*
William:	*fi ʾanhu dōr?*
ilmuwaẓẓafa:	*fi‿ddōr ittāni yafandim.*
William:	*wi fīha ḥammām?*
ilmuwaẓẓafa:	*aywa, kullᵊ ġuṛaf ilfunduʾ fīha ḥammām wi fīha tilifōn wi takyīf, lākin li‿lʾasaf ma-fihāš tilivizyōn.*
William:	*wi taman ilġurfa di kām ya-taṛa?*
ilmuwaẓẓafa:	*miyya‿wi xamsīn ginē(h) fi‿llēla.*
William:	*ya-taṛa fī bankᵊ hina fi‿lfunduʾ?*
ilmuwaẓẓafa:	*fī, bassᵊ ʾāfil dilwaʾti.*
William:	*ma-ɛlešš, bukṛa‿ṣṣubḥ, in šāʾ Aḷḷā, afūt ɛalē(h).*
ilmuwaẓẓafa:	*law samaḥt, iddīni‿lbasbōr bitāɛ ḥadritak!*
William:	*itfaḍḍali, ilbasbōr ahó.*
ilmuwaẓẓafa:	*itfaḍḍal, muftāḥ ilġurfa ahó!*
William:	*ya-taṛa‿lfiṭār issāɛa kām?*
ilmuwaẓẓafa:	*min sitta‿w nuṣṣᵊ‿l-ɛašaṛa. tiṣbaḥ ɛala xēr!*
William:	*w‿inti min ʾahlu!*

VOCABULARY

anhu	which one	*baɛdᵊ ma*	after (conj.)
ʾalam, ʾalām	pain	*dafaɛ, yidfaɛ ḥ*	to pay
ʾahl	family	*dafɛ*	payment
ʾigṛaʾāt	procedures, formalities	*daras, yidris ḥ*	to study
		dawli	international
ʾinsān	person	*dulāṛ, -āt*	dollar
bank, bunūk	bank	*fakahāni, -yya*	fruit seller
barīd	post, mail	*funduʾ, fanādiʾ*	hotel

ġurfa, ġuraf	room
ḫagaz, yiḫgiz ḫ	to reserve, to book
ḫagz	reservation, booking
ḫāgiz	to have reserved
ḫass, yiḫiss bi ḫ	to feel
idda, yiddi w ḫ	to give s/th to *s/o*
isti²bāl	reception
ištaġal	to work
kalb, kilāb	dog
kušk, akšāk	kiosk, booth
layyil, yilayyil	to become night
maḫall, -āt	shop
makān, amākin	room, space
maṭār, -āt	airport
mitallig	freezing, frozen
muftāḫ, mafatīḫ	key
rasmi	official
sallim, yisallim ʿala w	to greet
samaḫ, yismaḫ li w bi ḫ	to permit
surʿa	speed
bi-surʿa	quickly, speedily
ṣibiḫ, yiṣbaḫ	to awaken
šaġġāla	housemaid
šakl, aškāl	appearance
tallāga, -āṭ	fridge
ṭamāṭim (c. fem.)	tomato
wiṣil, yiwṣal	to arrive
xārig	abroad
xēr	goodness
ʿinwān, ʿanawīn	address; title (of book)
ʿumr, aʿmāṛ	age, lifetime

If you can't find a word in the vocabulary list, look it up in the glossary!

GRAMMAR

I. Participles

In stem I, verbs have an active participle with the pattern **KāTiB** and a passive participle with the pattern ma**KTūB**. The other stems only have one participle which may be either active or passive.

1. Active participle of stem I

(a) In stem I the active participle follows the pattern **KāTiB** (→ VI.III):

ḫagaz	→	*ḫāgiz*	having reserved
misik	→	*māsik*	having caught
ḫaṭṭ	→	*ḫāṭiṭ* (fem. *ḫaṭṭa*)	having put

(b) When forming the active participle of the verbs med. inf., a *-y-* appears as second radical:

		masc.	fem.	pl.	
ʾāl	→	*ʾāyil*	*ʾayla*	*ʾaylīn*	having said
bāʿ	→	*bāyiʿ*	*bayʿa*	*bayʿīn*	having sold

In the case of verbs with tert. inf., the third radical which is in fact a *-y-*, is not obvious in the masculine form of the participle, but it appears in the feminine and plural forms:

		masc.	fem.	pl.	
miši	→	*māši*	*mašya*	*mašyīn*	walking
nisi	→	*nāsi*	*nasya*	*nasyīn*	having forgotten

Be careful: the following participles are irregular: *gayy, gayya, gayyīn* "coming" (from *gih, yīgi* → XIII.II); *wākil, wakla, waklīn* "having eaten" (from *kal, yākul* → VII.III and IX.III); *wāxid, waxda, waxdīn* "having taken ~ caught" (from *xad, yāxud* → VII.III and IX.III).

2. Passive participle of stem I

(a) In stem I the passive participle follows the pattern ma**KT**ū**B**:

fihim	→	*mafhūm*	understood
ḫagaz	→	*maḫgūz*	reserved
fakk	→	*mafkūk*	loosened, undone

(b) In the case of verbs with tert. inf, the passive participle follows the pattern ma**KT**i (masc.), ma**KT**iyya (fem.), ma**KT**iyyīn (pl.):

ʾala	→	*maʾli*	fried
šawa	→	*mašwi*	grilled
ḫaša	→	*maḫši*	stuffed

(c) In the case of verbs with med. inf., no participle is formed. The participle form from stem VII is used instead (cf. 3 below):

I	*bāɛ*	→	VII	*itbāɛ*	→	*mitbāɛ*	sold
I	*šāl*	→	VII	*itšāl*	→	*mitšāl*	removed

3. Participles of the derived stems

(a) The participles of stems II and III are formed by replacing the prefix *yi-* of the imperfect by *mi-*:

imperfect		participle	
yisaddaʾ	→	*misaddaʾ*	believing
yiṛawwaḫ	→	*miṛawwaḫ*	returning home
yisāfir	→	*misāfir*	traveling
yikaffi	→	*mikaffi*	(being) sufficient
yiɛādi	→	*miɛādi*	(being) hostile

Depending on the meaning of the verb itself, the participles of stems II and III can be interpreted as active or passive.

Participles from stems II and III which end in *-i* have their feminine in *-iyya*, and their plural in *-iyyīn* in the same way as *nisba*-adjectives: *mistanni, mistanniyya, mistanniyyīn* "waiting."

(b) Most *t*-stems form their participles in the same way as stems II and III. They usually have the same passive or reflexive meaning as the verb from which they are derived:

V	*yitɛallim*	→	*mitɛallim*	educated
V	*yiggawwiz*	→	*miggawwiz*	married
VI	*yittākil*	→	*mittākil*	worn-out
VII	*yitbāɛ*	→	*mitbāɛ*	sold
4-rad.	*yitnarfis*	→	*mitnarfis*	irritated

In the case of weak verbs from the *t*-stems which end in *-a* in the imperfect, the final *-a* changes to *-i* when the participle is formed:

yitɛašša	→	*mitɛašši, mitɛaššiyya*	"having dined"
yistanna	→	*mistanni, mistanniyya*	"waiting"

4. Use of participles

(a) The participle is in fact a verb form. Suffixes which are added to the participle are object suffixes. This is why the first person singular suffix has to be *-ni* "me": *sāmiɛ* → *huwwa miš samiɛni* "he can't hear me," *fakrīn* → *intu fakrinni?* "can you (pl.) remember me?" For all other suffixes, singular and plural, there is no visible difference between the forms of the possessive and the object suffixes.

If the feminine form of the participle is used in combination with a suffix, then the final *-a* will be lengthened (and not changed to *-it* as happens with the feminine endings of nouns) (→ VIII.II): *šayfa* + *h* > *šayfā(h)*, *maska* + *ha* > *maskāha*, *samɛa* + *ni* > *samɛāni*.

(b) In the first instance, the active participle refers to a person who is engaged in doing something:

yilɛab	"he plays"	→	*lāɛib*	"player"
yirkab	"he mounts"	→	*rākib*	"passenger"
yiɛmil	"he works"	→	*ɛāmil*	"worker"
yišhad	"he witnesses"	→	*šāhid*	"witness"

(c) At the same time the active participle is a verb form which emphasizes the fact that an action has been completed and that the situation now being described is the resultant effect of this action:

action		**resultant effect**
libis burnēṭa he put on a hat	→	*lābis burnēṭa* he's wearing a hat (he's got a hat on)
ɛiriftu min biɛīd I recognized him from afar	→	*ana ɛarfu min zamān* I've known him for a long time
ḫagazt ilʔōḍa I reserved the room	→	*ana ḫāgiz ilʔōḍa* I've reserved the room

At the time of speaking the result of the action is still in effect and when translated, it may sometimes be replaced by a different verb (see examples above). In this case one speaks of the resultant effect of the participle. In English the present perfect is often used in such cases:

ana nāsi	"I've forgotten"
Ḫasan xāṭib	"Ḫasan is engaged (to be married)"

By contrast, the perfect in Arabic only indicates that something happened in the past. It does not reveal whether its effect is still in existence:

ḫagazt (perfect)	"I reserved" (once, at a certain moment)
but: *ana ḫāgiz*	"I've made a reservation"

(d) The following types of verbs express the present time by using the active participle:

* Verbs which refer to the senses such as "to see," " to hear," "to smell," "to feel", etc.

sāmiɛ?	"can you hear?"
ana šamma rīḫa ġarība	"I smell something strange"
ana ḫāsis bi-ʾalam fi-baṭni	"I feel a pain in my stomach"

* Verbs which refer to movement in a certain direction

hiyya rayḫa‿lmadrasa	"she's on her way to school" (right now)
humma‿msafrīn Aswān	"they're traveling to Aswan"
mīn illi ṭāliɛ issillim?	"who's that going up the stairs?"
siyadtak nāzil?	"are you getting off?"
áho gayy!	"there he comes!"

* Verbs which describe a particular state of mind or body

ana fāhim kullᵊ ḫāga	"I understand everything"
miš fākir	"I can't remember"
humma ʾaɛdīn	"they're sitting (down)"

(e) Depending on the context, the participles of some verbs can also refer to future time, where in English the present continuous is used:

inta gayyᵊ baɛdᵊ bukṛa?	"are you coming the day after tomorrow?"
hiyya‿msafra imta?	"when is she leaving?"
iḫna rayḫīn Sīna bukṛa	"we're going to Sinai tomorrow"

(f) In combination with *lissa* "still," the active participle is used to express the idea of "to have just done or been doing something":

iḫna lissa waklīn	"we've just eaten"
ana lissa wāṣil min Faṛansa	"I've just arrived from France"
hiyya lissa‿mkallimāni fi‿ttilifōn	"she's just phoned me"

(g) The participle from stem VII is seldom used in the case of strong verbs. One uses instead the passive participle from the base stem:

itwalad, yitwilid "to be born"	→	*mawlūd*	"born"
itġasal, yitġisil "to be washed"	→	*maġsūl*	"washed"

Thus **mitwilid* or **mitġisil* are not used.

(h) The passive participle can also express a possibility and form nouns:

mašrūb	"drinkable"	→	"a beverage"
mafhūm	"comprehensible	→	"a concept"

These form their plurals correspondingly either with *-āt* such as *mašrubāt* "beverages" or as broken plurals such as *mafahīm* "concepts."

II. *kān* in combination with other verbs

A sentence which already contains a verb can be moved into a past setting by using *kān.*

1. The combination of *kān* with the *bi*-imperfect or with a participle indicates duration of time in the past, in contrast to the perfect which refers to an action which happened once

iḫna nazlīn fi-sSavōy we're staying at the Savoy	→	*kunna nazlīn fi-sSavōy* we were staying at the Savoy
Maḫmūd biyiʾṛa‿ggurnāḷ Maḫmūd is reading the newspaper	→	*Maḫmūd kān biyiʾṛa‿ggurnāḷ* Maḫmūd was reading the newspaper
binsāfir kitīr we travel a lot	→	*kunna binsāfir kitīr* we used to travel a lot

2. When *kān* is followed by the perfect it expresses completed past time. *kān* frequently begins a clause and is followed immediately by the subject:

lamma wiṣil ilQāhira ***kānit*** *iddinya* ***layyilit***	when he arrived in Cairo, it was already night
lamma ʾumna mi‿nnōm ***kānit*** *iššamsᵊ* ***ṭilɛit***	when we got up, the sun had already risen

3. When combined with the *ḫa*-imperfect, *kān* indicates that something nearly happened or that there was an intention to do something:

kuntᵊ ḫamūt	I almost died
kānit ḫatīgi	she intended to come

III. Relative Clauses

There are two kinds of relative clause: (a) the relative clause introduced by *illi* which refers to a **defined antecedent** and immediately follows it, and (b) the relative clause without *illi* which follows an **undefined antecedent**. By defined we mean pronouns, nouns with a definite article or a possessive suffix, and proper nouns:

(a)	***iṛṛāgil*** *illi saʾal suʾāl*	the man who asked a question
	ana *‿lli šuftu*	I'm the one who saw him
(b)	*saʾaltᵊ* ***ṛāgil*** *māši fi‿ššāriɛ*	I asked a man who was walking down the street
	badawwaṛ ɛala ***ṭālib*** *ʾismu ɛAli*	I'm looking for a student whose name is ɛAli

1. The relative clause with *illi*

illi forms a connection between two clauses which share a common factor and it remains unchanged whatever the gender or number of the antecedent:

isʾal ***iṛṛāgil***	+ ***iṛṛāgil*** *hināk*	→	*isʾal iṛṛāgil illi‿hnāk* ask the man who is (standing) there!
dōl ***iggirān***	+ ***iggirān*** *saknīn fōʾ*	→	*dōl iggirān illi saknīn fōʾ* those are the neighbors who live upstairs

In the preceding examples, the antecedent was the subject of the subordinate clause. When the antecedent has a different function, a pronoun suffix referring to the antecedent has to be used in the subordinate clause.

	ma-ɛagabnīš ***ilfilm*** + *šufna* ***ilfilm*** *fi‿ttilivizyōn*
→	*ma-ɛagabnīš ilfilm illi šufnā(****h****) fi‿ttilifizyōn*
	the film which we saw on TV did not appeal to me
	fēn ***ikkutub*** + *ištarēt* ***ikkutub***
→	*fēn ikkutub illi ištaret****ha****?*
	where are the books which you bought?
	*ādi‿****ṛṛāgil*** + *badawwaṛ ɛala‿****ṛṛāgil***
→	*ādi‿ṛṛāgil illi badawwaṛ ɛalē(****h****)*
	there is the man (whom) I am looking for
	ḫāxud ***ilġurfa*** + ***ilġurfa*** *fīha takyīf*
→	*ḫāxud ilġurfa‿lli* ***fīha*** *takyīf*
	I'll take the room which has air-conditioning
	ḫāxud ***ilbaṭṭīxa*** + *wazn* ***ilbaṭṭīxa*** *sitta kīlu*
→	*ḫāxud ilbaṭṭīxa‿lli wazn****aha*** *sitta kīlu*
	I'll take the watermelon whose weight is 6 kg

2. The relative clause without *illi*

The relative clause without *illi* follows an undefined antecedent. This is treated in exactly the same way as the relative clause with *illi*. And where necessary it contains a suffixed pronoun which refers to the antecedent:

ɛāwiz ***ġurfa*** + ***ilġurfa*** *fīha takyīf*
→ *ɛāwiz ġurfa fīha takyīf*
I want a room which has air conditioning

ʾabilt^{ə} *magmūɛit* ***ṭalaba*** + *ma-šuftiš* ***iṭṭalaba*** *ʾabl*^{ə} *kida*
→ *ʾabilt*^{ə} *magmūɛit ṭalaba ma-šuftuhumš*^{ə} *ʾabl*^{ə} *kida*
I came across a group of students whom I had not seen before

ɛayza ***ġurfa*** + *ʾugrit* ***ilġurfa*** *aʾall*
→ *ɛayza ġurfa ʾugritha aʾall*
I want a room at a lower rent [which has a lower rent]

badawwaṛ ɛala ***bint*** + *šaɛr* ***ilbint*** *aḫmaṛ*
→ *badawwaṛ ɛala bint*^{ə} *šaɛraha aḫmaṛ*
I'm looking for a girl with red hair [whose hair is red]

iggawwiz waḫda ***maṣriyya*** + *abu‿****lmaṣriyya*** *duktūr*
→ *iggawwiz waḫda maṣriyya ʾabūha duktūr*
he married an Egyptian girl whose father is a doctor

INCREASE YOUR VOCABULARY

Islamic formulas

bismillāh iṛṛaḫmān iṛṛaḫīm — In the name of God, the Most Merciful! (said before undertaking any action)

assalāmu ɛalaykum wa ṛaḫmatu‿ḷḷāhi‿w baṛakātu — May God's mercy and blessing be upon you! (greeting)

reply: *wa ɛalēkumu‿ssalām* — blessings upon you too!

in šāʾ Aḷḷāh — God willing!
bi-ʾizn illāh — with God's permission!
fi-ʾamant‿illāh — under God's care! (taking leave)

la ḫawla wala quwwata ʾilla bi‿llāh	the power and the glory are God's alone! (great shock or sorrow)
mā šāʾ Aḷḷāh!	what God intends! (when admiring something; lovely!)
ilḫamdu li-llāh	praise be to God!
reply: *yistāhil ilḫamd!*	He is worthy of praise!
ḫamdilla ʿa‿ssalāma	thank God for the safe return! (on arriving from a journey or recovering from an illness)
reply: *Aḷḷāh yisallimak!*	God be with you!
ramaḍān karīm!	(greeting used during the fasting month of Ramaḍān)
reply: *Aḷḷāhu ʾakṛam!*	

EXERCISES

I. It has just happened! Use *lissa* with the active participle and add the correct suffix where necessary.

ṛāḩ fēn iggawāb? da‿na lissa katbu min šuwayya! *(katab)*

1. *ʾafalt ilbāb lē? da‿na lissa* ____________ *min šuwayya! (fataḩ)*
2. *Aḩmad ṛāḩ fēn? da‿na lissa* ______________ *min šuwayya! (šāf)*
3. *amḍi tāni lē? miš ana lissa* ______________ *ʾuddāmak! (maḍa)*
4. *illaḩma‿mtalliga, ana lissa* ______________ *min ilfirīzir. (ṭallaɛ)*
5. *ikkubbayāt di‿nḍīfa, ana lissa* ____________ *innaharḍa. (ġasal)*
6. *ilkutub fēn? da‿na lissa* ___________ *innaharḍa‿ṣṣubḩ! (ištara)*
7. *ana ma-šuftahāš, di lissa* __________________ *mi‿lxārig. (rigiɛ)*
8. *ana miš gaɛāna, ana lissa* _______________ *min šuwayya. (kal)*
9. *balāš ʾahwa min faḍlik, ana lissa* _________________ *šāy! (širib)*
10. *li‿lʾasaf, Samya miš mawgūda, di lissa* _____ *min xamas daʾāyiʾ! (xarag)*

II. Active participle or *bi*-imperfect?

1. *Muḩammad* __________________ *ilmadrasa kullᵉ yōm. (ṛāḩ)*
2. *ana* ______________________________ *rīḩa ġarība. (šamm)*
3. *hiyya* ________________________ *innaharḍa bi‿llēl. (sāfir)*
4. *ana* __________________ *kuwayyis bi‿nnaḍḍāra‿ggidīda. (šāf)*
5. *ɛala fēn in šāʾ Aḻḻā? - ana* __________________ *ilbalad. (nizil)*
6. *iḩna dayman* ____________________ *Iskindiriyya fi‿ṣṣēf. (sāfir)*
7. *ilkalb* __________________________ *aḩsan min ilʾinsān. (šamm)*
8. *ana* ______________________________ *bi-ʾalam fi-baṭni. (ḩass)*
9. *inta ḩatuʾɛud hina? - lā, ana* _____ *li‿dduktūr baɛdᵉ‿šwayya. (ṛāḩ)*

10. *kullᵊ yōm issāɛa ɛašaṛa ᵓAḥmad* ________________ *issūᵓ. (nizil)*

11. *ya-taṛa inti* ____________________ *mīn illi‿hnāk da? (šāf)*

12. *dayman lamma bašṛab ṃayya saᵓɛa* __________ *bi-ᵓalam fi-snāni. (ḥass)*

III. It's happened! Use the passive participle.

1. *ilbawwāb ġasal ilɛaṛabiyya, wi‿lɛaṛabiyya dilwaᵓti*_______*wi‿nḍīfa.*

2. *iṭṭabbāx ᵓala‿ssamak wi dilwaᵓti‿ssamak* ______ *wi gāhiz li‿lᵓakl.*

3. *Aḥmad itkasaṛit riglu‿w dilwaᵓti riglu* __________*wi‿miggabbisa.*

4. *šawēna‿llaḥma‿w dilwaᵓti‿llaḥma* _____________ *wi gahza!*

5. *ilbāb itᵓafal min sāɛa‿w dilwaᵓti ḥatlaᵓī(h)* ________________.

6. *ilbulīs manaɛ ilmurūr, yaɛni‿lmurūr dilwaᵓti* _______________.

7. *Aḥmad itwalad fi Ṭanṭa, yaɛni huwwa* _______ *wi mitṛabbi fi‿rrīf.*

8. *issabbāk fakk ilḥanafiyya‿w sabha* ________________ *wi ṛawwaḥ.*

9. *ḥagazt imbāriḥ ᵓōḍa fi‿lfunduᵓ, yaɛni dilwaᵓti‿lᵓōḍa* ______ *xalāṣ.*

10. *Ḥasan xaṭab Randa, yaɛni dilwaᵓti Randa* ______________ *rasmi.*

11. *Ḥasan ṭafa‿llamḅa, yaɛni illamḅa dilwaᵓti* ________ *wi ma-fīš nūr.*

12. *ilṃayya lāzim tiġli, ma-tišṛabūšᵊ ġēr ṃayya* ________________ *!*

13. *ilmudīr maḍa‿lᵓawṛāᵓ, yaɛni‿lᵓawṛāᵓ dilwaᵓti* _______ *wi gahza.*

14. *Samīr iggawwiz Samya, yaɛni humma dilwaᵓti* ______________.

IV. Did everyone do it? No, he is the only one who did it.

kulluhum itɛallimu? - *lā, huwwa bass illi‿tɛallim.*

1. *kulluhum mišyu?* - ______________________________.

2. *kulluhum safru?* - ______________________________.

3. *kulluhum nisyu?* - ______________________________.

4. *kulluhum ɛazzilu?* - ______________________.

5. *kulluhum maḍu?* - ______________________.

6. *kulluhum ṛawwaḫu?* - ______________________.

7. *kulluhum itnaʾalu?* - ______________________.

8. *kulluhum idday ʾu?* - ______________________.

9. *kulluhum rikbu‿lʾaṭr?* - ______________________.

10. *kulluhum simɛu‿lkalām?* - ______________________.

V. Answer the following using *illi* and a relative clause.

rikibti‿ilʾutubīs minēn? *(ilmaḫaṭṭa ʾuddām ilmustašfa)*
rikibt ilʾutubīs min ilmaḫaṭṭa‿lli ʾuddām ilmustašfa

1. *gibt iṭṭamāṭim di‿mnēn?* *(ilfakahāni‿f-šāriɛ Ḫasan Ṣabri)*

____

2. *ištarēt issagāyir di‿mnēn?* *(ikkušk^{ə} ʾuddām issinima)*

____

3. *ištarēt ilbadla di‿mnēn?* *(ilbutīk gambina ɛala ṭūl)*

____

4. *saʾalt^{ə} mīn?* *(ilɛaskari wāʾif ʾuddām ilbāb)*

____

5. *laʾet ilmafatīḫ fēn?* *(ɛala‿ttaṛabēẓa fi-ʾoḍt innōm)*

____

6. *nixušš^{ə} min ʾayy^{ə} bāb?* *(ilbāb ɛa‿lyimīn)*

____

7. *aṣallaḫ ʾayy^{ə} ḫanafiyya?* *(ilḫanafiyya bitnaʾʾaṭ ṃayya)*

____

8. *ɛawza titfaṛṛagi ɛala ʾayy^{ə} fustān?* *(ilfustān fi‿lfitrīna)*

____

9. *ɛawzīn ʾayy^{ə} gawāb?* *(iggawāb wiṣil innahaṛda‿ṣṣubḫ)*

____

10. *ɛawza taxdi ʾayy^{ə} ṣūra?* *(iṣṣūra fīha ṣaḫbiti)*

____

VI. Which one? Make relative clauses, and be careful with the pronoun suffixes.

iššaʾʾa fēn? - *inta ʾaggaṛt iššaʾʾa.*

iššaʾʾa‿lli ʾaggaṛtaha fēn?

1. *mīn iṛṛāgil?* - *iggawwizit iṛṛāgil.*

   *mīn irrāgil*____________________________________?

2. *fēn ilḫagāt?* - *gibti‿lḫagāt mi‿ssūʾ.*

   *fēn ilḫagāt*____________________________________?

3. *áho da‿lmaḫall!* - *itfaṛṛagna ʿala‿lmaḫall imbāriḫ.*

   *áho da‿lmaḫall*____________________________________!

4. *fēn ilmafatīḫ?* - *xadt ilmafatīḫ minni‿mbāriḫ.*

   fēn ilmafatīḫ ____________________________________?

5. *mīn iṛṛāgil?* - *kuntᵊ bitkallim iṛṛāgil.*

   mīn iṛṛāgil ____________________________________?

6. *ma-laʾetš ikkitāb.* - *kunti ʿayza‿kkitāb.*

   ma-laʾetš ikkitāb ____________________________________.

7. *hāt ilistimāṛa!* - *malēt ilistimāṛa min šuwayya.*

   hāt ilistimāṛa ____________________________________!

8. *warrīni‿ṣṣuwar!* - *ʿamalti‿ṣṣuwar fi Maṣr.*

   warrīni‿ṣṣuwar ____________________________________!

9. *ahé‿ttallāga!* - *inta ṣallaḫt ittallāga.*

   ittallāga ____________________________________ *ahé*!

10. *ilmaṭʿam kuwayyis giddan.* - *itʿaššēna fi‿lmaṭʿam imbāriḫ.*

    ilmaṭʿam ______________________________ *kuwayyis giddan.*

11. *lāzim nirgaʿ ilmaḫall.* - *daxalna‿lmaḫallᵊ da min šuwayya.*

    *lāzim nirgaʿ ilmaḫall*____________________________________.

VII. Form relative clauses and be careful with the pronoun suffixes.

kallimtilak iṛṛāgil. - *axu‿ṛṛāgil mudīr bank.*

kallimtilak iṛṛāgil illi ʾaxū(h) mudīr bank.

1. *ḫāxud ilfustān.* - *taman ilfustān mitēn ginē(h).*

   ḫāxud ilfustān ____________________________________.

2. *iḫna ʿawzīn ilmuftāḫ.* - *xadt ilmuftāḫ min Ḫasan.*

   iḫna ʿawzīn ilmuftāḫ ____________________________________.

3. *ḫāxud ilbadla* - *lōn ilbadla bunni.*

ḫāxud ilbadla ______________________.

4. *inta šāyif iṛṛāgil?* - *šakl iṛṛāgil wiḫiš?*

inta šāyif iṛṛāgil ______________________?

5. *ʿawzīn ilġurfa* - *balakōnit it ilġurfa ʿa‿nNīl.*

ʿawzīn ilġurfa ______________________.

6. *fēn ilfilūs?* - *ġayyaṛt ilfilūs mi‿lbank.*

fēn ilfilūs ______________________?

7. *aho da‿lkātib.* - *ʾarēt kitāb ilkātib fi‿lʾagāza.*

aho da‿lkātib ______________________.

8. *ittaṣaltᵊ bi‿ssitt.* - *kunna ʾabilna‿ssittᵊ fi‿lmaḫaṭṭa.*

ittaṣaltᵊ bi‿ssitt ______________________.

VIII. What exactly are you looking for? Form relative clauses as shown in the example.

ʿāwiz ʿaṛabiyya - *taman ilʿaṛabiyya maʿʾūl.*

ʿāwiz ʿaṛabiyya tamanha maʿʾūl.

1. *badawwaṛ ʿala ṭālib.* - *ism iṭṭālib Ḥasan.*

badawwaṛ ʿala ṭālib ______________________.

2. *badawwaṛ ʿala ṭabbāx.* - *iṭṭabbāx yiʿṛaf yuṭbux kuwayyis.*

badawwaṛ ʿala ṭabbāx ______________________.

3. *badawwaṛ ʿala badla.* - *albis ilbadla fi‿lḫafla.*

badawwaṛ ʿala badla ______________________.

4. *badawwaṛ ʿala ṭamāṭim.* - *iṭṭamāṭim tinfaʿ li‿ssalaṭa.*

badawwaṛ ʿala ṭamāṭim ______________________.

5. *badawwaṛ ʿala ṭālíba.* - *ism iṭṭālíba Mirvat.*

badawwaṛ ʿala ṭāliba ______________________.

6. *laʾēt šaʾʾa ḫilwa.* - *ʾaggaṛt iššaʾʾa ʿala ṭūl.*

laʾēt šaʾʾa ḫilwa ______________________.

7. *laʾēt kitāb kuwayyis.* - *ištarēt ikkitāb ʿala ṭūl.*

laʾēt kitāb kuwayyis ______________________.

8. *ʾaʿadtᵊ sanatēn fi-Maṣr.* - *itʿallimtᵊ fi‿ssanatēn dōl ilʿaṛabi.*

ʾaʿadtᵊ sanatēn fi-Maṣr ______________________.

9. *ya-tara fī filmᵊ‿kwayyis?* - *nitfarrag ɛala‿lfilm fi‿ttilivizyōn.*

ya-tara fī filmᵊ‿kwayyis ______________________________?

10. *ya-tara fī ʾutubīs?* - *nāxud ilʾutubīs min hina.*

ya-tara fī ʾutubīs ______________________________?

IX. Even more relative clauses!

1. *šuft imbāriḥ film.* - *ilfilmᵊ ɛagabni xāliṣ.*

šuft imbāriḥ film ______________________________.

2. *ana miḥtāga‿l-šaġġāla šaṭra.*- *iššaġġāla tiɛraf tuṭbux.*

ana miḥtāga‿l-šaġġāla šaṭra ______________________________.

3. *da ʾawwil maḥall.* - *daxalna‿lmaḥallᵊ‿f-Xān ilXalīli.*

da ʾawwil maḥall ______________________________.

4. *kān fī hina rāgil.* - *irrāgil saʾal ɛalēk.*

kān fī hina rāgil ______________________________.

5. *laʾēt funduʾ laṭīf.* - *niziltᵊ fi‿lfunduʾ da.*

laʾēt funduʾ laṭīf ______________________________.

6. *fī‿hnāk ɛaskari murūr.* - *mumkin nisʾal ilɛaskari da.*

fī‿hnāk ɛaskari murūr ______________________________.

7. *ɛandi walad tāni.* - *ɛumr ilwalad itnāšar sana.*

ɛandi walad tāni ______________________________.

8. *ɛanduhum bintᵊ tanya.* - *ɛumr ilbintᵊ ɛašar sinīn.*

ɛanduhum bintᵊ tanya ______________________________.

9. *ɛāwiz ašūf badla tanya.* - *lōn ilbadla ʾaḥla‿šwayya.*

ɛāwiz ašūf badla tanya ______________________________.

10. *ḥanlāʾi ʾinšāʾ Aḷḷāh maḥall* - *ɛand ilmaḥallᵊ buḍāɛa ʾarxaṣ.*

ḥanlāʾi ʾinšāʾ Aḷḷāh maḥall ______________________________.

X. Talk to someone and explain why you've come.

yikallim ilmudīr - *kuntᵊ ɛāwiz akallim ilmudīr*

1. *yištiri ṭawābiɛ barīd* - *kuntᵊ ɛāwiz* ________________

2. *yiʾullak ḥāga* - *kuntᵊ ɛāwiz* ________________

3. *yigaddid ilʾiqāma‿btaɛtu* - *kuntᵊ ɛāwiz* ________________

4. *yisʾal suʾāl* - *kuntᵊ ɛāwiz* ________________

5. *yāxud ilbasbōr bitāʿu* - *kuntᵊ ʿāwiz* ________________

6. *yiḥgiz makān kuwayyis* - *kuntᵊ ʿāwiz* ________________

7. *yitfarrag ʿa‿kkutub* - *kuntᵊ ʿāwiz* ________________

8. *yidfaʿ ilʾigāṛ* - *kuntᵊ ʿāwiz* ________________

9. *yidris fi‿ggamʿa* - *kuntᵊ ʿāwiz* ________________

10. *yisāfir Maṣr* - *kuntᵊ ʿāwiz* ________________

XI. I was going to come, but I changed my mind.

ma-safirtiš lē? - *kuntᵊ ḥasāfir,* *lākin ġayyaṛtᵊ fikri.*

1. *ma-štaġaltūš lē?* - ____________ *lākin ġayyaṛna fikrina.*

2. *ma-ggawwiztiš lē?* - ______________ *lākin ġayyaṛtᵊ fikri.*

3. *ma-ḥagaztīš makān lē?* - ______________ *lākin ġayyaṛtᵊ fikri.*

4. *ma-biʿtiš ilbēt lē?* - ______________ *lākin ġayyaṛtᵊ fikri.*

5. *ma-nziltūš issūʾ lē?* - ____________ *lākin ġayyaṛna fikrina.*

6. *ma-ruḥtiš Luʾṣur lē?* - ______________ *lākin ġayyaṛtᵊ fikri.*

7. *ma-rgiʿtiš badri lē?* - ______________ *lākin ġayyaṛtᵊ fikri.*

8. *ma-tnaʾaltūš lē?* - ____________ *lākin ġayyaṛna fikrina.*

9. *ma-ʾaʿadtiš hina lē?* - ______________ *lākin ġayyaṛtᵊ fikri.*

10. *ma-baʿattiš ilawlād lē?* - ______________ *lākin ġayyaṛtᵊ fikri.*

XII. Match one item from (a) with one item from (b).

	(a)	(b)
1.	*ʾāxud iššaʾʾa*	*niʿmilha ʿa‿ġada!*
2.	*di kānit ʾawwil maṛṛa*	*ma-fihāš tilivizyōn.*
3.	*ʿāwiz ʾōḍa*	*illi gibtaha‿nnahaṛda‿ṣṣubḥ.*
4.	*ana gayya ʾāxud ilʿaṛabiyya*	*illi kuntᵊ badawwaṛ ʿalē(h) .*
5.	*ʾādi‿lmuftāḥ*	*ašufhum fīha.*
6.	*fēn iddawa*	*illi fīha takyīf*
7.	*ḥāxud ilġurfa*	*ʾigaṛha aktaṛ min tultumīt ginē(h).*
8.	*ṭallaʿ mi‿lfirīzar laḥma*	*illi‿ddahūli‿dduktūr.*

9. *miš ʿāwiz ġurfa* *fīha tilifōn.*
10. *ma-ʾdarš aʾaggar šaʾʾa* *illi‿ʾgarha maʿʾūl.*

Answers:	1a + ___	2a + ___	3a + ___	4a + ___
	5a + ___	6a + ___	7a + ___	8a + ___
	9a + ___	10a + ___		

XIII. *kuntᵊ ḥatuʾʿud ʾaddᵊ ʾē‿f-Maṣr?* "How long were you going to stay in Egypt?" Give a short reply, as in the example below.

(2, yōm) *kuntᵊ ḥaʾʿud yomēn fi Maṣr.*

(3, yōm) ____________________

(7, sana) ____________________

(20, yōm) ____________________

(2, sana) ____________________

(15, šahṛ) ____________________

(5, šahṛ) ____________________

(9, ʾusbūʿ) ____________________

(11, ʾusbūʿ) ____________________

(6, sana) ____________________

(17, yōm) ____________________

(10, šahṛ) ____________________

(4, sāʿa) ____________________

XIV. Translate the following sentences.

1. The house that we had in Giza was tiny.

____

2. We've been living in Alexandria for two months now.

____

3. That's the house that we want to buy.

____

4. Breakfast will be ready at 7 o'clock.

____

5. We can take another bus.

____

6. They nearly died because of the heat.

____

7. The woman wore a long red dress.

____

8. The students were still here an hour ago.

____

9. You don't have to come before eight o'clock.

____

10. You (polite) can come any time you like.

____

11. Do you see the man who's wearing a green sweater? He's the doorman.

____

12. Is there a bank where I can change some money?

____

13. Can I buy a form and a revenue stamp from you?

____

14. Do you want the dress that's in the window (*fitrīna*)?

____

15. I'm taking the room that's on the 3rd floor.

____

16. I'll comc and have a look at the flat first.

____

17. The director needs a good secretary.

____

18. The number of your room is three hundred and twenty-five.

____

19. She wanted to (meant to) write a letter but she changed her mind.

____

20. When I arrived the official had (already) gone home.

____

LESSON XIII

READING PASSAGES

ḫādis faẓīɛ

1. *imbāriḫ bi‿llēl ṛawwaḫt ilbēt mitʾaxxaṛ šuwayya wi ka‿lɛāda fataḫt ittilivizyōn ɛašān atfaṛṛag ɛala našrit ilʾaxbāṛ.*

2. *ahammᵊ xabaṛ fi‿nnašṛa kān iġtiyāl raʾīs maglis iššaɛb. inḍarab fi‿ššāriɛ bi‿rruṣāṣ wi huwwa rākib ilɛaṛabiyya‿btaɛtu.*

3. *wi miš huwwa bass illi māt, talāta mi‿lḫuṛṛās itʾatalu‿f-nafs ilwaʾt, lākin issawwāʾ ma-gaṛalūš ḫāga.*

4. *illi ʾaṭlaqu‿nnāṛ ɛalē(h) kānu rakbīn mutusiklᵊ sarīɛ wi hirbu mubašáṛatan baɛd irtikāb ilgarīma. mabāḫis ʾamn iddawla bitdawwaṛ ɛalēhum fi-kullᵊ makān, wi‿lġāyit dilwaʾti ma-ʾidrūš yimsikūhum. iṛṛaʾīs bi-nafsu ṛāḫ ɛašān yišūf makān ilḫādis.*

5. *fī nās bitʾūl innuhum min iggamaɛāt ilmutaṭarrifa wi‿byitɛamlu maɛa gihāt agnabiyya wi‿byiddaṛṛabu ɛala ṭuruʾ iliġtiyāl fi‿lxārig.*

ɛand idduktūr

idduktūr: *ʾahlan ya Sāmi! salamtak! bāyin ɛalēk taɛbān ʾawi?*
Sāmi: *ana fiɛlan ɛayyān ʾawi ya duktūr. min imbāriḫ iṣṣubḫ w‿ana ḫāsis bi-ʾalam šidīd fi-baṭni.*
idduktūr: *ṭabb, itmaddid hina ɛašān akšif ɛalēk.*
Sāmi: *ḫāḍir ya duktūr!*
idduktūr: *ʾulli ḫāsis bi‿lʾalam fēn?*
Sāmi: *ilʾalam fi‿nnaḫya‿lyimīn ya duktūr!*
idduktūr: *ya-taṛa ɛandak suxuniyya wi‿btiɛraʾ wi ḫāsis bi-ṣudāɛ?*
Sāmi: *aywa ya duktūr, wi kamān ma-līš nifsᵊ li‿lʾakl!*
idduktūr: *min imta w‿inta ḫāsis bi‿lʾalam da?*
Sāmi: *min ʾusbūɛ taʾrīban. kān ɛandi nafs ilʾalam min ʾīmit šahṛ, bassᵊ ṛāḫ wi rigiɛ tāni dilwaʾti.*
idduktūr: *inta ɛandak iltihāb fi‿zzayda. lāzim tudxul ilmustašfa ḫālan wi titɛimillak ɛamaliyya‿f-aʾṛab waʾt.*
Sāmi: *wi‿lɛamaliyya di ḍarūri ya duktūr?*
idduktūr: *aywa, ḍarūri! maɛa‿ssalāma ya Sāmi, wi xud bālak min nafsak!*

VOCABULARY

ʾamn	safety
ʾaṭlaq, yuṭliq irruṣāṣ ɛala w	to shoot at
baṭn (f.), *buṭūn*	stomach
baɛḍ	each other; some
bān, yibān	to appear
bāyin ɛala w	to seem, to look ...
dawla, duwal	state
dawwaṛ ɛala ḥ	to look for
faẓīɛ, fuẓāɛ	terrible, dreadful
fiɛlan	really
gamāɛa, -āt	group
gaṛa, yigṛa li w ḥ	to happen (to s/o)
garīma, gaṛāyim	crime
gāmid	severe, strong
giha, -āt	party, institution
hirib, yihṛab	to escape, to flee
ḥaddid ḥ	to establish
ḥass, yiḥiss bi ḥ	to feel
ḥādis, ḥawādis	accident, event
ḥālan	immediately
ḥāris, ḥurrās	guard, bodyguard
iddaṛṛab	to be trained
iġtiyāl	murder
iltihāb, -āt	inflammation
inḍarab	to get shot, to be hit
irtikāb	committing
itʾatal	to be killed
itmaddid	to lie down
itɛamal	to be performed
itɛāmil	to work together
kašaf, yikšif ɛala w	to examine s/o (medically)
mabāḥis (pl.)	police investigation department
maglis, magālis	council
maṛṛ, yimurr ɛala w	to drop in on s/o
mawḍūɛ, -āt ~ mawaḍīɛ	matter, subject
mawɛid, mawaɛīd	appointment
māt, yimūt	to die
min ʾīmit	since, about
misik, yimsik ḥ	to arrest, to hold
mitʾaxxaṛ	late
mubašáratan	immediately
mutaṭarrif	extremist
mutusikl,-āt	motorbike
nafs	self; same
naḥya, nawāḥi	side, direction
našrit ilʾaxbāṛ	news broadcast
nifs	appetite, desire
ṛaʾīs, ruʾasa ~ ruʾasāʾ	president, chairman
ṛawwaḥ	to go home
ṛāḥa	rest
bi‿ṛṛāḥa	quietly, slowly
ruṣāṣ	bullet(s); lead (metal)
salāma	safety
salamtak!	get well!
suxuniyya	fever
ṣabi, ṣubyān	errand boy
ṣudāɛ	headache
šaɛb, šuɛūb	people
šidīd, šudād	heavy, severe
ṭarīʾa, ṭuruʾ	method, way
yōm	day
ilyomēn dōl	nowadays
zayda	appendix
zimīl, zumala ~ zumalāʾ	colleague
ɛamaliyya, -āt	operation
ɛāda, -āt	custom, habit
ɛiriʾ, yiɛraʾ	to sweat

GRAMMAR

I. *riglēn* + suffix (pseudo-dual)

The words (*rigl*) *riglēn* "feet, legs," (*ɛēn*) *ɛenēn* "eyes" and (*ʾīd*) *ʾidēn* "hands" look as though they are duals (→ VIII.I), but they function as plurals and can therefore have possessive suffixes added to them where necessary. In such cases the final *-n* of the plural ending *-ēn* is omitted.

riglēn	*riglē + ki*	>	*riglēki*	your (f.) feet
	riglē + hum	>	*riglēhum*	their feet
but:	*riglē + ya*	>	*riglayya*	my feet
	ʿenē + ya	>	*ʿenayya*	my eyes
	ʾidē + ya	>	*ʾidayya*	my hands

As for *riglayya*, *idayya*, etc, they are formed in the same way as *ʿalayya* (→ VIII.V).

In a genitive construction they are directly followed by the noun:

riglēn ittarabēza "the legs of the table" *ʿenēn ilbint* "the eyes of the girl"

II. Irregular verbs

The verbs *gih, yīgi* "to come," *idda, yiddi* "to give," *wiʾiʿ, yuʾaʿ* "to fall," and *wiʾif, yuʾaf* "to stop" "to stand" are irregular and do not conform to any pattern.

1. *gih ~ ga, yīgi* "to come": This verb is conjugated in the same way as the *a*-perfect and the *i*-imperfect of tert.inf. verbs (→ IX.III).

perfect			**imperfect**		
gih	*gēt*	*gēt*	*yīgi*	*tīgi*	*āgi*
gat	*gēti*		*tīgi*	*tīgi*	
gum	*gētu*	*gēna*	*yīgu*	*tīgu*	*nīgi*
imperative			**active participle**		
taʿāla, taʿāli, taʿālu			*gayy, gayya, gayyīn*		

With possessive suffixes, object suffixes, and with the *ma-...-š* of the negative, *gih* changes to *ga-*, and *gum* to *gu-* : *gāni* "he came to me," *ma-gāš* "he didn't come," *ma-gūš* "they didn't come."

The imperfect *yīgi, tīgi* etc. drops its *-ī-* when negated: *tīgi* → *ma-tgīš* "you shouldn't come," *yīgu* → *ma-ygūš* "they shouldn't come."

2. *idda, yiddi* "to give": The base form of the perfect is irregular, but it is conjugated in the same way as the *a*-perfect and the *i*-imperfect of tert. inf. verbs (→ IX.III).

perfect			**imperfect**		
idda	*iddēt*	*iddēt*	*yiddi*	*tiddi*	*addi*
iddit	*iddēti*		*tiddi*	*tiddi*	
iddu	*iddētu*	*iddēna*	*yiddu*	*tiddu*	*niddi*
imperative			**active participle**		
iddi, iddi, iddu			*middi, -yya, -yyīn*		

The verb *iddan, yiddan* "to call to prayer," too, does not fit into the normal verbal patterns, but follows the strong verb: *iddant* "I called to prayer", *yiddanu* "they call to prayer."

3. *wiʾiɛ, yuʾaɛ* "to fall" and *wiʾif, yuʾaf* "to stand" lose their *-w-* in the imperfect and the imperative. Their prefix is formed with *-u-* instead of *-i-*:

perfect			**imperfect**		
wiʾiɛ	*wiʾɛit*	*wiʾiɛt*	*yuʾaɛ*	*tuʾaɛ*	*aʾaɛ*
wiʾɛit	*wiʾiɛti*		*tuʾaɛ*	*tuʾaɛi*	
wiʾɛu	*wiʾiɛtu*	*wiʾiɛna*	*yuʾaɛu*	*tuʾaɛu*	*nuʾaɛ*
imperative			**active participle**		
uʾaɛ, uʾaɛi, uʾaɛu			*wāʾiɛ, waʾɛa, waʾɛīn*		

III. Verb stems *n*-VII, X and IV

1. inKaTaB, yin**K**i**T**i**B**: In addition to the *it* + base stem already mentioned in lesson XI.II, there is also an *in* + base stem, which has a passive meaning. This *n*-VII stem only occurs with a limited number of verbs and some set expressions such as:

	inkatab kitabha	"she's got engaged"
but	*itkatab iggawāb*	"the letter was written"
	inḍarab bi_rruṣāṣ	"he was struck by a bullet"
but	*iḍḍarab ḫittit ɛalʾa*	"he was given such a beating"

2. ista**KT**a**B**, yista**KT**a**B** and ista**KT**i**B**, yista**KT**i**B**: Stem X is formed with the help of the prefix *ista-*. An *-a-* or *-i-* appears in the last syllable, just as happened in stem II (→ XI.I). It often has the meaning of "to consider" or "to seek":

istaɛmil, yistaɛmil	"to use"	*istafhim, yistafhim*	"to inform oneself"
istaġrab, yistaġrab	"to be amazed"	*istaġla, yistaġla*	"to find s/th expensive"
istalṭaf, yistalṭaf	"to like"	*istaɛbaṭ, yistaɛbaṭ*	"to play the fool"

3. ʾa**KT**a**B**, yu**KT**i**B** ~ yi**KT**i**B** ~ yi**KT**a**B**: You will sometimes encounter verbs from stem IV which have been borrowed from Modern Standard Arabic. These verbs have *ʾa-* in the perfect, and generally *yu-* as the prefix in the imperfect:

ʾaṭlaq, yuṭliq innāṛ	"to shoot"	*ʾalqa, yulqi xiṭāb*	"to give a speech"
ʾaslam, yislam	"to become a Muslim"	*ʾaḍrab, yuḍrib*	"to strike"
ʾakṛam, yikrim	"to be generous to"	*ʾatāḫ, yutīḫ ~ yitīḫ*	"to allow"

4. Sometimes passive verbs are also borrowed from Modern Standard Arabic:

uġma, yuġma ɛalē(h)	"he fainted"	*tuškaṛ*	"accept my thanks!"
uġma ɛalēha	"she fainted"	*yuɛtabaṛ*	"it is considered to be"

IV. *nafs* "same" "the same" and "oneself"

1. The word "same" is expressed by *nafs* followed by a defined noun; *nafs* and the noun form a genitive construction:

nafs iṛṛāgil	the same man
nafs ilmudarrisīn	the same teachers
nafs iššēʾ	the same thing
nafs ilḫikāya	the same story
fi-nafs ilwaʾt	at the same time

2. If *nafs* is placed after a defined noun, it is always given a suffix which refers to that noun, and the meaning of *nafs* changes to "self":

iṛṛāgil nafsu	the man himself
ilmudarrisa nafsaha	the teacher herself

To indicate "myself" "yourself" etc, the preposition *bi-* is placed before *nafs*:

ana‿b-nafsi "I myself" *hiyya‿b-nafsaha* "she herself"

3. When placed after the verb, *nafs* followed by an appropriate suffix has the reflexive meaning of "oneself":

iḫna šayfīn nafsina fi‿lmirāya	"we see ourselves in the mirror"
biykallim nafsu ṭūl innahāṛ	"he talks to himself all day long"
biyfakkaṛ fi-nafsu‿w bass	"he only thinks of himself"

V. *wala* and *ʾayy*

When *wala* or *ʾayy* are used in a negative sentence with an undefined noun, they mean "nothing at all," "not a single," "no ... at all."

1. *wala* followed by a noun in the singular, usually refers to countable things:

ma-fīš wala šagaṛa fi‿gginēna di	"there isn't a single tree in this garden"
ma-fhimtiš wala kilma min kalāmak	"I haven't understood a single word of what you said"

2. *ʾayy* is used with non-countable and abstract nouns, as well as collectives (→ XIV.I) and plurals:

ana miš ḫāsis bi-ʾayyᵊ ʾalam	"I feel no pain at all"
ma-fīš ʾayyᵊ gaṛāyim ʿandina	"we don't have any crime at all"
ma-lhūš ʾayyᵊ ṛaʾyᵊ fi‿lmasʾala	"he has no opinion on the matter"

N.B. *Whether *wala* or *ʾayy* is used frequently depends upon what it is that the speaker wants to emphasize:

so:	*ma-fīš ʾayyᵊ namlᵊ hina*	"there really aren't any ants here"
but:	*ma-fīš wala namla hina*	"there isn't a single ant here"

VI. The circumstantial clause

1. Definition: In Arabic, a circumstantial clause is used to express an action or event which took place simultaneously with the situation or event expressed in the main clause. There are modal circumstantial clauses and temporal circumstantial clauses.

(a) A **modal** circumstantial clause always refers to the subject or object of the main clause, and describes its situation or state of mind at the time when the event in the main clause takes place.
N.B. In English this would not necessarily be expressed in a clause; a participle or prepositional phrase might be used instead.

(b) A **temporal** circumstantial clause refers to an event which happens at the same time as the event in the main clause. This event does not necessarily relate to the subject or object of the main clause.
N.B. in English the temporal circumstantial clause might be translated simply as a clause of time, but a participle phrase or an adverb might also be used.

(a) modal	*Ḥasan rigiɛ ilbēt wi huwwa zaɛlān* Ḥasan came home and he was angry [i.e. angrily, in a temper]
	sibnāha ʾaɛda fi‿gginēna We left her sitting in the garden
(b) temporal	*inḍarab bi‿rruṣāṣ wi huwwa rākib ilɛaṛabiyya‿btaɛtu* he was hit by bullets while he was sitting in his car
	Fawzi‿ggawwiz w‿ana fi‿lxārig Fawzi got married while I was abroad

2. Stucture
(a) The circumstantial clause follows the main clause. It usually has the structure: *wi* + subject + predicate. The predicate can be an adjectival, participial, prepositional, or verbal phrase with a *bi*-imperfect:

fāt ɛalayya fi‿lbēt	*w‿ana miš mawgūd*	"and I wasn't there"
"he came to my house"	*w‿ana‿msāfir*	"while I was traveling"
	w‿iḥna fi‿lxārig	"while we were abroad"
	w‿iḥna‿bnitġadda	"as we were having dinner"

sāb ilmaṭɛam wi huwwa lissa gaɛān "still hungry, he left the restaurant"

(b) A circumstantial clause can also be formed by using a prepositional phrase with the meaning "to have" (→ V.I), then it has the structure: *wi* + prepositional phrase:

rigiɛ wi‿mɛā‿flūs "he came back with some money"

3. Use
(a) A temporal circumstantial clause is used to express the simultaneity of the events in the main and in the subordinate clauses. It can be put

either in front of the main clause or after it. In both cases it would correspond to a clause of time in English and would be introduced by words such as "when," "while" or "as":

safirtᵊ Kanada w‿ana ṭālib "I went to Canada when I was a student"
or: *w‿ana ṭālib safirtᵊ Kanada*

(b) In a main clause containing a reference to a period in time, the latter can be placed first, and the main clause transformed into a temporal circumstantial clause with the structure *wi* + subject + predicate:

baḥāwil akallimak fi‿ttilifōn baʾāli sāɛa
→ *baʾāli sāɛa w‿ana baḥāwil akallimak fi‿ttilifōn*
"I've been trying to call you by phone for a whole hour"

ana ḥāsis bi-ʾalam šidīd fi-baṭni min imbāriḥ iṣṣubḥ
→ *min imbāriḥ iṣṣubḥ w‿ana ḥāsis bi-ʾalam šidīd fi-baṭni*
"I've had this terrible stomach ache since yesterday morning"

(c) If a modal circumstantial clause follows a verb of movement such as *ṛawwaḥ, rigiɛ, ṛāḥ, miši, gih, nizil, ṭiliɛ, daxal,* or *xaṛag*, you can omit *wi* + pronoun provided that the circumstantial clause refers to the **subject** of the main clause. In English such clauses are frequently expressed by a present participle:

xaṛagtᵊ min ɛandu miš ɛārif ṛāsi min riglayya (= *w‿ana miš ɛārif...*)
"I left him not knowing if I was on my head or my heels"

ɛadda ɛa‿lʾismᵊ rākib ḥumāṛu (= *w‿huwwa rākib ḥumāṛu*)
"he passed the police station riding his donkey"

When the circumstantial clause is both modal and prepositional, *wi* can also be omitted:

daxalit maɛāha ṣaniyyit ilʾahwa (= *wi‿mɛāha ṣaniyyit ilʾahwa*
"she came in with a tray of coffee"

(d) When a circumstantial clause follows a verb referring to one of the senses such as *šāf, yišūf* and *simiɛ, yismaɛ*, you can omit *wi* + subject provided that the circumstantial clause refers to the **object** of the main clause:

šāfit iṛṛāgil wi huwwa xārig mi‿lbēt → *šāfit iṛṛāgil xārig mi‿lbēt*
"she saw the man leaving the house"

kuntᵊ samɛā(h) wi huwwa‿byindah ɛalēk → *kuntᵊ samɛā‿byindah ɛalēk*
"I could hear him calling you"

VII. Verbs with two objects

1. Nouns as objects

(a) Verbs such as *idda, yiddi* "to give" and *warra, yiwarri* "to show" can have two objects, where the first object refers to "people" who receive something, and the second object refers to "things" which are received:

	person	thing
iddēt	*Ḫasan*	*ilfilūs*
I gave	Ḫasan	the money
warrēt	*issuwwāḫ*	*ilmatḫaf*
I showed	the tourists	the museum

Other verbs of this type are:

ʿallim w ḫ "to teach s/o s/th" — *fahhim w ḫ* "to explain s/th to s/o"
sallif w ḫ "to lend s/o s/th" — *nāwil w ḫ* "to hand s/th to s/o"
sallim w ḫ "to hand s/o s/th" — *wakkil w ḫ* "to feed s/o s/th"

fahhimt iṛṛāgil ilmuškila	"I explained the problem to the man"
ʿallimit uxtaha iṭṭabīx	"she taught her sister how to cook"
ḫanwakkil ilʾawlād ʾē?	"what shall we give the children to eat?"
nawilt ilʾusṭa‿lmifakk	"I handed the workman the screwdriver"

(b) It is possible to reverse the order, and put the "thing" first and the "person" second, but in such cases the person must be preceded by the preposition *li-* "to," which automatically gives emphasis to the person:

	thing	person
iddēt	*ilfilūs*	*li-Ḫasan*
I gave	the money	to Ḫasan
warrēt	*ilmatḫaf*	*li‿ssuwwāḫ*
I showed	the museum	to the tourists

*sallift*ᵊ *mīt ginē(h) li-ṣaḫbi*	"I lent 100 pounds to my friend"
*nawilt ilmifakk*ᵊ *li‿lʾusṭa*	"I handed the screwdriver to the workman"

2. Suffixes as objects

Verbs of this type can also be followed by object suffixes instead of nouns.

(a) The noun representing the "thing" can be replaced by a direct object suffix which is attached directly to the verb, while the noun designating the "person" follows as an indirect object preceeded by *li* (→ 1,b above):

iddēt ilfilūs li-Ḫasan	→	*iddetha‿l-Ḫasan*
I gave the money to Ḫasan		I gave it to Ḫasan
warri lkitāb li-ḅaḅāki	→	*warrī‿l-ḅaḅāki*
show the book to your father		show it to your father

sallimhum li‿lbulīs	"he handed them to the police"
lāzim tiwarrīha l-ḅaḅāki	"you must show it to your father"

(b) When the noun designating the "person" is replaced by a suffix, then the suffix can either:

* be placed directly after the verb as a direct object
* or introduced by *li-* as an indirect object:

iddētu‿lfilūs	~	*iddetlu‿lfilūs*	I gave him the money
warrīha‿ššaᵓᵓa	~	*warrilha‿ššaᵓᵓa*	show her the flat!

ḫaddīlak fikra ʿa‿lli ḫaṣal	"I'll give you an idea of what happened"
ḫayiddīni‿lbasbōr	"he will give me the passport"

Note that: In the case of the 1st person singular, it is the direct object *-ni* that is commonly used (and not *li-* with the indirect object): *iddāni‿lʿaṛabiyya* rather than *iddāli‿lʿaṛabiyya* "he gave me the car."

(c) If both "person" and "thing" are represented by suffixes, then the "thing" must be attached to the verb as a direct object suffix, while the suffix designating the person follows as an indirect object preceeded by *li-* .

iddēt ilfilūs li-Ḫasan	→	*iddethālu* I gave it to him
warra‿lmatḫaf li‿ssuwwāḫ	→	*warrahulhum* he showed it to them

The forms of the suffixes are somewhat different from usual (→ X.VI).

STEM FORMS OF THE VERB

STRONG VERBS

I *katab, yiktib* *misik, yimsik*	II *kassaṛ, yikassaṛ* *ɛallim, yiɛallim*	III *ʾābil, yiʾābil* *sāfir, yisāfir*
VII *itkatab, yitkitib* *itmasak, yitmisik*	V *itkassaṛ, yitkassaṛ* *itɛallim, yitɛallim*	VI *itʾābil, yitʾābil* *itbādil, yitbādil*
n-VII *inbaṣaṭ, yinbiṣiṭ* *inḍarab, yinḍirib*	X *istaġṛab, yistaġṛab* *istaɛmil, yistaɛmil*	IX *iḫmaṛṛ, yiḫmaṛṛ* *ismaṛṛ, yismaṛṛ*
VIII *iftakaṛ, yiftikir* *ištaġal, yištaġal*		IV *ʾaṭlaq, yuṭliq* *ʾakṛam, yikrim*

WEAK VERBS

I *fakk, yifukk* *dāx, yidūx* *šāl, yišīl* *rama, yirmi* *miši, yimši*	II *ʾammim, yiʾammim* *dawwax, yidawwax* *šayyil, yišayyil* *ṛabba, yiṛabbi* *mašša, yimašši*	III *šāwir, yišāwir* *dāyiʾ, yidāyiʾ* *dāra, yidāri*
VII *itfakk, yitfakk* *itʾāl, yitʾāl* *itbāɛ, yitbāɛ* *itrama, yitrimi*	V *itʾammim, yitʾammim* *iṣṣawwaṛ, yiṣṣawwaṛ* *itġayyaṛ, yitġayyaṛ* *itmašša, yitmašša*	VI *itšāwir, yitšāwir* *iddāyiʾ, yiddāyiʾ* *iddāra, yiddāra*
n-VII *inḫall, yinḫall* *inḫāz, yinḫāz* *inḫana, yinḫini*	X *istalazz, yistalazz* *istafād, yistafād* *istaġla, yistaġla*	IX *iswadd, yiswadd* *ibyaḍḍ, yibyaḍḍ* *iḫlaww, yiḫlaww*
VIII *iḫtall, yiḫtall* *ixtāṛ, yixtāṛ* *ištaka, yištiki*		IV *ʾatāḫ, yutīḫ* *ʾalqa, yulqi*

EXERCISES

I. Is that another one? No, it's the same one.

da‿ktāb tāni? - *lā, da nafs ikkitāb!*

1. *šāfu ɛaṛabiyya tanya?* - *lā, ________________!*
2. *fī sabab tāni?* - *lā, ________________!*
3. *da maraḍ tāni?* - *lā, ________________!*
4. *ʾaggaṛti šaʾʾa tanya?* - *lā, ________________!*
5. *ḫatāxud ʾutubīs tāni?* - *lā, ________________!*
6. *ḫayīgi‿f-yōm tāni?* - *lā, ________________!*
7. *ḫatrūḫu ḫafla tanya?* - *lā, ________________!*
8. *huwwa ʾallak kalām tāni?* - *lā, ________________!*
9. *iššaʾʾa‿btaɛtak fi‿ɛmāṛa tanya?* - *lā, ________________!*
10. *inti ḫatnāmi‿f-ʾōḍa tanya?* - *lā, ________________!*

II. Yes, they're doing it themselves! Confirm what is being said.

inta‿lli ḫatrūḫ? - *aywa, ana‿b-nafsi.*

1. *inti‿lli ḫatgībi‿lfilūs?* - *aywa, ________________.*
2. *intu‿lli ḫatʾaggaṛu‿ššaʾʾa?* - *aywa, ________________.*
3. *huwwa‿lli ḫayṣallaḫ ittakyīf?* - *aywa, ________________.*
4. *hiyya‿lli ḫatibɛatli xabaṛ?* - *aywa, ________________.*
5. *humma‿lli ḫayištaġalu hina?* - *aywa, ________________.*
6. *iḫna‿lli kunna ɛayzīn kida?* - *aywa, ________________.*
7. *inta‿lli naḍḍaft ilʾōḍa?* - *aywa, ________________.*

III. Two things happen simultaneously. Show this by using a circumstantial clause.

kān hina, lamma kuntu baṛṛa → kān hina w‿intu baṛṛa.

1. *ḥassᵊ‿b-ᵓalam, lamma kān biyitɛašša.*

____

2. *šuftaha, lamma kuntᵊ batfassaḥ fi‿nnādi.*

____

3. *šufnā xārig, lamma kunna ᵓaɛdīn fi‿lbalakōna.*

____

4. *kunna binfakkaṛ fīha, lamma kunna fi‿ggamɛa.*

____

5. *fātu ɛala Asyūṭ, lamma kānu ṛayḥīn Aswān.*

____

6. *lamma kuntᵊ ṛayḥa‿ssūᵓ, ᵓabiltuhum fi‿ssikka.*

____

7. *saᵓalu ɛala ḥaḍritak, lamma kuntᵊ miš mawgūd.*

____

8. *ɛamaltu ᵓē, lamma kuntᵊ‿msafra?*

____

9. *lamma kunna‿bnišṛab iššāy, gōzi ḥakāli kullᵊ šēᵓ.*

____

10. *lamma kuntᵊ baḥaḍḍar ilfiṭār, laᵓēt innᵊ ma-fīš šāy fi‿lbēt.*

____

IV. Rewrite de sentences using a circumstantial clause.

lamma ᵓalli kida, kān farḥān → ᵓalli kida‿w huwwa farḥān.

1. *lamma daxal maktabu, kān zaɛlān.*

____

2. *lamma ᵓallaha kida, kānu‿byitmaššu.*

____

3. *lamma sallimtᵊ ɛalē(h), kuntᵊ farḥāna.*

____

4. *lamma xaṛagna, kān maɛāna ɛišrīn ginē(h).*

____

5. *lamma ṛāḥu Maṣr, kānu lissa‿ṣġayyaṛīn.*

____

6. *lamma‿smiʕnāha, kānit bitkallim Ḥasan.*

____

7. *lamma šufnāhum, kānu‿byitmaššu ʕa‿kkurnīš.*

____

8. *lamma‿nḍarab bi‿rruṣāṣ, kān rākib ilʕaṛabiyya.*

____

9. *lamma ʔaṛa‿ggurnāḷ, kān ʔāʕid fi‿lbalakōna.*

____

10. *lamma‿štara‿lʕaṛabiyya di, kān fi-ʔUṛubba.*

____

V. Form circumstantial clauses by combining sentences from (a) and (b).

	(a)	(b)
1.	*šāf miṛātu*	*wi humma ʔaʕdīn fi‿lbalakōna*
2.	*ʔibni gih yizurni*	*wi‿mṛātu‿mʕā*
3.	*xadna ṣūra ḥilwa‿lʕAli*	*wi hiyya‿btirkab ʕaṛabiyyitha*
4.	*ṭalab ilḥisāb*	*w‿ana fi‿lmustašfa*
5.	*ilʕaskari ʔabaḍ ʕalē*	*wi‿ḥna lissa ʔaʕdīn ʕa‿ssufṛa*
6.	*wiʔiʕ fi‿lmayya*	*wi huwwa‿byitfaṛṛag ʕa‿lmaʕbad*
7.	*rigiʕ min Faṛansa*	*w‿iḥna binʕaddi ʕa‿kkubri*
8.	*ḥakit li-gozha kullᵊ ḥāga*	*wi huwwa biyḥāwil yihṛab*

1a + ______	2a + ______	3a + ______	4a + ______
5a + ______	6a + ______	7a + ______	8a + ______

VI. Use a circumstantial clause to indicate the length of time.

ma-banamšᵊ min talat t-iyyām →
min talat t-iyyām w‿ana ma-banamš

1. *ʕandu suxuniyya min imbāriḥ.*

____

2. *baštaġal sawwāʔ min sanatēn.*

____

3. *ana‿f-Maṣrᵊ min šahṛᵊ Māris.*

____

4. *ʿandi ṣudāʿ min imbāriḥ iṣṣubḥ.*

____

5. *ana mistanniyyāki min sāʿa‿w nuṣṣ.*

____

6. *biyitfaṛṛagu ʿa‿ttilivizyōn min issāʿa tamanya.*

____

7. *ṃāṃa fi‿lmustašfa min talat t-iyyām.*

____

8. *baḥāwil atʿallim ilʿaṛabi min mudda ṭawīla.*

____

9. *biyiddaṛṛabu fi‿lxārig min talat šuhūr.*

____

10. *iḥna saknīn fi‿zZaʾazīʾ min ʿašaṛ sinīn.*

____

VII. Write a suitable form of *gih* or *idda* in each blank.

1. *Jane* ______________ *Maṣrᵊ min sanatēn.* *(gih)*
2. *ilʾutubīs lissa ma-*______________*-š.* *(gih)*
3. *bukṛa* ______________*-lak ilʾigāṛ.* *(idda)*
4. ______________ *-ni‿lmuftāḥ ya madām!* *(idda)*
5. ______________ *hina min faḍlik!* *(gih)*
6. *iḍḍiyūf* ______________ *imbāriḥ.* *(gih)*
7. *ya-taṛa humma* ________ *walla lissa ma-* ________ *-š?* *(gih)*
8. ______________ *Ḥasan ilmuftāḥ lē, ya Maha?* *(idda)*
9. ______________*-u‿lmuftāḥ wi mišyit.* *(idda)*
10. *ana* ______________ *ḥālan!* *(gih)*
11. ______________ *badri kida lē, ya Samya?* *(gih)*
12. *mumkin* ______________ *-ni fikra ʿan ilmawḍūʿ da?* *(idda)*

VIII. Answer in the negative using *wala* or *ᵓayy*.

ya-taṛa fī ward? - *laᵓ, ma-fīš wala warda.*

1. *ya-taṛa‿fhimtu kalāmi?* - *laᵓ, ________________ kilma.*

2. *ɛandik fikṛa ɛan ilmawḍūɛ da?* - *laᵓ, ________________ fikṛa*

3. *inti ḫassa‿b-ᵓalam fi-riglik?* - *laᵓ, ________________ ᵓalam.*

4. *fī tuffāḫ fi‿ttallāga?* - *laᵓ, ________________ tuffāḫa.*

5. *maɛāk sagāyir?* - *laᵓ, ________________ sigāṛa.*

6. *ɛandak badla ɛašān ilḫafla?* - *laᵓ, ________________ badla.*

7. *ilᵓōḍa di fīha šababīk?* - *laᵓ, ________________ šibbāk.*

8. *maɛāk ittazākir bitaɛt‿ilḫafla?* - *laᵓ, ________________ tazākir.*

9. *fī šuᵓaᵓ faḍya fi‿lɛAgami?* - *laᵓ, ____________ šaᵓᵓa faḍya.*

10. *ɛanduku‿drūs innahaṛda?* - *laᵓ, ________________ durūs.*

11. *fī mutusiklāt fi‿ggaṛāž?* - *laᵓ, ______________ mutusikl.*

12. *ḫaṣalit garīma fi‿lMaɛādi?* - *laᵓ, ________________ gaṛāyim.*

IX. Of course they've already done it! Give a logical reply.

iddēt ilwalad ilfilūs?
ṭabɛan, iddētu‿lfilūs.

1. *huwwa Ḫasan idda ṣaḫb‿ilbēt ilᵓigāṛ?*

   ṭabɛan, ____.

2. *hiyya Maha ᵓiddit ibnaha‿lmuftāḫ?*

   ṭabɛan, ____.

3. *ḫatwarri ṣaḫbitak ilbalad?*

   ṭabɛan, ____.

4. *huwwa warra‿ssuwwāḫ Xān ilXalīli?*

   ṭabɛan, ____.

5. *salliftᵊ Ḥasan kitābak?*

ṭabɛan, ______________________________________.

6. *fahhimt iṛṛāgil ilmawḍūɛ?*

ṭabɛan, ______________________________________.

7. *nawilti Sayyid ilmalḥ?*

ṭabɛan, ______________________________________.

8. *ḥatsallif Samīr ilmīt ginē(h)?*

ṭabɛan, ______________________________________.

9. *ɛallimtu‿ṭṭalaba illuġa‿lɛaṛabiyya?*

ṭabɛan, ______________________________________.

10. *sallimtu‿lmuwaẓẓaf mafatīḥ ilmaktab?*

ṭabɛan, ______________________________________.

11. *warrēt iṭṭālibāt ilmaktaba?*

ṭabɛan, ______________________________________.

12. *iddētu‿Mḥammad‿lfilūs?*

ṭabɛan, ______________________________________.

Repeat the above, this time giving a reply in the negative:
laʾ, ma-ddetūš ilfilūs.

X. Organize the words into sentences.

1. *bi‿llēl, šuwayya, ṛawwaḥu, mitʾaxxaṛ, imbāriḥ.*

____

2. *ittilivizyōn, tišūf, fataḥit, ɛašān, našrit ilʾaxbāṛ.*

____

3. *ɛala, nafs, itfaṛṛagna, ilfilm, fi, imbāriḥ, ittilivizyōn.*

____

4. *bitāɛ, ɛaṛabiyya, iddīni, ilmuftāḥ, law samaḥt!*

____

5. *iššuġl, fūt, wi, ya Maḫmūd, ʕalēna, ṛāyiḫ, inta!*

6. *ilʕaṛabiyya, irruṣāṣ, wi, bi, huwwa, ḍarabū, rākib.*

7. *kān, šahṛ, ʕandi, nafs, ilʔalam, min.*

8. *aʔṛab, lāzim, izzayda, fi, waʔt, tiʕmil, ʕamaliyyit.*

9. *yimkin, nisāfir, baʕd, Aswān, bukṛa.*

10. *wiʔiʕ, riglu, imbāriḫ, wi, itkasaṛit, ibni.*

XI. Translate the following sentences.

1. He wanted to go and fetch the children himself.

2. Thank God nothing happened to the chauffeur!

3. We want to watch TV now!

4. There isn't a single girl in the class.

5. I've had a headache since this morning.

6. I've got (I feel) a severe pain in my legs.

7. My father died while I was abroad.

8. I had thirty pounds with me.

9. He bought two books and gave them to *Layla.*

10. I'll change the money next week.

11. The child had a high fever.

12. I won't buy that pullover for you, *Samya*!

13. Our appointment (*maɛād*), don't forget it *Ḥasan*!

14. Where have you been *Maha*? I haven't seen you for so long.

15. I have to watch the news every day.

16. The police looked for him everywhere, but they didn't find him.

17. They sat at home while it was raining (outside).

18. *Ṭāriʔ* didn't feel like (*nifs*) eating.

19. The police have come to ask about *Aḥmad* and *Ṭāriʔ*.

20. She came inside with a book in her hand.

LESSON XIV

READING PASSAGE

ziyāṛit wafdᵊ rasmi

1. *lamma‿ṣḥīt innahaṛda‿ṣṣubḥ, laʾēt nafsi zahʾān wi ma-līš nifs aɛmil ʾayyᵊ ḥāga.*

2. *fa sibt ilbēt wi mašaklu, wi ruḥt atmašša ɛa‿kkurnīš.*

3. *lamma‿wṣilt ikkurnīš laʾēt iddinya zaḥma ɛa‿lʾāxir, wi‿lʾaɛlām miɛallaʾa‿f-kullᵊ makān, wi‿lɛasākir ṛayḥīn gayyīn zayyᵊ ma‿ykūn fi mūlid walla ɛīd w‿ana miš wāxid bāli.*

4. *ma-fīš xamas daʾāyiʾ wi‿ddinya‿tʾalabit wi wiʾfit ɛala rigl: kalaksāt wi dawša wi hēṣa.*

5. *fa saʾaltᵊ wāḥid m‿illi waʾfīn ɛa‿rraṣīf ʾē‿lḥikāya, ʾalli ʾinnᵊ fi wafdᵊ rasmi min ʾIṭalya ḥayfūt min hina. ilwafdᵊ da wiṣil maṭāṛ ilQāhira innahaṛda‿ṣṣubḥ, wi kān f‿istiʾbālu ṛaʾīs iggumhuriyya wi ɛadad kibīr min ilmasʾulīn.*

6. *lamma‿lwafdᵊ ɛadda wi huwwa‿f-ṭarīʾu‿l-ʾAṣrᵊ ɛAbdīn, kān fi aktaṛ min ɛišrīn ɛaṛabiyya wi ɛasākir wi ẓubbāṭ wi yufaṭ maktūb ɛalēha "Miṣru turaḥḥibu bi-ḍuyūfihā."*

7. *baɛdᵊ kida ɛirift inn ilwafdᵊ da gih bi-munasbit iftitāḥ muʾtamaṛ ilɛilaqāt iliqtiṣadiyya w‿innu ʾām bi‿ttawqīɛ ɛala ɛaʾdᵊ bi-xṣūṣ mašruɛāt ṣinaɛiyya muštaṛaka bēn Maṣrᵊ w‿ʾIṭalya.*

8. *baɛd ilwafdᵊ ma ɛadda rigɛit ilḥayā fi‿ššawāriɛ ka‿lɛāda wi kaʾannᵊ ma-fīš ḥāga ḥaṣalit.*

VOCABULARY

ʾAṣrᵊ ɛAbdīn	Abdin Palace	*kaʾann*	as if
ʾāxir	last, latest	*kalaks, -āt*	claxon, hooter, horn
ɛa‿lʾāxir	extremely	*kifāya*	enough
bi-xṣūṣ	concerning	*ikkurnīš*	the esplanade
dawša	noise	*masʾūl*	responsible
ḍēf, ḍuyūf	guest	*mašrūɛ, -āt ~ mašarīɛ*	project
gumhuriyya	republic	*Miṣr ~ Maṣr*	Egypt
hēṣa	commotion	*miɛallaʾ*	hanging
hudūʾ	quietness	*muʾtamaṛ, -āt*	conference
ḥasab, yiḥsib ḥ	to reckon, to think	*muštaṛak*	joint, common
ḥayā	life	*mūlid*	holy day
iftitāḥ	opening inauguration	*ṛaḥḥab bi w ḥ*	to welcome (s/o)
iqtiṣādi	economic	*raṣīf, arṣifa*	pavement, sidewalk
itʾalab	to be turned upside down	*ṣiḥi, yiṣḥa*	to wake up
itmašša	to walk along to stroll	*ṣināɛi*	industrial
		šaraḥ, yišṛaḥ ḥ	to explain
ka-	(such) as	*tawqīɛ*	signature

wafd, wufūd	delegation
wi⊃if, yu⊃af ¿ala rigl	to be in an uproar
xad, yāxud bālu (min)	to watch to pay attention (to)
xiyāṛ (c.)	cucumbers
yafṭa, yufaṭ	banner, notice board
zah⊃ān	bored
ziyāṛa, -āt	visit
¿a⊃d, ¿u⊃ūd	treaty
¿adad, a¿dād	amount, number
¿alam, a¿lām	flag, banner
¿allim, yi¿allim ḅ ~ *w*	to mark s/th to teach s/o
¿āda, -āt	custom
¿ilāqa, -āt	relationship
¿īd, a¿yād	official celebration

GRAMMAR

I. Collectives and materials

1. Definition: Collectives (c.) are the names for groups of things and refer to a species in general, rather than one single item or unit (n.u.). For example *bēḍ* and *burtu⊃ạn* are "eggs" and "oranges" in general. In order to indicate one individual egg, the suffix *-a* is added to the collective noun, e.g. *bēḍa* "an egg," *burtu⊃āna* "an orange." Sometimes the ending *-āya* is also used to indicate one individual unit: *ṭamāṭim* → *ṭamaṭmāya* "a (small) tomato."

The plural and the dual are formed from the n.u.:

bēḍ → *bēḍa* → *beḍāt* → *beḍtēn*
baṣal → *baṣala* → *baṣalāt* → *baṣaltēn.*

In the same way, the name of a material can be used, with the addition of the suffix *-a*, to refer to a piece of that material e.g: *gild* "leather" → *gilda* "a leather washer," *ṣabūn* "soap" → *ṣabūna* "one piece of soap."

	collective (c.)	**single unit** (n.u.)
date palms	*naxl*	*naxla, -āt*
eggs	*bēḍ*	*bēḍa, -āt*
fishes	*samak*	*samaka, -āt*
flowers	*ward*	*warda, -āt*
lemons	*lamūn*	*lamūna, -āt*
mangoes	*manga* (fem.)	*mangāya, -āt*
onions	*baṣal*	*baṣala, -āt*
oranges	*burtu⊃ạn*	*burtu⊃āna, -āt*
potatoes	*baṭāṭis* (fem.)	*baṭaṭsāya, -āt*
tomatoes	*⊃ūṭa* (fem.)	*⊃uṭāya, -āt*
	ṭamāṭim (fem.)	*ṭamaṭmāya, -āt*
trees	*šagaṛ*	*šagaṛa, -āt*
water melons	*baṭṭīx*	*baṭṭīxa, -āt*
	material	**single item**
leather	*gild*	*gilda, -āt*
paper	*wara⊃*	*wara⊃a, -āt*
soap	*ṣabūn*	*ṣabūna, -āt*
wood	*xašab*	*xašaba, -āt*

2. Use of collectives and materials:

(a) To express "three eggs" for instance, you should combine the name for the single unit with a number according to the rules given in lesson VI.V.

aṛbaɛ beḍāt	"four eggs"	*ḫidāšaṛ baṭṭīxa*	"eleven watermelons"
xamastāšaṛ bēḍa	"fifteen eggs"	*talatīn naxla*	"thirty palm trees"

(b) After *kām* "how many" "several," the n.u. is used (→ V.VI.4):

ɛāwiz kām lamūna?	"how many lemons do you want?"
iddīni kām waraʾa kida!	"give me some sheets of paper!"

(c) After *šuwayya* "some" "a little" "a few," the collective is used:

iddīni‿šwayyit ruzz, ya‿Mḫammad "give me some rice, Muḫammad!"

Note that if a word does not have a collective form, the plural is used after *šuwayya* :

ɛandi‿šwayyit ṣuwar ḫilwīn ʾawi "I've got a few really nice photos"

(d) When ordering in a restaurant you should combine the collective with the long version of the numbers 3 to 10 (→ V.VI.2):

talāta samak	"three portions of fish!"
xamsa baṭṭīx	"five portions of water melon!"
itnēn ruzz	"two portions of rice"

II. Negative particles

1. *miš*

(a) In a nominal sentence *miš* is placed before the predicate. In a verbal sentence, *miš* is placed before the *ḫa*-imperfect, and in a participle phrase it is placed before the participle:

ɛAli miš fi‿lmaktaba	"Ali is not in the library"
ana miš mudarris	"I'm not a teacher"
ɛAli miš miggawwiz	"ɛAli's not married"
ilḫafla miš innahaṛda	"the party is not today"
ilwafdᵊ miš ḫayɛaddi min hina	"the delegation won't be coming past here"
ana miš wāxid bāli	"I don't quite understand"

(b) *miš* also introduces rhetorical questions when a positive reply is expected, and it is used even with verbs which would normally form the negative with *ma-.. -š* :

miš ilɛīd innahaṛda	"surely the holy day is today?"
miš da‿bɛīd ɛalēk šuwayya	"isn't that a bit far for you?"
miš ʾultilak kida imbāriḫ	"didn't I tell you that yesterday?"
miš tiskut aḫsan	"wouldn't you rather shut up?"

2. *ma-...-š*

(a) *ma-...-š* can be used to negate the perfect, the *bi*-imperfect and the imperfect:

ma-gūš imbāriḫ	"they didn't come yesterday"
ma-biyḫibbiš yiʾūm badri	"he doesn't like getting up early"
ma-tʾulšᵊ kalām fāriġ	"don't talk rubbish!"

Note that *miš* may be used with the *bi*-imperfect as well: *miš bitrudd* "she doesn't answer."

(b) *ma-...-š* is also used for the negation of prepositional phrases with the meaning "to have" or "there is" "there are" (→ V.II). In these cases the preposition is inserted between *ma-* and *-š* :

ma-ʿandināš ṭamāṭim dilwaʾti	"we haven't got any tomatoes now"
ma-fīš ḫāga ḫaṣalit	"nothing happened"
ma-waṛayīš ḫāga	"I've got nothing to do"
ma-ʿalehāš ḍarība	"there's no tax on that"
Ḫasan ma-minnūš fayda	"Ḫasan is of no use at all"

Note that the suffix *-ya* "me" changes to *-yi* in such cases: *waṛāya* "behind me" → *ma-waṛayīš*; *maʿāya* → *ma-mʿayīš.*

(c) *ma-...-š* can sometimes replace *miš* if the subject to be negated is a personal pronoun: *inta miš ʿārif* → *ma-ntāš ʿārif* "you don't know."

In the case of *ana* the negative is *ma-nīš* : *ana miš ʿārif* → *ma-nīš ʿārif* "I don't know."

3. *ma-*

After particles expressing a wish such as *yarēt* "if only...," and exclamations such as *waḻḻāhi* "by God" or *ʿumr* "ever," the negative is formed with *ma-* (without *-š*):

ma-getš	→	*yarētak ma-gēt*	if only you hadn't come
ma-šuftūš	→	*ʿumri ma-šuftu*	I've never seen him
miš ḫayixlaṣ	→	*ʿumru ma-ḫayixlaṣ*	it will never end

4. *wala*

If a negative sentence contains two parallel phrases and the negative applies to both of them, then they should be linked by *wala* meaning "neither ... nor ...":

biyiʿṛaf yiʾṛa‿w yiktib he can read and write	→	*ma-byiʿṛafšᵊ yiʾṛa wala yiktib* he can neither read nor write
ʿandina bēḍ wi ṭamāṭim we have eggs and tomatoes	→	*ma-ʿandināš bēḍ wala ṭamāṭim* we have neither eggs nor tomatoes

5. *la ... wala...*

As already mentioned in 4 above, parallel negative phrases can be linked by *wala*. In these cases the first negative particle can be *miš, ma-...-š* or *la* :

miš kuwayyisa‿w miš wiḥša →	*miš kuwayyisa wala wiḥša* *la‿kwayyisa wala wiḥša*
not good and not bad	neither good nor bad
ma-biyšufšᵊ‿w ma-byismaɛš →	*ma-biyšufšᵊ wala‿byismaɛ* *la biyšūf wala‿byismaɛ*
he can't see and he can't hear	he can neither see nor hear

When *la* is used, it can also be put at the front of the sentence:

huwwa la‿kbīr wala‿ṣġayyaṛ →	*la huwwa‿kbīr wala‿ṣġayyar* "he's neither big nor little"
la huwwa wala‿mṛātu gayyīn innahaṛda	"neither he nor his wife are coming today"

III. Verbs followed by a simple imperfect

1. In Arabic certain types of verbs are directly followed by a simple imperfect, whereas in English the infinitive would be used. For example, after a verb of movement in a certain direction (→ VIII.VI and XI.IV), in Arabic a simple imperfect is used to express a purpose. In these cases the subject of the main verb and the subject of the imperfect are one and the same:

ilwalad ṛāḥ yištiri ɛēš	"the boy went to buy bread"
nisīt aʾullak ḥāga	"I forgot to tell you something"
ḥawilt attiṣil bi-syadtak	"I tried to phone you"
kān ṭabɛan biyīgi‿yzūru	"naturally he came to visit him"
ʾaɛadt atfaṛṛag ɛa‿ttilivizyōn	"I sat down to watch TV"

2. After verbs such as *xalla, yixalli* and *sāb, yisīb* "to let"; *baɛat, yibɛat* "to send" and *ṭalab, yuṭlub min w* "to ask s/o to do s/th," a simple imperfect is used if the object of the main verb is the subject of the imperfect verb. The main verb then agrees with the subject and the imperfect agrees with the object. In English the infinitive of purpose would be used in such cases:

sibt ilwalad yiṛawwaḥ	"I let the boy go home"
xallāni arūḥ li‿dduktūr	"he made me go to the doctor"
hiyya baɛtāni ʾaṣallaḥ ilḥanafiyya	"she sent me to repair the faucet"
ṭalabit minnu‿ywaṣṣalha lmaṭār	"she asked him to take her to the airport"

With *xalla* and *sāb* in the sense of "to make someone do something," the perfect may be used when referring to past time: *xallētu maḍa‿ ggawāb* "I made him sign the letter."

EXERCISES

I. Answer saying: there's still one left

ilbaṭṭīx xiliṣ! - *lā, fī* *baṭṭīxa waḥda* *kamān .*

1. *ilwaraʾ xiliṣ!* - *lā, fī* ____________________ *kamān.*

2. *ilburtuʾān xiliṣ!* - *lā, fī* ____________________ *kamān.*

3. *ilbaṣal xiliṣ!* - *lā, fī* ____________________ *kamān.*

4. *ilbaṭāṭis xilṣit!* - *lā, fī* ____________________ *kamān.*

5. *ilmōz xiliṣ!* - *lā, fī* ____________________ *kamān.*

6. *ilʾūṭa xilṣit!* - *lā, fī* ____________________ *kamān.*

7. *issamak xiliṣ!* - *lā, fī* ____________________ *kamān.*

8. *illamūn xiliṣ!* - *lā, fī* ____________________ *kamān.*

9. *ilbēḍ xiliṣ!* - *lā, fī* ____________________ *kamān.*

II. Answer saying: but I only ate one ...

inta kalt ilʾūṭa kullaha? - *lā, kalt*^{ə} *ʾuṭāya waḥda* *bass.*

1. *inta kalt ilmōz kullu?* - *lā, kalt* ________________ *bass.*

2. *inti kalti‿lmanga kullaha?* - *lā, kalt* ________________ *bass.*

3. *inti kalti‿lburtuʾān kullu?* - *lā, kalt* ________________ *bass.*

4. *inta kalt ilbēḍ kullu?* - *lā, kalt* ________________ *bass.*

5. *inta kalt iṭṭamāṭim kullaha?* - *lā, kalt* ________________ *bass.*

6. *inti xadti‿llamūn kullu?* - *lā, xadt* ________________ *bass.*

7. *inta xadt ilward*^{ə} *kullu?* - *lā, xadt* ________________ *bass.*

8. *inta kalt ilbaṭāṭis kullaha?* - *lā, kalt* ________________ *bass.*

9. *inta xadt ilwaraʾ kullu?* - *lā, xadt* ________________ *bass.*

III. How much is that altogether?

talat baṭṭixāt wi kamān tisɛa yibʾu itnāšaṛ baṭṭīxa.

1. *xamas lamunāt wi kamān sitta yibʾu* ____________________.
2. *aṛbaɛ naxlāt wi kamān tamanya yibʾu* ____________________.
3. *sabaɛ baʾaṛāt wi kamān baʾaṛa yibʾu* ____________________.
4. *sitt^{ə} samakāt wi kamān sabɛa yibʾu* ____________________.
5. *taman šagaṛāt wi kamān sabɛa yibʾu* ____________________.
6. *sitt^{ə} beḍāt wi kamān tisɛa yibʾu* ____________________.
7. *aṛbaɛ baṣalāt wi kamān baṣaltēn yibʾu* ____________________.

IV. Exactly how many of these are there?

fī naxl^{ə}‿ktīr hina! - yaɛni kām naxla biẓẓabṭ?

1. *fī lamūn kitīr hina! - yaɛni* ____________________ *bi‿ẓẓabṭ?*
2. *fī baʾaṛ kitīr hina! - yaɛni* ____________________ *bi‿ẓẓabṭ?*
3. *fī samak kitīr hina! - yaɛni* ____________________ *bi‿ẓẓabṭ?*
4. *fī mōz kitīr hina! - yaɛni* ____________________ *bi‿ẓẓabṭ?*
5. *fī šagaṛ kitīr hina! - yaɛni* ____________________ *bi‿ẓẓabṭ?*
6. *fī ward^{ə}‿ktīr hina! - yaɛni* ____________________ *bi‿ẓẓabṭ?*
7. *fī burṭuʾān kitīr hina! - yaɛni* ____________________ *bi‿ẓẓabṭ?*
8. *fī bēḍ kitīr hina! - yaɛni* ____________________ *bi‿ẓẓabṭ?*

V. There aren't more than two or three ...

ya-taṛa, fī naxl^{ə}‿ktīr hina? - lā, ma-fīš aktaṛ min naxlitēn talāta.

1. *ya-taṛa, fī šagaṛ kitīr hina? - lā, ma-fīš aktaṛ min* ______________.
2. *ya-taṛa, fī samak kitīr hina? - lā, ma-fīš aktaṛ min* ______________.
3. *ya-taṛa, fī baṣal kitīr hina? - lā, ma-fīš aktaṛ min* ______________.
4. *ya-taṛa, fī manga‿ktīr hina? - lā, ma-fīš aktaṛ min* ______________.

5. *ya-taṛa, fī baʾaṛ kitīr hina?* - *lā, ma-fīš aktaṛ min* ____________.

6. *ya-taṛa, fī baṭāṭis kitīr hina?* - *lā, ma-fīš aktaṛ min* ____________.

7. *ya-taṛa, fī bēḍ kitīr hina?* - *lā, ma-fīš aktaṛ min* ____________.

8. *ya-taṛa, fī lamūn kitīr hina?* - *lā, ma-fīš aktaṛ min* ____________.

VI. Well then, leave it!

ilbaṭṭīxa di miš ḥilwa - *balāš* *baṭṭīx* *baʾa!*

1. *ilmangāya di miš ḥilwa.* - *balāš* ________________ *baʾa!*
2. *ilʾuṭāya di miš ḥilwa.* - *balāš* ________________ *baʾa!*
3. *ilbaṭaṭsitēn dōl miš ḥilwīn.* - *balāš* ________________ *baʾa!*
4. *ittalat mozāt dōl miš ḥilwīn.* - *balāš* ________________ *baʾa!*
5. *illamūna di miš ḥilwa.* - *balāš* ________________ *baʾa!*
6. *ilwarditēn dōl miš ḥilwīn.* - *balāš* ________________ *baʾa!*
7. *issamaktēn dōl miš ḥilwīn.* - *balāš* ________________ *baʾa!*
8. *iṭṭamaṭmāya di miš ḥilwa.* - *balāš* ________________ *baʾa!*

VII. Use the correct form (n.u., pl., or c.) of the following words:

mōz, baṣal, baṭṭīx, lamūn, buṛtuʾān, ward, ʾūṭa, baʾaṛ, baṭāṭis, bēḍ, waraʾ, ṣabūn, samak, ṛuzz

1. *baḥibb* ______________________________.
2. ________________________ *waḥda‿kfāya ʾawi.*
3. *iddīni kaman šuwayyit* ____________________!
4. *il*________________________ *ġāli‿lyomēn dōl.*
5. *iddīni xamas* __________________ *min faḍlak!*
6. *ma-fīš aktaṛ min* ____________________ *hina.*
7. *ana ʿawza talat* __________________________.

8. *iddīni kām* __________________ *law samaḫt!*

9. *ma-fīš ġēr* ________________________ *itnēn.*

10. *maʿāk kām* _______________, *ya‿btāʿ issamak?*

11. *ʿawzīn šuwayyit* ________________ *min faḍlak.*

12. *ʿišrīn* _______________________ *kifāya ʾawi.*

13. *ma-baḫibbiš ilbaṭāṭis,* _______ *waḫda‿kfāya ʾawi.*

14. *da fallāḫ faʾīr, ʿandu* ____________ *waḫda bass.*

VIII. Trees are green, so this tree is green too!

iššagaṛ lōnu ʾaxḍar, yaʿni iššagaṛa di xaḍra barḍu.

1. *ilmōz lōnu ʾaṣfar, yaʿni‿lmōza di* __________________ *barḍu.*
2. *iṭṭamāṭim lonha ʾaḫmaṛ, yaʿni‿ṭṭamaṭmāya di* __________ *barḍu.*
3. *ilbaṭṭīx lōnu ʾaḫmaṛ, yaʿni‿lbaṭṭīxa di* ________________ *barḍu.*
4. *ilwaraʾ da lōnu ʾabyaḍ, yaʿni‿lwaraʾa di* _____________ *barḍu.*
5. *ilbēḍ da lōnu ʾabyaḍ, yaʿni‿lbēḍa di* _________________ *barḍu.*
6. *ilbaʾaṛ lōnu ʾiswid, yaʿni‿lbaʾaṛa di* _________________ *barḍu.*
7. *issamak da lōnu ʾazraʾ, yaʿni‿ssamaka di* _____________ *barḍu.*
8. *ilmanga lonha burtuʾāni, yaʿni‿lmangāya di* ____________ *barḍu.*

IX. Give a negative reply to the following questions.

1. *iddinya kānit zaḫma ʿa‿kkurnīš?*

   ____

2. *šuftu‿lʿasākir illi waʾfīn ʿa‿lbāb?*

   ____

3. *ya-taṛa humma waxdīn balhum?*

   ____

4. *ya-taṛa Samya bitšūf kuwayyis?*

   ____

5. *intu ʾaṣlan min hina?*

____

6. *ilwafdᵊ ḥayʿaddi min iššāriʿ da?*

____

7. *ya-taṛa dōl ẓubbāṭ walla ʿasākir?*

____

8. *humma masʾulīn ʿan ilmašruʿāt di?*

____

9. *fī ʿīd walla mūlid innahaṛda?*

____

10. *ikkitāb da‿kwayyis walla wiḥiš?*

____

11. *ya-taṛa di‿mṛātu walla bintu?*

____

12. *ilmudarris ḥayišṛaḥ iddarsᵊ da kamān maṛṛa?*

____

13. *intu samʿīn iṣṣōṭ ilġarīb da?*

____

14. *ya-taṛa fī ʾaklᵊ‿w šurbᵊ fi‿lḥafla?*

____

X. Neither one nor the other! Use *la ... wala ...* .

ʿawza ʾūṭa walla‿xyāṛ? *la ʿawza ʾūṭa wala‿xyāṛ.*

1. *ʿawza mōz walla manga?* ______________________.

2. *gibti‿lbaṣal wi‿ṭṭamāṭim?* ______________________.

3. *maʿāk ʾalam wi waraʾa?* ______________________.

4. *intu ʿawzīn kabrīt walla wallāʿa?* ______________________.

5. *ḥayīgi bukṛa walla baʿdu?* ______________________.

6. *ya-taṛa, ʿandukum zēt wi sukkaṛ?* ______________________.

7. *huwwa Samīr itnaʾal wi ʿazzil?* ______________________.

8. *mīn da, Ḥasan walla Samīr?* ______________________.

9. *anzil w‿arūḫ issūʾ?* ______________________________.

10. *iddētu‿lmuftāḫ wi‿rruxṣa?* ________________________.

11. *laʾetīha ʿand ilfakahāni walla ʿand ilxuḍari?* ______________.

12. *ilfustān wāsiʿ walla dayyaʾ ʿalēki?* _____________________ .

XI. Combine one phrase from (a) with a suitable phrase from (b).

	(a)	(b)
1.	*hiyya ʿawzāni*	*tiʿṛaf tiktib*
2.	*iftakaṛtaha*	*yisibūna*
3.	*kānit bitiḫsibhum*	*āgi bukṛa*
4.	*ʿawzinkum*	*tikūn niḍīfa*
5.	*ʿāwiz ittallāga*	*bitikkallim faransāwi*
6.	*iftakaṛtik*	*maṣriyyīn*
7.	*kuntᵊ baḫsibak*	*tirgaʿu badri*
8.	*ma-kanitšᵊ ʿawzāhum*	*bitiġsili‿lmawaʿīn*

1a + ______	2a + ______	3a + ______	4a + ______
5a + ______	6a + ______	7a + ______	8a + ______

XII. Did you do it? No, but I tried! Reply using *ḫāwil* or *nisi* and the correct suffix.

xallaṣt iššuġl? - *laʾ, lākin ḫawilt axallaṣu.*

1. *gibt ikkutub* - *laʾ,* _____________________ .

2. *dafaʿit ilḫisāb?* - *laʾ, lākin* __________________ .

3. *malētu‿stimāṛit ilʾiqāma?* - *laʾ,* ______________________ .

4. *ittaṣaltu bi‿dduktūr?* - *laʾ, lākin* __________________ .

5. *ʿallimtᵊ ʿa‿lwaraʾa* - *laʾ,* _____________________ .

6. *ḫaketilhum ilḫikāya?* - *laʾ, lākin* __________________ .

7. *itfaṛṛagtu ʿa‿lfilm imbāriḫ?* - *laʾ,* _____________________ .

8. *ʿamalt ilwāgib?* - *laʾ, lākin* __________________ .

9. *ʿaddētu ʿala‿ṣḥabkum?* - *laʾ,* ____________________ .

10. *fihimti‿ddarsᵊ da‿kwayyis* - *laʾ, lākin* ________________ .

XIII. Use the correct form of the verb in brackets.

xallāni astanna li-muddit sāʿa *(istanna)*

1. *sibha* ________________ *ilxārig li-waḥdaha!* *(rāḥ)*
2. *xallīna* ________________ *iššuġlᵊ‿w rawwaḥ inta!* *(ʿamal)*
3. *sibni* ________________ *ill‿ana ʿawzu!* *(ʾāl)*
4. *xallīhum* ________________ *iggawabāt kullaha!* *(katab)*
5. *ma-tsibhāš* ________________ *ilḥagāt ilwiḥša di!* *(ištara)*
6. *xallīni* ________________ *bi-hudūʾ!* *(ištaġal)*
7. *ma-txallinīš* ________________ *minnak!* *(ziʿil)*
8. *xallīha* ________________ *ikkutub maʿāha!* *(gāb)*
9. *ma-tsibhūš* ________________ *li-waḥdu bi‿llēl!* *(xarag)*
10. *sibtaha* __________ *wi* ______________ *(fattaḥ, ʾaffil)*

fi‿ššababīk zayyᵊ ma hiyya ʿawza.

XIV. Organize the words into logical sentences.

1. *taʿbanīn, šuwayya, ʿalēku, bāyin.*

____

2. *ʿandaha, imbāriḥ, ṣudāʿ, kān.*

____

3. *ḥadritak, ginē(h), mumkin, li, tifukk, mīt?*

____

4. *ilḥāga, kullaha, kida, lē, ġilyit?*

____

5. *kīlu, ilʾūṭa, ʾirš, tisʿīn, tamanu.*

____

6. *iṣṣubḫ, xaṛagt, innahaṛda, šuwayya, atfassaḫ.*

____

7. *ilwafd, ʾAṣrᵊ ɛAbdīn, baɛdᵊ ma, wiṣil, ṛāḫ, ɛala ṭūl.*

____

8. *yištiru, nafs, kānu, ɛawzīn, ilɛaṛabiyya.*

____

9. *ma-...-š, bi‿llēl, banām, xāliṣ.*

____

10. *sabaɛ, baštaġal, baʾāli, hina, sinīn.*

____

11. *bāyin, fiɛlan, ɛayyān, ɛalēk.*

____

12. *zaḫma, ɛala, kānit, iddinya, ikkurnēš, ʾawi.*

____

13. *ma-, safirna, yaretna, imbāriḫ!*

____

14. *kānu, mafrūša, yiʾaggaṛu, šaʾʾa, ɛawzīn.*

____

15. *iṛṛāgil da, ma-, šufnā, ɛumrina.*

____

16. *bukṛa, ilfarš, mumkin, nišūf, nīgi?*

____

17. *sabɛa, ana, muntaẓir, bukṛa, issāɛa, ḫaḍritik.*

____

18. *ana, ma-, waḷḷāhi, ilḫafla, ṛāyiḫ !*

____

XV. Translate the following sentences.

1. They let their son travel alone.

____

2. Egypt has no economic relations with your country.

____

3. Potatoes have got very expensive these days.

____

4. People who have a cold shouldn't go to work.

____

5. The president came to *Asyūṭ* on the occasion of the festivities.

____

6. Let me make you a cup of coffee!

____

7. Don't forget to pay the bill, *Muḥammad*!

____

8. There is only one orange in the fridge.

____

9. I forgot to tell you something important.

____

10. There was a big crowd, as if something had happened.

____

11. I've never seen anything like that (before)!

____

12. If only I hadn't gone to the party yesterday!

____

13. Don't make me get angry with you!

____

14. The CID are looking for extremist movements in the country.

____

15. In our town we have no airport, neither big nor small.

____

16. If only I hadn't bought this old house!

____

17. The minister met neither the Italian delegation nor the English one.

____

18. I didn't sell my house, neither did I buy another house.

____

LESSON XV

READING PASSAGES

iliqtiṣād ilmaṣri

1. *Maṣr^{ə} zayy^{ə} ma-ntu εarfīn kānit quwwa‿qtiṣadiyya‿kbīra fi‿lmāḍi, fi-εahd^{ə} Mḫammad εAli Bāša.*

2. *baεd^{ə} kida ḫaṣal tadahwur iqtiṣādi‿kbīr fi‿lbalad bi-sabab ilistiεmāṛ ilʾagnabi. lamma gih Gamāl εAbd inNāṣir ḫāwil yirfaε min mustawa‿lmaεīša wi yibni‿liqtiṣād ilmaṣri min gidīd.*

3. *lamma qaṛṛaṛ taʾmīm qanāt isSuwēs sanat ʾalf^{ə} tusεumiyya sitta‿w xamsīn εašān yizawwid iddaxl ilqawmi, ʾāmit idduwal ilʾagnabiyya bi-εudwān εala Maṣr.*

4. *baεd ilḫarb^{ə} banit Maṣr isSadd ilεĀli wi da kān ʾingāz kibīr fi-magāl tawlīd ikkahṛaba‿llazma li‿ṣṣināεa wi‿f-magāl irrayy^{ə} wi‿zziṛāεa.*

5. *ġēr kida, Maṣr^{ə} εandaha dilwaʾti maṣādir tanya li‿ddaxl ilqawmi zayy^{ə} rusūm qanāt isSuwēs wi taḫwilāt ilmaṣriyyīn illi‿byištaġalu fi‿dduwal ilεaṛabiyya‿ššaqīqa, wi kamān issiyāḫa‿lli daxlaha biywaffaṛ li‿lbalad ilmalayīn min ilεumla‿ṣṣaεba.*

6. *bi‿nnisba li‿lmustaʾbal, law ihtammit Maṣr^{ə} bi‿zziṛāεa mumkin tistaġna εan ilistiṛād mi‿lxārig, wi ʾiza ḫassinit nawεiyyit ilʾintāg mumkin tiṣaddar xuḍrawāt wi fawākih li-bilād issūʾ ilʾurubbiyya‿lmuštaṛaka.*

7. *amma bi‿nnisba li‿ssiyāḫa, law banit Maṣr^{ə} fanādiʾ mutawassiṭa, fa da ḫayzawwid min εadad issuwwāḫ min kull^{ə} ʾanḫāʾ ilεālam.*

yōm ʾagāza

1. *Hiba‿w Maha ma-kanš^{ə} εanduhum muḫaḍrāt imbāriḫ wi kānu faḍyīn ṭūl innahāṛ.*

2. *ḫawāli‿ssāεa εašaṛa xadu taks^{ə}‿w nizlu‿lbalad.*

3. *Hiba kānit εawza tištiri‿hdiyya l-axūha‿ṣṣuġayyaṛ wi Maha kān nifsaha fi fustān gidīd.*

4. *fi ʾawwil maḫall^{ə} daxalū(h), Hiba šāfit maʾlama xašab fīha ʾalamēn ruṣāṣ wi ʾalam ḫibr^{ə} min nōε kuwayyis fa‿štaritha εala ṭūl.*

5. *amma Maha fa-daxalit sitt^{ə} maḫallāt ʾabl^{ə} ma‿tlāʾi fustān ʾuṭn^{ə} gamīl tilbisu fi‿ṣṣēf.*

6. *wi hiyya‿btidfaε ilḫisāb šāfit fi‿lfitrīna gazma gild^{ə} εagabitha ʾawi, fa‿štaritha kamān.*

7. *ḫaṭṭu kull^{ə} ḫāga‿f-šanṭa‿ blastik kānit maεāhum wi rigεu‿lbēt bi-surεa, liʾinn^{ə} maεād ilġada kān ʾaṛṛab.*

VOCABULARY

ʾabl^{ə} ma	before (conj.)
ʾaṛṛab, yiʾaṛṛab min ḫ	to approach
ʾingāz, -āt	achievement
ʾintāg	production
ballaġ ḫ	to warn; to notify
bana, yibni ḫ	to build
bi-sabab	because of
daxl	income
dawa, adwiya	medicine
fakha, fawākih	fruit
fāṣil	to bargain
fitrīna	shop window
ḫarb (f.), *ḫurūb*	war
ḫaṛāmi, -yya	thief, robber
ḫassin ḫ	to improve
ḫaṣal, yiḫṣal	to happen
ḫawāli	about, approximately
ihtamm bi ḫ	to show interest in s/o ~ s/th
iqtiṣād	economy
istaġna, yistaġna εan ḫ ~ w	to manage without s/th ~ s/o
istiṛād	import
istiεmāṛ	colonialism
iswira, asāwir	bracelet
kahṛaba	electricity
liʾann	because
maʾlama, maʾālim	pencil box
magāl,-āt	area
maṛṛ, yimurr εala w	to pass by s/o
maṣdaṛ, maṣādir	source
mawʾaf, mawāʾif	parking place, bus stop
maεād, mawaεīd	appointment
maεīša	living
milyōn, malayīn	million
min gidīd	again, once more
mugrim,	criminal
muḫaḍra, -āt	lecture
munādi, -yya	parking attendent

mustaʾbal	future
mustawa, -yāt	level, standard
mutawassiṭ	average, medium
māḍi	past (noun)
naḫās ~ niḫās	copper
nawεiyya	type, sort
nifs... fi	to want to to feel like
qanāt isSuwēs	Suez Canal
qaṛṛaṛ ḫ	to decide
qawmi	national
quwwa, -āt	power, force
rafaε, yirfaε min ḫ	to enhance
rakan, yirkin (ḫ)	to park
rayy	irrigation
rusūm	toll, duty
sadd, sudūd	dam
safīna, sufun	ship
sihir, yishaṛ	to stay up late
sūʾ tafāhum	misunderstanding
ṣaddar ḫ	to export
ṣināεa, -āt	industry
šaqīq	full brother
taʾmīm	nationalization
tadahwur	decline
taḫwīla, -āt	transfer
tawlīd	generation (electr.)
timsāl, tamasīl	statue
ṭāẓa	fresh
waffaṛ ḫ	to provide with
xašab	wood
xuḍrawāt (pl.)	vegetables
zawwid min ḫ	to increase
zākir	to study
ziṛāεa	agriculture
εagab, yiεgib w	to please
εahd, εuhūd	time, era
εarīs, εirsān	bridegroom
εāli	high
εudwān εala	aggression against
εālam	world
εuluww	height
εumla ṣaεba	hard currency

GRAMMAR

I. Verbal clauses introduced by *inn* "that"

1. After verbs and expressions referring to senses, feelings, or emotions, and also after verbs such as "to say," "to think," "to believe,"

"to be of the opinion," the word *inn* "that" is used to introduce the subsequent clause:

Samya ḫatiggawwiz	→	*ʾalūli ʾinnᵊ Samya ḫatiggawwiz*
"Samya is going to get married"		"they told me that Samya was going to get married"

List of words and expressions in this category:

ʾāl inn ...	he said that ...	*aẓunn inn ...*	I assume that ...
fākir inn ...	he thinks that	*bāyin inn ...*	it seems that...
fihim inn ...	he understood that ...	*mamnūʿ inn ...*	it is forbidden to
		min raʾyi ʾinn ...	it's my opinion that ...
iftakar inn ...	he believed that		
mitʾakkid inn ...	he's convinced that ...	*mithayyaʾli ʾinn ..*	it seems to me that ...
misaddaʾ inn ...	he believed that	*muḫtamal inn ..*	it's probable that
nisi ʾinn ...	he forgot that ...	*ṣaḫīḫ inn ...*	it's true that ...
simiʿ inn	he heard that ...	*wāḍiḫ inn ...*	it's obvious that ...
šāf inn ...	he saw that ...	*yiẓhar inn ...*	it seems that ...
xāyif inn ...	he fears that ...	*ġarīb inn ...*	it's strange that ...
ʿārif inn...	he knows that ...	*ʿagabni fīh ʾinn*	it pleased me that he ...

2. If the word *inn-* introduces a verbal clause, and if this clause does not have a noun as its subject, then *inn-* must be followed by a suffix which refers to the subject:

ḫawwišu‿flūs	→	*wāḍiḫ innu**hum** ḫawwišu‿flūs*
"they have saved money"		"it is obvious that they have saved some money"
huwwa šāri ʿaṛabiyya	→	*ʾalitli ʾinn**u** šāri ʿaṛabiyya*
"he has bought a car"		"she told me that he had bought a car"

3. If the word *inn-* introduces a prepositional clause meaning "to have" or "there is" "there are," one can use *inn* without a suffix, or *innu* :

ma-fīš filūs → *ʾalli ʾinnᵊ ma-fīš filūs* "he told me that there was no money"
or: *ʾalli ʾinnu ma-fīš filūs*

4. After expressions such as *ʾāl, xāyif,* as well as *yiẓhar, mithayyaʾli, aẓunn, bāyin, mamnūʿ, muḫtamal,* the conjunction *inn-* can be omitted:

bāyin ʿalē ma-fhimšᵊ ḫāga	"it seems he has understood nothing"
mithayyaʾli Samya ḫatiggawwiz ʿan ʾurayyib	"it appears to me that Samya is going to get married soon"
mamnūʿ tirkin ilʿaṛabiyya hina	"it is forbidden to park your car here"

5. In the case of *iftakaṛ* and *fākir* "to think that" "to believe that," the conjunction *inn* can also be omitted and the subject of the subordinate clause can be directly attached to the introductory verb in the form of a suffix:

iftakaṛt inn ilʿaṛabiyya ḫatkūn gahza	"I thought that the car would be ready"
iftakaṛt ilʿaṛabiyya ḫatkūn gahza	"I thought the car would be ready"
iftakaṛtaha ḫatkūn gahza	"I thought it would be ready"

Note that this construction also occurs after *ʿāwiz* (→ VII.IV):

ana ʿawzak tigīni bukṛa “I want you to come to me tomorrow”

6. As for *nisi, yinsa*, this verb means:

* “to forget that ...” when it is followed by *inn-*

nisīt inn^{ə} Maṣr^{ə} ʿandaha maṣādir tanya kamān
“I forgot that Egypt also had other sources”

* and “to forget to ...” when followed by an imperfect

nisīt asallim ʿalēhum “I forgot to greet them”

II. Conditional clauses

In Arabic, conditions fall into two broad categories: those which refer to a real possibility and can be realized (realis), and those which are hypothetical (contrafactive) and cannot be realized (irrealis). Both types can be introduced by *iza, law,* and occasionally *in.*

1. Realis

(a) The conjunction *iza* can be followed either by the perfect or by *kān* with an imperfect, a participle, a nominal phrase, or a prepositional phrase. The conjunction *law* on the other hand can also be followed by a simple imperfect:

miš misaddaʾni? isʾal Faṭma	→	*iza ma-kuntiš misaddaʾni, isʾal Faṭma!* If you don’t believe me, ask Faṭma!
ma-fīš waʾt? nīgi bukṛa tāni	→	*iza ma-kānš^{ə} fī waʾt, nīgi bukṛa tāni!* If there isn’t (enough) time, we’ll come again tomorrow!
tiḥibb^{ə} timši? itfaḍḍal!	→	*iza kunt^{ə}‿tḥibb^{ə} timši, itfaḍḍal!* *iza ḥabbēt timši, itfaḍḍal!* *law ḥabbēt timši, itfaḍḍal!* *law tiḥibb^{ə} timši, itfaḍḍal!* If you want to go, then go!

(b) As far as order is concerned, the conditional clause can stand either before or after the main clause:

iza kānit ilmaḥallāt fatḥa ḥaninzil ilbalad
“If the shops are open, we’ll go to town”
law šuft^{ə} Samīr ʾullu yittiṣil bīna
“If you see Samīr, tell him to call us”

taʿāla innahaṛda bi‿llēl, iza kān ʿandak waʾt
“come this evening, if you’ve got time”
kunt aḥibb atfaṛṛag ʿa‿kkutub, iza kān mumkin
“I’d like to look at the books, if that’s possible”

2. Irrealis

(a) As with realizable conditional clauses, unrealizable and contrafactive conditional clauses are introduced by *iza* or *law*. But in the case of the irrealis, *iza* and *law* are mostly followed by *kān*, and the main clause itself is always introduced by *kān*:

law kān ɛandi‿flūs kunt ištarēt ilɛaṛabiyya di
"If I had (some) money, I'd buy this car"

The condition can refer to present or future time [as in (a) below] or to past time [as in (b) below].

When it refers to past time, the main clause always has *kān* + perfect:

(a) *law kuntᵊ fākir, kunt aʾullak*
if I remembered I'd tell you

law kān ilbēt da‿btāɛi, kunt abiɛhūlak
if that house was mine I'd sell it to you

(b) *law kān ɛandu waʾt, kān gih*
if he had had time, he would have come

iza ma-kuntiš inta ʾultili, kān ḫaddᵊ tāni ʾalli
if you hadn't told me, someone else would have told me

law kānit iddinya ṣēf, kān mumkin nistaḫamma fi‿lbaḫṛ
"if it was summer we would be able to swim in the sea"

iza kuntᵊ bitḫibbini‿b-ṣaḫīḫ kunt iggawwiztini min zamān
"if you really loved me you would have married me a long time ago"

In practice, these rules are not always strictly applied, and whether the condition is realizable or not must often be deduced from the context.

(b) Negative conditional clauses in the irrealis can also be expressed by using *lōla* (= *law lā*) which is always followed by a noun or a suffix:

lōla Gamāl ɛAbd inNāṣir, kānit qanāt isSuwēs ma-tʾammimitš
"but for ɛAbd inNāṣir, the Suez Canal would not have been nationalized"

lolāk ma-kunnāš fihimna ḫāga
"but for you, we would have understood nothing"

Also note the expression: *ana law minnak* "if I were you ...."

3. Indirect questions

The words *iza* + *kān* can also be used to introduce indirect questions where the word "whether" would be used in English:

miš ɛārif iza kānit Samya gayya walla laʾ
I don't know whether Samya's coming or not

kuntᵊ ɛāwiz aɛṛaf iza kānit mawgūda walla laʾ
I wanted to know whether she was present or not

III. *badal*-constructions

The term *badal*-construction is used when a noun is added to another noun in order to qualify it, usually by referring to the material from which it is made, e.g. *gild* "leather," *waraʾ* "paper," *dahab* "gold," *ʾuṭn* "cotton" etc. The second noun is not inflected for number and gender, but it does receive an article if it qualifies a word which is defined.

mandīl waraʾ	a paper handkerchief
ilmandīl ilwaraʾ	the paper handkerchief
ilmanadīl ilwaraʾ	the paper handkerchiefs
ʾamīṣ ʾuṭn	a cotton shirt
ilʾamīṣ ilʾuṭn	the cotton shirt
ilʾumṣān ilʾuṭn	the cotton shirts

Other examples:

šanṭa‿blastik	"a plastic bag"	*issikka‿lḫadīd*	"the railway"
ʾalam ruṣāṣ	"a (lead) pencil"	*ilfustān ilḫarīr*	"the silk dress"

In addition, *badal*-constructions may be formed from words which do not refer to materials, but give another specification:

ixwāti‿lbanāt "my sisters"	*ižžīb ilbanṭalōn* "culottes"
[lit: my brothers the girls]	[lit: the skirt the trousers]

IV. The verbal noun or *maṣdar*

Verbal nouns or *maṣdar*s are derived from verbs:

fihim	"to understand"	→	*fahm*	"understanding"
ṣaddar	"to export"	→	*taṣdīr*	"export"
intaẓar	"to wait"	→	*intiẓāṛ*	"waiting"

They can have an active or a passive meaning:

balāš kidb!	"no lying!"
liʿaṛabiyya ʿawza ġasīl	"the car needs washing"

1. Forming of the *maṣdar*

(a) When forming the *maṣdar* from the base stem, several different patterns can be used. The most common ones are:

KaTB	*wazn*	*(wazan)*	*fahm*	*(fihim)*	*ʾakl*	*(kal)*
KiTB	*diḫk*	*(diḫik)*	*libs*	*(libis)*	*kidb*	*(kidib)*
KuTB	*šurb*	*(širib)*	*ḫubb*	*(ḫabb)*	*buʿd*	*(biʿid)*
KaTāB	*samāʿ*	*(simiʿ)*	*fasād*	*(fisid)*	*ḍalāl*	*(ḍall)*
KaTīB	*ġasīl*	*(ġasal)*	*ṭabīx*	*(ṭabax)*	*xabīz*	*(xabaz)*
KuTāB	*ʾuʿād*	*(ʾaʿad)*	*suʾāl*	*(saʾal)*	*sukāt*	*(sikit)*
KuTūB	*rugūʿ*	*(rigiʿ)*	*duxūl*	*(daxal)*	*nuzūl*	*(nizil)*
KiTāBa	*kitāba*	*(katab)*	*ʾiṛāya*	*(ʾaṛa)*	*ziyāṛa*	*(zāṛ)*
KaTaBān	*ṭayarān*	*(ṭār)*	*lamaʿān*	*(lamaʿ)*	*ġalayān*	*(ġili)*

Weak verbs often follow the pattern **KaTaB**ān when forming the *masdar: dāṛ* → *dawaṛān* "turning"; *ṭār* → *ṭayarān* "flying."

gih → *migiyy* "coming" and *ṛāḥ* → *miṛwāḥ* "going" are irregular.

(b) Verbs from stems II and V share the same *maṣdar*, and verbs from stems III and VI also share a *maṣdar* :

II and V taKTīB

ɛallim	→	*taɛlīm*	"instruction"	*ṣallaḥ*	→	*taṣlīḥ*	"repair"
itɛallim	→	*taɛlīm*	"intstruction"	*itṣallaḥ*	→	*taṣlīḥ*	"repair"

III and VI muKaTBa ~ miKaTBa

ɛāmil	→	*muɛamla*	"treatment"	*ʾābil*	→	*muʾabla*	"meeting"
itɛāmil	→	*muɛamla*	"treatment"	*itʾābil*	→	*muʾabla*	"meeting"
wāfiʾ	→	*miwafʾa*	"agreement"	*ḥāwil*	→	*miḥawla*	"trial"
iddāyiʾ	→	*midayʾa*	"annoying"				

Sometimes the pattern **KiTāB** can be found in the *maṣdar* of stem III:

ɛālig	→	*ɛilāg*	"treatment"	*dāfiɛ*	→	*difāɛ*	"defense"
ḥāwir	→	*ḥiwāṛ*	"dialogue"				

(c) Stems IV and *n*-VII, as well as stems VIII and X, all form a *maṣdar* which is recognizable by the presence of the vowel *-i-* followed by a *-ā-* in the final syllable:

ʾangaz	→	*ʾingāz*	"achievement"	*ittafaʾ*	→	*ittifāʾ*	"agreement"
ʾaṭlaq	→	*ʾiṭlāq*	"shooting"	*ittaṣal*	→	*ittiṣāl*	"connection"
inbaṣaṭ	→	*inbiṣāṭ*	"pleasure"	*istaʾbil*	→	*istiʾbāl*	"reception"
ihtamm	→	*ihtimām*	"concern"	*istaɛmil*	→	*istiɛmāl*	"usage"

Note that the *maṣdars* of *ištara* "to buy" and *ištaġal* "to work" are taken from the base stem: *šira* "buying" and *šuġl* "work."

(d) 4-radical verbs form their *maṣdars* according to the pattern **KaTBaLa**:

dardiš	→	*dardaša*	"chatter"	*narfis*	→	*narfasa*	"nervousness"
ittaryaʾ	→	*taryaʾa*	"mocking"	*laxbaṭ*	→	*laxbaṭa*	"confusion"

2. Use of the *maṣdar*

When combined with words such as *ʾabl* "before," *baɛd* "after," and *liḥadd* "until," the *maṣdar* can be used to form temporal phrases:

ʾabl^{ə} wuṣūl ilwafd	before the arrival of the delegation
baɛd^{ə} dafɛ irrusūm	after payment of the duty
liḥadd^{ə} taʾmīm qanāt isSuwēs	until the nationalization of the Suez Canal

SOME VERBAL NOUNS

ᵓaddim, taᵓdīm	offering
ᵓafal, ᵓafl	closing
ᵓaggaṛ, taᵓgīr	hiring; renting
ᵓaṛa, ᵓiṛāya	reading
ᵓaṭlaq, ᵓiṭlāq	shooting
ᵓaɛad, ᵓuɛād	sitting; staying
ᵓām, ᵓiyām	standing up
ᵓāxiz, muᵓaxza	offense
bāɛ, bēɛ	selling
dafaɛ, dafɛ	paying
dardiš, dardaša	chattering
daxal, duxūl	entering
dāṛ, dawaṛān	turning
diħik, diħk	laughing
ḍarab, ḍarb	hitting
fakk, fakk	untying
fataħ, fatħ	opening
fāṣil, fiṣāl	bargaining
gaddid, tagdīd	renewing
gahhiz, taghīz	preparing
ġasal, ġasīl	washing
ġayyaṛ, taġyīr	changing
ġili, ġalayān	boiling (water)
ġili, ġiluww	becoming expensive
ħabb, ħubb	loving
ħagaz, ħagz	reserving
ħaḍḍar, taħḍīr	preparing
ħassin, taħsīn	improving
ħāwil, miħawla	attempting
ibtada, ibtidāᵓ ~ bidāya	beginning
iddāyiᵓ, midayᵓa	being annoyed
iggawwiz, gawāz	marriage
istaᵓbil, istiᵓbāl	reception
istalam, istilām	receiving
istaɛmil, istiɛmāl	using
ištaġal, šuġl	working
ištaṛa, šira	buying
itᵓaxxaṛ, taᵓxīr	being late
itnaᵓal, naᵓl	transferring
itnarfis, narfasa	being irritated
ittaṣal, ittiṣāl bi w	contacting
ittafaᵓ, ittifāᵓ	agreement
ittaryaᵓ, taryaᵓa ɛala w	mocking

itɛallim, taɛlīm	learning
iɛtazaṛ, iɛtizāṛ li w	apologizing
kal, ᵓakl	eating
kasaṛ, kasṛ	breaking
katab, kitāba ~ katb	writing
kašaf, kašf ɛala ħ	examining
libis, libs	wearing (clothes)
masaħ, masħ	sweeping
māt, mōt	death
misik, mask	catching
naḍḍaf, tanḍīf	cleaning
nām, nōm	sleeping
nizil, nuzūl	descending
ṛadd, ṛadd	giving back replying
rakkib, tarkīb	fixing
ṛāħ, miṛwāħ	going
rigiɛ, rugūɛ	returning
rikib, rukūb	mounting
saᵓal, suᵓāl	asking
sihir, sahaṛ	staying up
saraᵓ, sirᵓa	stealing
sāfir, safaṛ	traveling
simiɛ, samāɛ	hearing
ṣaddar, taṣdīr	export
ṣallaħ, taṣlīħ	repairing
šawa, šawy	grilling
širib, šurb	drinking
ṭabax, ṭabīx	cooking
ṭaffa, taṭfiyya	turning off
ṭalab, ṭalab	requesting
ṭār, ṭayarān	flying
ṭiliɛ, ṭulūɛ	climbing
wiṣil, wuṣūl	arriving
waṣṣal, tawṣīl	bringing
wazan, wazn	weighing
waḍḍab, tawḍīb	cleaning up
xaṛag, xurūg	leaving
xāf, xōf min ħ	fearing
zāṛ, ziyāṛa	visiting
ẓabaṭ, ẓabṭ	adjusting
ɛamal, ɛamal	making
ɛirif, maɛrifa	knowing

EXERCISES

I. Make conditional sentences using the realis.

ʕāwiz tištiri fakha ḥilwa? lāzim tistanna‿šwayya.
→ *iza kuntᵊ ʕāwiz tištiri fakha ḥilwa, lāzim tistanna‿šwayya.*

1. *ʕāwiz baṭṭīxa‿kwayyisa? lāzim tibʕat Hāni‿ssūʔ.*

____

2. *Maṣrᵊ ʕawza‿tṣaddar ilxuḍrawāt? lāzim tiḥassin nawʕiyyit ilʔintāg.*

____

3. *tiḥibbᵊ‿tfāṣil? lāzim tikūn šāṭir.*

____

4. *ḥāsis bi-ʔalam fi-baṭnak? xalli‿dduktūr yikšif ʕalēk.*

____

5. *ʕandak iltihāb fi‿zzayda? lāzim tiʕmil ʕamaliyya ʕala ṭūl.*

____

6. *miš lāʔi ṭamāṭim fi‿ssūʔ? rūḥ izZamālik.*

____

7. *Maha ʕawza tinzil issūʔ? lāzim tāxud taks.*

____

8. *tinzil issūʔ badri? ḥatlāʔi xuḍār ṭāza.*

____

9. *ʕawzīn tigaddidu ilʔiqāma? lāzim tirūḥu‿lMugammaʕ.*

____

10. *ḥabbēt tišūf našrit ilʔaxbāṛ? lāzim tiftaḥ ittilivizyōn dilwaʔti.*

____

II. The car's been stolen. It wouldn't have been stolen if ...!
Make logical conditional sentences using the irrealis.

ʔafalt iggaṛāž?
→ *law kuntᵊ ʔafalt iggaṛāž ma-kanitš ilʕaṛabiyya‿tsaraʔit*

1. *nadahti‿lmunādi?* ____________________

2. *sibtu‿ššanṭa maftūḥa?* ____________________

3. *sibtaha fi‿ggaṛāž?* ____________________

4. *rakantīha‿f-mawʔaf tāni?* ______

5. *iddētu‿lmunādi‿lmuftāḫ?* ______

6. *ʔafalt ilbāb bi‿lmuftāḫ?* ______

7. *rakantaha ɛa‿nnaṣya?* ______

8. *iggaṛāž maftūḫ?* ______

9. *rigiɛtᵊ mitʔaxxaṛ?* ______

10. *šilt ilbaṭṭariyya?* ______

III. Make logical conditional sentences using the irrealis.

miš ḫarkab ilʔutubīs liʔannᵊ fī zaḫma
→ *law ma-kanšᵊ fī zaḫma, kuntᵊ‿rkibt ilʔutubīs.*

1. *ma-štaretšᵊ ɛaṛabiyya‿gdīda liʔannᵊ ma-ɛandīš filūs.*

______

2. *ma-safirnāš Iskindiriyya liʔann iggawwᵊ miš ḫilw.*

______

3. *ḫaṣal sūʔ tafāhum liʔann Willy ma-byikkallimš ilɛaṛabi‿kwayyis.*

______

4. *ḫarkin ilɛaṛabiyya hina liʔannᵊ fī munādi.*

______

5. *ma-ġayyaṛtiš ilkutub liʔann ilmaktaba miš fatḫa‿nnahaṛda.*

______

6. *ma-getšᵊ‿mɛāk liʔinnᵊ ma-ɛandīš waʔt.*

______

7. *ʔidirna‿nrūḫ ilMaɛādi liʔinnᵊ fī mitru (metro).*

______

8. *ḫanzil ilbalad bi‿lɛaṛabiyya liʔinnᵊ fī mawʔaf ɛaṛabiyyāt.*

______

9. *miš ḫaʔɛud fi‿lbēt innahaṛda liʔinnᵊ fī šuġl.*

______

10. *ma-nsitš ilmaɛād bitaɛna liʔinnik ittaṣalti biyya.*

______

IV. Combine a word from (a) with a phrase from (b). Use *inn* if necessary.

(a)	*ṣaɛb*	*yiɛgibni*	*ṣaḫīḫ*	*mamnūɛ*	*lāzim*	*ɛagība*
	bāyin	*ġarība*	*ḍarūri*	*yiẓhar*	*wāḍiḫ*	*ma-yṣaḫḫiš*

(b) *ilʾutubīs lissa ma-gāš*
kānit li-waḫdaha
tifaṛṛagna ɛala kullᵊ ḫāga
kull ilʾiwaḍ maḫgūza
ḫatsafru‿mɛāna
ilmaḫallāt fatḫa bi‿llēl
yimsiku‿lmugrimīn
Faṭma ma-gatš innahaṛda
tīgi min ġēr taṣrīḫ
tirgaɛu mi‿ssafaṛ min ġēr hadāya

1. ______________________________

2. ______________________________

3. ______________________________

4. ______________________________

5. ______________________________

6. ______________________________

7. ______________________________

8. ______________________________

9. ______________________________

10. ______________________________

V. Turn these sentences around so that they form indirect commands.

inta lāzim tīgi bukṛa, ana ɛawza kida → *ana ɛawzāk tīgi bukṛa!*

1. *lāzim nuʾɛud dilwaʾti, ṃāṃa ɛawza kida.*

____

2. *hiyya ḫatiggawwiz, abūha kān ɛāwiz kida.*

____

3. *ana ḫāxud ilfilūs di‿mɛāya, Samya kānit ɛawza kida.*

____

4. *inti ṣaḫbit ilbēt, ana kuntᵊ fakṛa kida.*

____

5. *inta ma-bitḫibbiš iššukulāṭa* (chocolate), *iftakaṛtᵊ kida.*

____

6. *ilʕarabiyya lāzim titġisil, ana ʕāwiz kida.*

____

7. *ana miš mawgūd, humma kānu fakrīn kida.*

____

8. *lāzim ʔāxud ʔagāza, ilmudīr ʕāwiz kida.*

____

9. *lāzim arūḫ ilmadrasa, ṃāṃa‿w ḅāḅa ʕawzīn kida.*

____

10. *lāzim tiṭbuxi dilwaʔti, iḫna ʕawzīn kida.*

____

VI. What are they made of? Combine one word from (a) with a suitable word from (b). Do the exercise twice, first without and then with the definite article.

(a) *ʔuṭn, naḫās, ḫadīd, ʔasfalt, gild, ṣūf, dahab, kawitš, ḫarīr, faḍḍa, ʕāg, naylon, ruṣāṣ, ʔalabastaṛ*

(b) *sāʕa, ʔalam, badla, ṭarīʔ, kīs, iswira, mandīl, sikka, žakitta, timsāl, abrīʔ, ṭaʔṭūʔa, gazma, ṣaniyya, ʔamīṣ, bilūza*

kīs waraʔ	*ilkīs ilwaraʔ*
______________	______________
______________	______________
______________	______________
______________	______________
______________	______________
______________	______________

VII. What you would like to have? Name the material it's made of.

huwwa da dahab? ana kunt ^{e} ʕawza ʔiswira dahab.
→ *ʔāsif, ilʔasāwir iddahab xilṣit.*

1. *huwwa da ʔalabastaṛ? ana kunt ^{e} ʕāwiz timsāl* ______________.

ʔāsif, ittamasīl ______________________________ *xilṣit.*

2. *huwwa da ṣūf? ana kunt ^{e} ʕāwiz bulōfar* ______________.

ʔāsif, ilbulofaṛāt ______________________________ *xilṣit.*

3. *huwwa da ḥarīr? ana kuntᵊ ʿāwiz mandīl ________________.*

ʾāsif, ilmanadīl ________________________________ xilṣit.

4. *huwwa da dahab? ana kuntᵊ ʿāwiz sāʿa ________________.*

ʾāsif, issaʿāt ________________________________ itbāʿit.

5. *huwwa da ʾuṭn? ana kuntᵊ ʿawza‿blūza ________________.*

ʾasfa, ilbiluzāt ________________________________ xilṣit.

6. *huwwa da‿nḥās? iḥna kunna ʿawzīn ṣaniyya ________________.*

ʾāsif, iṣṣawāni ________________________ kullaha‿tbāʿit.

7. *huwwa da gild? ana kuntᵊ ʿawza šanṭa ________________ṭabīʿi.*

ʾāsif, iššunaṭ ________________________________ xilṣit.

8. *huwwa da ʾuṭn? ana kuntᵊ ʿawza ʾamīṣ ________________.*

ʾasfa, ilʾumṣān ________________________________ xilṣit.

VIII. Stop doing that! Use the appropriate verbal noun.

baṭṭal tišṛab sagāyir! - *baṭṭal šurb sagāyir!*

1. *baṭṭal tidḥak ʿa‿nnās!* - ________________
2. *balāš tiġsil ilʿaṛabiyya!* - ________________
3. *balāš tuṭbuxi‿nnahaṛda!* - ________________
4. *baṭṭal tuʾʿud ʿa‿lʾahāwi!* - ________________
5. *balāš tishaṛ illēla!* - ________________
6. *baṭṭal tākul illuḥūm!* - ________________
7. *balāš titʾaxxaṛ kullᵊ yōm!* - ________________
8. *balāš tinaḍḍaf ilʾuwaḍ innahaṛda!* - ________________
9. *balāš tifāṣil fi‿ssūʾ!* - ________________
10. *balāš tistaʿmil iddawa da!* - ________________
11. *balāš tiṣallaḥ ilḥanafiyya!* - ________________
12. *balāš tidardišu fi‿lfaṣl!* - ________________

IX. Use a *maṣdar* to ask what we should do next.

dilwaʔti ḫaṣallaḫ ikkahṛaba. - *wi baʕdᵊ taṣlīḫ ikkahṛaba ḫatiʕmil ʔē?*

1. *dilwaʔti ḫanišṛab ilʔahwa.* - ______________________ *ḫatiʕmilu ʔē?*

2. *dilwaʔti ḫaġsil ilʕaṛabiyya.* - ______________________ *ḫatiʕmil ʔē?*

3. *dilwaʔti ḫanišwi‿llaḫma.* - ______________________ *ḫatiʕmilu ʔē?*

4. *dilwaʔti ḫanākul.* - ______________________ *ḫatiʕmilu ʔē?*

5. *dilwaʔti ḫanzūr aṣḫabna.* - ______________________ *ḫatiʕmilu ʔē?*

6. *dilwaʔti ḫaġayyar ilfilūs.* - ______________________ *ḫatiʕmil ʔē?*

7. *dilwaʔti ḫaḫaḍḍar ilfiṭār.* - ______________________ *ḫatiʕmil ʔē?*

8. *dilwaʔti ḫanʔābil ilwafd.* - ______________________ *ḫatiʕmilu ʔē?*

9. *dilwaʔti ḫarūḫ adfaʕ ilʔigāṛ.* - ______________________ *ḫatiʕmil ʔē?*

10. *dilwaʔti ḫaṣallaḫ ittallāga.* - ______________________ *ḫatiʕmil ʔē?*

11. *dilwaʔti ḫazākir šuwayya.* - ______________________ *ḫatiʕmil ʔē?*

X. Ask questions, using *ʔē, kām,* and *ʔaddᵊ ʔē* with the following words:

wazn	"weight"	*ʕumr*	"age"	*ṭūl*	"length"
ʕadad	"amount"	*ʕuluww*	"height"	*taman*	"price"
lōn	"color"	*irtifāʕ*	"height"	*ʔigāṛ*	"rent"
šakl	"form, shape"	*masāfa*	"distance"		

iṛṛāgil da *waznu kām kīlu?*

1. *ilbadla di* ______________________

2. *banṭalōnak iggidīd* ______________________

3. *ṣaḫbitik Fawziyya* ______________________

4. *ya Ḥasan bitḥibbᵉ Samīḥa* ____________________

5. *ɛarīs Samya* ____________________

6. *iššaʾʾa‿ggidīda* ____________________

7. *burg ilQāhira* ____________________

8. *Hiba* ____________________

9. *min hina li‿lbalad* ____________________

10. *iṭṭalaba ɛandukum* ____________________

XI. I wanted to ask if ... Make indirect questions.

ya-taṛa‿ddinya zaḥma? - *kuntᵉ ɛāwiz asʾal iza kānit iddinya zaḥma walla laʾ!*

1. *ya-taṛa Ḥasan mawgūd?* - ____________________
2. *ilʾūṭa gamda ya-taṛa?* - ____________________
3. *fī ɛanduku baṣal?* - ____________________
4. *ya-taṛa‿lmudīr mawgūd?* - ____________________
5. *fī baṭṭīxa ʾaʾallᵉ min xamsa kīlu?* - ____________________
6. *ya-taṛa‿lmanga ḥilwa?* - ____________________
7. *mumkin ninzil hina?* - ____________________
8. *tiʾdaṛ tiġsilli‿lɛaṛabiyya?* - ____________________
9. *ya-taṛa‿lʾaṭrᵉ waṣal?* - ____________________

XII. Make conditional sentences replacing the *maṣdar* with a verb.

ɛawzīn tiʾaggaṛu šaʾʾa - *lāzim ilmirwāḥ li‿ssimsāṛa* →
iza kuntu ɛawzīn tiʾaggaru šaʾʾa, lāzim tirūḥu li‿ssimsāṛa.

1. *ɛawza‿tsafri bukṛa* - *lāzim ilʾiyām min innōm badri*

____

2. *ɛawzīn tištiru bēt gidīd* - *lāzim bēɛ ilbēt ilʾadīm ilʾawwil*

____

3. *ʕāwiz tiʔra kutub gidīda* - *mumkin miṛwāḥak ilmaktaba*

____

4. *intu ʕaṭšanīn* - *mumkin šurbᵊ ḥāga saʔʕa*

____

5. *Ḥasan ʕāwiz yisāfir bukṛa* - *lāzim ḥagzᵊ tazkaṛa fi‿lʔaṭr*

____

6. *Samya ʕawza tuxrug bi‿llēl* - *lāzim libsᵊ‿blōvar ṣūf*

____

7. *Maṣrᵊ ʕawza‿tzawwid iddaxl* - *lāzim taḥsīn nawʕiyyit ilʔintāg*

____

8. *Samīr ʕāwiz yiʕṛaf ilḥaʔīʔa* - *lāzim suʔāl Maha*

____

9. *iḥna ʕawzīn niwṣal badri* - *lāzim rukūb taks*

____

10. *Karīma ʕawza‿tsāfir* - *lāzim ṭalab vīza*

____

XIII. Make conditional sentences using the irrealis. Be careful of agreement and meaning.

ʕandaha‿zzayda‿w ʕašān kida daxalit ilmustašfa.
→ *law ma-kanšᵊ ʕandaha‿zzayda, ma-kanitsᵊ daxalit ilmustašfa.*

1. *iḥna faḍyīn innahaṛda‿w ʕašān kida ruḥna‿ssinima.*

____

2. *ḥaṣal ḥādis wi ʕašān kida‿ttaṣalu bi‿lbulīs.*

____

3. *iddinya miš zaḥma‿w ʕašān kida‿tmaššēt ʕa‿lkurnīš.*

____

4. *inti ḥassa‿b-ʔalam fi-baṭnik wi ʕašān kida ruḥti li-dduktūr!*

____

5. *inta taʕbān ʔawi‿w ʕašān kida ma-ruḥtiš iššuġl.*

____

6. *ʕanduku ʔagāza‿w ʕašān kida safirtu‿lBaḥr ilʔAḥmaṛ.*

____

7. *fataḥna‿ttilivizyōn wi‿tfaṛṛagna ʕala našrit ilʔaxbāṛ.*

____

8. *ilwafdᵊ ʿadda min hina‿w ʿašān kida‿tfaṛṛagna ʿalē(h).*

____

9. *ma-līš nifsᵊ fi‿lʾaklᵊ‿w ʿašān kida ma-ʾaʿadtiš ʿa‿ssufṛa.*

____

10. *ma-ʿandūš ʿaṛabiyya‿w ʿašān kida ma-ruḥnāš Sīna.*

____

11. *ma-ʿandināš waʾtᵊ‿w ʿašān kida ma-ruḥnāš ilḥafla.*

____

12. *Aḥmad miš ḥāgiz makān fi‿lmaṭʿam wi ʿašān kida ma-laʾāš taṛabēza faḍya.*

____

13. *maʿād ilġada ʾaṛṛab wi ʿašān kida ṛawwaḥna.*

____

14. *iḥna binḥibb iṣṣaḥra‿w ʿašān kida‿štaṛakna fi‿rriḥla.*

____

XIV. Organize the words into sentences.

1. *isSaʿudiyya, sinīn, mudarris, fi, baʾāli, xamas, baštaġal.*

____

2. *law, aḥsan, gētu, šuwayya, kān, badri, kuntu.*

____

3. *ilmudīr, tiḥibbi, tišūfi, iza, lāzim, šuwayya, kunti, tistanni.*

____

4. *ʾigaṛha, iza, maʿʾūl, kān, iššaʾʾa, ḥāxud, di.*

____

5. *lolāk, ʾē, ʿirifna, niʿmil, ma-kunnāš.*

____

6. *muḥaḍrāt, kunna, law, ʿandina, ilkulliyya, kān, ruḥna.*

____

7. *aẓunn, isSadd ilʿĀli, inn, bi‿nnisba li, muhimm, Maṣr.*

____

8. *imbāriḥ, gild, wi, šanṭa, Fawziyya, gazma, ištarit, ḥilwīn.*

____

9. *dafʿ irrusūm, min, issufun, qanāt isSuwēs, bitmurr, baʿd.*

____

XV. Translate the following sentences.

1. I gave the porter the key to the flat.

2. Give it to them, then!

3. I want to show them the library.

4. When are you going to give (back) the money that I lent you?

5. I have neither my passport nor my driving license with me.

6. He explained a subject to us which was (quite) new for (*ʿala*) us.

7. He has neither bought the vegetables, nor has he cooked them.

8. If I'd had time, I would have visited you.

9. When we were in Aswan it was very hot.

10. I don't know her and she doesn't know me either.

11. When *Samīr* gets back from Kuwait, he's going to marry *Hiba*.

12. Cotton shirts are best in (*fi*) this heat.

13. If the lift is broken, we shall have to go up by the stairs on foot.

14. If Egypt hadn't built cheaper hotels, the tourists wouldn't have come.

15. If the car had been repaired, the accident wouldn't have happened.

LESSON XVI

READING PASSAGES

ittaɛlīm fi-Maṣr

1. *kān maḥw ilʾummiyya fi‿lmudun wi fi‿lquṛa ɛan ṭarīʾ ittaɛlīm min ahammᵊ ʾahdāf sawṛit ʾalfᵊ tusɛumiyya‿tnēn wi xamsīn.*

2. *ɛašān kida ʾamaṛ wazīr ittarbiyya wi‿ttaɛlīm bi-ʾinšāʾ madāris magganiyya‿gdīda, ɛilāwa ɛala‿lmadāris ilḥukumiyya‿lmawgūda wi‿lmadāris ilxāṣṣa.*

3. *bi‿nnisba li-baṛāmig ittaɛlīm ʾamaṛ ilwazīr bi-taʾlīf kutub gidīda bi‿lɛaṛabi ɛan tarīx wi guġṛafyit ilbilād ilɛaṛabiyya, wi ʾaṣbaḥit ilmawāddᵊ di ʾigbāri‿f-gamīɛ ilmadāris.*

4. *amma‿ttaɛlīm fi‿ggamɛa fa-baʾa maggāni li‿lmaṣriyyīn wi‿l-kull ilmuwāṭinīn ilɛaṛab. wi ẓaharit kutub gidīda bi‿lluġa‿lɛaṛabiyya fi‿lmawādd ilɛilmiyya, liʾinn ilmarāgiɛ ilʾagnabiyya kānit ʾaḥyānan ṣaɛba ɛala ʾabnāʾ iššaɛb.*

5. *di kānit ʾawwil xaṭawāt fi taṭawwur niẓām ittaɛlīm fi-Maṣr, wi‿ttaṭawwur da ma zāl gāri‿lġāyit ma yiwṣal li-mustawa‿ynāsib ɛadāt wi ʾahdāf ilbilād ilɛaṛabiyya.*

ilfaṛaḥ ilmaṣri

1. *min yōm ma Samya‿txaṭabit wi xaṭibha Maḥmūd biyištaġal fi‿sSaɛudiyya.*

2. *ʾawwil ma yirgaɛ ḥayḥaddidu maɛād ilfaṛaḥ wi yiggawwizu ɛala ṭūl.*

3. *baɛdᵊ ma yiggawwizu ḥaysafru ʾAswān ɛašān yimaḍḍu‿hnāk šahṛ ilɛasal bitaɛhum.*

4. *wi baɛdᵊ kida ḥayirgaɛu Maṣrᵊ‿f-šaʾʾithum iggidīda, lākin miš ḥayʾaḍḍu maɛa baɛḍᵊ ġēr šahrēn liʾinnᵊ Maḥmūd muḍṭarrᵊ yirgaɛ isSaɛudiyya‿lġāyit ma yintihi ɛaʾd ilɛamal bitāɛu, wi Samya lāzim tistilim šuġlaha iggidīd fi‿lmustašfa.*

5. *ɛa‿ṣṣēf taʾrīban ḥaykūn Maḥmūd rigiɛ wi ḥayathum ka-ẓōg wi zōga ḥatibtidi‿b-ḥaʾʾᵊ‿w ḥaʾīʾi.*

VOCABULARY

ʾaḍḍa, yiʾaḍḍi ḥ	to spend time	*hadaf, ahdāf*	goal, aim
ʾaṣbaḥ, yiṣbaḥ ḥ	to become	*ḥaddid, yiḥaddid*	to set, to fix
ʾaṣṣ, yiʾuṣṣ ḥ	to cut	*itxaṭabit, titxiṭib*	to get engaged (of women)
ʾigbāri	compulsory	*ibtada, yibtidi ḥ*	to begin
ʾinšāʾ	establishing	*ma zāl*	is still, yet
bāku, bakuwāt	package	*maḍḍa, yimaḍḍi ḥ*	to spend
bi-ḥaʾʾᵊ‿w ḥaʾīʾi	really	*maggāni*	free of charge
faṛaḥ, afṛāḥ	wedding	*maḥw ilʾummiyya*	combatting illiteracy
gāri	going on		
guġṛafya	geography		

maṛgaɛ, maṛāgiɛ	source (literary)	*taṭawwur*	evolution
maɛād, mawaɛīd	appointment	*wazīr, wuzaṛa*	minister
mādda, mawādd	material; topic	*xad, yāxud ɛala ḫ*	to get used to
muḍṭarr	forced, obliged	*xaṭīb*	fiancé
muwāṭin, -īn	citizen	*xaṭwa, xaṭawāt*	step
niẓām, nuẓum	system	*xāṣṣ*	private
sixin, yisxan	to grow warm	*zōg, azwāg*	husband
isSaɛudiyya	Saudi Arabia	*ẓahaṛ, yiẓhar*	to appear
ṣaydaliyya, -āt	pharmacy	*ɛaʔdᵊ ɛamal*	contract (for work)
šahṛ ilɛasal	honeymoon		
taʔlīf	writing, composing	*ɛan ṭarīʔ*	via, through
		ɛasal	honey
taʔrīban	approximately	*ɛilmi*	scientific

GRAMMAR

I. *illa* and *ġēr* "only" "except" "no other"

The simplest way to express "only" or "except" is by using the word *bass* in an affirmative sense:

talāta bass	"only three"
ilmaṭar biyinzil ɛandina fi‿ššita bass	"in our (country) it only rains in winter"

But if one wants to give the emphasis to the word "only," one must use a negative followed by *illa* or *ġēr* meaning "except":

ilmaṭar biyinzil ɛandina fi‿ššita bass	
→ *ilmaṭar ma-byinzilšᵊ ɛandina illa fi‿ššita*	it doesn't rain in our (country) except in winter
fāḍil rubɛᵊ sāɛa bass	
→ *miš fāḍil ġēr rubɛᵊ sāɛa*	there is only a quarter of an hour left
maɛāya‿lxamsīn ʔiršᵊ dōl bass	
→ *ma-mɛayīš ġēr ilxamsīn ʔiršᵊ dōl*	I've got nothing on me except these 50 piasters

In contrast to *illa, ġēr* can be combined with a possessive suffix:

ma-ḫaddiš ġērak	"nobody (else) but you"

II. *anhū, anhī, anhūm* "which ... ?" "which one?"

The interrogative words *anhū* (m.), *anhī* (f.) and *anhūm* ~ *anhūn* (pl.) "which" "which one" can be placed (a) after a defined noun or (b) before an undefined noun. In both cases they agree with the noun they refer to:

(a)	*ilbāb anhū*	*ilɛaṛabiyya anhī*	*iṭṭalaba anhūm* ~ *anhūn*
(b)	*ánhu bāb*	*ánhi ɛaṛabiyya*	*ánhu ṭalaba* ~ *ánhi ṭalaba*
	which door?	which car?	which students?

Note that in (b)

* The stress is on the first syllable
* When referring to people in the plural, *ánhu* as well as *ánhi* can be used:

ánhi zabāyin? "which clients?" *ánhu mudarrisīn?* "which teachers?"

III. *kida* "thus" "this way" "that"

In the first instance, *kida* means "thus" "like that" "this way":

kida aḫsan "it's better this way" *kida miš ḫayinfaɛ* "that won't do"

kida can also be translated by "that" especially when it follows a preposition:

aḫsan min kida ma-fīš	"there's nothing better than that"
maɛna kida ʾinn.....	"that means that ..."

baɛdᵊ kida	"after that"	*ʾablᵊ kida*	"before that"
ɛašān kida	"that's why"	*zayyᵊ kida*	"like that"

Note that the expression "in spite of that" is always expressed by *maɛa zālik* (never *maɛa kida*).

IV. *baɛḍ* "each other" and *baɛḍ* "some" "several" "a few"

1. *baɛḍ* expresses reciprocity

* with verbs as in:

imta ḫanšūf baɛḍᵊ tāni?	"when shall we meet (each other) again?"
biybuṣṣu‿l-baɛḍ	"they look at each other"
bitiɛrafu baɛḍ?	"do you know each other?"

* with prepositions as in:

Salwa wi Randa saknīn gambᵊ baɛḍ	"Salwa and Randa live near each other"
kānu mašyīn waṛa baɛḍ	"they were walking one after the other"

In the same way *fōʾ baɛḍ* "one above the other" and *maɛa baɛḍ* "with each other."

2. In more formal speech, *baɛḍ* is used to express "several" "some" "certain" in combination with a defined noun in the plural:

baɛḍ innās "certain people" *fi-baɛḍ ilmunasbāt* "on some occasions"

N.B. * Instead of *baɛḍ*, in less formal speech *kām* is often used with an undefined singular noun to express "some" "a few":

ḫaʾɛud hina kām yōm wi baɛdᵊ kida ḫasāfir tāni
"I'll stay here for a few days and then set off again"

ma-ɛandūš ġēr kām ṣāḫib hina
"he's only got a few friends here"

* Remember: In interrogative sentences *kām* means "how many":

ḫatuʾʿud hina kām yōm? "how many days are you staying here?"

* Pay attention to the difference in pronunciation between *baʿd* "after" and *baʿḍ* "some" "several."

V. Subordinate clauses of time

1. In Arabic the conjunctions which introduce a subordinate clause of time frequently consist of a preposition followed by the particle *ma* :

baʿdᵊ ma	after	*ʾablᵊ ma*	before
sāʿit ma	the moment that, when	*waʾtᵊ ma*	at the time when
yōm ma	on the day when	*kullᵊ ma*	whenever, every time
min sāʿit ma	since the moment that	*min yōm ma*	since the day that
min waʾtᵊ ma	since the time that	*liġāyit ma*	until
liḫaddᵊ ma	until	*ʾawwil ma*	as soon as

The subject of the subordinate clause of time can be placed before or after the particle *ma* :

ʾablᵊ Ḥasan ma yīgi ~ *ʾablᵊ ma Ḥasan yīgi* "before Ḥasan comes"
ʾabl inta ma timši ~ *ʾablᵊ ma timši* "before you go"

2. Use

(a) *kullᵊ ma* "whenever" "each time that" may only be combined with the simple imperfect:

kullᵊ ma yirkin ilʿaṛabiyya‿hnāk yisīb ilfaṛāmil sayba
"every time he parks the car there, he leaves the handbrake off"

kullᵊ ma‿yšufni yifṛaḫ
"every time he sees me, he's happy"

(b) *baʿdᵊ ma* "after" is used with the perfect to express past time, and with the simple imperfect to express future time:

baʿd ilwafdᵊ ma ʿadda rigʿit ilḫayā fi‿ššawāriʿ ka‿lʿāda
"after the delegation had passed, life in the streets returned to normal"

baʿd irraʾīs ma yistaʾbil iḍḍuyūf ḫayrūḫu‿lʾaṣr iggumhūri
"after the president has welcomed the guests, they will go to the Palace of the Republic"

(c) *ʾablᵊ ma* "before" is used with the simple imperfect even when it refers to past time:

ṛāḫ ilmaṭār ʾabl ilwafdᵊ ma yiwṣal
"he got to the airport before the delegation arrived"

ʿadda ʿalēna ʾablᵊ ma‿yṛawwaḫ
"he dropped in to see us before going home"

(d) *ʾawwil ma* "as soon as" is used with the imperfect or the perfect:

ʾawwil ma tiwṣal ilmidān, tiḫawwid yimīn
"as soon as you get to the square, turn right"

ʾawwil ma‿wṣiltᵊ nadaht ilmunādi
"as soon as I arrived I called the parking attendant

(e) *lamma* "when" "whenever," *sāɛit ma* "the moment when," *yōm ma* "the day when," *waʾtᵊ ma* "the time when" can refer to past or future time and thus be combined with the perfect or the imperfect:

lamma‿nɛūz baṭṭīx niʾullu ya Hāni rūḥ giblina baṭṭīxa
"whenever we want some water melons we say: Hāni, go and get a water melon for us"

lamma waṣalt ikkurnīš laʾēt iššāriɛ zaḥma ɛa‿lʾāxir
"when I arrived at the Corniche I found the street extremely crowded"

yōm ma kān igginē(h) ginē(h)
"in the days when a pound was (still) a pound"

(f) *min sāɛit ma* "since the moment that," *min yōm ma* "since the day that," *min waʾtᵊ ma* "since the time that" are always combined with the perfect:

min yōm ɛAli ma ḥaggᵊ baṭṭal šurb
"since the day that ɛAli went on a pilgrimage he stopped drinking"

min sāɛit ma‿štaġaltᵊ hina baʾūm iṣṣubḥᵊ badri
"since the time I started to work here I've had to get up early"

(g) *lamma, liḥaddᵊ ma, liġāyit ma* "until" can be combined with the perfect or the imperfect:

fiḍlu mašyīn liġāyit ma wiṣlu‿ssūʾ	"they kept on walking until they got to the market"
lāzim nistanna lamma yīgi‿lʾutubīs	"we must wait till the bus comes"

VI. Other subordinate clauses

1. *ɛalašān* ~ *ɛašān* (→ XI.IV.3b) and *liʾinn* ~ *liʾann* "because," "because of," are causal conjunctions. *liʾinn* ~ *liʾann* can be followed by a verbal, nominal, or prepositional sentence, while the rules used in the case of *inn* (→ XV.I.1 and 2) also apply to sentences introduced by *liʾinn* ~ *liʾann* :

... *liʾinnina taɛbanīn ʾawi*	"... because we're very tired"
... *liʾinnuhum yistahlu*	"... because they deserve it"
... *liʾinnᵊ Samīra bintᵊ‿kwayyisa*	"... because *Samīra* is a nice girl"

Be careful: *ɛalašān* ~ *ɛašān* used with the simple imperfect indicates purpose, not reason (→ XI.IV.3b).

2. *maɛa ʾinn - walaw ʾinn* "however" "even if" "even though" are used with all types of sentence while the rules used in the case of *inn* are also applied to them:

fihimt kullᵊ ḥāga maɛa ʾinn ilɛarabi‿btāɛi miš ʾawi
"I understood everything even though my Arabic isn't very good"

wiʾift atfarrag walaw ʾinni kuntᵊ mistaɛgil ʾawi
"I stood and watched even though I was in a hurry"

3. *zayyᵊ ma‿ykūn* and *ka˒ann* ~ *ka˒inn* "as if" are used to introduce unrealizable comparisons:

zayyᵊ ma‿ykūn fī ʕīd walla ḥāga	"as if there were a feast or something"
ka˒innᵊ ma-fīš ḥāga ḥaṣalit	"as if nothing had happened"

4. *zayyᵊ ma* "just as" is used with the perfect, a participle, or the simple imperfect:

zayyᵊ ma‿nti šayfa ma-fīš ḥāga	"as you (fem.) see, there is nothing"
zayyᵊ ma‿ntu ʕarfīn	"as you (pl.) know"
zayyᵊ ma tīgi tīgi	"come what may"

5. *badal ma* ~ *bidāl ma* "instead of" is always used with the simple imperfect:

badal ma yu˒ʕud fi‿lbēt xaṛag yitmašša‿šwayya
"instead of sitting at home, he went for a walk"

badal ma tittiṣil bī, rūḥ zūru
"instead of calling him, pay him a visit"

6. *min ġēr ma* "without" is always used with the simple imperfect:

rigiʕ mi‿sSaʕudiyya min ġēr ma‿ygīb ḥāga
"he came back from Saudi Arabia without bringing anything (back)"

Note that in Arabic "without" can also be expressed by means of a negative circumstantial clause:

Samya‿txaṭabit min ġēr ma‿ʕraf → *Samya‿txaṭabit w‿ana miš ʕārif*
"Samya got engaged without my knowing"

VII. Borrowings from Standard Arabic

When listening to the speech of educated Egyptians you will often come across words which do not comply with the rules given in *kullu tamām*. These words are usually borrowings from Standard Arabic, which sometimes differs from colloquial Arabic in its rules. For instance, Standard Arabic does not elide *-i-* nor shorten long vowels, as in the case of *ʕāmma* "public (f.)," *xāṣṣa* "private (f.)," *ṭālíba* "student (f.)," *ilQāhíra* "Cairo," *gāmiʕāt* "universities," *ʕā˒ilāt* "families," *muwāṭinīn* "citizens" etc.

The glottal stop ˒ may also be preserved, whereas in ordinary speech it would be elided: *il˒ayyām* "the days" instead of *il-iyyām.*

As to morphology, *nisba*-adjectives receive feminine and plural suffixes just as other adjectives do: *madāris magganiyya* "free schools."

EXERCISES

I. Which one? It makes no difference, whichever you like!

āxud anhu taks? - *xud ʾayy^ə taks^ə min ittaksiyyāt!*

1. *arkab anhu ʾutubīs?* - ______________________
2. *albis anhi badla?* - ______________________
3. *nāxud anhu dawa?* - ______________________
4. *nirkab anhi ʿaṛabiyya?* - ______________________
5. *aftaḥ anhu bāku?* - ______________________
6. *axušš anhi ṣaydaliyya?* - ______________________
7. *asʾal anhu ʿaskari?* - ______________________
8. *niʾaggaṛ anhi šaʾʾa?* - ______________________
9. *anām fi-ʾanhi ʾōḍa?* - ______________________
10. *arūḥ ʾanhi madrasa?* - ______________________

II. Fill in the blanks using *anhu, anhi, anhūm*.

1. *iḥna miš ʿarfīn nāxud* ____________ *ʾutubīs.*
2. *ya-taṛa,* ____________ *ʿaṛabiyya ʾarxaṣ?*
3. *ʿawzīn titkallimu maʿa* ____________ *ṭalaba?*
4. *ḥatirkabu* ____________ *ʾaṭr?*
5. *ya Sāmi, nifsak tišūf* ____________ *film?*
6. *intu‿xtartu‿lmaṭʿam* ____________ *?*
7. *ḥatrūḥ ginent‿ilḥayawanāt maʿa* ____________ *ʾawlād?*
8. *Ḥasan miš ʿārif lāzim yištaġal fi* ____________ *madrasa.*
9. *ʿawzīn tištiru* ____________ *taṛabēẓa?*
10. *ʾarētu* ____________ *kutub?*

III. Use *baʿḍ* "each other" correctly in the following sentences.

ilfakahāni gamb ilxuḍari yaʿni humma litnēn gambᵊ baʿḍ

1. *ʿAli sākin gambᵊ Maḥmūd yaʿni* ______________________
2. *Samya gat maʿa Samīra yaʿni* ______________________
3. *Aḥmad kān biyitʿašša maʿa Maḥmūd yaʿni* ______________
4. *Samīr ʾābil Muḥammad ʿa‿ssalālim yaʿni* ______________
5. *ana ḥašūfak baʿdᵊ bukṛa yaʿni‿ḥna* ______________
6. *Fikri‿biyfahhim ʿAli wi ʿAli‿biyfahhim Fikri yaʿni* __________
7. *Maḥmūd ṛāḥ ilMugammaʿ, wi Sayyid ṛāḥ maʿā(h) yaʿni* ________
8. *Sayyid biyidris wi Badrᵊ‿byidris maʿā(h) yaʿni* ____________
9. *Maha xadit ʿala Sanāʾ wi Sanāʾ xadit ʿala Maha yaʿni* __________
10. *ilfustān da zayy ilfustān da yaʿni* ______________
11. *huwwa ʿagabha w‿hiyya ʿagabitu yaʿni* ______________
12. *imbāriḥ kalna samak wi ʾawwil imbāriḥ kamān yaʿni yomēn waṛa* ______________ *samak!*

IV. Use *ġēr* and the suitable suffix to express "no other" "only" etc.

irrubʿᵊ‿gnē(h) da, miš fāḍil maʿāna ġēru.

1. *iššanṭa di, ana miš šayfa šanṭa* ______________
2. *ilmaḥallāt di, ana miš ʿarfa maḥallāt* ______________
3. *da‿bni wi di binti, ma-ʿandīš awlād* ______________
4. *yiẓhar gēna badri ʾawi, ma-fīš* ______________ *fi‿lmaktab.*
5. *ana ʾuxtu‿lwaḥīda, wi ma-lūš* ______________
6. *intu samʿinni, lākin ma-ḥaddiš* ______________ *samiʿni.*
7. *ana ʿāwiz aštiri‿lkutub di bass, miš ʿāwiz aštiri kutub* __________
8. *inta ṣadīqi‿lwaḥīd, ma-līš ṣadīq* ______________

9. *issikirtēra di‿kwayyisa, miš ɛawzīn sikirtēra* ________________

10. *ahum dōl iṭṭalaba‿btuɛna, ma-ɛandināš ṭalaba* ________________

11. *ittilivizyōn da miš ḫilw lākin ma-ɛandināš* ____________________

12. *inti ʔuxti‿w ḫabibti‿w ma-līš* ______________________ *fi‿ddunya.*

13. *ilʔummiyya hiyya sabab ilmašākil, ma-fīš* ___________________

14. *maɛād ilfaṛaḫ itḫaddid, miš binfakkaṛ fi maɛād* ________________

15. *faḍillina šahrēn bass, ma-fīš* _______________________________

V. Only three days! Use the negative with *ġēr* or *illa*.

ḫaʔɛud talat t-iyyām bass. - *miš ḫaʔɛud ġēr talat t-iyyām.*

- *miš ḫaʔɛud illa talat t-iyyām.*

1. *ɛandi xamsa‿gnē(h) bass.* - ____________________________.

2. *šuftu maṛṛa waḫda bass.* - ____________________________.

3. *ɛagabni‿lbulōfar da bass.* - ____________________________.

4. *ɛanduhum ilmudēl da bass.* - ____________________________.

5. *bināxud ʔagāza fi‿ṣṣēf bass.* - ____________________________.

6. *ɛawzīn salamtak bass.* - ____________________________.

7. *arkab taks^{ə} fāḍi bass.* - ____________________________.

8. *ilḫagāt di mawgūda ɛandina bass.* - ____________________________.

9. *ilmaṭar biyinzil ɛandina fi‿ššita bass.* - ______________________.

10. *ʔaɛad fi-Maṣr^{ə} sanatēn bass.* - ____________________________.

11. *ḫakūn fi-Maṣr^{ə} yomēn bass.* - ____________________________.

12. *baktib bi‿lʔalam ilḫibr^{ə} bass.* - ____________________________.

VI. What a disappointment! Use *lamma* with the perfect or the imperfect and pay close attention to the meaning.

aḫibb aṭlaɛ šaʾʾiti - *alāʾi‿lʾaṣansēr ɛaṭlān.*
→ *lamma ḫabbēt aṭlaɛ šaʾʾiti laʾēt ilʾaṣansēr ɛaṭlān.*

1. *adxul ilḫammām* - *alāʾi‿lmayya maʾṭūɛa.*

___

2. *abtidi ʾaḫaḍḍar ilfiṭār* - *gaṛas ilbāb yiḍrab.*

___

3. *aḫibb aɛmil fingān ʾahwa* - *ma‿laʾīš bunnᵊ fi‿lbēt.*

___

4. *aʾɛud afṭar* - *yibtidi gaṛas ittilifōn yirinn.*

___

5. *arūḫ maktab iggawazāt* - *ilmuwaẓẓaf ġāyib.*

___

6. *aḫibb awallaɛ innūr* - *ma-fīš kahṛaba.*

___

7. *axrug mi‿lbēt* - *iddinya bitmaṭṭar.*

___

8. *arkab ilʾaṭr* - *ma-laʾīš fī amākin faḍya*

___

9. *azurha fi‿lmustašfa* - *uxti ɛamla ɛamaliyya.*

___

10. *anzil issūʾ* - *alāʾi‿lmaḫallāt bitiʾfil.*

___

VII. Every morning! Using *baɛdᵊ ma*, combine each of the sentences below in turn with the one that follows, and pay careful attention to the meaning.

aṣḫa‿ṣṣubḫ - arūḫ ilḫammām - āxud dušš - aġsil sināni - abtidi albis hidūmi - aḫaḍḍar ilfiṭār - afṭar - arūḫ iššuġl - ašṛāb šāy - aʾṛa‿ggurnāl - aktib šiwayyit gawabāt

aṣḫa‿ṣṣubḫ - arūḫ ilḫammām → *baɛdᵊ ma‿ṣḫa‿ṣṣubḫᵊ barūḫ ilḫammām*

___

___

___

___

____

____

____

____

____

VIII. Yesterday was just the same! Using *baɛdᵊ ma*, combine the following sentences in pairs, just as you did in exercise VII.

aṣḥa‿ṣṣubḥ - arūḥ ilḥammām - āxud dušš - aġsil sināni - abtidi albis hidūmi - aḥaḍḍar ilfiṭār - afṭar - arūḥ iššuġl - ašṛāb šāy - aʔṛa‿ggurnāl - aktib šuwayyit gawabāt

aṣḥa‿ṣṣubḥ - arūḥ ilḥammām → *baɛdᵊ ma‿ṣḥīt iṣṣubḥᵊ ruḥt ilḥammām*

____

____

____

____

____

____

____

____

____

IX. *mašākil ilmurūr* "traffic problems." Write a suitable conjunction in each of the blanks.

liḥaddᵊ ma, min ʔawwil ma, ɛašān, liġāyit ma, lamma, baɛdᵊ ma, kullᵊ ma, min sāɛit ma, maɛa ʔinn, lamma, badal ma, lamma

1. ____________ *ṣḥīt min innōm ḥassēt bi-ṣudāɛ šidīd.*
2. *dawwaṛtᵊ ɛala‿sbirīna ʔaxudha* ____________ *yixiff iṣṣudāɛ šuwayya, lākin ma-kanšᵊ fī wala‿sbirināya fi‿lbēt.*
3. ____________ *xadtᵊ dušš, ḥassēt inni ʔaḥsan bi-ktīr.*
4. *fiṭirtᵊ wi‿nziltᵊ mi‿lbēt. rikibt ilɛaṛabiyya‿btaɛti‿w* ____________ *ḥabbēt aftaḥ ilkuntakt laʔēt ilbaṭariyya faḍya.*

5. ______________ *ašaġġal ilmutūr yirūḥ wāʾif ʿala ṭūl.*

6. *ṭalabtᵊ mi‿lbawwāb yizuʾʾili‿lʿaṛabiyya*______________ *ʾāmit wi‿lḥamdu lillāh.*

7. *ʿand ilkubri‿lʿilwi ibtada ilmutūr yisxan, fa-daxaltᵊ‿šmāl* ______________ *da kān mamnūʿ.*

8. *wi* ____________ *aʿaddi ʿala‿tTaḥrīr futtᵊ ʿala Gardin Siti.*

9. ____________ *wiṣiltᵊ ʾaxīṛan šuġli kānit issāʿa tisʿa.*

10. *yaʿni* ___________ *‿nziltᵊ min ilbēt*___________ *‿wṣilt ilmaktab kān fāt aktaṛ min sāʿa‿w nuṣṣ.*

X. What should he do first? Give him advice or tell him what to do.

aġsil šaʿṛi‿lʾawwil walla ʾaʾuṣṣu? → *iġsilu ʾablᵊ ma‿tʾuṣṣu!*

1. *axallaṣ iššuġl ilʾawwil walla ʾaṛawwaḥ?*

____

2. *aḥaḍḍar ilfiṭār ilʾawwil walla ʾāxud dušš?*

____

3. *atġadda‿lʾawwil walla ʾanām?*

____

4. *aʿmil iššāy walla ʾalbis hidūmi‿lʾawwil?*

____

5. *arūḥ iššuġlᵊ walla ʾafṭar ilʾawwil?*

____

6. *atfaṛṛag ʿa‿ttilivizyōn walla ʾaʾṛa‿ggurnāḷ ilʾawwil?*

____

7. *aġsil sināni walla ʾāxud dušš ilʾawwil?*

____

8. *argaʿ ilbēt walla ʾatʿašša‿lʾawwil?*

____

9. *anzil issūʾ walla ʾaḥaḍḍar ilġada‿lʾawwil?*

____

10. *aṛawwaḥ walla ʾawaṣṣal Suʿād ilʾawwil?*

____

11. *aktib iggawabāt walla‿rūḥ li‿lmudīr ilʾawwil?*

____

12. *agīb istimāṛa walla‿ʿmil ṣuwar ilʾawwil?*

____

XI. Organize the words into sentences.

1. *ilʾutubīs, ʾawwil ma, rikibnā, wiṣil, ʿala ṭūl.*

____

2. *maʿa ʾinni, ruḥt, atmašša, taʿbān, ʿa‿kkurnēš, kunt.*

____

3. *ʿārif, zayyᵊ ma, inta, ilmurūr, Maṣr, fi, ṣaʿb.*

____

4. *yikūnu, bi-surʿa, biyigru, zayyᵊ ma, mistaʿgilīn.*

____

5. *gahhiz, ʾablᵊ ma, issūʾ, tinzil, ya Ḥasan, ilfiṭār!*

____

6. *iggawwizu, igGīza, saknīn, min yōm ma, humma, fi, wi.*

____

7. *liġāyit ma, li, imši, ʾāxir iššāriʿ, tiwṣal!*

____

8. *wiṣil, sāʿit ma, kalām, min, ma-baṭṭalš.*

____

9. *ʾawwil ma, gih, ʿalayya, šafni, yisallim.*

____

10. *kullᵊ ma, issuʾāl, yiḥmaṛṛᵊ wiššu, asʾalu, da.*

____

XII. Translate the following sentences.

1. Even though I had a headache, I started to work.

____

2. When *Samīr* comes back from Kuwait, he will marry *Samya*.

____

3. When we were in Aswan it was very hot.

____

4. The delegation had passed by before I arrived at the *Taḫrīr* Square.

5. "What would you like to drink?" – "It doesn't matter, either tea or coffee."

6. Education was made compulsory for all citizens.

7. *Samya* doesn't want to get married because (*liʾann*) she's still young.

8. After I have finished my studies at school, I shall go to University.

9. The girl continued to wait until the teacher asked her to come in.

10. "*Faṭma*, please bring the cups with you!" "What cups?"

11. *Samīr*, you must finish your work before your friends come!

12. Every time he comes, he tells strange stories.

13. This train only stops at the main stations.

14. I don't want to go on a journey unless you come with me.

15. *Mirvat* and *Hāla* looked at each other without speaking.

16. He speaks to nobody except (those) people he knows really well.

17. We've got to study seven topics at the University this year.

18. Economic development has reached a high level.

19. She appealed to him from the first moment he saw her.

20. Nobody's coming today except you.

LESSON XVII

Arabic Script

In order to prepare students for the study of Modern Standard Arabic (MSA), Arabic script is introduced starting with lessons XI through XVI. It is intended in the first instance to familiarize the students with Arabic letters and with the basic rules of reading and writing.

In the Arab world, MSA is used for the written text. In Egypt, however, there is also a considerable body of literature written in dialect.

Since there is a marked difference between the two varieties of Arabic, only those words which are the same in both, or which differ from each other very slightly, will be used in this lesson.

Basic facts:

- ☞ the alphabet consists of 28 letters
- ☞ Arabic is written from right to left
- ☞ only consonants and long vowels are written.
- ☞ doubled consonants are only written once
- ☞ short vowels are sometimes indicated by diacritical signs

In Arabic the word *yiktib* is written {yktb} يكتب, *mudarris* is {mdrs} مدرس , *kibīr* is {kbyr} كبير , *surūr* is {srwr} سرور . Since the short vowels are not written, every Arabic word can be read in more than one way. For example{ktb} كتب could represent *katab* or *kutub;* {mdrsh} مدرسة could either be *madrasa* or *mudarrisa.* This is why it is only possible to read fluently and correctly if you have a good knowledge of the language.

Letter formation:

Most letters can be written in four different ways depending on whether they are written separately and stand on their own, or whether they occur at the beginning, middle or end of a word and thus connect to another letter on the left, on the right, or on both sides. Some letters cannot connect on the left to the letter which follows them and so their medial form is the same as their final form. Some letters differ from one another simply by the number of dots written above or below them. They fall naturally into four groups, which will be described below.

Arabic is written "morphologically". This means that if the stress shifts and causes a long vowel to be pronounced as a short one, the vowel still retains its original shape and is written long, e.g., *mawgūd* + *īn* → *mawgūdīn* موجودين "present" (not *mawgudīn*), *kātib* + *a* → *kātiba* كاتبة "female writer" (not *katba*) and *bēt+nā* → *bētnā* بيتنا. "our house" (not *betna*)

I. First group of letters (with lesson XI)

name	sound	separate	final	medial	initial
bāʾ	*b*	ب	ـب	ـبـ	بـ
yāʾ	*y, ī, i, ē, e, ā*	ي	ـى or ـي	ـيـ	يـ
nūn	*n*	ن	ـن	ـنـ	نـ
tāʾ	*t*	ت	ـت	ـتـ	تـ
ṯāʾ	*ṯ*	ث	ـث	ـثـ	ثـ
ʾalif	*ʾa, ʾā, ʾi, a, ā, i*	ا	ـا	ـا	ا
wāw	*w, ū, u, ō, o*	و	ـو	ـو	و
mīm	*m*	م	ـم	ـمـ	مـ

The letters ا and و are non-connectors, which means that they cannot be linked to the letter on their left. Together with the letter ي they are used to represent the long vowels *ā ō ū ē ī*, and to indicate short vowels in words borrowed from other languages.

ا is also used to indicate one of the short vowels *a-*, *i-* or *u-* at the beginning of a word.

ث , which is represented by *ṯ* is pronounced 'th' as in the English word 'thin.' In informal speech it is frequently pronounced as *t* and in cultured informal speech as *s*.

Final *yā'* can be written with ـي or without dots ى depending on whether it is to be pronounced *ī* or *ā* (*ʾalif maqṣūra*), e.g. بنى *banā* "he built," but بيتي *bētī* "my house." However, in Egypt final *yā'* is almost always written without dots.

Reading exercise:

ibn		ابن	*bāb*		باب
bātā	"Bata"	باتا	*ṯāliṯ*	"third"	ثالث
yōm		يوم	*yimīn*	"right"	يمين
anā		انا	*nōm*		نوم
bint		بنت	*nabāt*	"plant"	نبات
ṯaman	"price"	ثمن	*mabnā*		مبنى

Writing exercise:

nōm, tamām, min, bāb, mōt, ṯāliṯ , mabnā, ibn, bātā, nām, bēt bintī nāmit, bāb bētī, anā bint, ṯāliṯ mabnā.

Reading exercise:

بنات نام تمام من نبات ابن

مبنى ثمن مات بنت انا انت

تمام باب بيت يوم يمين نوم

II. Second group of letters (with lesson XII)

name	sound	separate	final	medial	initial
kāf	*k*	ك	ـك	ـكـ	كـ
lām	*l, ḷ*	ل	ـل	ـلـ	لـ
dāl	*d*	د	ـد	ـد	د
ḏāl	*ḏ, d, z*	ذ	ـذ	ـذ	ذ
rāʾ	*r, ṛ*	ر	ـر	ـر	ر
zāy	*z*	ز	ـز	ـز	ز
hāʾ	*h*	ه	ـه	ـهـ	هـ
fem. ending *-a* or *-it*		ة	ـة		

د ذ ر and ز are non-connectors and cannot be linked to the letter on their left. In MSA ذ *ḏ* must be pronounced 'th' as in the English words 'this, thy.' In everyday speech this is often replaced by *z*.

Both *ṛ* and *r* are written ر.

The feminine ending *-a* is written ة . In Egypt the dots are frequently omitted e.g. مكتبه *maktaba* "library," but when they form part of a genitive construction they must be written and are pronounced *-it*: مكتبة ناهد *maktabit Nāhid* "Nāhid's library."

The article *il-* (*al-* in MSA) is always written ال even when the *i-* is not pronounced as in *wi‿lbēt* والبيت, or when the *l-* is assimilated with the following consonant as in *innūr* النور "the light."

When *ʾalif* ا follows ل *lām* it is written لا *lā* "no." The letter *lām* may also be combined with the letter *mīm* as in لم *lam,* "not" and with the letters *mīm* and *ʾalif* as in لما *lammā* "when."

Reading exercise:

inNīl	النيل	*ḏahab*	"gold"	ذهب
maṛṛa	مرة ~ مره	*kalb*	"dog"	كلب
maṛṛāt	مرات	*haṛam*	"pyramid"	هرم
kōkākōlā	كوكاكولا	*awlād*		اولاد

ʾuktōbar		اكتوبر	*kalām*		كلام
bard		برد	*warda*	"flower"	وردة
ʾalam	"pain"	الم	*tadkaṛa*	"ticket"	تذكرة
ilkalām		الكلام	*ilward*		الورد
ilkalb		الكلب	*innūr*		النور

Writing exercise:

tazkaṛa (*z* = d̲), *baṛaka* (*-a* = ة), *kān, kunt, kitāb, nizil, nazzil, haṛam, muhimm, hināk, lāzim, mumkin, mawlūd, nādī, walad, awlād, balad, bilād, kitīr* (*t* = t̲), *ʾahl, hirib*

kitāb ilbint, wādī innīl, maktabī hinā, maktab Randā, biyūt kibīra.

Reading exercise:

برد	دكتور	بنزين	تذكرة	كلمة	الكلاب
بنك	لبنان	النيل	كلام	البنوك	الكتاب
نور	زمان	تراب	ذهب	كوداك	كوكاكولا
مهم	كبير	يناير	مولود	ممكن	اكتوبر

III. Third group of letters (with lesson XIII)

name	sound	separate	final	medial	initial
ɛayn	ɛ	ع	ـع	ـعـ	عـ
ġayn	ġ	غ	ـغ	ـغـ	غـ
ḫā'	ḫ	ح	ـح	ـحـ	حـ
xā'	x	خ	ـخ	ـخـ	خـ
ğīm	g, ğ, ž	ج	ـج	ـجـ	جـ
sīn	s	س	ـس	ـسـ	سـ
šīn	š	ش	ـش	ـشـ	شـ
fā'	f	ف	ـف	ـفـ	فـ
qāf	q , ʾ	ق	ـق	ـقـ	قـ

Both *ʾalif* and *qāf* are pronounced ʾ in the dialect of Cairo. However, the ʾ = q will always be represented by the letter *qāf* ق in MSA.

Reading exercise:

šawāriɛ		شوارع	*šuġl*	"work"	شغل
ilɛamal	"the work"	العمل	*mawāɛīd*		مواعيد
duxūl	"entrance"	دخول	*mamnūɛ*	"forbidden"	ممنوع
tadxīn	"smoking"	تدخين	*yōm iggumɛa*		يوم الجمعة
qāl	"he said"	قال	*qalam*	"pen"	قلم
yōm iggumɛa		يوم الجمعة	*kinīsa*		كنيسة
iġtiyāl		اغتيال	*ilmabāḫiṯ*		المباحث
iġtiyāl		اغتيال	*ilxārig*		الخارج
funduq		فندق	*raqm*		رقم
Iskindiriyya		اسكندرية	*ilQāhira*		القاهرة
tilifōn		تليفون	*šaqqa*		شقة
madrasa		مدرسة	*mustašfā*		مستشفى
ittaḫrīr		التحرير	*Rūsyā*		روسيا
sūbar		سوبر	*nādī*		نادي
ilʾ awlād		الاولاد	*madrasa*		المهندسين
gāmiɛa		جامعة	*gamāɛāt*		جماعات
xurūg	"exit"	خروج	*istiɛlāmāt*		استعلامات
aḥsan		احسن	*ilMaɛādi*		المعادي

Writing exercise:

funduʾ (ʾ = q), *fanādiʾ* (ʾ = q), *maɛhad, maɛāhid, ḫādis* (*s* = ṯ), *ḫawādis* (*s* = ṯ), *istiɛlāmāt, istiʾbāl* (ʾ = q), *iġtiyāl, mabāḫis* (*s* = ṯ), *gamāɛa* (-a = ة), *šuɛūb, xaṛag, dawla* (-a = ة), *ɛaṛab, walad Muḫammad, Maḫmūd, Samīr, Aḫmad, Ḫasan, Samīḫa* (-a = ة) *mawāɛīd ilɛamal, nādī‿lMuhandisīn, yōm issabt, šawāriɛ ilmadīna* (-a = ة), *madrast‿ilbanāt* (-*t* = ة)

Reading exercise:

ممنوع التدخين	جامع	القاهرة	اسكندرية
يوم الخميس	المهندسين	حوادث	المعادي
ممنوع الدخول	التحرير	الجيزة	جامعة
يوم السبت	بنزين	الشعب	الدول
شقة مفروشة	شوارع	مرة	الاغتيال
يوم الجمعة	كنيسة	شعوب	مباحث
فندق النيل	مهندس	احسن	سوبر
مواعيد العمل	دخول	خروج	مستشفى
مدرسة البنات	استعلامات	اسوان	استقبال
ميدان التحرير	محمود	محمد	سمير

IV. Fourth group of letters (with lesson XIV)

name	sound	separate	final	medial	initial
ṣād	*ṣ*	ص	ـص	ـصـ	صـ
ḍād	*ḍ*	ض	ـض	ـضـ	ضـ
ṭā'	*ṭ*	ط	ـط	ـطـ	طـ
ẓā'	*ẓ*	ظ	ـظ	ـظـ	ظـ
hamza	ʾ	ء			إ or أ

In spoken Arabic it often happens that non-emphatic letters are pronounced emphatically, due to the spreading effect of emphatic sounds. In the written form, these accidentally emphatic sounds (often *s, d, t, z,* or *r*) do not change; they retain their original, non-emphatic form. So one may say *Aṣyūṭ*, but one will always write *Asyūṭ* اسيوط.

When the *hamza* occurs at the beginning of a word, it is put above the *ʾalif* if the vowel which follows is *-a-* or *-u-*, and beneath the *ʾalif* when the following vowel is *-i-*.

Reading exercise:

ʾAṣr inNīl		قصر النيل	*Ṭābā*		طابا
Asyūṭ		أسيوط	*Maṣr*		مصر
iššurṭa	"police"	الشرطة	*Ṭanṭā*		طنطا
ṣālūn		صالون	*ʾĪṭālyā*		ايطاليا
ilmaṭār		المطار	*faḍḍa*	"silver"	فضة
ilbarīd ilgawwī		البريد الجوي	*ṭālib*		طالب
Kurnīš		كورنيش	*qahwa*		قهوة
iqtiṣād		اقتصاد	*alʾUqṣur* (= *Luʾṣur*)	"Luxor"	الأقصر

Writing exercise:

ɛāda (-a = ة), *ɛādāt, Samīḫa* (-a = ة), *ɛalam, ɛalāqa* (-a = ة), *ɛalāqāt, ɛāš, tuffāḫa* (-a = ة), *mūlid, tawqīɛ, mašrūɛ, mašārīɛ, baṣala* (-a = ة), *wafd, wufūd, duktūr, hirib, gamāɛa* (-a = ة), *dawla* (-a = ة), *nafs, šurṭa* (-a = ة), *ḍuhr* (*ḍ* = *ẓ*), *samak, wiṣil, ḍarab*

maṭār ilQāhira (-a = ة) *iddawlī, maglis iššaɛb, šahr Ramaḍān, ahṛām igGīza* (-a = ة), *ʾidāṛit ilmurūr* (-it = ة), *ʾidāṛit iggawāzāt* (-it = ة)

Reading exercise: ☜

مشروع	مشاريع	عساكر	مولد	إدارة الجامعة
عدد	بسيط	أطلق	مشاكل	نشرة الاخبار
قهوة	عقد	عقود	صناعة	البريد الجوي
وفد	وفود	افتتاح	حكاية	الوفد المصري
المطار	العلاقة	الشرطة	بسرعة	كورنيش النيل
شهر	متطرف	خبر	بطن	قصر الثقافة
الاخبار	وقت	تدريب	مكان	يوم السبت
ضيوف	علاقة	زيارة	توقيع	مواعيد العمل
العدد كامل				مصر ترحب بكم

V. The alphabet (with lesson XV)

☜

value	name	letter	value	name	letter
ṭ	*ṭāʾ*	ط	*ā, ʾi, ʾa, ʾu*	*ʾalif*	ا
ẓ, ḍ	*ẓāʾ*	ظ	*b*	*bāʾ*	ب
ε	*εayn*	ع	*t*	*tāʾ*	ت
ġ	*ġayn*	غ	*ṯ, t, s*	*ṯā’*	ث
f	*fāʾ*	ف	*g, ğ, ž*	*gīm*	ج
q, ʾ	*qāf*	ق	*ḥ*	*ḥāʾ*	ح
k	*kāf*	ك	*x*	*xāʾ*	خ
l	*lām*	ل	*d*	*dāl*	د
m	*mīm*	م	*ḏ, d, z*	*ḏāl*	ذ
n	*nūn*	ن	*r, ṛ*	*rāʾ*	ر
h -a	*hāʾ*	ه	*z*	*zāyn*	ز
w, ū, u, ō, o	*wāw*	و	*s*	*sīn*	س
y, ī, i, ē, e	*yāʾ*	ي	*š*	*šīn*	ش
ā	*ʾalif maqṣūra*	ى	*ṣ*	*ṣād*	ص
-a, -it	*tāʾ marbūṭa*	ة	*ḍ*	*ḍād*	ض

Numbers:

٠	٩	٨	٧	٦	٥	٤	٣	٢	١
0	9	8	7	6	5	4	3	2	1

Be careful: groups of figures are written from left to right.

٧٤٠١	٢٧٥٤٦	٦٤٥	١٩٩٢	٦٨٤٠٢
7401	27546	645	1992	68402

In the case of dates, the figures of each group are written from left to right, but the date as a whole is read from right to left:

٢٠٠٣/١٢/٢٧ = 27-12-2003

Read the following proper names:

مصطفى	عمر	فاطمة	حسن
محمود	خالد	كامل	سامي
صفوت	كمال	حسين	علي
سمير	احمد	مها	عبد الله
سامية	زينب	اشرف	عادل
عبد الناصر	جمال	غالي	ابراهيم
السادات	انور	مبارك	حسني

Ħasan, Fāṭima, عUmaṛ, Muṣṭafā, Sāmi, Kāmil, Xālid, Maħmūd, عAlī, Ħisēn, Kamāl, Ṣafwat, عAbdaḷḷah, Maha, Aħmad, Samīr, عĀdil, Ašṛaf, Zēnab, Samya, Ibrāhīm, Ġāli, Gamāl, عAbd inNāṣir, Ħusnī, Mubāṛak, Anwaṛ, isSādāt

Read the following place names:

تونس	مراكش	فاس	الأزهر
البحرين	سوريا	العريش	الزمالك
سيناء	المغرب	القاهرة	دمشق
فلسطين	تركيا	ليبيا	الجزائر
اليمن	السودان	لبنان	الاردن
أسوان	بيروت	اسرائيل	العراق
عمان	بغداد	الرياض	الخرطوم
قناة السويس	اليونان	ايران	اليابان

المعادي الدقي الجيزة مصر الجديدة

المملكة العربية السعودية جمهورية مصر العربية

ilʾAzhaṛ, Fās, Maṛṛākiš, Tūnis, izZamālik, ilɛArīš, Surya, ilBaḥrēn, Dimašq, ilQāhira, ilMaġrib, Sīnāʾ, igGazāʾir, Lībyā, Turkiyā, Filasṭīn, ilʾUrdun, Lubnān, isSūdān, ilYaman, ilɛIrāq, Israʾīl, Bayrūt, Aswān, ilXarṭūm, irRiyāḍ, Baġdād, ɛAmmān, ilYābān, ʾĪrān, ilYunān, qanāt isSuwēs, ilMaɛādī, idDuqqī, igGīza, Maṣr iggidīda, ilMamlaka‿lɛAṛabiyya‿sSaɛūdiyya, Gumhūriyyit Miṣr ilɛArabiyya

Writing exercise:
ilʾustāz (*z* = *ḏ*), *ʾidāṛa* (*-a* = ة), *maɛhad, ḥukūma* (*-a* = ة), *ilʾahṛām, ġasīl, ittārīx, ḥiwāṛ, ilʾaxbāṛ, markaz, muhandis, iggawāzāt, gumhūriyya* (*-a* = ة); *mīdān ittaḥrīr, issikka‿lḥadīd* (*-a* = ة), *ilḥamdu lillāh* (*ā* = a), *issānawiyya‿lɛāmma* (*-s* = *ṯ*, *-a* = ة), *sanat 1990* (*-at* = ة), *tilīfōn nimra 842377* (*-a* = ة), *ġurfa raqam 342* (*-a* = ة), *nimra 23* (*-a* = ة); *daṛagit ilḥaṛāra 32* (*-it, -a* = ة); *bi-surɛit tamānīn fi‿ssāɛa* (*t* = *ṯ*, *-it* en *-a* = ة)

VI. Reading exercise (with lesson XVI)

The following words and phrases can be found in the reading passages in chapters XII to XVI, try to read them.

(١)	التلفزيون	مجلس الشعب
(٢)	أطلق النار عليه	في الخارج
(٣)	مباحث أمن الدولة	في كل مكان
(٤)	ارتكب الجريمة	نشرة الاخبار
(٥)	زيارة وفد رسمي	مطار القاهرة
(٦)	مصر ترحب بضيوفها	قصر عابدين
(٧)	مؤتمر العلاقات الاقتصادية	استقبال
(٨)	المشروعات الصناعية	الجمهورية
(٩)	الاقتصاد المصري	في عهد محمد علي
(١٠)	بسبب الاستعمار	تدهور اقتصادي
(١١)	جمال عبد الناصر	مستوى المعيشة

(١٢)	قناة السويس	السد العالي
(١٣)	الدخل القومي	الدول العربية الشقيقة
(١٤)	نوعية الانتاج	السوق الأوروبية المشتركة
(١٥)	بالنسبة للسياحة	كل أنحاء العالم

(١٥)	التعليم في مصر	محو الأمية
(١٦)	وزير التربية والتعليم	المدارس الخاصة
(١٧)	جميع المدارس	تاريخ البلاد العربية
(١٨)	كل المواطنين العرب	نظام التعليم

(١٩)	كوبري التحرير	فندق النيل
(٢٠)	مدينة نصر	ميدان العتبة
(٢١)	شارع نادي الصيد	الجامعة الأمريكية
(٢٢)	كلية الطب	مستشفى الدقي

GLOSSARY

(approximately 1800 Arabic words)

You will find the letters to be in the following order :

a	ᵓ	*b*	*d*	*ḍ*	*f*	*g*	*ġ*
h	*ḫ*	*i*	*k*	*l*	*m*	*n*	*q*
r	*s*	*ṣ*	*š*	*t*	*ṭ*	*u*	*v*
w	*x*	*y*	*z*	*ẓ*	*ž*	*ɛ*	

The long vowel follows the corresponding short vowel:

a *ā* *e* *ē* *i* *ī* *o* *ō* *u* *ū*

abbreviations:

act.	active
adj.	adjective
adv.	adverb
c.	collective noun
f.	feminine
imperf.	imperfect
inter.	interrogative
intr.	intransitive
inv.	invariable
m.	masculine
n.	noun
n.u.	single unit (nomen unitatis)
part.	participle
pass.	passive
pl.	plural
pr.	pronoun
rel.	religious
rel. pr.	relative pronoun
sg.	singular
tr.	transitive
v.	verb

Note: verbs are given as perfect, imperfect, and verbal noun: *katab, yiktib, kitāba*

Note: definitions in the glossary relate to the context in which the words appear in this book

ARABIC - ENGLISH

a

aʾall	less, least
aʾṛab	closer, closest
abb ~abu, abbahāt	father
absaṭ	simpler, simplest
abyaḍ, bēḍa, bīḍ	white
afandim	yes? what were you saying?
agdād (pl.)	ancestors
agmal	more ~ most beautiful
aġla	more ~ most expensive
ahamm	more ~ most important
ahó, ahé, ahúm	there is...
aḥdas	more ~ most modern
aḥmaṛ, ḥamṛa, ḥumr	red
aḥsan	better, best
aḥwal, ḥōla, ḥūl	cross-eyed
akbaṛ	bigger, biggest older, oldest
akṛam	more ~ most generous
aktaṛ	more, most
alazz	tastier, tastiest
Aḷḷāh	God
Aḷḷāh yibārik fīk	God bless you
Aḷḷāh yixallīk	God keep you
ilḥamdu lillāh	thanks be to God
bi‿smi‿llāh iṛṛaḥmān iṛṛaḥīm	in the name of God the Beneficent,the Merciful
in šāʾ Aḷḷāh	God willing
ma šāʾ Aḷḷāh	what God intends
amma ... fa	as for...
ana	I
anhū, anhī, anhūm	which one(s)?
aṛbaɛa	four
arxaṣ	cheaper, cheapest
ashal	easier, easiest
asmaṛ, samṛa, sumr	dark-skinned
asnāʾ	during
asṛaɛ	faster, fastest
asɛad	happier, happiest

aṣġaṛ	smaller, smallest younger, youngest
aṣlaɛ, ṣalɛa, ṣulɛ	bald
aṣfaṛ, ṣafra, ṣufr	yellow
ašʾaṛ, šaʾṛa, šuʾr	blond
ašwal, šōla, šūl	left-handed
ašyak	more ~ most elegant
aṭraš, ṭarša, ṭurš	deaf
aṭwal	taller, tallest longer, longest
aṭyab	friendlier, friendliest
awʾāt	sometimes
awlād (pl.)	children; boys
awsaɛ	wider, widest
awḥaš	uglier, ugliest worse, worst
axaff	lighter, lightest
axḍar, xaḍra, xuḍr	green
aẋx ~ axu, ixwān ~ ixwāt ṣubyān	brother
aywa	yes
azraʾ, zarʾa, zurʾ	blue
azka	cleverer, cleverest
aɛma, ɛamya, ɛumy	blind
aɛṛag, ɛarga, ɛurg	lame
ạ̄	yes

ʾ

ʾabadan	never
la --	not at all
ʾabl	before
ʾabrīl	April
ʾadam	foot (measure)
ʾaddᵊ ʾē?	how much? to what extent? ~ big? ~ long?
ʾadāb (pl.)	literature, arts
ʾaddim, yiʾaddim li w ḥ	present s/th to s/o offer s/th to s/o
ʾadīm, ʾudām	old (things)
ʾaḍa, yiʾḍi ḥ	spend (time)
ʾaḍḍa, yiʾaḍḍi ḥ	spend (time)
ʾafal, yiʾfil (ḥ), ʾafl	close (s/th)
ʾagāza, -āt	holiday
ʾaggaṛ, yiʾaggaṛ ḥ	rent s/th
-- li w ḥ	rent s/th to s/o

ʾagnabi, ʾagānib	foreigner
ʾaġusṭus	August
ʾahl, ʾahāli	family people
ʾahlan wa sahlan	welcome!
ʾahwa	coffee
ʾahwa, ʾahāwi	coffee house
ʾaḫyānan	sometimes
ʾakl	food, eating
ʾakram, yikrim w	be generous to s/o
ʾala, yiʾli ḫ, ʾaly	fry s/th
ʾalabasṭar	alabaster
ʾalam, ʾalām	pain
ʾalam, aʾlām ~ iʾlām ~ ʾilíma	pen
-- gāff	ballpoint
-- ruṣāṣ	pencil
-- ḫibr	fountain pen
ʾalaɛ, yiʾlaɛ ḫ, ʾalɛ	strip s/th take off s/th
ʾalb, ʾulūb	heart
ʾalf, alāf	thousand
ʾall, yiʾill, ʾilla	decrease (v.) diminish
ʾallil, yiʾallil ḫ ~ min ḫ	reduce s/th cut down on s/th
ʾAlmanya	Germany
ʾalmāni, ʾalmān	German
ʾalqa, yulqi ilqabḍ ɛala w	arrest s/o
ʾamal, ʾamāl	hope
ʾamaṛ	moon
ʾamaṛ, yuʾmur w bi ḫ, ʾamṛ	order s/o to do s/th
ʾamāna	loyalty
ʾamīṣ, ʾumṣān	shirt
ʾammim, yiʾammim ḫ	nationalize s/th
ʾamn	security
ʾAmrīka	America, USA
ʾamrikāni, ʾamrikān	American
ʾamrīki, -yyīn	American
ʾangaz, yingiz ḫ	carry out s/th execute s/th
ʾaṛa, yiʾṛa ḫ, ʾiṛāya	read s/th
ʾaṛaf	nuisance
ʾarḍ, ʾarāḍi	ground, soil
ʾaṛṛab, yiʾaṛṛab, ʾurb	approach (v.)
-- ɛala ḫ	be nearly s/th
ʾasaf	regret, remorse
li‿l--	unfortunately
ʾasāṛ (pl.)	antiquities
ʾasfalt	asphalt
ʾaslam, yuslim ~ yislam	become Muslim
ʾastīka, ʾasatīk	eraser
ʾaṣanṣēr, -āt	elevator
ʾaṣl	origin
ʾaṣl ...	because ...
ʾaṣlan	originally
ʾaṣr, ʾuṣūr	palace
ʾAṣrᵊ ɛAbdīn	Abdin Palace
ʾaṣṣ, yiʾuṣṣ ḫ, ʾaṣṣ	cut s/th
ʾatal, yiʾtil w, ʾatl	kill s/o
ʾaṭaɛ, yiʾṭaɛ ḫ, ʾaṭɛ	tear s/th
ʾaṭr, ʾuṭurāt ~ ʾuṭúra	train
ʾaṭlaq, yuṭliq innāṛ ɛala w	shoot at s/o
ʾaw	or
ʾawām	quickly
ʾawi	very
miš --	not so good
ʾawwal ~ ʾawwalāni	first (adj.)
ʾawwil	first (adj.) beginning of
il--	first (adv.)
ʾaxīr	last
ʾaxīran	finally
ʾaxxaṛ, yiʾaxxaṛ w ~ ḫ	delay s/o ~ s/th cause s/o or s/th to regress
ʾayy	any; which ...?
ʾaɛad, yuʾɛud, ʾuɛād	sit; stay
ʾābil, yiʾābil w	meet s/o
ʾādir	being able to
ʾāl, yiʾūl li w ḫ	tell s/o s/th say s/th to s/o
ʾām, yiʾūm, ʾiyām	get up, stand up
ʾāsif	sorry
ʾāwim, yiʾāwim w ~ ḫ	resist s/o ~ s/th
ʾāxir	last (adj.); end of
ɛa‿lʾāxir	extremely
ʾāxiz, yiʾāxiz w	blame s/o
ʾāɛid	sitting
ʾē	what?
ʾidāṛa, -āt	administration directorate
ʾidaṛt‿iggawazāt	passport office

ʾidir, yiʾdaṛ	be able to
-- ɛala w ~ ḫ	master s/o ~ s/th
ʾifṭāṛ	main meal during *Ramaḍān*
ʾigāṛ	rent (n.)
ʾigṛāʾ, -āt	formality, measure
ʾigbāri	compulsory
ʾihmāl	negligence
ʾimḍa, -āt	signature
ʾimla	dictation
ʾingāz, -āt	achievement acquisition
ʾIngiltiṛa	England
ʾingilīzi, ʾingilīz	Englishman English
ʾinsān	human being
ʾinšāʾ	foundation
ʾintāg	production
ʾiqāma	residence permit
ʾiṛāya	reading (n.)
ʾirš, ʾurūš	piastre
-- sāġ	one piastre
ʾism, aʾsām	police station
ʾiswira, ʾasāwir	bracelet
ʾišr	skin; peel
ʾIṭalya	Italy
ʾiṭāli, -yyīn	Italian
ʾizāza, ʾazāyiz	bottle
ʾizn	permission
ʾīd (f.), *ʾidēn*	hand
ʾōḍa, ʾuwaḍ	room
ʾōḍit ʾuɛād	living room
ʾōḍit gulūs	living room
ʾōḍit nōm	bedroom
ʾōḍit sufṛa	dining room
ʾuddām	in front of opposite
ʾugṛa	wages
ʾuktōbaṛ	October
ʾulayyil	little, few
ʾumāš, -āt *~ aʾmiša*	fabric
ʾumbūba, ʾanabīb	canister (gas)
ʾummiyya	illiteracy
ʾurayyib (min ḫ)	nearby, close (to s/th)
ʾurb	closeness
ʾUṛubba	Europe
ʾurubbi, -yyīn	European
ʾusbūɛ, ʾasabīɛ	week
ʾustāz, ʾasadza	Mr.; professor
ʾUsturalya	Australia
ʾusturāli, -yyīn	Australian
ʾuṣayyaṛ	short, little
ʾuṣād	in front of opposite
ʾutubīs, -āt	bus
ʾuṭn	cotton
ʾuṭṭ, ʾuṭṭa, ʾuṭaṭ	cat
ʾūṭa (c.f.)	tomatoes

b

baʾa	so, then
baʾa, yibʾa ḫ	become
baʾālak..?	how long ... have you been ...?
baʾšīš	tip (money)
baʾaṛ (c.)	cows
badla, bidal	suit
badri	early
baḫr, buḫūr	sea
ilBaḫr ilʾAḫmaṛ	Red Sea
ilBaḫr ilʾAbyaḍ ilMutawassiṭ	Mediterranean Sea
balad (f.), *bilād*	country; town; village
balakōna, -āt	balcony
balāš	free; don't ...!
bi- --	for free
ballaġ, yiballaġ *w ḫ*	communicate s/th to s/o
ballaġ, yiballaġ ɛan w ~ ḫ	report s/o ~ s/th
balṭu, balāṭi	coat
Balžīka	Belgium
balžīki, -yyīn	Belgian
bana, yibni ḫ, buna	build s/th
banafsigi	purple
bank, bunūk	bank
banṭalōn, -āt	trousers (a pair)
banzīn	gasoline
baṛaka, -āt	blessing
bard	cold
barḍu	also, as well
barīd	mail
ṣandūʾ --	mailbox
barīza, barāyiz	10 piastre coin
baṛṛa	outside
baṛṛad, yibaṛṛad	cool down (weather)
basaṭ, yibsiṭ w	please s/o make s/o happy
basbōr, -āt ~ -tāt	passport
basīṭ, busaṭa	simple
basīṭa!	it's a simple matter!
bass	only; but; however
baṣal (c.)	onions

baṣīr	sighted
baṣṣ, yibuṣṣ li w, baṣṣ	look at s/o
bašmuhandis, -īn	chief engineer
baṭal, abṭāl	hero
baṭāṭis (c. f.)	potatoes
baṭīʾ, buṭāʾ	slow
baṭn (f.), *buṭūn*	stomach
baṭṭal, yibaṭṭal ḥ	stop doing s/th
baṭṭariyya, -āt	battery
baṭṭāl	bad
baṭṭīx (c.)	watermelons
bawwāb, -īn	doorman, janitor
bayyin, yibayyin ḥ	reveal s/th
baɛat, yibɛat li w ḥ	send s/o s/th
baɛd	after
-- *kida*	after that
-- *ma*	after (conj.)
baɛdēn	then
baɛḍ	some; each other
bāb, abwāb ~ ibwāb	door
ḅāba	dad
bāku, -wāt ~ bawāki	package
bāl	thought
wāxid bālu	paying attention
bārid	cold
bārik, yibārik fi w	bless s/o
-- *li w*	congratulate s/o
Bāša, -wāt	Pasha
bāt, yibāt, biyāt	spend the night
bāyin ɛala w	apparently ...
bāyiẓ	out of order
bāɛ, yibīɛ ḥ, bēɛ	sell s/th
Bē, Bahawāt	Bey
bēḍ (c.)	eggs
bēn	between
bēt, biyūt ~ buyūt	house
bi	with, by
bi‿nnisba li w ~ ḥ	regarding s/o ~ s/th
bi‿ẓẓabṭ	precisely
bilastik	plastic
bilūza, -āt	blouse
bint, banāt	girl; daughter
birnāmig, baṛāmig	program
bitāɛ, bitāɛit, bitūɛ	belonging to ...
biɛīd, buɛād (min ~ ɛan)	distant, far (from)
bīra	beer
bukṛa	tomorrow
baɛd --	day after tomorrow
bulīs	police
bulōfar, -āt	sweater, pullover
bunn	coffee beans
bunni	brown
burg, abṛāg	tower
burnēṭa, baranīṭ	hat
burtuʾān (c.)	oranges
burtuʾāni	orange (color)
busṭa	mail, post
būṣ (c.)	reed
būṣa, -āt	inch

d

da	that (m.), this (m.)
daʾn (f.), *duʾūn*	beard, chin
dabaḥ, yidbaḥ ḥ, dabḥ	slaughter s/th
dafaɛ, yidfaɛ li w ḥ dafɛ	pay s/o s/th
dahab	gold
damġa, -āt	fiscal stamp
damm	blood
daṛaga, -āt	degree
daṛagit ilḥaṛāṛa	temperature (grade)
daras, yidris ḥ, dars	study s/th
dardiš, yidardiš, dardaša	chatter
dars, durūs	lesson
dawa, adwiya	medicine
dawla, duwal	state (country)
dawli	international
dawša	noise, fuss
dawwaṛ, yidawwaṛ ḥ	turn s/th around
-- *ɛala w ~ ḥ*	look for s/o ~ s/th search for s/o ~ s/th
dawwax, yidawwax w	make s/o dizzy
daxal, yidxul ḥ, duxūl	enter s/th
daxl	income
dayman	always
dayyaʾ	narrow
dāfi	warm
dāfiɛ, yidāfiɛ ɛan w ~ ḥ	defend s/o ~ s/th
dāṛ, yidūr, dawaṛān	turn (intr.)
dāṛ, diyāṛ	residence
Dāṛ ilKutub	National Library

dāra, yidāri ḫ	conceal s/th
-- عala w ~ ḫ	cover up s/o ~ s/th
dās, yidūs ḫ, dōs	run over s/th
-- عala ḫ	trample s/th
dāyiʾ, yidāyiʾ w	annoy s/o irritate s/o
dāx, yidūx, dōxa	become dizzy
di	that (f.), this (f.)
diʾīʾa, daʾāyiʾ	minute
diḫik, yidḫak, diḫk	laugh (v.)
-- عala w	fool s/o
diḫk	laugh (n.)
difāع	defense
dilwaʾti	now
dinya	world
id-- bard	it's cold
id-- bitmaṭṭar	it's raining
id-- ḍalma	it's dark
id-- ḫaṛṛ	it's hot
id-- katma	the weather is oppressive
id--a zaḫma	it's crowded
diṛāsa, -āt	study
disimbir	December
dōl	these, those
dōr, adwāṛ ~ idwāṛ	floor
id-- ilʾarḍi	ground floor
duġri	straight on
duktūr, dakatra	doctor
-- bāṭini	physician
dukturā	doctorate
dulāb, dawalīb	cupboard, closet
dulāṛ, -āt	dollar
dunya	world
dušš, idšāš	shower

ḍ

ḍalma	darkness; dark
ḍarab, yiḍrab w ~ ḫ, ḍarb	beat s/o ~ s/th
-- w bi‿nnāṛ	shoot at s/o
ḍarība, ḍarāyib	tax
ḍarūri	necessary
ḍēf, ḍiyūf ~ ḍuyūf	guest
ḍiḫik, yiḍḫak, ḍiḫk	laugh (v.)
-- عala w ḍiḫk	fool s/o
ḍuhr	noon
baعd iḍ--	afternoon

f

fa	so; then; hence
faʾīr, fuʾaṛa	poor
fabṛāyir	February
faḍḍa	silver
faḍl	favor
min faḍlak	please
fahhim, yifahhim w ḫ	explain s/th to s/o
fakahāni, -yya	fruit seller
fakha (c.), *fawākih*	fruit
fakk, yifukk ḫ, fakk	untie s/th dismantle s/th change (money)
fakka	small change
fakkaṛ, yifakkaṛ	think
-- fi w ~ ḫ	think of s/o ~ s/th
fallāḫ, -īn	farmer (Egypt)
fanilla, -āt	undershirt
faṛaḫ	joy
faṛaḫ, afṛāḫ	wedding
Faṛansa	France
faṛansāwi	Frenchman French
faṛḫān	happy, glad
faṛmala, faṛāmil	brake (n.)
farš	furniture
farxa, firāx	chicken
fataḫ, yiftaḫ ḫ, fatḫ	open s/th
faṣl, fuṣūl	classroom; season
fatūṛa, fawatīr	bill, check
fayda, fawāyid	use
fawwil, yifawwil	fill up with fuel
faẓīع, fuẓāع	terrible, dreadful
fāḍi	empty; free
fāṣil, yifāṣil, fiṣāl	bargain (v.)
fāt, yifūt	pass by
-- عala w ~ ḫ	drop in on s/o ~ s/th
fēn	where?
fi	in, during
fibṛāyir	February
fiḍi, yifḍa	become empty become free
fiḍil, yifḍal	remain go on (doing s/th)
fihim, yifham ḫ, fahm	understand s/th
fikra, afkāṛ	idea, thought
film, aflām	movie
filūs (pl.)	money
fingān, fanagīn	cup
firīzar, -āt	freezer

fiṣāl	bargaining
fitrīna, -āt	shop window
~ fatarīn	
fiṭār	breakfast
fiṭir, yifṭar	have breakfast
fiṭār ~ futūr	
fiɛlan	indeed
fī(h)	there is ~ are
fōᵓ	above, on (top of)
funduᵓ, fanādiᵓ	hotel
furṣa, furaṣ	opportunity
fustān, fasatīn	dress
fuṭūr	breakfast
fūl (c.)	beans
-- midammis	cooked beans
fūṭa, fuwaṭ	towel

g

gabal, gibāl	mountain
gabbis, yigabbis ḫ	put s/th in plaster
gaddid, yigaddid ḫ	renew s/th extend s/th
gahhiz, yigahhiz ḫ	prepare s/th
gahl	ignorance
gallabiyya, galalīb	long garment (Egypt)
gamāɛa, -āt	group
gamb	next to
gamīl, gumāl	beautiful
gamɛa, gāmiɛāt	university
ganayni, -yya	gardener
ganūb	south
ganūbi	southern
gaṛa, yigṛa li w ḫ	happen to s/o
gaṛas, agṛās	bell, doorbell
~ igṛāṣ	
gaṛāž, -āt	garage
garīda, gaṛāyid	newspaper
garīma, gaṛāyim	crime
gawāb, -āt	letter
gawāz, -āt	permit (n.)
gawla, -āt	tour
gaww	weather
gawwi	meteorological
gayy	coming
gazma, gizam	shoes (a pair)
fardit --	shoe (one)
gaɛān	hungry
gāb, yigīb li w ḫ	bring s/o s/th
gāhiz	ready
gāmid	hard; intense
gāmiɛ, gawāmiɛ	mosque
gāṛ, girān	neighbor
gāri	going on
gāyiz	possible; possibly
gāɛ, yigūɛ, gūɛ	be hungry
gibna, giban	cheese
gidd, gudūd	grandfather
~ agdād	ancestors (only pl.)
giddan	very, quite
gidīd, gudād	new
-- lang	brand new
min --	once again
min ᵓawwil wi --	all over again
gih, yīgi, migiyy	come
giha, -āt	direction establishment
gihāz, aghiza	device
gild	skin; leather
gilda, -āt	leather washer
ginē, -hāt	pound (Egypt)
ginēna, ganāyin	garden
ginent‿ ilḫayawanāt	zoo
gīl, agyāl	generation
giri, yigri, gary	run
gōz, igwāz	husband
guġrafya	geography
gumhūri	republican
gumhuriyya	republic
gumla, gumal	sentence
gumruk, gamārik	customs
gurnāl, garanīl	newspaper
guwwa	inside

ġ

ġada (m.)	lunch
ġalaṭ (inv.)	wrong
ġalṭa, -āt	mistake
ġalayān	boiling
ġani, aġniya	rich
ġarb	west
ġarbi	western
ġarīb, aġṛāb	foreigner
ġarīb	odd, peculiar
ġasal, yiġsil ḫ, ġasīl	wash s/th
ġasīl	laundry
ġayyaṛ, yiġayyaṛ ḫ	alter s/th change s/th convert (money)
ġayyim, yiġayyim	become cloudy
ġāli	expensive
ġālíban	probably

ġāmiʾ	dark (adj.)
ġēr	except (for)
min --	without
ġili, yiġla, ġuluww	become expensive
ġili, yiġli, ġalayān	boil
ġurfa, ġuṛaf	room

h

hadaf, ahdāf	goal
hamdān	exhausted
haṛam, ahṛām	pyramid
hawa	air, wind
hādi	calm, quiet
hāmm	important
hēṣa	commotion
hidi, yihda, hudūʾ	calm down become quiet
hidiyya, hadāya	present, gift
hidūm (pl.)	clothes, clothing
hina	here
hināk	there
hindi, hunūd	Indian
hunūd ḥumr	Native Americans
hirib, yihṛab (min ḥ), hurūb	flee (s/th)
hiyya	she
hotēl, -āt	hotel
hudūʾ	quietness
Hulanda	Holland The Netherlands
hulandi	Dutchman Dutch
humma	they
huwwa	he

ḥ

ḥaʾīʾa	truth
ḥaʾīʾi	truly
ḥabb, yiḥibb w ~ ḥ, ḥubb	love s/o ~ s/th
ḥadd	someone somebody
ma-ḥaddiš	nobody
ḥaddid, yiḥaddid ḥ	determine s/th
ḥadīd	iron
ḥadīs	modern
ḥadīs, aḥadīs	conversation interview
ḥadsa, ḥawādis	accident
ḥaḍḍaṛ, yiḥaḍḍaṛ ḥ	prepare s/th
ḥaḍritak	you (polite)
ḥafla, ḥafalāt	party
ḥagaṛ, ḥigāṛa	stone; battery
ḥagaz, yiḥgiz ḥ, ḥagz	reserve s/th
ḥagg, yiḥigg, ḥigg	go on a pilgrimage
ḥaka, yiḥki li w ḥ	tell s/o s/th
ḥalāl (inv.)	allowed (rel.)
ḥalāwa	sweetmeats
ḥall, yiḥill ḥ, ḥall	solve s/th
ḥammām, -āt	bath; bathroom
ḥanafiyya, -āt	tap; faucet
ḥaṛaka, -āt	movement
ḥaṛām (inv.)	forbidden (rel.)
ḥaṛām ʿalēk	shame on you! have mercy!
ḥaṛāmi, -yya	thief
ḥaṛāṛa	temperature
ḥaṛb (f.), *ḥurūb*	war
ḥarīr, ḥarāyir	silk
ḥarīr	silken
ḥaṛṛ	warmth; warm
ḥasab, yiḥsib ḥ	calculate s/th
-- w ḥ	consider s/o s/th
ḥass, yiḥiss bi ḥ	feel s/th
ḥassin, yiḥassin ḥ	improve s/th
ḥaṣal, yiḥṣal (li w), ḥuṣūl	occur, happen (to s/o)
ḥaša, yiḥši ḥ ḥ	stuff s/th with s/th
ḥatta	even
ḥaṭṭ, yiḥuṭṭ ḥ, ḥaṭṭ	place s/th, put s/th
ḥawalēn	around
ḥawāli	approximately
ḥawwid, yiḥawwid	turn (direction)
ḥawwiš, yiḥawwiš ḥ	save (money)
ḥayawān, -āt	animal
ḥayawi	lively
ḥayā	life
ḥayy, aḥyāʾ	district, quarter
ḥādis, ḥawādis	incident; accident
ḥāḍir	okay; at your service present (adj.)
ḥāga, -āt	thing, matter something
ḥāl, aḥwāl	situation
ḥālan	immediately
ḥāliyyan	presently
ḥāris, ḥuṛṛās	guard
ḥāwil, yiḥāwil ḥ	try (to do) s/th
ḥēṭa, ḥiṭān	wall
ḥibr	ink
ḥikāya, -āt	story
ḥilm, aḥlām	dream

ḥilw	sweet; pretty
Ḥilwān	Helwan: Cairo suburb
ḥisāb, -āt	bill, check
ḥitta, ḥitat	piece; neighborhood
ḥiwāṛ, -āt	dialogue
ḥizām, ḥizíma	belt
ḥōš, aḥwāš	courtyard
ḥukūma, -āt	government
ḥumāṛ, ḥimīr	donkey
ḥurr, aḥṛāṛ	free
ḥurriyya	freedom

i

ibn, abnāʾ	son
-- *ḥalāl*	decent person
ibtada, yibtidi	start (intr.)
-- *ḥ* ~ *fi ḥ*	make a start to s/th start s/th
ibtidāʾi	elementary; initial
idda, yiddi w ḥ	give s/o s/th
iddan, yiddan	call to prayer
iddaṛṛab, yiddaṛṛab	train (intr.)
-- *εala ḥ*	train for s/th
iddāra, yiddāra	hide oneself
iddāyiʾ, yiddāyiʾ	be annoyed
idDuʾʾi	Doqqi: quarter in Giza
iḍḍarab, yiḍḍirib	be hit
iftakaṛ, yiftikir w ~ ḥ	remember s/o ~ s/th
iftitāḥ	inauguration
iggaddid, yiggaddid	be renewed be extended
iggawwiz, yiggawwiz w	marry s/o
igGīza	Giza: West-Bank Cairo
igtimāε, -āt	meeting, assembly
iġtiyāl	assassination
ihtamm, yihtamm bi w ~ ḥ	have an interest in s/o ~ s/th
ihtimām	interest
iḥna	we
iḥtāg, yiḥtāg ḥ ~ li ḥ	need s/th
ikkallim, yikkallim	talk (intr.) speak (intr.)
-- *maεa w εan ~ fi ḥ*	discuss s/th with s/o
illa	except (for)
illi	which, who, whom
ilMaεādi	Maadi: Cairo suburb
ilMugammaε	Mugamma: central administrative building in Cairo
ilMuhandisīn	Mohandiseen: quarter in Giza
ilQāhíra	Cairo
iltihab, -āt	inflammation
iltaḥaq, yiltiḥiq bi ḥ	enrol in s/th
iltiḥāq	enrolment
ilYunān	Greece
ilεaṛabi	Arabic
ilεAtaba	Ataba: quarter in Central Cairo
imbāriḥ	yesterday
ʾawwil --	day before yesterday
imta	when?
imtiyāz, -āt	distinction privilege
in	if
inbasaṭ, yinbisiṭ	enjoy oneself
inbasaṭ, yinbisiṭ bi ḥ	be pleased with s/th
inḍarab, yinḍirib bi‿nnāṛ	get shot at
infataḥ, yinfitiḥ	open (pass.)
Ingiltira	England
ingilīzi, ingilīz	Englishman English
inkatab, yinkitib	be written
inn	that
innahaṛda	today
inNimsa	Austria
inšaḷḷa	God willing
inta	you (m.)
intaẓar, yintiẓir w ~ ḥ	wait for s/o ~ s/th
inti	you (f.)
intiẓār	waiting (n.)
intu	you (pl.)
iqtiṣād	economy
iqtiṣādi	economical
irtakab, yirtikib ḥ	commit s/th
irtifāε	height
isfing (c.)	sponge
irtikāb	committing (n.)
Iskindiriyya	Alexandria
ism, asāmi	name
istaʾāl, yistaʾīl	resign
istaʾbil, yistaʾbil w	receive s/o (visitors)

istaʾzin, yistaʾzin w	ask s/o for permission; take one's leave
istafād, yistafīd min w ~ ḫ	profit from s/o ~ s/th
istafhim, yistafhim ɛan ḫ	inquire about s/th
istaġall, yistaġill w ~ ḫ	exploit s/o ~ s/th; take advantage of s/o ~ s/th
istaġla, yistaġla ḫ	consider s/th expensive
istaġna, yistaġna ɛan w ~ ḫ	manage without s/o ~ s/th
istaġṛab, yistaġṛab min ḫ	be surprised by s/th
istaḫaʾʾ, yistaḫaʾʾ ḫ	deserve s/th
istaḫamma, yistaḫamma	bathe (v.)
istaḫmil, yistaḫmil (w ~ ḫ)	put up (with s/o ~ s/th); hold out
istalaf, yistilif ḫ	borrow s/th
istalam, yistilim ḫ	receive s/th
istalṭaf, yistalṭaf w	find s/o pleasant
istamaṛṛ, yistamiṛṛ	continue
istanna, yistanna	wait
istarayyaḫ, yistarayyaḫ	rest (v.)
istarxaṣ, yistarxaṣ ḫ	consider s/th cheap
istaɛgil, yistaɛgil	hurry (v.)
istaɛmil, yistaɛmil ḫ	use s/th
istāhil, yistāhil ḫ	deserve s/th
istiʾbāl	reception
istimāṛa, -āt	form, application
istiṛād	import
istiɛgāl	rush
istiɛmāl	use, usage
istiɛmāṛ	colonialism
iswid, sōda, sūd	black
iṣṣallaḫ, yiṣṣallaḫ	get repaired
iššaṛṛaf, yiššaṛṛaf bi ḫ	be honored by s/th
ištaġal, yištaġal	work (v.)
ištaka, yištiki	complain (v.)
-- w	make a complaint about s/o
ištara, yištiri ḫ, šira	buy s/th
ištarak, yištirik fi ḫ	participate in s/th
ištāʾ, yištāʾ li w ~ ḫ, šōʾ	long for s/o ~ s/th

itʾalab, yitʾilib	be turned upside down
itʾammim, yitʾammim	be nationalized
itʾatal, yitʾitil	be killed
itʾaṭaɛ, yitʾiṭiɛ	be torn
itʾaxxaṛ, yitʾaxxaṛ	be late
itʾābil, yitʾābil	meet (each other)
itʾāl, yitʾāl	be said
itbāɛ, yitbāɛ	be sold
itfakk, yitfakk	be loosened; be changed (money)
itfaṛṛag, yitfaṛṛag ɛala ḫ	watch s/th
itfassaḫ, yitfassaḫ fusḫa	stroll (v.); go out
itfataḫ, yitfitiḫ	open (pass.)
itġadda, yitġadda	lunch (v.)
itġasal, yitġisil	be washed
itġayyaṛ, yitġayyaṛ	change (intr.)
itḫāsib, yitḫāsib	settle accounts
itkallim, yitkallim	speak; talk
itkatab, yitkitib	be written
itlaff, yitlaff	be wrapped
itlamm, yitlamm	gather (intr.)
itmaddid, yitmaddid	lie down
itmala, yitmili	be filled; become full
itmasak, yitmisik	get arrested
itmašša, yitmašša	stroll (v.)
itnaʾal, yitniʾil	be transfered
itnaffis, yitnaffis	breathe (v.)
itnarfis, yitnarfis (ɛala w)	get irritated; get angry (on s/o)
itnasa, yitnisi	be forgotten
itnēn	two
litnēn	both
itṛabba, yitṛabba	grow up, be raised
itrakkib, yitrakkib	be installed
itrama, yitrimi	be thrown away
itsamma, yitsamma	be named
itsammim, yitsammim	be poisoned
itsāmiḫ, yitsāmiḫ	forgive one another
itṣallaḫ, yitṣallaḫ	be repaired
itṣawwar, yitṣawwar (ḫ)	have one's picture taken; imagine (s/th)
itṣāliḫ, yitṣāliḫ	reconcile (with each other)

itšaṛab, yitširib	be drunk (consumed)
itšāl, yitšāl	be removed
itšāwir, yitšāwir	consult with s/o
ittafaʔ, yittifiʔ ʕala ḥ	agree upon s/th
ittaryaʔ, yittaryaʔ ʕala w, taryaʔa	mock s/o
ittaṣal, yittiṣil bi w	contact s/o
ittiḥād	union
ittākil, yittākil	be eaten
	be worn out
ittāxid, yittāxid	be taken; be shocked
ittifāʔ, -āt	agreement, treaty
itwalad, yitwilid	be born
itwassaʕ, yitwassaʕ	expand
itxaṭabit, titxiṭib	get engaged (f.)
itxāniʔ, yitxāniʔ (maʕa w)	quarrel (with s/o)
itʕamal, yitʕimil	be done
itʕallim, yitʕallim ḥ	learn s/th
itʕaṛṛaf, yitʕaṛṛaf ʕala w	make s/o's acquaintance
itʕašša, yitʕašša	dine
itʕāmil, yitʕāmil maʕa w	deal with s/o
iṭṭabax, yiṭṭibix	be cooked
ixtafa, yixtifi	disappear
ixtāṛ, yixtāṛ w ~ ḥ	choose s/o ~ s/th
iza	if
izZamālik	Zamalek: quarter in Cairo
izzāy	how?
izzayyak	how are you?
iẓẓabaṭ, yiẓẓibiṭ	become adjusted
iʕtazaṛ, yiʕtizir li w ʕan ḥ	apologize to s/o for s/th

k

ka-	like, as
kaʔann	as if, as though
kabrīt (c.)	matches
kaffa, yikaffi w	be sufficient for s/o
kahṛaba	electricity
kal, yākul ḥ, ʔakl	eat s/th
kalaks, -āt	claxon, horn
kalām	talk
ʔayy --	nonsense; just any old thing
kalb, kilāb	dog
kallim, yikallim w	speak to s/o
kamān	also, as well
kanaba, -āt	couch, sofa
Kanada	Canada
kanadi	Canadian
kaṛam	generosity
karafatta, -āt	tie
karīm, kuṛama	generous
kart, kurúta	card
kasaṛ, yiksaṛ ḥ, kasr	break s/th
kašaf, yikšif ʕala w ~ ḥ, kašf	examine s/o check s/th
katab, yiktib ḥ, kitāba	write s/th
katma (inv.)	oppressive (weather)
kattaṛ, yikattaṛ ḥ ~ min ḥ	increase s/th
kawitš	rubber; tires
kaza‿w kaza	so and so
kām	how many ~ much?
	some
kān, yikūn	be
kātib, kuttāb	writer
kibīr, kubāṛ	big
-- fi‿ssinn	old (people)
kida	like that, in that way
kifāya	enough
kilma, kalimāt	word
kinīsa, kanāyis	church
kitāb, kutub	book
kitir, yiktaṛ, kutr	increase (v.)
kitīr, kutāṛ	many, much
bi‿ktīr	much more
kīlu	kilogram
	kilometer
kīs, akyās ~ ikyās	bag
kōka	cola
kubbāya, -āt	glass
kubri, kabāri	bridge
-- ʕilwi	flyover
kufta	meatballs
kuḥli	dark blue
kull	all; whole; every
-- ḥāga	everything
--wāḥid	everyone
kulliyya, -āt	faculty
kulliyyit ilʔadāb	faculty of arts
kulliyyit ilʔḥuʔūʔ	faculty of law
kurnīš inNīl	corniche: road along the Nile

kuṛṛāsa, kaṛarīs	notebook
kursi, karāsi	chair
kušk, akšāk	kiosk
kuwayyis	good

l

laʾ ~ lā ~ laʾʾa	no
la muʾaxza	sorry, excuse me
la.... wala	neither... nor....
laʾa, yilāʾi ḫ	find s/th
laʾīm, luʾama	sly
laban, albān	milk
laff, yiliff ḫ, laff	wrap s/th
laḫaʾ, yilḫaʾ ḫ	catch up with s/th
laḫam, yilḫim ḫ, liḫām	weld s/th
laḫma	meat
lamaɛ, yilmaɛ, lamaɛān	shine
lamḅa, lumaḍ	light bulb
lamma	when
lamūn (c.)	lemon
laṭīf, luṭāf	kind, pleasant
law	if
laxbaṭ, yilaxbaṭ	confuse s/o
w ~ ḫ, laxbaṭa	mix up s/th
layyil, yilayyil	become night
lazīz, luzāz	delicious, tasty
lākin	but
lāzim	necessary; must
lē	why?
lēl	evening; night
bi‿llēl	in the evening at night
nuṣṣ illēl	midnight
lēla, layāli	evening (n.u.) night (n.u)
li	for, to
li-waḫdu	alone, by himself
liʾann ~ liʾinn	because
libis, yilbis ḫ, libs	put on s/th; wear s/th
liġāyit	till, until
liḫadd	till, until
lissa	still; just (recently)
liṣṣ, luṣūṣ	thief
litnēn	both
liɛib, yilɛab (bi ḫ), liɛb	play (with s/th)
lōḫa, -āt	blackboard; painting
lōn, alwān	color
Lubnān	Lebanon
lubnāni	Lebanese
lukanḍa, -āt	hotel
luṭf	kindness

m

mā- ... -š	not
ma-zāl	still
maʾfūl	closed
maʾlama, maʾālim	pencil box
maʾli	fried
mabāḫis (pl.)	police investigation department
mablūl	wet
mabna (m.), *mabāni*	building
mabṛūk	congratulations!
mabsūṭ	happy, satisfied
madīna, mudun	city
madrasa, madāris	school
--‿btidāʾi	elementary school
-- sanawi	secondary school
maḍa, yimḍi (ḫ ~ ɛala ḫ)	sign (s/th)
maḍḍa, yimaḍḍi ḫ	spend s/th (time)
mafhūm	understood
mafhūm, mafahīm	notion
mafkūk	loose; disassembled
mafrūš	furnished
maftūḫ	open
magāl,-āt	area, field
maggāni	free
maglis, magālis	council
-- iššaɛb	parliament
magmūɛa, -āt	group
magnūn, maganīn	crazy
maḫall, -āt	shop
maḫaṭṭa, -āt	station
maḫgūz	reserved
maḫši	stuffed
maḫṭūṭ	placed
maḫw	eradication
makān, amākin	place
mala, yimla ḫ, malw	fill out s/th
malābis (pl.)	clothes
malḫ	salt
mallīm, malalīm	millieme: 1/10 piastre
mamnūɛ	forbidden
manaxīr (f.)	nose
manaɛ, yimnaɛ ḫ manɛ	forbid s/th
-- w min ḫ	forbid s/o (to do) s/th

mandīl, manadīl	handkerchief
manga (c. f.)	mango
manṭiʾa, manāṭiʾ	region, area
maraḍ, amrāḍ	sickness, disease
margaɛ, maṛāgiɛ	source, studybook
marīḍ	sick
marīḍ, marḍa	patient
markib (f.), *marākib*	boat, ship
maṛṛ, yimuṛṛ ɛala w, maṛṛ	drop in on s/o
maṛṛa, -āt	once, one time
bi‿lmaṛṛa	at the same time
kamān --	once again
kaza --	several times
masʾūl	responsible
masʾūl, -īn	man in charge official (n.)
masal, amsāl	proverb
masal, amsila	example
masalan	for example
masaḫ, yimsaḫ ḫ, masḫ	swab s/th wipe off s/th
masāfa, -āt	distance
masṭara, masāṭir	ruler
masūṛa, mawasīr	pipe
maṣdaṛ, maṣādir	source
maṣnaɛ, maṣāniɛ	factory
Maṣr	Egypt; Cairo
Maṣr igGidīda	Heliopolis
maṣri	Egyptian
mašrūb, -āt	beverage
mašrūɛ, -āt ~ mašariɛ	project
mašwi	grilled
matḫaf, matāḫif	museum
maṭar, amṭār	rain
maṭār, -āt	airport
maṭbax, maṭābix	kitchen
maṭṭar, yimaṭṭar	rain (v.)
maṭɛam, maṭāɛim	restaurant
mawʾaf, mawāʾif	parking; bus stop
mawḍūɛ, -āt ~ mawaḍīɛ	subject, theme
maksūr	broken
maktab, makātib	desk; office
maktaba, -āt	library
mawgūd	present (adj.)
mawlūd	born
mawlūd, mawalīd	infant
mawwin, yimawwin w bi ḫ	supply s/o with s/th
mawwit, yimawwit w ~ ḫ	kill s/o
mawɛid, mawaɛīd	appointment
ṃayya	water
-- maɛdaniyya	mineral water
mayyit, -īn	dead
maẓbūṭ	exact; exactly
mažistēr	master's degree
maɛʾūl	reasonable, logical
miš --	unbelievable
maɛa	with
maɛazālik	nevertheless
maɛād, mawaɛīd	appointment
maɛbad, maɛābid	temple
maɛhad, maɛāhid	institute
maɛīša	living (n.)
ma-ɛlešš	it doesn't matter
maɛlūma, -āt	data; information (pl.)
maɛna (m.), *maɛāni*	meaning
maɛrifa, maɛārif	knowledge
mādda, mawādd	substance subject (study)
māḍi	past
ṃāma	mama
māniɛ, mawāniɛ	hindrance
māris	March
māši	agreed!
māši	on foot
māt, yimūt, mōt	die
māyu	May
miʾaddim	fast (watch)
miʾaxxaṛ	slow (watch)
midawwaṛ	round, circular
midayʾa	nuisance
middāyiʾ	annoyed
midān, mayadīn	square
mifakk, -āt	screwdriver
migabbis	plastered
miggawwiz	married
miġayyim	cloudy
iddinya --a	it's cloudy
miḫawla, -āt	attempt
miḫtāg li w ~ ḫ	needing s/o ~ s/th
mikaffi	sufficient
milli	millimeter
milyōn, malayīn	million
min	from; out of; than
-- ʾīmit...	about ... ago
minēn	where from?
miṛawwaḫ	going home
miṛwāḫ	going (n.)
miṛāt...	wife of ...
mirāya, -āt	mirror
misaddaʾ	believing
misāfir	traveling
misik, yimsik w ~ ḫ, mask	grab s/o ~ s/th arrest s/o

mistanni	waiting
mistaṛayyaḫ	relaxed
mistaɛgil	being in a hurry
miṣammim	determined
Miṣr	Egypt
miš	not
miši, yimši, mašy	walk (v.); leave (intr.)
mišwāṛ, mašawīr	errand
mitʾakkid	sure
mitʾaxxaṛ	late
mitallig	frozen
mitbāɛ	sold
mithayyaʾ li w	it seems to s/o
mitnarfis	angry, irritated
mitr, amtāṛ~ imtāṛ	meter
mitṛabbi	raised
mitšakkir	thank you
mittākil	worn out
mitɛallim	educated
mitɛawwid ɛala w ~ ḫ	used to s/o ~ s/th
miwāfiʾ	agreeing
mixalli	letting
miyya, -āt	hundred
miɛaksa	teasing (n.)
miɛallaʾ	hanging
mīn	who?
mīza, -āt	advantage
mōt	death
mōz (c.)	bananas
muʾabla, -āt	meeting
muʾtamaṛ, -āt	conference
mubāṛak	blessed
mubāšáṛatan	immediately
mudarris, -īn	teacher
mudda	period
mudēl, -āt	model
mudīr, -īn	manager, director
muḍṭarr	forced
muftāḫ, mafatīḫ	key
mugrim, -īn	criminal
muhandis, -īn	engineer
muhimm	important
muḫaḍra, -āt	lecture
muḫafẓa, -āt	governorate
muḫāmi, -yyīn	lawyer
muḫāsib, -īn	bookkeeper
muḫtamal	probably
mukalma, -āt	telephone call
mumassil, -īn	actor
mumkin	possible
munasba, -āt	occasion
bi-munasbit ...	on the occasion of
munādi, -yya	parking attendant
munāsib	appropriate, suited
muntaẓir	waiting
muqīm	staying, residing
muršid, -īn	guide
murūr	traffic
mustaqirr	stable, steady
mustašfa, -yāt	hospital
mustawa, -yāt	level
mustaḫīl	impossible
muškila, mašākil	problem
muštaṛak	common
mutašakkir	thank you
mutaṭarrif, -īn	extremist
mutawassiṭ	average
mutšakkir	thank you
mutūṛ, -āt	motor; motorcycle
muwaẓẓaf, -īn	civil servant
muwāṭin, -īn	citizen
mūlid, mawālid	celebration (rel.)
mūsim, mawāsim	season

n

naʾal, yinʾil w ~ ḫ, naʾl	transfer s/o ~ s/th
naʾʾa, yinaʾʾi ḫ	select s/th
naʾʾaṭ, yinaʾʾaṭ (ḫ)	drip
nabāt, -āt	plant (n.)
nabi, anbiya	prophet
nadah, yindah w ~ li w, nadh	call s/o
naḍḍaf, yinaḍḍaf ḫ	clean s/th
naḍḍāra, -āt	glasses
nafax, yunfux ḫ ~ fi ḫ, nafx	blow (into) s/th
nafaɛ, yinfaɛ, nafɛ	to be useful
nafs	self
nahṛ, anhāṛ	river
nahāṛ	daytime
naḫās	copper
naḫya, nawāḫi	side; direction
naml (c.)	ants
nammaṛ, yinammaṛ ḫ	number s/th
narfis, yinarfis w, narfasa	irritate s/o
naṣṣ, nuṣūṣ	text
naṣya, nawāṣi	street corner
ɛa‿nnaṣya	on the street corner
našāṭ, -āt ~ anšiṭa	activity
našṛa, našaṛāt	broadcast
našrit ilʾaxbāṛ	news broadcast

natīga, natāyig	result; calendar
nawwaṛ, yinawwaṛ (ḫ)	illuminate (s/th)
nawwim, yinawwim w	put to sleep
nawɛiyya, -āt	sort, type; quality
naxl (c.)	palm trees
naylon ~ naylu	nylon
nazzil, yinazzil ḫ	bring s/th down
nāᵓiṣ	missing; minus
nādi, andiya ~ nawādi	club
nām, yinām, nōm	sleep (v.)
nāṛ (f.), *niṛān*	fire
nās (pl.)	people
nāsib, yināsib w	suit s/o
nāwil, yināwil w ḫ	hand s/th to s/o
niᵓiṣ, yinᵓaṣ, naᵓaṣān	decrease (v.); be missing
nibīt	wine
niḍīf, nuḍāf	clean
nifiɛ, yinfaɛ w, nafɛ	be useful to s/o
nifs + suffix *fi ḫ*	desire s/th
nihāya, -āt	end
niḫās	copper
nimra, nimar	number
nimsāwi	Austrian
nisi, yinsa ḫ ~ w, nisyān	forget s/o ~ s/th
niskafē	nescafé
nizil, yinzil (ḫ ~ min ḫ, nuzūl	go down (s/th) get off (s/th)
niẓām, nuẓum	system
nufimbir	November
nōm	sleep (n.)
nōɛ, anwāɛ	kind, sort
nuṣṣ, inṣāṣ	half
nūnu	baby
nūr, anwāṛ	light

q

qanā, qanawāt	channel, canal
qanāt isSuwēs	Suez Canal
qaṛāṛ, -āt	decision
qarn, qurūn	century
qaṛṛaṛ, yiqaṛṛaṛ ḫ	decide s/th
qaṛya, quṛa	village
qawmi	national
qism, aqsām	department
qiṣṣa, qiṣaṣ	story
quṛᵓān	Koran
quwwa, -āt	power, force

r

raᵓaba, riᵓāb	neck
raᵓīs, ruᵓasāᵓ ~ ruᵓasa	president, chairman
ṛaᵓy, ᵓaṛāᵓ	opinion; advice
ṛabba, yiṛabbi w	to raise s/o
rabīɛ	spring
ṛadd, yirudd ɛala w ~ ḫ, ṛadd	reply to s/o ~ s/th
ṛafaɛ, yirfaɛ ḫ, ṛafɛ	lift up s/th raise s/th
raff, rufūf	shelf
raggaɛ, yiraggaɛ ḫ	give back s/th
ṛaḫam, yirḫam w, ṛaḫma	to have mercy on s/o
ṛaḫma	mercy
ṛaḫḫab, yiṛaḫḫab bi w ~ ḫ	welcome s/o ~ s/th
rakan, yirkin ḫ, rakn	park s/th
rakkib, yirakkib ḫ	install s/th
-- *w ḫ*	let s/o embark in s/th
rama, yirmi ḫ, ramy	throw (away) s/th
rann, yirinn, rann	ring (intr.)
rasmi	official; officially
raṣīf, arṣífa	pavement
ṛawwaḫ, yiṛawwaḫ	go home
rayy	irrigation
rayyis	chief
ṛābiɛ	fourth
ṛāgil, riggāla	man
ṛāḫ, yirūḫ ḫ, miṛwāḫ	go to s/th
-- *li w*	go to s/o
ṛāḫa	rest
bi‿ṛṛāḫa	slowly; softly
ṛās (f.), *rūs*	head
ṛāyiḫ	going
rigiɛ, yirgaɛ ḫ, rugūɛ	return (somewhere)
rigl (f.), *riglēn*	foot; leg
ɛala --	in an uproar
ɛala riglē	on foot
rigīf (ɛēš)	loaf of bread
riḫla, -āt ~ ṛaḫalāt	excursion
rikib, yirkab ḫ, rukūb	ride s/th; get in s/th
rixīṣ, ruxāṣ	cheap
rīf, aryāf	countryside
rīfi	rural
rīḫ, riyāḫ	wind

rīḫa, ṛawāyiḫ	scent
rubʕ, irbaʕ	quarter (1/4)
rufayyaʕ	thin
ṛumād	ash
ṛumādi	gray
rusūm (pl.)	charge
Rusya	Russia
rūsi, rūs	Russian
ruṣāṣ	lead (metal)
ruṣāṣi	gray
ruxṣa, ruxaṣ	(driving) license
ruzz (c.)	rice

s

saʔal, yisʔal w ḫ, suʔāl	ask s/o s/th
-- *ʕala w*	ask about s/o
sabab, asbāb	reason, cause
bi--- ḫ	because of s/th
sabaġ, yusbuġ ḫ, sabġ	dye s/th
sabbāk, -īn	plumber
sabbūṛa	blackboard
sabʕa	seven
sadd, yisidd ḫ, sadd	block s/th
sadd, sudūd	dam
isSadd ilʕĀli	High Dam
saddaʔ, yisaddaʔ w ~ ḫ	believe s/o ~ s/th
safaṛ	journey
safīna, sufun	ship
sahl	easy
saḫāb (c.), *suḫub*	clouds
sakk, yisukk ḫ, sakk	lock s/th
sakṛān	drunk
salām	peace
salām, -āt	greeting
salāma	safety
salamtak	get well!
maʕa ssalāma	goodbye
salaṭa, -āt	salad
sallif, yisallif w ḫ,	lend s/th to s/o
sallim, yisallim w ḫ	hand s/th to s/o
-- *ʕala w*	greet s/o
sama, -wāt	heaven; sky
samak (c.)	fish
samaḫ, yismaḫ li w bi ḫ	allow s/o (to do) s/th
law samaḫt	please!
samāʕ	hearing
sana, sanawāt ~ sinīn	year
sanawi	secondary; annual
sanawiyya ʕāmma	final school exam
sandūʔ, sanadīʔ	chest
sanṭi	centimeter
sanya, sawāni	second (time unit)
saraʔ, yisraʔ ḫ, sirʔa	steal s/th
saṛṛaḫ, yisaṛṛaḫ ḫ	comb s/th
saṭr, suṭūr ~ usṭur	line
sawa	together
sawṛa, -āt	revolution
sawwāʔ, -īn	chauffeur
saxxān, -āt	boiler
sayyaḫ, yisayyaḫ ḫ	make s/th melt
sayyida, -āt	lady
saʕīd, suʕada	happy
sāʔiḫ, suwwāḫ	tourist
sāb, yisīb w ~ ḫ	leave s/th, let s/o
sābit	stable (adj.)
sābiʕ	seventh
sādis	sixth
sāfir, yisāfir	travel to (v.) go on a journey
sāḫ, yisīḫ	melt
sāwa, yisāwi ḫ	be equal to s/th be worth s/th
sāʕa, -āt	clock; watch; hour
sāʕid, yisāʕid w	help s/o
-- *fi ḫ*	help doing s/th
sibtimbir	September
sigāṛa, sagāyir	cigarette
siggāda, sagagīd	carpet
sihir, yishaṛ, sahaṛ	stay up late go out (late)
sikin, yuskun fi, sakan	live in s/th
sikit, yuskut, sukūt	stop speaking, shut up
sikka, sikak	road
issikka‿lḫadīd	railways
sillim, salālim	stairs
simiʕ, yismaʕ w ~ ḫ, samāʕ ~ samʕ	hear s/o ~ s/th
simsāṛ, samasṛa	house agent
sinima, -hāt	cinema
sinn	age
sinna, sinān ~ asnān	tooth
sirʔa	theft
sitāṛa, satāyir	curtain
sitt, -āt	woman, lady
sitti	my grandmother

sitta	six
sixin, yisxan, suxuniyya	become hot have a fever
siyadtak	you (polite)
siyāḫa	tourism
siɛr, asɛāṛ	price
Sīna	Sinai
suʾāl, asʾila	question
sudāni	Sudanese; peanuts
sufṛa, sufaṛ	dining table
sufṛagi, -yya	waiter
sukkaṛ (c.)	sugar
surūr	pleasure
bi-kull --	with pleasure
Surya	Syria
sūri, -yyīn	Syrian
surɛa, -āt	speed
bi---	quickly
Suwisra	Switzerland
suwisri	Swiss
suxn	warm
suxuniyya	fever
sūʾ, aswāʾ	market
sūʾ tafāhum	misunderstanding

ṣ

ṣabāḫ	morning
-- ilxēr	good morning (greet)
-- innūr	good morning (reply)
ṣabbaḫ, yiṣabbaḫ ɛala w	greet s/o (in the morning)
ṣabi, ṣubyān	errand boy
ṣabr	patience
ṣabūn (c.)	soap
ṣaddar, yiṣaddar ḫ	export s/th
ṣaff, ṣufūf	row; class
ṣaḫāfa	press
ṣaḫīḫ	true; truly
ṣaḫḫ (inv.)	right, correct
ṣala, -wāt	prayer
ṣalla, yiṣalli, ṣala	pray
ṣallaḫ, yiṣallaḫ ḫ	repair s/th
ṣalōn, -āt	sitting room
ṣammim, yiṣammim ɛala ḫ	insist on s/th
ṣandal, ṣanādil	sandals (a pair)
ṣanf, aṣnāf	sort, quality
ṣaniyya, ṣawāni	tray
ṣawwar, yiṣawwar ḫ	photograph s/th
ṣaydala	pharmacy (study)
ṣaydali, ṣayadla	pharmacist
ṣaydaliyya, -āt	pharmacy
ṣaɛb	difficult
ṣāḫib, aṣḫāb ~ iṣḫāb	friend; owner
ṣaḫb_ilbēt	landlord
ṣāla, -āt	hall
ṣālit istiʾbāl	reception hall
ṣāliḫ, yiṣāliḫ w	make up with s/o
ṣāliḫ li ḫ	suitable for s/th
ṣēf	summer
ṣēfi	summer (adj.)
ṣifa, -āt	characteristic quality
ṣifr, aṣfāṛ ~ iṣfāṛ	zero
ṣiḫi, yiṣḫa	wake up
ṣiḫḫa	health
ṣināɛa, -āt	industry
ṣināɛi	industrial artificial
ṣubāɛ, ṣūbaɛ, ṣawābiɛ	finger
ṣubḫ	morning
ṣudāɛ	headache
ṣudfa, ṣudaf	coincidence
bi_ṣṣudfa	by chance
ṣuġayyaṛ	small; little; young
ṣulb	steel
ṣūf, aṣwāf	wool
ṣūf	woollen
ṣūra, ṣuwar	picture

š

šaʾʾa, šuʾaʾ	appartment
šagaṛ (c.), *ašgāṛ*	trees
šaġġāla, -āt	maid
šahad, yišhad, šahāda	testify
šahāda	testimony
šahāda, -āt	certificate diploma
šahṛ, šuhūr~ ušhur	month
-- ilɛasal	honeymoon
šakaṛ, yuškur w, šukr	thank s/th
šakl, aškāl	form, shape
šakwa, šakāwi	complaint
šamāl	north
šamāli	northern
šamm, yišimm ḫ, šamm	smell s/th
šams (f.)	sun
šanṭa, šunaṭ	bag, suitcase

šaqīq, ašiqqa	full brother
šaṛaf	honor
šaṛaḫ, yišraḫ ḫ, šaṛḫ	explain s/th
šarᵓ	east
šarᵓi	eastern
šaṛāb, -āt	stockings (a pair)
šarika, -āt	firm, company
šarq	east
išŠarq ilᵓAwsaṭ	Middle East
šarṭ, šurūṭ	condition
šawa, yišwi ḫ, šawy	grill s/th
šayyil, yišayyil w ḫ	get s/o to carry s/th
šaɛb, šuɛūb	people
šaɛbi	popular, folk
šaɛr (c.)	hair
šābb, šubbān	young man
šābba, -āt	young woman
šāf, yišūf w ~ ḫ	see s/o ~ s/th
šāl, yišīl ḫ, šēl	carry (away) s/th
šāriɛ, šawāriɛ	street
šāṭiᵓ, šawāṭiᵓ	coast, beach
šāṭir, šaṭrīn ~ šuṭṭār	clever, smart
šāwir, yišāwir w	ask s/o for advice
-- li w	wave to s/o
šāy	tea
šēᵓ, ašyāᵓ	thing, something
šēᵓ lā yuṭāq	unbearable!
šēk, -āt	check
šiᵓīᵓ, ašiᵓᵓa	full brother
šibbāk, šababīk	window
šidīd, šudād	severe
šimāl	left
širib, yišṛab ḫ, šurb	drink s/th
šita	winter; rain
šiṭān, šayaṭīn	devil
šīk	chic, elegant
šubbāk, šababīk	window
šuġl, ašġāl	work
šuġlāna	job
šukr	gratitude; thanks
šukṛan	thank you
šurb	drinking (n.)
šurba	soup
šurṭa	police
šuwayya	somewhat
šuwayyit ṃayya	some water
šuwayyit ṛuzz	some rice

t

taᵓmīm	nationalization
taᵓrīban	approximately, nearly
taᵓxīr	delay (n.)
tadahwur	decline (n.)
tadrīb	training (n.)
tadxīn	smoking (n.)
tafkīr	thinking (n.)
tagdīd	extension; renewal
taġyīr	change; changing
taḫrīr	liberation
taḫsīn	improvement
taḫt	under, below
taḫwīla, -āt	transfer
taks, tukúsa ~ taksiyāt	taxi
takyīf	airconditioning
talāta	three
talg	ice; snow
tallāga, -āt	refrigerator
tallig, yitallig	freeze
taman, atmān	price
tamanya	eight
tamām	perfect
kullu --	everything is okay
tammim, yitammim ɛala ḫ	check s/th
tamrīn, -āt	exercise; training
tanḍīf	cleaning (n.)
taṛabēẓa, -āt	table
tarbiyya ~ tarbiya	upbringing education
tarīx	history
tarīx, tawarīx	date
tarkīb	fixing (n.)
taryaᵓa	mockery
taslīm	delivery reclaim (baggage)
taṣdīr	export (n.)
taṣlīḫ, -āt	reparation
taṣrīḫ, ṭaṣarīḫ	permission, permit, license
taṭawwur, -āt	development
tawlīd	generation (of energy)
tawqīɛ, -āt	signature
taxaṣṣuṣ	specialization
tazkaṛa, tazākir	ticket
taɛāla	come!
taɛbān	tired
taɛlīm	education
tābiɛ, yitābiɛ ḫ	pursue s/th
tālit	third

tāmin	eighth
tāni	second; another again, once again
tāsiɛ	ninth
tiʾīl, tuʾāl	heavy
tilifōn, -āt	telephone
tilivizyōn, -āt	television
tilmīz, talamza	pupil
tilt	third (1/3)
timsāl, tamasīl	statue
tisɛa	nine
tixīn, tuxān	thick; fat
tīn (c.)	figs
tuffāḥ (c.)	apples
tultumiyya	three hundred
tuṛāb	dust
Turkiya	Turkey
turki, taṛakwa	Turk, Turkish
tuxn	thickness
tūt (c.)	mulberries

ṭ

ṭaʾṭūʾa, ṭaʾaṭīʾ	ashtray
ṭab ...	fine ...
ṭabašīr (c.)	chalk
ṭabax, yuṭbux ḥ, *ṭabx ~ ṭabīx*	cook s/th
ṭabīb, aṭibba	doctor
ṭabīx	cooking (n.)
ṭabīɛa	nature
ṭabīɛi	natural
ṭabūr, ṭawabīr	queue
ṭabɛan	of course
ṭafa, yiṭfi ḥ, ṭafy	turn off s/th
ṭaffa, yiṭaffi ḥ	extinguish s/th
ṭaffāya, -āt	ashtray
ṭalab, yuṭlub, *w ~ ḥ, ṭalab*	ask for s/th order s/th
-- ḥ min w	ask s/o (to do) s/th
ṭallaɛ, yiṭallaɛ ḥ	bring s/th up take s/th out
ṭalyāni, ṭalayna	Italian
ṭamāṭim (c. f.)	tomatoes
ṭarāwa	coolness
ṭarbūš, ṭarabīš	tarbush (hat)
ṭari, -yya, ṭurāy	soft
ṭarīʾ, ṭuruʾ	road
ɛan -- ḥ	via; by means of
ṭarīʾa, ṭuruʾ	method, manner
ṭawīl, ṭuwāl	long; tall
ṭayyib	kind; good okay! fine!
ṭaɛm	taste
ṭābiɛ, *ṭawābiɛ barīd*	stamp
ṭālib, ṭullāb *~ ṭalaba*	student (m.)
ṭālíba, -āt	student (f.)
ṭār, yiṭīr, ṭayarān	fly (v.)
ṭāza (inv.)	fresh (food)
ṭibb	medicine
ṭifl, aṭfāl	child
ṭiliɛ, yiṭlaɛ (ḥ), *ṭulūɛ*	get out; appear ascend (s/th) go up
ṭūl	length
-- innahāṛ	all day long
-- illēl	all night long
-- ɛumri	my whole life long
ɛala --	immediately; straight on

u

umm, -ahāt	mother
usṭa, -wāt	craftsman
uxt, ixwāt banāt	sister

v

veranda, -āt	veranda, porch
vīza, -āt	visa

w

wa	and
waʾt, awʾāt	time
-- farāġ	spare time
waḍḍab, *yiwaḍḍab ḥ*	arrange s/th put s/th in order
wafd, wufūd	delegation
waffaṛ, yiwaffaṛ ḥ	save s/th
wagaɛ, yiwgaɛ w, *wagaɛ*	hurt s/o
wagaɛ, awgāɛ	pain
waḥdu	alone, by himself
wakkil, yiwakkil *w ḥ*	feed s/th to s/o
wala	not a single
-- ḥāga	nothing
-- ḥitta	nowhere
-- wāḥid	no one
walad, awlād	boy
walla	or

wallaع, yiwallaع ḫ	light s/th
	switch on s/th
wallāعa, -āt	lighter
waṛa	behind
waraʾ (c.), *ʾawrāʾ*	paper
ward (c.), *wurūd*	flowers
warra, yiwarri w ḫ	show s/o s/th
waṣal, yiwṣal ḫ ~ li ḫ, wuṣūl	arrive at s/th
waṣl, wuṣúla	receipt
waṣṣal, yiwaṣṣal w ḫ	take s/o somewhere
-- *ḫ li w*	deliver s/th to s/o
wazan, yiwzin ḫ, wazn	weigh s/th
wazīr, wuzaṛa	minister
wazn	weight
wādi, widyān	valley
wāḍiḫ	clear
wāfiʾ, yiwāfiʾ (عala ḫ)	agree (to s/th)
wāgib, -āt	duty; homework
wāḫid	one
wāsiع	wide
wi	and
wiʾif, yuʾaf, wuʾūf	stand up
	come to a stop
wiʾif عala rigl	be in an uproar
wiʾiع, yuʾaع, wuʾūع	fall down
widn (f.), *widān*	ear
wiḫiš	ugly; bad
wilāya, -āt	province
ilWilayāt ilMuttaḫida	USA
wisix	dirty
wiṣil, yiwṣal (ḫ), wuṣūl	arrive (at)
wišš, wušūš	face
-- *iṣṣubḫ*	early in the morning
wizāṛa, -āt	ministry
wuṣūl	arrival

x

xabaṛ, axbāṛ	message, news
xabba, yixabbi ḫ	hide s/th
xad, yāxud ḫ	take s/th
-- *bard*	catch a cold
-- *bālu min ḫ*	pay attention to s/th
-- *عala w ~ ḫ*	get used to s/o ~ s/th
xafa, yixfi ḫ, xafy	hide s/th
xaff, yixiff	recover
xafīf, xufāf	light (weight)
xalāṣ	enough!
xalla, yixalli w ~ ḫ	allow s/o ~ s/th
	preserve s/o
	make s/o do s/th
xallaṣ, yixallaṣ ḫ	finish s/th
xamsa	five
xaṛag, yuxrug, xurūg	go outside
	exit (v.)
xarīf	autumn
xaṣrān	out of order
xašab	wood
	wooden
xašš, yixušš ḫ	enter s/th
	turn (direction)
xaṭab, yuxṭub w	ask for s/o's hand in marriage
xaṭwa, xaṭawāt	step
xaṭṭ	script, handwriting
xaṭṭ, xuṭūṭ	line
xazna, xizan	cash desk; safe
xazzān, -āt	reservoir (water)
xāf, yixāf min w ~ ḫ, xōf	fear s/o ~ s/th
	be afraid of s/o ~ s/th
xāl, xilān	uncle (maternal)
xāla, -āt	aunt (maternal)
xāliṣ	very, extremely
xāmis	fifth
xārig	outside
ilxārig	abroad
xāṣṣ	private
xāṣṣatan	especially
xātim, xawātim	ring
xēr	bounty, good deed
xidma, xadamāt	service
ʾayy --	at your service!
xiliṣ ~ xuluṣ, yixlaṣ	be finished, end,
	come to an end
xisir, yixsaṛ	break down
	be spoiled
xiṭāb, -āt	speech
xiyāṛ (c.)	cucumbers
xōf	fear
xuḍari, -yya	greengrocer
xuḍāṛ (c.), *xuḍrawāt*	vegetables

y

ya	vocative particle
ya ... ya ...	either ... or ...

yafandim	Sir, Madam
yafṭa, yufaṭ	noticeboard signboard
yaḻḻa	come on! let's go!
yanāyir	January
yarēt	if only
ya-tara ...	I wonder ...
yaɛni	that is to say
yimīn	right (direction)
yimkin (inv.)	perhaps
yiẓhar (inv.)	apparently
yōm, ayyām	day
~ iyyām	
ilyomēn dōl	these days
yulyu	July
yunyu	June
yunāni	Greek

z

zaʾʾ, yizuʾʾ w ~ ḫ, zaʾʾ	push s/o ~ s/th
zahʾān	bored
zaḫma (inv.)	crowded
zaki, azkiya	intelligent
zamān	previously long ago
zann, yizinn, zann	whine
zaraɛ, yizraɛ ḫ, zarɛ	plant s/th
zarɛ (c.)	plants
zatūn (c.)	olives
zawbaɛa, zawābiɛ	storm
zawwid, yizawwid ḫ ~ min ḫ	increase s/th
zawwid, yizawwid w bi ḫ	provide s/o with s/th
zayda	appendix
zayy	as, like
-- baɛḍu	it doesn't matter
-- ma	as though
zaɛlān min w	angry with s/o
-- ɛala w	sorry for s/o
zād, yizīd, ziyāda	increase (v.)
zākir, yizākir ḫ	study s/th
zāṛ, yizūr w ~ ḫ, ziyāṛa	visit s/o ~ s/th pay a visit to s/o ~ s/th
zibāla	garbage
zibūn, zabāyin	client, customer
zimīl, zumala ~ zumalāʾ	colleague schoolmate
ziṛāɛa	agriculture
ziṛāɛi	agricultural
ziyāṛa, -āt	visit
ziɛil, yizɛal min w, zaɛal	be angry with s/o
zōʾ	manners, tact
zōg, azwāg	husband
zōga, zawgāt	wife

ẓ

ẓabaṭ, yuẓbuṭ ḫ, ẓabṭ	adjust
bi‿ẓẓabṭ	precisely
ẓahar, yiẓhaṛ, ẓuhūr	appear
yiẓhar ɛala w	apparently s/o is ...
ẓābiṭ, ẓubbāṭ	officer
ẓarf, ẓurūf	envelope circumstance
ẓarīf, ẓurāf	pleasant, kind
ẓurf	kindness

ž

žakitta, -āt	jacket
žīb, -āt	skirt

ɛ

ɛaʾd, ɛuʾūd	contract
-- ɛamal	labor contract
ɛadad, aɛdād	number, amount
ɛadal, yiɛdil ḫ, ɛadl	set s/th straight
ɛadd, yiɛidd ḫ, ɛadd	count
ɛadda, yiɛaddi ḫ	cross s/th
-- ɛala w ~ ḫ	pass by s/o
ɛaddād, -āt	electricity meter taxi meter
ɛads (c.)	lentils
ɛafrīt, ɛafarīt	demon, devil
ɛafwan	not at all!
ɛagab, yiɛgib w	appeal to s/o
ɛagala	rush (n.)
ɛagala, -āt	wheel
ɛagala, ɛagal	bicycle
ɛagūz, ɛawagīz	old (people) elderly
ɛahd, ɛuhūd	era
ɛala ~ ɛa	on

ɛa_lʔāxir	extremely
ɛa_nnaṣya	on the street corner
ɛa_rrīḥa	lightly sugared (coffee)
-- *fēn*	where to?
-- *kēfak*	as you wish!
-- *mahlak*	slow down!
-- *rigl*	in an uproar
-- *riglē(h)*	walking, on foot
-- *ṭūl*	immediately straight on
ɛalam, aɛlām	flag
ɛalašān	for, because in order to
ɛallaʔ, yiɛallaʔ ḥ	hang up s/th
ɛallim, yiɛallim w ḥ	teach s/o s/th
-- *ḥ* ~ *ɛala ḥ*	mark s/th
ɛamal, aɛmāl	deed; work
ɛamal, yiɛmil ḥ, ɛamal	do s/th, make s/th
ɛamaliyya, -āt	operation
ɛamm, aɛmām ~ *ɛimām*	uncle (paternal)
ɛamma, -āt	aunt (paternal)
ɛan	from; about
ɛand	at
ɛandak hina	stop here!
ɛaraʔ	sweat
ɛaṛabi, ɛaṛab	Arab
ɛaṛabi	Arabic
ɛaṛabiyya, -āt	car
ɛarḍ	breadth, width
ɛarḍ, ɛurūḍ	show, presentation
ɛarīs, ɛirsān	bridegroom
ɛaṛūsa, ɛaṛāyis	bride; doll
ɛasal	honey
ɛasali	hazel (color)
ɛaskari, ɛasākir	policeman, soldier
ɛaṣīr	juice
ɛaša (m.)	dinner
ɛašaṛa	ten
ɛašān	for, because in order to
-- *xaṭrak*	for your sake!
ɛaṭlān	out of order
ɛaṭšān	thirsty

ɛayyān	sick
ɛayyil, ɛiyāl	child
ɛazzil, yiɛazzil, ɛizāl	move (house)
ɛāʔil	sensible
ɛāda, -āt	custom common practice
ɛādi, -yya, -yyīn	ordinary, common
ɛāg	ivory
ɛākis, yiɛākis w	tease s/o
ɛālam	crowd
ɛāli	high
ɛāmil, yiɛāmil w	treat s/o
ɛāmm	general, common
ɛāš, yiɛīš, ɛīša	live
ɛāšir	tenth
ɛāwiz ~ *ɛāyiz*	wanting, wishing
ɛāz, yiɛūz ḥ	want, wish
ɛēla, -āt ~ *ɛāʔilāt*	family
ɛēn (f.), *ɛenēn* ~ *ɛuyūn*	eye
ɛēš (c.)	bread
ɛilāqa, -āt	relationship
ɛilāwa ɛala ḥ	moreover
ɛilba, ɛilab	box
ɛilm	science
ɛilmi	scientific
ɛimāṛa, -āt	block of flats
ɛinwān, ɛanawīn	address; title (of a book)
ɛiriʔ, yiɛraʔ, ɛaṛaʔ	sweat
ɛirif, yiɛṛaf w ~ *ḥ, maɛrifa*	know s/o ~ s/th
-- + imperf.	know how to
ɛišrīn	twenty
ɛiṭiš, yiɛṭaš, ɛaṭaš	be thirsty
ɛiyāda, -āt	clinic
ɛīd, aɛyād	feast
ɛīša	living (n.)
ɛidwān ~ *ɛudwān*	aggression
ɛuluww	height
ɛumda (m.), *ɛumad*	headman (village)
ɛumla, -āt	currency
-- *ṣaɛba*	hard currency
ɛumr, aɛmāṛ	life span
ɛumru ma...	never did he ...

ENGLISH - ARABIC

a

Abdin Palace	*ʾAṣrᵊ ɛAbdīn*
able: be -- to	*ʾidir, yiʾdaṛ*
being -- to	*ʾādir*
about	*ɛan; min*
-- ... ago	*min ʾīmit ...*
above	*fōʾ*
abroad	*ilxārig*
accident	*ħādis, ħawādis*
	ħadsa, ħawādis
achievement	*ʾingāz, -āt*
acquaintance	*maɛrifa, maɛārif*
make s/o's --	*itɛaṛraf, yitɛaṛraf ɛala w*
acquisition	*ʾingāz, -āt*
activity	*našāṭ, -āt*
actor	*mumassil, -īn*
address	*ɛinwān, ɛanawīn*
adjust s/th	*ẓabaṭ, yuẓbuṭ ħ, ẓabṭ*
become --ed	*iẓẓabaṭ, yiẓẓibiṭ*
administration	*ʾidāṛa, -āt*
advantage	*mīza, -āt*
take -- of s/o ~ s/th	*istaġall, yistaġill w ~ ħ*
advice	*ṛaʾy, ʾaṛāʾ*
afraid	*xāyif*
be -- of s/o ~ s/th	*xāf, yixāf min w ~ ħ, xōf*
after	*baɛd*
-- that	*baɛdᵊ kida*
--...ing	*baɛdᵊ ma ...*
afternoon	*baɛd iḍḍuhr*
again	*tāni; kamān maṛṛa*
all over --	*min ʾawwil wi‿gdīd*
against	*ɛala ~ ɛa*
age	*sinn*
aggression	*ɛidwān ~ ɛudwān*
agree upon s/th	*ittafaʾ, yittifiʾ ɛala ħ*
-- to s/th	*wāfiʾ, yiwāfiʾ ɛala ħ*
agreed	*māši*
agreeing	*miwāfiʾ*
agreement	*ittifāʾ, -āt*
agricultural	*ziṛāɛi*
agriculture	*ziṛāɛa*
air	*hawa*
airconditioning	*takyīf*
airport	*maṭār, -āt*

alabaster	*ʾalabasṭar*
Alexandria	*Iskindiriyya*
all	*kull*
-- day long	*ṭūl innahāṛ*
allow s/o ~ s/th	*xalla, yixalli w ~ ħ*
-- s/o to do s/th	*samaħ, yismaħ li w bi ħ*
allowed (rel.)	*ħalāl* (inv.)
alone	*waħdu; li-waħdu*
also	*kamān; barḍu*
alter s/th	*ġayyaṛ, yiġayyaṛ ħ*
always	*dayman*
America	*ʾAmrīka*
American	*ʾamrikāni, ʾamrikān*
	ʾamrīki, -yyīn
amount	*ɛadad, aɛdād*
ancestors	*agdād ~ gudūd*
and	*wi ~ wa*
anew	*min gidīd*
angry	*zaɛlān; mitnarfis*
angry with s/o	*zaɛlān min w*
be -- with s/o	*ziɛil, yizɛal min w, zaɛal*
be -- on s/o	*itnarfis, yitnarfis ɛala w*
animal	*ħayawān, -āt*
annoy s/o	*dāyiʾ, yidāyiʾ w*
annoyance	*midayʾa*
annoyed	*middāyiʾ*
be --	*iddāyiʾ, yiddāyiʾ*
annual	*sanawi*
another	*tāni*
antiquities	*ʾasāṛ*
ants	*naml* (c.)
any	*ʾayy*
anything	*ʾayyᵊ ħāga*
apologize to s/o for s/th	*iɛtazaṛ, yiɛtizir li w ɛan ħ*
apparently	*yiẓhar* (inv.)
	bāyin ɛala w
appartment	*šaʾʾa, šuʾaʾ*
appeal to s/o	*ɛagab, yiɛgib w*
appear	*ẓahar, yiẓhaṛ, ẓuhūr*
appendix	*zayda*
apples	*tuffāħ* (c.)
application form	*istimāṛa, -āt*
appointment	*mawɛid ~ maɛād, mawaɛīd*
approach (intr.)	*ʾaṛṛab, yiʾaṛṛab, ʾurb*

appropriate	*munāsib*
approximately	*ḫawāli; taʾrīban*
April	*ʾabrīl*
Arab	*ʿarabi, ʿarab*
Arabic	*ʿarabi, ilʿarabi*
area	*manṭiʾa, manāṭiʾ*
	magāl, -āt
around	*ḫawalēn*
arrange s/th	*waḍḍab, yiwaḍḍab ḫ*
arrest s/o	*ʾabaḍ, yuʾbuḍ ʿala w*
	misik, yimsik w
	ʾalqa, yulqi ʾilqabḍ ʿala w
get --ed	*itmasak, yitmisik*
arrival	*wuṣūl*
arrive (at)	*waṣal ~ wiṣil, yiwṣal ḫ, wuṣūl*
artificial	*ṣināʿi*
as	*zayy; ka-*
-- for...	*amma ... fa*
-- if	*kaʾann; zayyᵊ ma*
-- though	*kaʾann; zayyᵊ ma*
-- well	*kamān; barḍu*
-- you wish	*ʿala kēfak!*
	zayyᵊ ma-tḫibb!
ascend s/th	*ṭiliʿ, yiṭlaʿ ḫ ṭulūʿ*
ashtray	*ṭaʾṭūʾa, ṭaʾaṭīʾ*
	ṭaffāya, -āt
ask s/o s/th	*saʾal, yisʾal w ḫ, suʾāl*
-- about s/o	*saʾal ʿala w*
-- for s/o ~ s/th	*ṭalab, yuṭlub w ~ ḫ, ṭalab*
-- s/o s/th	*ṭalab min w ḫ*
-- s/o for advice	*šāwir, yišāwir w*
-- s/o for permission	*istaʾzin, yistaʾzin w*
asleep	*nāyim*
make s/o fall --	*nawwim, yinawwim w*
asphalt	*ʾasfalt*
assassination	*ʾatl; iġtiyāl*
assemble s/th	*rakkib, yirakkib ḫ*
assembly	*igtimāʿ, -āt*
at	*ʿand*
Ataba	*ilʿAtaba*
attempt	*miḫawla, -āt*
August	*ʾaġusṭus*
aunt (maternal)	*xāla, -āt*
aunt (paternal)	*ʿamma, -āt*
Australia	*ʾUsturalya*
Australian	*ʾusturāli*
Austria	*inNimsa*
Austrian	*nimsāwi*
autumn	*xarīf*
average	*mutawassiṭ*

b

baby	*nūnu; ṭifl, aṭfāl*
bad	*wiḫiš; baṭṭāl*
bag	*šanṭa, šunaṭ*
	kīs, akyās ~ ikyās
balcony	*balakōna, -āt*
bald	*aṣlaʿ, ṣalʿa, ṣulʿ*
ballpoint	*ʾalam gāff*
bananas	*mōz* (c.)
bank	*bank, bunūk*
bargain (v.)	*fāṣil, yifāṣil, fiṣāl*
bath	*ḫammām, -āt*
bathe	*istaḫamma, yistaḫamma*
bathroom	*ḫammām, -āt*
battery	*baṭṭariyya, -āt*
	ḫagaṛ, ḫigāṛa
be	*kān, yikūn*
beach	*šāṭiʾ, šawāṭiʾ*
beans	*fūl* (c.)
cooked --	*fūl midammis*
beard	*daʾn* (f.), *duʾūn*
beat s/o ~ s/th	*ḍarab, yiḍrab w ~ ḫ, ḍarb*
beautiful	*gamīl, gumāl*
	ḫilw
more ~ most --	*agmal; aḫla*
because	*ʿalašān ~ ʿašān*
	liʾann ~ liʾinn
-- of s/th	*bi-sabab ḫ*
become	*baʾa, yibʾa*
bedroom	*ʾōḍit nōm*
beer	*bīra*
before	*ʾabl*
begin (v.)	*ibtada, yibtidi*
beginning	*bidāya*
-- of	*ʾawwil*
behind	*waṛa*
Belgian	*balžīki*
Belgium	*Balžīka*
believe s/o ~ s/th	*saddaʾ, yisaddaʾ w ~ ḫ*
-- that s/o s/th	*ḫasab, yiḫsib w ḫ*
believing	*misaddaʾ*
bell	*gaṛas, agṛās ~ igṛāṣ*
belonging to ...	*bitāʿ, bitāʿit, bitūʿ*
below	*taḫt*
belt	*ḫizām, ḫizíma*

best	*aḥsan*
better	*aḥsan*
between	*bēn*
beverage	*mašrūb, -āt*
Bey	*Bē, Bahawāt*
bicycle	*ʕagala, ʕagal*
big	*kibīr, kubāṛ*
	ṭawīl, ṭuwāl
how --	*ʔaddᵊ ʔē?*
bigger -- biggest	*akbaṛ*
bill (check)	*fatūṛa, fawatīr*
	ḥisāb, -āt
black	*iswid, sōda, sūd*
blackboard	*lōḥa, -āt*
	sabbūṛa
blame s/o	*ʔāxiz, yiʔāxiz w*
bless s/o	*bārik, yibārik fi w*
blessed	*mubāṛak*
blessing	*baṛaka, -āt*
blind	*aʕma, ʕamya, ʕumy*
block s/th	*sadd, yisidd ḥ,*
	sadd
block of flats	*ʕimāṛa, -āt*
blond	*ašʔaṛ, šaʔṛa, šuʔr*
blood	*damm*
blouse	*bilūza, -āt*
blow s/th	*nafax, yunfux*
	ḥ ~ fi ḥ, nafx
blue	*azraʔ, zarʔa, zurʔ*
dark --	*kuḥli*
boat	*markib* (f.),
	marākib
boil	*ġili, yiġli, ġalayān*
boiler	*saxxān, -āt*
boiling	*ġalayān*
book	*kitāb, kutub*
bookkeeper	*muḥāsib, -īn*
bored	*zahʔān*
born	*mawlūd*
be --	*itwalad, yitwilid*
borrow s/th	*istalaf, yistilif ḥ*
both	*litnēn*
bottle	*ʔizāza, ʔazāyiz*
bounty	*xēr*
box	*ʕilba, ʕilab*
boy	*walad, awlād*
bracelet	*ʔiswira, ʔasāwir*
brake (n.)	*faṛmala, faṛāmil*
bread	*ʕēš* (c.)
loaf of --	*riġīf, riġífa ~ irġifa*
breadth	*ʕarḍ*
break s/th	*kasaṛ, yiksaṛ ḥ, kasr*
-- down	*xisir, yixsaṛ*
breakfast	*fiṭār ~ fuṭūr*
have --	*fiṭir, yifṭar, fiṭār*
breathe	*itnaffis, yitnaffis*
bride	*ʕaṛūsa, ʕaṛāyis*
bridegroom	*ʕarīs, ʕirsān*
bridge	*kubri, kabāri*
bring s/o s/th	*gāb, yigīb li w ḥ*
-- s/th down	*nazzil, yinazzil ḥ*
-- s/th up	*ṭallaʕ, yiṭallaʕ ḥ*
broadcast	*našṛa, našaṛāt*
broken	*maksūr*
brother	*ạxx ~ axu, ixwān*
	~ ixwāt ṣubyān
full --	*šaqīq, ašiqqa*
	šiʔīʔ, ašiʔʔa
brown	*bunni; asmaṛ*
build s/th	*bana, yibni ḥ,*
	buna
building	*mabna* (m.),
	mabāni
bus	*ʔutubīs, -āt*
bus stop	*mawʔaf, mawāʔif*
but	*lākin; bass*
buy s/th	*ištara, yištiri ḥ,*
	šira
by	*bi*
-- chance	*bi‿ṣṣudfa*
-- himself	*li-waḥdu*
-- means of	*ʕan ṭarīʔ*

c

Cairo	*ilQāhira; Maṣr*
calculate s/th	*ḥasab, yiḥsib ḥ*
calendar	*natīga, natāyig*
call s/o	*nadah, yindah*
	w ~ li w, nadh
-- to prayer	*iddan, yiddan*
calm (adj.)	*hādi, hadya,*
	hadyīn
calm down	*hidi, yihda, hudūʔ*
Canada	*Kanada*
Canadian	*kanadi, yyīn*
canal	*qanā ~ qanāt,*
	qanawāt
canister (gas)	*ʔumbūba, ʔanabīb*
car	*ʕaṛabiyya, -āt*
card	*kart, kurúta*
carpet	*siggāda, sagagīd*
carry (away) s/th	*šāl, yišīl ḥ, šēl*
-- out s/th	*ʔangaz, yingiz ḥ*
get s/o -- s/th	*šayyil, yišayyil*
	w ḥ
cash desk	*xazna, xizan*
cat	*ʔuṭṭ* (m.), *ʔuṭṭa*
	(f.), *ʔuṭaṭ*

catch s/o ~ s/th	*misik, yimsik w ~ ḫ, mask*
-- up with s/th	*laḫaᵓ, yilḫaᵓ ḫ*
cause (n.)	*sabab, asbāb*
celebration (rel.)	*mūlid, mawālid*
centimeter	*sanṭi*
century	*qarn, qurūn*
certificate	*šahāda, -āt*
chair	*kursi, karāsi*
chairman	*raᵓīs, ruᵓasāᵓ ~ ruᵓasa*
chalk	*ṭabašīr* (c.)
change (intr.)	*itġayyaṛ, yitġayyaṛ*
-- s/th	*ġayyaṛ, yiġayyaṛ ḫ*
-- (money)	*fakk, yifukk ḫ, fakk*
be --ed (money)	*itfakk, yitfakk*
change (n.)	*taġyīr*
small --	*fakka*
channel	*qanā, qanawāt*
characteristic	*ṣifa, -āt*
charge	*rusūm* (pl.)
chatter (v.)	*dardiš, yidardiš, dardaša*
chauffeur	*sawwāᵓ, -īn*
cheap	*rixīṣ, ruxāṣ*
consider s/th --	*istarxaṣ, yistarxaṣ ḫ*
cheaper ~ cheapest	*arxaṣ*
check s/th	*tammim, yitammim ɛala ḫ*
check	*šēk, -āt*
check (bill)	*ḫisāb, -āt*
cheese	*gibna, giban*
chest (box)	*sandūᵓ, sanadīᵓ*
chic	*šīk*
chicken	*farxa, firāx*
chief	*rayyis*
chief engineer	*bašmuhandis, -īn*
child	*ṭifl, aṭfāl*
	ɛayyil, ɛiyāl
children	*awlād*
chin	*daᵓn* (f.), *duᵓūn*
choose s/o ~ s/th	*ixtāṛ, yixtāṛ w ~ ḫ*
church	*kinīsa, kanāyis*
cigarette	*sigāṛa, sagāyir*
cinema	*sinima, -hāt*
circular (adj.)	*midawwaṛ*
circumstance	*ẓarf, ẓurūf*
citizen	*muwāṭin, -īn*
city	*madīna, mudun*
civil servant	*muwaẓẓaf, -īn*
class	*ṣaff, ṣufūf*
classroom	*faṣl, fuṣūl*

claxon	*kalaks, -āt*
clean s/th	*naḍḍaf, yinaḍḍaf ḫ*
clean (adj.)	*niḍīf, nuḍāf*
cleaning (n.)	*tanḍīf*
clear (adj.)	*wāḍiḫ*
clever	*šāṭir, šaṭrīn ~ šuṭṭār;*
	zaki, azkiya
cleverer ~ cleverest	*azka; ašṭar*
client	*zibūn, zabāyin*
clinic	*ɛiyāda, -āt*
clock	*sāɛa, -āt*
close (s/th)	*ᵓafal, yiᵓfil ḫ, ᵓafl*
close (to)	*ᵓurayyib (min)*
closed	*maᵓfūl, ᵓāfil*
closeness	*ᵓurb*
closer ~ closest	*aᵓṛab*
closet	*dulāb, dawalīb*
clothes	*hidūm*
	malābis
clothing	*hidūm* (pl.)
	malābis (pl.)
clouds	*saḫāb* (c.), *suḫub*
cloudy	*miġayyim*
become --	*ġayyim, yiġayyim*
it's --	*iddinya‿mġayyima*
club	*nādi, andiya ~ nawādi*
coast	*šāṭiᵓ, šawāṭiᵓ*
coat	*balṭu, balāṭi*
coffee	*ᵓahwa*
-- beans	*bunn*
-- house	*ᵓahwa, ᵓahāwi*
coincidence	*ṣudfa, ṣudaf*
cola	*kōka; bibsi*
cold (n.)	*bard*
it's --	*iddinya bard*
catch a ~	*xad, yāxud bard*
cold (adj.)	*bārid*
colleague	*zimīl, zumala ~ zumalāᵓ*
colonialism	*istiɛmāṛ*
color	*lōn, alwān ~ ilwān*
comb s/th	*saṛṛaḫ, yisaṛṛaḫ ḫ*
come (v.)	*gih, yīgi, migiyy*
-- here	*taɛāla hina!*
-- on	*yaḷḷa!*
coming	*gayy*
commit s/th	*irtakab, yirtikib ḫ*
committing (n.)	*irtikāb*
common	*muštaṛak*
	ɛādi, -yya, -yyīn
-- practice	*ɛāmm*
commotion	*hēṣa*

communicate	*ballaġ, yiballaġ*
s/th to s/o	*w ḫ*
company	*šarika, -āt*
complain	*ištaka, yištiki*
(about s/th)	*(min ḫ)*
complaint	*šakwa, šakāwi*
make a --	*ištaka, yištiki w*
about s/o	
compulsory	*ʾigbāri*
conceal s/th	*dāra, yidāri ḫ*
condition	*šarṭ, šurūṭ*
conference	*muʾtamaṛ, -āt*
confuse s/o	*laxbaṭ, yilaxbaṭ*
	w, laxbaṭa
congratulate s/o	*bārik, yibārik li w*
congratulations!	*mabṛūk!*
consider s/o s/th	*ḫasab, yiḫsib w ḫ*
consult s/o	*šāwir, yišāwir w*
-- with s/o	*itšāwir, yitšāwir*
contact s/o	*ittaṣal, yittiṣil bi w*
continue	*istamaṛṛ, yistamiṛṛ*
contract	*ɛaʾd, ɛuʾūd*
labor contract	*ɛaʾdᵊ ɛamal*
conversation	*ḫadīs, aḫadīs*
	muḫadsa, -āt
convert (money)	*ġayyaṛ, yiġayyaṛ ḫ*
cook s/th	*ṭabax, yuṭbux ḫ,*
	ṭabx ~ ṭabīx
be --ed	*iṭṭabax, yiṭṭibix*
cooking (n.)	*ṭabīx*
cool down	*baṛṛad, yibaṛṛad*
	(weather)
coolness	*ṭarāwa*
copper	*naḫās ~ niḫās*
corniche: road	*kurnīš inNīl*
along the Nile	
correct	*ṣaḫḫ* (inv.)
cotton	*ʾuṭn*
couch	*kanaba, -āt*
council	*maglis, magālis*
country	*balad* (f.), *bilād*
countryside	*rīf, aryāf*
courtyard	*ḫōš, aḫwāš*
cover up s/o	*dāra, yidāri*
~ s/th	*ɛala w ~ ḫ*
cows	*baʾaṛ* (c.)
craftsman	*usṭa, -wāt*
crazy	*magnūn, maganīn*
crime	*garīma, gaṛāyim*
criminal	*mugrim, -īn*
cross s/th	*ɛadda, yiɛaddi ḫ*
cross-eyed	*aḫwal, ḫōla, ḫūl*
crow (v.)	*iddan, yiddan*
crowded	*zaḫma* (inv.)
it's --	*iddinya zaḫma*

cucumbers	*xiyāṛ* (c.)
cup	*fingān, fanagīn*
cupboard	*dulāb, dawalīb*
currency	*ɛumla, -āt*
hard --	*ɛumla ṣaɛba*
curtain	*sitāṛa, satāyir*
custom	*ɛāda, -āt*
customer	*zibūn, zabāyin*
customs	*gumruk, gamārik*
cut s/th	*ʾaṣṣ, yiʾuṣṣ ḫ, ʾaṣṣ*
-- down on s/th	*ʾallil, yiʾallil*
	ḫ ~ min ḫ

d

dad	*ḅāba*
dam	*sadd, sudūd*
High Dam	*isSadd ilɛĀli*
dark: it's --	*iddinya ḍalma*
dark-skinned	*asmaṛ, samṛa,*
	sumr
darkness	*ḍalma*
data	*maɛlūma, -āt*
date	*tarīx, tawarīx*
daughter	*bint, banāt*
day	*yōm, ayyām ~*
	iyyām
all -- long	*ṭūl innahāṛ*
-- after	*baɛdᵊ bukṛa*
tomorrow	
-- before	*ʾawwil imbāriḫ*
yesterday	
these --s	*ilyomēn dōl*
daytime	*nahāṛ*
dead	*mayyit, -īn*
deaf	*aṭraš, ṭarša, ṭurš*
deal with s/o	*itɛāmil, yitɛāmil*
	maɛa w
death	*mōt*
December	*disimbir*
decent person	*ibnᵊ ḫalāl*
decide s/th	*qaṛṛaṛ, yiqaṛṛaṛ ḫ*
decision	*qaṛāṛ, -āt*
decline (n.)	*tadahwur*
decrease (v.)	*ʾall, yiʾill, ʾilla*
	niʾiṣ, yinʾaṣ,
	naʾṣ ~ naʾaṣān
deed	*ɛamal, aɛmāl*
defense	*difāɛ*
defend s/o ~ s/th	*dāfiɛ, yidāfiɛ*
	ɛan w ~ ḫ
degree	*daṛaga, -āt*
delay s/o ~ s/th	*ʾaxxaṛ, yiʾaxxaṛ*
	w ~ ḫ

delay (n.)	*taᵓxīr*
delegation	*wafd, wufūd*
delicious	*lazīz, luzāz*
deliver s/th to s/o	*waṣṣal, yiwaṣṣal ḥ li w*
delivery	*taslīm; tawṣīl*
demon	*¿afrīt, ¿afarīt*
department	*qism, aqsām*
deserve s/th	*istaḥaᵓᵓ, yistaḥaᵓᵓ ḥ; istāhil, yistāhil ḥ*
desire s/th	*nifs* + suffix *fi ḥ*
desk	*maktab, makātib*
determine s/th	*ḥaddid, yiḥaddid ḥ*
determined	*miṣammim*
development	*taṭawwur, -āt*
device	*gihāz, aghiza*
devil	*šiṭān, šayaṭīn*
	¿afrīt, ¿afarīt
dialogue	*ḥiwāṛ, -āt*
dictation	*ᵓimla*
die	*māt, yimūt, mōt*
difficult	*ṣa¿b*
diminish	*ᵓall, yiᵓill, ᵓilla*
dine	*it¿ašša, yit¿ašša*
dining room	*ᵓōḍit sufṛa*
dining table	*sufṛa, sufaṛ*
dinner	*¿aša* (m.)
diploma	*šahāda, -āt*
direction	*giha, -āt*
	naḥya, nawāḥi
director	*mudīr, -īn*
directorate	*ᵓidāṛa, -āt*
dirty	*wisix*
disappear	*ixtafa, yixtifi*
disassembled	*mafkūk*
disease	*maraḍ, amrāḍ*
dismantle s/th	*fakk, yifukk ḥ, fakk*
distance	*masāfa, -āt*
	bu¿d
distant (from)	*bi¿īd, bu¿ād (min ~ ¿an)*
distinction	*imtiyāz, -āt*
district	*ḥayy, aḥyāᵓ*
dizzy	*dāyix*
become --	*dāx, yidūx, dōxa*
make s/o --	*dawwax, yidawwax w*
do s/th	*¿amal, yi¿mil ḥ, ¿amal*
be done	*it¿amal, yit¿imil*
doctor	*duktūr, dakatra*
	ṭabīb, aṭibba
doctorate	*dukturā*

dog	*kalb, kilāb*
doll	*¿arūsa, ¿arāyis*
dollar	*dulāṛ, -āt*
donkey	*ḥumāṛ, ḥimīr*
door	*bāb, abwāb ~ ibwāb*
doorbell	*gaṛas, agṛās ~ igṛāṣ*
doorman	*bawwāb, -īn*
Doqqi	*idDuᵓᵓi*
dreadful	*fazī¿, fuzā¿*
dream	*ḥilm, aḥlām*
dress	*fustān, fasatīn*
drink s/th	*širib, yišrab ḥ, šurb*
be drunk (consumed)	*itšaṛab, yitširib*
drinking (n.)	*šurb*
drip	*naᵓᵓaṭ, yinaᵓᵓaṭ*
drop in on s/o	*maṛṛ, yimurr ¿ala w*
	fāt, yifūt ¿ala w
drunk	*sakṛān*
during	*asnāᵓ, fi*
dust	*turāb*
Dutch ~ Dutchman	*hulandi*
duty	*wāgib, -āt*
dye s/th	*sabaġ, yusbuġ ḥ, sabġ*

e

each other	*ba¿ḍ*
ear	*widn* (f.), *widān*
early	*badri* (inv.)
-- morning	*iṣṣubḥᵊ badri*
	wišš iṣṣubḥ (metaphor)
earth	*ᵓarḍ*
easier ~ easiest	*ashal*
east	*šarᵓ ~ šarq*
eastern	*šarᵓi*
easy	*sahl*
eat s/th	*kal, yākul ḥ, ᵓakl*
be --en	*ittākil, yittākil*
eating (n.)	*ᵓakl*
economical	*iqtiṣādi*
economy	*iqtiṣād*
educated	*mit¿allim*
education	*tarbiya ~ tarbiyya*
	ta¿līm
eggs	*bēḍ* (c.)
Egypt	*Maṣr ~ Miṣr*

Egyptian	*maṣri*
eight	*tamanya*
eighth	*tāmin*
either ... or ...	*ya ... ya ...*
elderly	*ɛagūz, ɛawagīz*
electricity	*kahṛaba*
electricity meter	*ɛaddād, -āt*
elegant	*šīk*
more ~ most --	*ašyak*
elementary	*ibtidāʾi*
-- school	*madrasa‿btidāʾi*
elevator	*ʾaṣanṣēr, -āt*
embark: let s/o -- in s/th	*rakkib, yirakkib w ḫ*
empty (adj)	*fāḍi, faḍya, faḍyīn*
become --	*fiḍi, yifḍa*
end (v.)	*xiliṣ ~ xuluṣ, yixlaṣ*
end (n.)	*nihāya, -āt*
-- of ...	*ʾāxir ...*
engage: get --d	*xaṭab, yuxṭub w* (of men), *itxaṭabit, titxiṭib* (of women), *xuṭūba*
engineer	*muhandis, -īn*
England	*Ingiltira ~ ʾIngiltiṛa*
English ~ Englishman	*ingilīzi ~ ʾingilīzi, ingilīz ~ ʾingilīz*
enjoy oneself	*inbasaṭ, yinbiṣiṭ*
enough	*kifāya*
enough!	*xalāṣ!*
enrol in s/th	*iltaḫaq, yiltiḫiq bi ḫ*
enrolment	*iltiḫāq*
enter s/th	*daxal, yidxul ḫ, duxūl; xašš, yixušš ḫ ~ fi ḫ*
envelope	*ẓarf, ẓurūf*
equal (v.)	*sāwa, yisāwi ḫ*
era	*ɛahd, ɛuhūd*
eradication	*maḫw*
eraser	*ʾastīka, ʾasatīk*
errand	*mišwāṛ, mašawīr*
-- boy	*ṣabi, ṣubyān*
especially	*xāṣṣatan*
establishment	*giha, -āt*
Europe	*ʾUṛubba*
European	*ʾurubbi*
even	*ḫatta*
evening	*lēl*
-- (n.u.)	*lēla, layāli*
in the --	*bi‿llēl*

every	*kull*
everyone	*kull innās*
	kull^{ə} wāḫid
everything	*kull^{ə} ḫāga*
-- is okay	*kullu tamām*
exact	*maẓbūṭ*
	ṣaḫḫ (inv.)
exactly	*bi‿ẓẓabṭ*
exam: final school --	*sanawiyya ɛāmma*
examine s/o ~ s/th	*kašaf, yikšif ɛala w ~ ḫ, kašf*
example	*masal, amsila*
for --	*masalan*
except (for)	*ġēr; illa*
excursion	*riḫla, -āt ~ raḫalāt*
excuse me	*la muʾaxza*
execute s/th	*ʾangaz, yingiz ḫ*
	naffiz, yinaffiz ḫ
exercize (n.)	*tamrīn, -āt*
exhausted	*hamdān*
exit (v.)	*xaṛag, yuxrug, xurūg*
expand	*itwassaɛ, yitwassaɛ*
expensive	*ġāli, ġalya, ġalyīn*
more ~ most --	*aġla*
become --	*ġili, yiġla, ġuluww*
consider s/th --	*istaġla, yistaġla ḫ*
explain s/th to s/o	*šaraḫ, yišraḫ ḫ li w, šarḫ*
	fahhim, yifahhim w ḫ
exploit s/o ~ s/th	*istaġall, yistaġill w ~ ḫ*
export s/th	*ṣaddar, yiṣaddar ḫ*
export (n.)	*taṣdīr*
extend s/th	*gaddid, yigaddid ḫ*
be --ed	*iggaddid, yiggaddid*
extension	*tagdīd*
extent: to what --	*ʾadd^{ə} ʾē?*
extinguish s/th	*ṭaffa, yiṭaffi ḫ*
extremely	*xāliṣ, ɛa‿lʾāxir*
extremist	*mutaṭarrif*
eye	*ɛēn* (f.), *ɛenēn ~ ɛuyūn*

f

fabric	*ʾumāš, -āt ~ aʾmiša*
face	*wišš, wušūš*
factory	*maṣnaɛ, maṣāniɛ*

faculty	*kulliyya, -āt*
-- of arts	*kulliyyit ilʾadāb*
-- of law	*kulliyyit ilʾḥuʾūʾ*
fall down	*wiʾiɛ, yuʾaɛ, wuʾūɛ*
family	*ɛēla, -āt; ɛāʾila, -āt; ʾahl, ʾahāli*
far (from)	*biɛīd, buɛād (min ~ ɛan)*
farmer	*fallāḥ, -īn*
fast	*sarīɛ*
	miʾaddim (watch)
faster ~ fastest	*asraɛ*
fat	*tixīn, tuxān*
	simīn, sumān
father	*abb ~ abu, abbahāt*
faucet	*ḥanafiyya, -āt*
favor	*faḍl*
fear s/o ~ s/th	*xāf, yixāf min w ~ ḥ, xōf*
fear	*xōf*
feast	*ɛīd, aɛyād*
February	*fabṛāyir ~ fibṛāyir*
feed s/th to s/o	*wakkil, yiwakkil w ḥ*
feel s/th	*ḥass, yiḥiss bi ḥ*
fever	*suxuniyya*
few	*ʾulayyil*
a -- ...	*šuwayyit ...*
field	*magāl,-āt*
fifth	*xāmis*
figs	*tīn* (c.)
fill out s/th	*mala, yimla ḥ, malw*
be --ed	*itmala, yitmili*
-- up with fuel	*fawwil, yifawwil*
final school exam	*sanawiyya ɛāmma*
finally	*ʾaxīran*
find s/o ~ s/th	*laʾa, yilāʾi w ~ ḥ*
finger	*ṣubāɛ ~ ṣūbaɛ, ṣawābiɛ*
finish s/th	*xallaṣ, yixallaṣ ḥ*
be --ed	*xiliṣ ~ xuluṣ, yixlaṣ*
fire	*nāṛ* (f.), *niṛān*
firm (company)	*šarika, -āt*
first (adj.)	*ʾawwil ~ ʾawwal*
	ʾawwalāni
first (adv.)	*ilʾawwil*
fiscal stamp	*damġa, -āt*
fish	*samak* (c.)
five	*xamsa*
five hundred	*xumsumiyya*
fix s/th	*ṣallaḥ, yiṣallaḥ ḥ*
be --ed	*itṣallaḥ, yitṣallaḥ*
fixing (n.)	*tarkīb, taṣlīḥ*
flag	*ɛalam, aɛlām*
flee (v.)	*hirib, yihṛab, hurūb*
floor	*dōr, adwāṛ ~ idwāṛ*
flowers	*ward* (c.), *wurūd*
fly (v.)	*ṭār, yiṭīr, ṭayarān*
flyover	*kubri ɛilwi*
folk (adj.)	*šaɛbi*
food	*ʾakl*
fool s/o	*diḥik, yidḥak ɛala w, diḥk*
foot	*rigl* (f.), *riglēn*
on --	*māši, mašya, mašyīn*
	ɛala riglē(h)
foot (measure)	*ʾadam*
for	*li; ɛalašān ~ ɛašān*
--your sake	*ɛašān xaṭrak*
forbid s/th	*manaɛ, yimnaɛ ḥ, manɛ*
-- s/o (to do) s/th	*manaɛ w min ḥ*
forbidden	*mamnūɛ*
	ḥaṛām (rel.)
force	*quwwa, -āt*
forced	*muḍṭarr*
foreigner	*ʾagnabi, ʾagānib*
	ġarīb, aġṛāb
forget s/o ~ s/th	*nisi, yinsa w ~ ḥ, nisyān*
be forgotten	*itnasa, yitnisi*
forgive one another	*itsāmiḥ, yitsāmiḥ*
form (n.)	*istimāṛa, -āt*
formality	*ʾigṛāʾ, -āt*
foundation	*ʾinšāʾ*
fountain pen	*ʾalam ḥibr*
four	*aṛbaɛa*
fourth	*ṛābiɛ*
France	*Faṛansa*
free	*ḥurr, aḥṛāṛ*
	fāḍi, faḍya, faḍyīn (time)
	maggāni (money)
for --	*bi-balāš*
become --	*fiḍi, yifḍa* (time)
freedom	*ḥurriyya*
freeze (s/th)	*tallig, yitallig (ḥ)*
freezer	*firīzar, -āt*
French ~ Frenchman	*faṛansāwi*

fresh (food)	*ṭāza* (inv.)
fried	*maʔli*
friend	*ṣāḫib, aṣḫāb ~ iṣḫāb*
	ṣadīq, aṣdiqāʔ
friendlier ~ friendliest	*aṭyab*
friendly	*ṭayyib*
from	*min*
front: in -- of	*ʔuddām, ʔuṣād*
frozen	*mitallig*
fruit	*fakha* (c.), *fawākih*
fruit seller	*fakahāni, -yya*
fry s/th	*ʔala, yiʔli ḫ, ʔaly*
full	*malyān*
become --	*itmala, yitmili*
furnished	*mafrūš*
furniture	*farš*
fuss	*dawša; hēṣa*
g	
galabiya (garment)	*gallabiyya, galalīb*
garage	*gaṛāž, -āt*
garbage	*zibāla*
garden	*ginēna, ganāyin*
gardener	*ganayni, -yya*
gasoline	*banzīn*
gather (intr.)	*itlamm, yitlamm*
general (adj.)	*ɛāmm*
generation (n.)	*gīl, agyāl*
-- (of energy)	*tawlīd (kahṛaba)*
generosity	*kaṛam*
generous	*karīm, kuṛama*
be -- to s/o	*ʔakram, yikrim w*
more ~ most --	*akṛam*
geography	*guġrafya*
German	*ʔalmāni, ʔalmān*
Germany	*ʔAlmanya*
get in s/th	*rikib, yirkab ḫ, rukūb*
-- off s/th	*nizil, yinzil ḫ ~ min ḫ, nuzūl*
-- up	*ʔām, yiʔūm, ʔiyām*
-- used to s/th	*xad, yāxud ɛala ḫ*
-- well!	*salamtak!*
gift	*hidiyya, hadāya*
girl	*bint, banāt*
give s/o s/th	*idda, yiddi w ḫ*
-- back s/th	*raggaɛ, yiraggaɛ ḫ*
Giza	*igGīza*
glad	*faṛḫān, mabsūṭ*
glass	*kubbāya, -āt*
-- (material)	*ʔizāz*
glasses	*naḍḍāra, -āt*
go to s/th	*ṛāḫ, yirūḫ ḫ, miṛwāḫ*
-- s/o	*ṛāḫ li w*
-- down s/th	*nizil, yinzil ḫ ~ min ḫ, nuzūl*
-- home	*ṛawwaḫ, yiṛawwaḫ*
-- on (doing s/th)	*fiḍil, yifḍal* + verb
-- out	*itfassaḫ, yitfassaḫ fusḫa*
-- out (late)	*sihir, yishar, sahaṛ*
-- outside	*xaṛag, yuxrug, xurūg*
-- up s/th	*ṭiliɛ, yiṭlaɛ ḫ, ṭulūɛ*
goal	*hadaf, ahdāf*
God	*Aḷḷāh*
-- bless you	*Aḷḷāh yibārik fīk*
-- keep you	*Aḷḷāh yixallīk*
-- willing	*in šāʔ Aḷḷāh ~ inšaḷḷa*
what ~ intends	*ma šāʔ Aḷḷāh*
in the Name of	*bi‿smi‿llāh*
-- the Beneficent, the Merciful	*iṛṛaḫmān iṛṛaḫīm*
thanks be to --	*ilḫamdu lillāh*
going (n.)	*miṛwāḫ*
going	*ṛāyiḫ*
-- home	*miṛawwaḫ*
-- on	*gāri*
gold	*dahab*
golden	*dahabi*
good	*kuwayyis, ṭayyib* (people)
-- morning	*ṣabāḫ ilxēr*
	ṣabāḫ innūr
not so --	*miš ʔawi*
goodbye	*maɛa‿ssalāma*
government	*ḫukūma, -āt*
governor	*muḫāfiẓ, -īn*
governorate	*muḫafẓa, -āt*
grab s/o ~ s/th	*misik, yimsik w ~ ḫ, mask*
grandfather	*gidd, gudūd ~ agdād*
gratitude	*šukr*
gray	*ṛumādi, ruṣāṣi*
Greece	*ilYunān*
Greek	*yunāni*
green	*axḍar, xaḍra, xuḍr*
greengrocer	*xuḍari, -yya*

greet s/o	*sallim, yisallim ɛala w*
-- s/o in the morning	*ṣabbaḥ, yiṣabbaḥ ɛala w*
greeting	*salām, -āt*
grill s/th	*šawa, yišwi ḥ, šawy*
grilled	*mašwi*
ground	*ᵓarḍ, ᵓarāḍi*
-- floor	*dōr ᵓarḍi*
group	*gamāɛa, -āt*
	magmūɛa, -āt
grow up	*iṭṛabba, yiṭṛabba*
guard	*ḥāris, ḥuṛṛās*
guest	*ḍēf, ḍiyūf ~ ḍuyūf*
guide	*muršid, -īn*

h

hair	*šaɛr* (c.)
half	*nuṣṣ, inṣāṣ*
hall	*ṣāla, -āt*
hand	*ᵓīd* (f.), *ᵓidēn*
hand s/th to s/o	*nāwil, yināwil w ḥ*
	sallim, yisallim w ḥ
handkerchief	*mandīl, manadīl*
handwriting	*xaṭṭ*
hang up s/th	*ɛallaᵓ, yiɛallaᵓ ḥ*
hanging	*miɛallaᵓ*
happen to s/o	*gaṛa, yigṛa li w ḥ*
	ḥaṣal, yiḥṣal li w ḥ, ḥuṣūl
happier ~ happiest	*asɛad*
happy	*faṛḥān, mabsūṭ, saɛīd, suɛada*
make s/o --	*basaṭ, yibsiṭ w*
hard	*gāmid*
hat	*burnēṭa, baranīṭ*
hazel (color)	*ɛasali*
he	*huwwa*
head	*ṛās* (f.), *rūs*
headache	*ṣudāɛ*
headman (village)	*ɛumda* (m.), *ɛumad*
health	*ṣiḥḥa*
hear s/o ~ s/th	*simiɛ, yismaɛ w ~ ḥ, samɛ ~ samāɛ*
hearing (n.)	*samāɛ*
heart	*ᵓalb, ᵓulūb*
heaven	*sama, -wāt*
heavy	*tiᵓīl, tuᵓāl*
height	*irtifāɛ; ɛuluww*
Heliopolis	*Maṣr igGidīda*
help s/o	*sāɛid, yisāɛid w*
-- s/o doing s/th	*sāɛid, yisāɛid w fi ḥ*
Helwan	*Ḥilwān*
hence	*fa*
here	*hina*
hero	*baṭal, abṭāl*
hide s/th	*xabba, yixabbi ḥ*
	xafa, yixfi ḥ, xafy
-- oneself	*iddāra, yiddāra*
high	*ɛāli, ɛalya, ɛalyīn*
hindrance	*māniɛ, mawāniɛ*
history	*tarīx*
hit s/o ~ s/th	*ḍarab, yiḍrab w ~ ḥ, ḍarb*
be --	*iḍḍarab, yiḍḍirib*
hold out	*istaḥmil, yistaḥmil*
holiday	*ᵓagāza, -āt*
	ɛuṭla
Holland	*Hulanda*
homework	*wāgib, -āt*
honey	*ɛasal*
honeymoon	*šahṛ ilɛasal*
honor (n.)	*šaṛaf*
be --ed	*iššaṛṛaf, yiššaṛṛaf*
hope	*ᵓamal, ᵓamāl*
horn	*kalaks, -āt*
hospital	*mustašfa, -yāt*
hot	*suxn*
become --	*sixin, yisxan, suxuniyya*
it's -- (weather)	*iddinya ḥaṛṛ*
hotel	*funduᵓ, fanādiᵓ*
	hotēl, -āt
	lukanḍa, -āt
hour	*sāɛa, -āt*
house	*bēt, biyūt ~ buyūt*
house agent	*simsāṛ, samasṛa*
how	*izzāy ~ izzayy?*
-- much?	*ᵓaddᵉ ᵓē?*
-- are you?	*izzayyak?*
-- many ...?	*kām ...?*
however	*bass*
human being	*ᵓinsān*
hundred	*miyya, -āt*
hungry	*gaɛān*
be --	*gāɛ, yigūɛ, gūɛ*
hurry (v.)	*istaɛgil, yistaɛgil*
being in a --	*mistaɛgil*
hurt s/o	*wagaɛ, yiwgaɛ w, wagaɛ*
husband	*gōz, igwāz*
	zōg, azwāg

i

I	*ana*
ice	*talg*
idea	*fikṛa, afkāṛ*
if	*in, iza, law*
-- only + pr.	*yarēt* + suffix
ignorance	*gahl*
illiteracy	*ᵓummiyya*
illuminate s/th	*nawwaṛ, yinawwaṛ ḥ*
imagine s/th	*itṣawwar, yitṣawwar ḥ*
immediately	*ḥālan, ɛala ṭūl mubāšáṛatan*
import	*istiṛād*
important	*muhimm; hāmm*
more ~ most --	*ahamm*
impossible	*mustaḥīl*
	miš mumkin
improve s/th	*ḥassin, yiḥassin ḥ*
improvement	*taḥsīn*
in	*fi*
-- order to	*ɛalašān ~ ɛašān*
inauguration	*iftitāḥ*
inch	*būṣa*
incident	*ḥādis, ḥawādis*
income	*daxl*
increase (intr.)	*zād, yizīd, ziyāda*
	kitir, yiktaṛ, kutr
-- s/th	*kattaṛ, yikattaṛ ḥ ~ min ḥ*
	zawwid, yizawwid ḥ ~ min ḥ
indeed	*fiɛlan*
India	*ilHind*
Indian	*hindi, hunūd*
industrial	*ṣināɛi*
industry	*ṣināɛa, -āt*
infant	*mawlūd, mawalīd*
inflammation	*iltihāb, -āt*
information	*maɛlumāt* (pl.)
ink	*ḥibr*
inquire about s/th	*istafhim, yistafhim ɛan ḥ*
inside	*guwwa*
insist on s/th	*ṣammim, yiṣammim ɛala ḥ*
install s/th	*rakkib, yirakkib ḥ*
institute	*maɛhad, maɛāhid*
intelligent	*zaki, azkiya*
intense	*gāmid*
interest	*ihtimām*
have an -- in s/o ~ s/th	*ihtamm, yihtamm bi w ~ ḥ*
international	*dawli*
interview	*ḥadīs, aḥadīs*
iron	*ḥadīd*
irrigation	*rayy*
irritate s/o	*dāyiᵓ, yidāyiᵓ w*
	narfis, yinarfis w, narfasa
get --ed	*itnarfis, yitnarfis*
irritated	*mitnarfis*
Italian	*ᵓiṭāli, -yyīn*
	ṭalyāni, ṭalayna
Italy	*ᵓIṭalya*
ivory	*ɛāg*

j

jacket	*žakitta, -āt*
jam	*miṛabba*
janitor	*bawwāb, -īn*
January	*yanāyir*
job	*šuġl*
	šuġlāna
journey	*safaṛ, riḥla*
go on a -- (to)	*sāfir, yisāfir*
joy	*faṛaḥ, inbisāṭ*
juice	*ɛaṣīr*
July	*yulyu*
June	*yunyu*
just (recently)	*lissa*

k

key	*muftāḥ, mafatīḥ*
kill s/o	*ᵓatal, yiᵓtil w, ᵓatl*
	mawwit, yimawwit w ~ ḥ
be --ed	*itᵓatal, yitᵓitil*
kilogram	*kīlu*
kilometer	*kīlumitr*
kind (n.)	*nōɛ, anwāɛ*
kind (adj.)	*laṭīf, luṭāf*
	ẓarīf, ẓurāf
	ṭayyib
kindness	*luṭf, ẓurf*
kiosk	*kušk, akšāk*
kitchen	*maṭbax, maṭābix*
know s/o ~ s/th	*ɛirif, yiɛraf w ~ ḥ, maɛrifa*
-- how to	*ɛirif, yiɛraf* + imperf.
knowledge	*maɛrifa, maɛārif*
	ɛilm
Koran	*quṛᵓān*

l

lady	*sitt, āt*
	sayyida, -āt
lame	*aɛrag, ɛarga, ɛurg*
landlord	*ṣāḫib bēt*
last (adj.)	*ᵓāxir*
late (adv.)	*mitᵓaxxaṛ*
be --	*itᵓaxxaṛ, yitᵓaxxaṛ*
laugh (v.)	*diḫik, yidḫak, diḫk*
lawyer	*muḫāmi, -yyīn*
lead (metal)	*ruṣāṣ*
learn s/th	*itɛallim, yitɛallim ḫ*
least	*aᵓall*
leather	*gild*
leave (intr.)	*miši, yimši, mašy*
-- s/o ~ s/th	*sāb, yisīb w ~ ḫ*
take one's --	*istaᵓzin, yistaᵓzin w ~ min w*
Lebanese	*lubnāni*
Lebanon	*Lubnān*
lecture	*muḫaḍra, -āt*
left	*šimāl*
left-handed	*ašwal, šōla, šūl*
leg	*rigl* (f.), *riglēn*
lemon	*lamūn* (c.)
lend s/th to s/o	*sallif, yisallif w ḫ*
length	*ṭūl*
lentils	*ɛads* (c.)
less	*aᵓall*
lesson	*dars, durūs*
let s/th	*sāb, yisīb ḫ*
-- s/o do s/th	*xalla, yixalli w* + impf.
--'s go	*yaḷḷa!*
letter	*ḫaṛf, ḫurūf*
	gawāb, -āt
	xiṭāb, -āt
level	*mustawa, -yāt*
liberation	*taḫrīr*
library	*maktaba, -āt*
National --	*Dāṛ ilkutub*
license	*taṣrīḫ, taṣarīḫ*
driving --	*ruxṣa, ruxaṣ*
lie down	*itmaddid, yitmaddid*
life	*ḫayā*
-- span	*ɛumr, aɛmāṛ*
lift up s/th	*ṛafaɛ, yirfaɛ ḫ, ṛafɛ*
light s/th	*wallaɛ, yiwallaɛ ḫ*
light (n.)	*nūr, anwāṛ*
light (weight)	*xafīf, xufāf*
light bulb	*lamḅa, lumaḍ*
lighter (n.)	*wallāɛa, -āt*
lighter ~ lightest	*axaff*
like	*zayy, ka-*
-- that	*kida*
line	*saṭr, suṭūr ~ usṭur*
	xaṭṭ, xuṭūṭ
literature	*ᵓadab, ᵓadāb*
little	*ᵓulayyil* (quantity)
	ṣuġayyaṛ
	ᵓuṣayyaṛ (length)
live (v.)	*ɛāš, yiɛīš, ɛīša*
-- in s/th	*sikin, yuskun fi ḫ, sakan*
lively	*ḫayawi*
living (n.)	*maɛīša*
	ɛīša
living room	*ᵓōḍit ᵓuɛād*
	ᵓōḍit gulūs
loaf of bread	*riġīf (ɛēš)*
lock s/th	*sakk, yisukk ḫ, sakk*
	ᵓafal, yiᵓfil ḫ, ᵓafl
logical	*maɛᵓūl*
long for s/o ~ s/th	*ištāᵓ, yištāᵓ li w ~ ḫ, šōᵓ*
long (adj.)	*ṭawīl, ṭuwāl*
-- ago	*zamān*
longer ~ longest	*aṭwal*
look at s/o	*baṣṣ, yibuṣṣ li w, baṣṣ*
-- for s/o ~ s/th	*dawwaṛ,yidawwaṛ ɛala w ~ ḫ*
loose	*mafkūk*
loosen: be --ed	*itfakk, yitfakk*
love s/o ~ s/th	*ḫabb, yiḫibb w ~ ḫ, ḫubb*
loyalty	*ᵓamāna*
lunch	*ġada* (m.)
lunch (v.)	*itġadda, yitġadda*

m

Maadi	*ilMaɛādi*
Madam!	*yafandim!*
	ya madām!
	ya sitt!
maid	*šaġġāla, -āt*
mail	*barīd; busṭa*
mailbox	*ṣandūᵓ barīd ~ busṭa*
make s/th	*ɛamal, yiɛmil ḫ, ɛamal ~ ɛumūla*
-- up with s/o	*ṣāliḫ, yiṣāliḫ w*
make s/o do s/th	*xalla, yixalli w yiɛmil ḫ*

mama	*ṃāma*
man	*ṛāgil, riggāla*
man in charge	*mas⁾ūl, -īn*
manage without s/o ~ s/th	*istaġna, yistaġna ʕan w ~ ḥ*
manager	*mudīr, -īn*
mango	*manga* (c.)
manner	*ṭarī⁾a, ṭuru⁾*
manners	*zō⁾* (m.sg.)
many	*kitīr, kutāṛ*
how --...?	*kām ...?*
March	*māris*
mark s/th	*ʕallim, yiʕallim ḥ ~ ʕala ḥ*
market	*sū⁾, aswā⁾*
married	*miggawwiz*
marry s/o	*iggawwiz, yiggawwiz w*
master s/o ~ s/th	*⁾idir, yi⁾daṛ ʕala w ~ ḥ*
master's degree	*mažistēr*
matches	*kabrīt* (c.)
matter	*ḥāga, -āt*
it doesn't --	*zayyᵊ baʕdu*
	ma‿ʕlešš
	miš muhimm
May	*māyu*
meal	*wagba, wagabāt*
main -- during *Ramaḍān*	*⁾ifṭāṛ ~ fiṭār*
meaning	*maʕna* (m.), *maʕāni*
measure (n.)	*⁾igṛā⁾, -āt*
measurement	*ma⁾ās, -āt*
meat	*laḥma*
meatballs	*kufta*
medicine (drug)	*dawa, adwiya*
medicine (study)	*ṭibb*
Mediterranean Sea	*ilBaḥr il⁾Abyaḍ ilMutawassiṭ*
meet s/o	*⁾ābil, yi⁾ābil w*
-- (each other)	*it⁾ābil, yit⁾ābil*
meeting	*igtimāʕ, -āt*
	mu⁾abla, -āt
melt	*sāḥ, yisīḥ*
make s/th --	*sayyaḥ, yisayyaḥ ḥ*
mercy	*ṛaḥma*
have -- on s/o	*ṛaḥam, yirḥam w, ṛaḥma*
have --	*ḥaṛām ʕalēk!*
message	*xabaṛ, axbāṛ*
meteorological	*gawwi*
meter	*mitr, amtāṛ ~ imtāṛ*
method	*ṭarī⁾a, ṭuru⁾*
Middle East	*išŠarq il⁾Awsaṭ*
midnight	*nuṣṣ illēl*
milk	*laban, albān*
millieme	*mallīm, malalīm*
millimeter	*milli*
million	*milyōn, malayīn*
minister	*wazīr, wuzaṛa*
ministry	*wizāṛa, -āt*
minus	*nā⁾iṣ; ⁾illa*
minute	*di⁾ī⁾a, da⁾āyi⁾*
mirror	*mirāya, -āt*
missing	*nā⁾iṣ*
be --	*ni⁾iṣ, yin⁾aṣ, na⁾aṣān*
mistake	*ġalṭa, -āt*
	xaṭa⁾, axṭā⁾
misunderstanding	*sū⁾ tafāhum*
mix up s/th	*laxbaṭ, yilaxbaṭ ḥ, laxbaṭa*
mock s/o ~ s/th	*ittarya⁾, yittarya⁾ ʕala w ~ ḥ, tarya⁾a*
mockery	*tarya⁾a*
model	*mudēl, -āt*
modern	*ḥadīs*
more ~ most --	*aḥdas*
Mohandiseen	*ilMuhandisīn*
money	*filūs* (pl.)
month	*šahṛ, šuhūr ~ ušhur*
moon	*⁾amaṛ*
more	*aktaṛ*
moreover	*ʕilāwa ʕala kida*
morning	*ṣubḥ; ṣabāḥ*
mosque	*gāmiʕ, gawāmiʕ*
most	*aktaṛ*
mother	*umm, -ahāt*
motor	*mutūṛ, -āt*
motorcycle	*mutūṛ, -āt*
mountain	*gabal, gibāl*
move (house)	*ʕazzil, yiʕazzil, ʕizāl*
movement	*ḥaṛaka, -āt*
movie	*film, aflām*
	sinima, -hāt
Mr.	*ustāz, ⁾asadza*
much	*kitīr*
-- more	*bi-ktīr*
Mugamma	*ilMugammaʕ*
mulberries	*tūt* (c.)
museum	*matḥaf, matāḥif*
Muslim:	*muslim, -īn*
become --	*⁾aslam, yuslim ~ yislam*
must	*lāzim*

n

name s/o ~ s/th	*samma, yisammi w ~ ḥ*
be --d	*itsamma, yitsamma*
name (n.)	*ism, asmāᵓ ~ asāmi*
narrow	*dayyaᵓ*
national	*qawmi*
nationalization	*taᵓmīm*
nationalize s/th	*ᵓammim, yiᵓammim ḥ*
be --d	*itᵓammim, yitᵓammim*
Native Americans	*hunūd ḥumr* (only pl.)
natural	*ṭabīɛi*
nature	*ṭabīɛa*
nearly	*taᵓrīban*
nearby	*ᵓurayyib*
necessary (adv.)	*ḍarūri; lāzim*
neck	*raᵓaba, riᵓāb*
need s/th	*iḥtāg, yiḥtāg ḥ ~ li ḥ*
needing s/o ~ s/th	*miḥtāg li w ~ ḥ*
negligence	*ᵓihmāl*
neighbor	*gāṛ, girān*
neighbor (f.)	*gāṛa, -āt*
neighborhood	*ḥayy, aḥyāᵓ*
	ḥitta, ḥitat
neither... nor....	*la ... wala ...*
nescafé	*niskafē*
Netherlands	*Hulanda*
never	*ᵓabadan*
never did he ...	*ɛumru ma ...*
nevertheless	*maɛazālik*
new	*gidīd, gudād*
brand --	*gidīd lang*
news	*xabaṛ, axbāṛ*
news broadcast	*našrit ᵓaxbāṛ*
newspaper	*garīda, gaṛāyid*
	gurnāl, garanīl
	ṣaḥīfa, ṣuḥuf
next to	*gamb*
night	*lēl*
-- (n.u)	*lēla, layāli*
at --	*bi‿llēl*
become --	*layyil, yilayyil*
nine	*tisɛa*
ninth	*tāsiɛ*
no	*laᵓ ~ lā ~ laᵓᵓa*
nobody	*wala ḥadd*
	ma-ḥaddiš
noise	*dawša*
nonsense	*ᵓayyᵊ kalām*
noon	*ḍuhr*
north	*šamāl*
northern	*šamāli*
nose	*manaxīr* (f.)
not	*mā- ... -š*
	miš
-- a single ...	*wala ...*
-- at all	*la ᵓabadan*
	ɛafwan (reply to *šukṛan*)
-- even	*wala*
-- so good	*miš ᵓawi*
notebook	*kuṛṛāsa, kararīs*
nothing	*wala ḥāga*
noticeboard	*yafṭa, yufaṭ*
notion	*mafhūm, mafahīm*
novel	*riwāya, -āt*
November	*nufimbir*
now	*dilwaᵓti*
nowhere	*wala ḥitta*
nuisance	*ᵓaṛaf*
	midayᵓa
number s/th	*nammaṛ, yinammaṛ ḥ*
number (n.)	*nimra, nimar*
	raqam, arqām
	ɛadad, aɛdād
nylon	*naylu ~ naylon*

o

occasion	*munasba, -āt*
on the -- of	*bi-munasbit....*
occur	*ḥaṣal, yiḥṣal ḥ li w, ḥuṣūl*
October	*ᵓuktōbar*
odd	*ġarīb*
of course	*ṭabɛan*
offer s/th to s/o	*ᵓaddim, yiᵓaddim ḥ li w*
office	*maktab, makātib*
officer	*ẓābiṭ, ẓubbāṭ*
official (n.)	*masᵓūl, -īn*
official (adj.)	*rasmi*
officially	*rasmi*
okay	*ḥāḍir ; ṭayyib*
old (people)	*kibīr fi‿ssinn*
	ɛagūz, ɛawagīz
old (things)	*ᵓadīm, ᵓudām*
older ~ oldest	*akbaṛ; aᵓdam*
olives	*zatūn* (c.)
on	*ɛala ~ ɛa*
on (top of)	*fōᵓ*

once	*maṛṛa, -āt*
-- again	*kamān maṛṛa tāni*
one	*wāḫid*
onions	*baṣal* (c.), *baṣala*
only	*bass*
open s/th	*fataḫ, yiftaḫ ḫ, fatḫ*
open (pass.)	*infataḫ, yinfitiḫ itfataḫ, yitfitiḫ*
open (part.)	*fātiḫ, maftūḫ*
operation	*ɛamaliyya, -āt*
oppressive: the weather is ---	*iddinya katma*
opinion	*ṛaʾy, ʾaṛāʾ*
opportunity	*furṣa, furaṣ*
opposite	*ʾuddām; ʾuṣād*
or	*ʾaw; walla*
orange (color)	*burtuʾāni*
oranges	*burtuʾān* (c.)
order s/th	*ṭalab, yuṭlub ḫ, ṭalab*
-- s/o to do s/th	*ʾamaṛ, yuʾmur w bi ḫ, ʾamṛ*
out of --	*bāyiẓ, ɛaṭlān, xasṛān, xaṛbān*
ordinary	*ɛādi, -yya, -yyīn*
origin	*ʾaṣl*
originally	*ʾaṣlan*
out of	*min*
outside	*baṛṛa; xārig*
owner	*ṣāḫib, aṣḫāb ~ iṣḫāb*

P

package	*bāku, -wāt ~ bawāki*
pain	*ʾalam, ʾalām*
painting	*lōḫa, -āt*
palace	*ʾaṣr, ʾuṣūr*
palm trees	*naxl* (c.)
paper	*waraʾ* (c.), *ʾawrāʾ*
park s/th	*rakan, yirkin ḫ, rakn*
parking	*mawʾaf, mawāʾif*
parking attendant	*munādi, -yya*
parliament	*maglis iššaɛb*
participate in s/th	*ištarak, yištirik fi ḫ*
party	*ḫafla, ḫafalāt*
Pasha	*Bāša, Bašawāt*
pass by s/o ~ s/th	*ɛadda, yiɛaddi ɛala w ~ ḫ*
passport	*basbōr, -āt ~ -tāt*
passport office	*ʾidaṛt_iggawazāt*

past	*māḍi*
patience	*ṣabr*
patient (n.)	*marīḍ, marḍa*
pavement	*raṣīf, arṣifa*
pay s/th to s/o	*dafaɛ, yidfaɛ ḫ li w, dafɛ*
-- attention to s/th	*xad, yāxud bālu min ḫ*
-- a visit to s/o ~ s/th	*zāṛ, yizūr w ~ ḫ, ziyāṛa*
paying attention	*wāxid bālu*
peace	*salām*
peanuts	*(fūl) sudāni*
peculiar	*ġarīb*
peel	*ʾišr*
pen	*ʾalam, aʾlām ~ iʾlām ~ ʾilíma*
pencil	*ʾalam ruṣāṣ*
pencil box	*maʾlama, maʾālim*
people	*nās* (pl.) *ʾahl, ʾahāli šaɛb, šuɛūb*
perfect	*tamām; mumtāz*
perhaps	*yimkin*
period	*mudda*
permission	*taṣrīḫ, taṣarīḫ; ʾizn*
ask s/o for --	*istaʾzin, yistaʾzin w ~ min w*
permit (n.)	*gawāz, -āt taṣrīḫ, taṣarīḫ*
pharmacist	*ṣaydali, ṣayadla*
pharmacy	*ṣaydaliyya, -āt*
pharmacy (study)	*ṣaydala*
photograph s/o ~ s/th	*ṣawwar, yiṣawwar w ~ ḫ*
physician	*duktūr bāṭíni*
piaster	*ʾirš, ʾurūš*
one --	*ʾiršᵊ sāġ*
ten -- coin	*barīza, barāyiz*
picture	*ṣūra, ṣuwar*
have one's -- taken	*itṣawwar, yitṣawwar*
piece	*ḫitta, ḫitat*
pilgrim	*ḫagg, ḫuggāg*
pilgrimage	*ḫigg*
go on a --	*ḫagg, yiḫigg, ḫigg*
pipe	*masūṛa, mawasīr*
place	*makān, ʾamākin ḫitta, ḫitat*
place s/th	*ḫaṭṭ, yiḫuṭṭ ḫ, ḫaṭṭ*
placed	*maḫṭūṭ*
plant (n.)	*nabāt, -āt*
plant s/th	*zaraɛ, yizraɛ ḫ, zarɛ*
plants	*zarɛ* (c.)

plaster	*gibs*
put s/th in --	*gabbis, yigabbis ḫ*
plastered	*migabbis*
plastic	*bilastik*
play (with s/th)	*liɛib, yilɛab (bi ḫ), liɛb*
pleasant	*laṭīf, luṭāf*
	ẓarīf, ẓurāf
find s/o --	*istalṭaf, yistalṭaf w*
please s/o	*basaṭ, yibsiṭ w*
be --ed with s/th	*inbasaṭ, yinbisiṭ bi ḫ*
please	*min faḍlak*
	law samaḫt
pleasure	*surūr*
with --	*bi-kullᵊ_srūr*
plumber	*sabbāk, -īn*
poison	*simm, sumūm*
be --ed	*itsammim, yitsammim*
police	*bulīs; šurṭa*
-- investigation department	*ilmabāḫis*
police station	*ʾism, aʾsām*
policeman	*ɛaskari, ɛasākir*
poor	*faʾīr, fuʾaṛa*
popular	*šaɛbi*
porch	*veranda, -āt*
possible	*mumkin; gāyiz*
possibly	*gāyiz*
post	*busṭa; barīd*
potatoes	*baṭāṭis* (c. f.)
pound	*ginē, -hāt*
power	*quwwa, -āt*
pray	*ṣalla, yiṣalli, ṣala*
prayer	*ṣala, -wāt*
call to --	*iddan, yiddan*
precizely	*bi_ẓẓabṭ*
prepare s/th	*gahhiz, yigahhiz ḫ*
	ḫaḍḍaṛ, yiḫaḍḍaṛ ḫ
present s/th to s/o	*ʾaddim, yiʾaddim ḫ li w*
present (adj.)	*mawgūd, ḫāḍir*
present (gift)	*hidiyya, hadāya*
presentation	*ɛarḍ, ɛurūḍ*
presently	*ḫālíyyan*
preserve s/o	*xalla, yixalli w*
president	*raʾīs, ruʾasāʾ ~ ruʾasa*
press	*ṣaḫāfa*
pretty	*ḫilw*
	gamīl, gumāl
previously	*zamān*
price	*siɛr, asɛāṛ*
	taman, atmān
private	*xāṣṣ*
privilege	*imtiyāz, -āt*
probably	*ġālíban; muḫtamal*
problem	*muškila, mašākil*
production	*ʾintāg*
products	*muntagāt*
professor	*ʾustāz, ʾasadza*
profit from s/o ~ s/th	*istafād, yistafīd min w ~ ḫ*
profit (n.)	*fayda*
program	*birnāmig, baṛāmig*
project	*mašrūɛ, -āt ~ mašarīɛ*
prophet	*nabi, anbiya*
proverb	*masal, amsāl*
provide s/o with s/th	*zawwid, yizawwid w bi ḫ*
pullover	*bulōfar, -āt*
pupil	*tilmīz, talamza*
purple	*banafsigi*
pursue s/th	*tābiɛ, yitābiɛ ḫ*
push s/o ~ s/th	*zaʾʾ, yizuʾʾ w ~ ḫ, zaʾʾ*
put s/th	*ḫaṭṭ, yiḫuṭṭ ḫ, ḫaṭṭ*
-- s/th in order	*waḍḍab, yiwaḍḍab ḫ*
-- on s/th	*libis, yilbis ḫ, libs*
-- to sleep	*nawwim, yinawwim w*
-- up with s/o ~ s/th	*istaḫmil, yistaḫmil w ~ ḫ*
pyramid	*haṛam, ahṛām*

q

quality (sort)	*nawɛiyya*
	ṣanf, aṣnāf
characteristic --	*ṣifa, -āt*
quarrel with s/o	*itxāniʾ, yitxāniʾ maɛa w, xināʾ*
quarter	*ḫayy, aḫyāʾ*
quarter (1/4)	*rubɛ, irbāɛ*
three --s	*talat t-irbaɛ*
question	*suʾāl, asʾila*
queue	*ṭabūr, ṭawabīr*
quickly	*ʾawām; bi-surɛa*
quiet	*hādi, hadya, hadyīn*
become --	*hidi, yihda, hudūʾ*
quietness	*hudūʾ*
quite (adv.)	*giddan*

r

railways	*issikka‿lḫadīd*
rain (v.)	*maṭṭar, yimaṭṭar*
it's --ing	*iddinya bitmaṭṭar*
rain (n.)	*maṭar, amṭār*
	šita
raise s/th	*ṛafaɛ, yirfaɛ ḫ, ṛafɛ*
-- s/o	*ṛabba, yiṛabbi w*
be --ed	*itṛabba, yitṛabba*
raised	*mitṛabbi*
read s/th	*ʾaṛa, yiʾṛa ḫ,*
	ʾiṛāya
reading (n.)	*ʾiṛāya*
ready	*gāhiz*
reason	*sabab, asbāb*
reasonable	*maɛʾūl*
receipt	*waṣl, wuṣúla*
receive s/th	*istalam, yistilim ḫ*
-- s/o	*istaʾbil,*
	yistaʾbil w
reception	*istiʾbāl*
reception hall	*ṣālit istiʾbāl*
reclaim (baggage)	*taslīm iššunaṭ*
reconcile	*itṣāliḫ, yitṣāliḫ*
recover (sickness)	*xaff, yixiff*
red	*aḫmaṛ, ḫamṛa,*
	ḫumr
reduce s/th	*ʾallil, yiʾallil*
	ḫ ~ min ḫ
reed	*būṣ* (c.)
refrigerator	*tallāga, -āt*
regarding s/o ~ s/th	*bi‿nnisba li w ~ ḫ*
region	*manṭiʾa, manāṭiʾ*
regress: cause s/o or s/th to --	*ʾaxxaṛ, yiʾaxxaṛ*
	w ~ ḫ
regret	*ʾasaf*
relationship	*ɛilāqa, -āt*
relaxed	*mistaṛayyaḫ*
remain (v.)	*fiḍil, yifḍal*
remember s/o ~ s/th	*iftakaṛ, yiftikir*
	w ~ ḫ
remorse	*ʾasaf*
remove s/th	*šāl, yišīl ḫ, šēl*
be --ed	*itšāl, yitšāl*
renew s/th	*gaddid, yigaddid ḫ*
be --ed	*iggaddid,*
	yiggaddid
renewal	*tagdīd*
rent s/th to s/o	*ʾaggaṛ, yiʾaggaṛ*
	ḫ li w
rent (n.)	*ʾigāṛ*
repair s/th	*ṣallaḫ, yiṣallaḫ ḫ*
be --ed	*itṣallaḫ, yitṣallaḫ*
	iṣṣallaḫ, yiṣṣallaḫ
reparation	*taṣlīḫ, -āt*
reply to s/o ~ s/th	*ṛadd, yirudd*
	ɛala w ~ ḫ, ṛadd
reply (n.)	*ṛadd, rudūd*
report s/o ~ s/th	*ballaġ, yiballaġ*
	ɛan w ~ ḫ
republic	*gumhuriyya*
republican	*gumhūri*
reserve s/th	*ḫagaz, yiḫgiz ḫ,*
	ḫagz
reserved	*maḫgūz*
reservoir (water)	*xazzān, -āt*
residence permit	*ʾiqāma*
residing	*muqīm*
resign	*istaʾāl, yistaʾīl*
resist s/o ~ s/th	*ʾāwim, yiʾāwim*
	w ~ ḫ
responsible	*masʾūl*
rest	*ṛāḫa*
-- (remains)	*bāʾi*
rest (v.)	*istarayyaḫ,*
	yistarayyaḫ
restaurant	*maṭɛam, maṭāɛim*
result	*natīga, natāyig*
return (v.)	*rigiɛ, yirgaɛ, rugūɛ*
reveal s/th	*bayyin, yibayyin ḫ*
revolution	*sawṛa, -āt*
rice	*ruzz* (c.)
rich	*ġani, aġniya*
ride s/th	*rikib, yirkab ḫ,*
	rukūb
ridicule s/o	*ittaryaʾ, yittaryaʾ*
	ɛala w, taryaʾa
right (direction)	*yimīn*
right!	*ṣaḫḫ!*
ring (n.)	*xātim, xawātim*
ring (intr.)	*rann, yirinn, rann*
river	*nahṛ, anhāṛ*
road	*sikka, sikak*
	ṭarīʾ, ṭuruʾ
room	*ʾōḍa, ʾuwaḍ*
	ġurfa, ġuṛaf
round (adj.)	*midawwaṛ*
row	*ṣaff, ṣufūf*
rubber	*kawitš*
ruler	*masṭara, masāṭir*
run (v.)	*giri, yigri, gary*
-- over s/th	*dās, yidūs ḫ, dōs*
rural	*rīfi*
rush (n.)	*istiɛgāl, ɛagala*
Russia	*Rusya*
Russian	*rūsi, rūs*

s

safe	*xazna, xizan*
safety	*salāma*
salad	*salaṭa, -āt*
salt	*malḫ*
sandals (a pair)	*ṣandal, ṣanādil*
satisfied	*mabsūṭ*
save s/th	*waffaṛ, yiwaffaṛ ḫ*
-- (money)	*ḫawwiš, yiḫawwiš ḫ*
say s/th to s/o	*ʾāl, yiʾūl ḫ li w*
be said	*itʾāl, yitʾāl*
scent	*rīḫa, ṛawāyiḫ*
school	*madrasa, madāris*
schoolmate	*zimīl, zumala ~ zumalāʾ*
science	*ʕilm, ʕulūm*
scientific	*ʕilmi*
screwdriver	*mifakk, -āt*
script	*xaṭṭ*
sea	*baḫr, buḫūr*
Red --	*ilBaḫr ilʾAḫmaṛ*
search for	*dawwaṛ, yidawwaṛ*
s/o ~ s/th	*ʕala w ~ ḫ*
season	*faṣl, fuṣūl*
	mūsim, mawāsim
second (time unit)	*sanya, sawāni*
second	*tāni*
secondary	*sanawi*
secondary school	*madrasa sanawi*
security	*ʾamn*
see s/o ~ s/th	*šāf, yišūf w ~ ḫ*
seem: it --s to s/o	*mithayyaʾ li w*
select s/th	*naʾʾa, yinaʾʾi ḫ*
self	*nafs*
sell s/th	*bāʕ, yibīʕ ḫ, bēʕ*
be sold	*itbāʕ, yitbāʕ*
send s/th to s/o	*baʕat, yibʕat ḫ li w*
sensible	*ʕāʾil*
sentence	*gumla, gumal*
September	*sibtimbir*
service	*xidma, xadamāt*
can I be of any --?	*ʾayyᵊ xidma?*
set s/th straight	*ʕadal, yiʕdil ḫ*
settle accounts	*itḫāsib, yitḫāsib*
seven	*sabʕa*
seventh	*sābiʕ*
severe	*šidīd, šudād*
	gāmid
shame on you	*ḫaṛām ʕalēk!*
shape	*šakl, aškāl*
she	*hiyya*
shelf	*raff, rufūf*
shine (v.)	*lamaʕ, yilmaʕ, lamaʕān*
ship	*markib (f.), marākib*
	safīna, sufun
shirt	*ʾamīṣ, ʾumṣān*
shocked: be --	*ittāxid, yittāxid*
shoes (a pair)	*gazma, gizam*
one shoe --	*fardit gazma*
shoot at s/o	*ʾaṭlaq, yuṭliq innāṛ ʕala w; ḍarab, yiḍrab w bi‿nnāṛ*
get shot at	*inḍarab, yinḍirib bi‿nnāṛ*
shop	*maḫall, -āt*
shop window	*fitrīna, -āt ~ fatarīn*
short	*ʾuṣayyaṛ*
show (n.)	*ʕarḍ, ʕurūḍ*
show s/th to s/o	*warra, yiwarri w ḫ*
shower	*dušš, idšāš*
shut up (v.)	*sikit, yiskut, sukūt*
sick	*marīḍ, ʕayyān*
sickness	*maraḍ, amrāḍ*
side	*naḫya, nawāḫi*
sidewalk	*raṣīf, arṣífa*
sighted	*baṣīr*
sign s/th	*maḍa, yimḍi ḫ ~ ʕala ḫ*
signature	*ʾimḍa, -āt*
	tawqīʕ, -āt
signboard	*yafṭa, yufaṭ*
silk	*ḫarīr, ḫarāyir*
silken	*ḫarīr*
silver	*faḍḍa*
simple	*basīṭ, busaṭa*
it's a -- matter	*basīṭa!*
Sinai	*Sīna*
since	*min*
sir!	*yafandim!*
sister	*uxt, ixwāt (banāt)*
sit (v.)	*ʾaʕad, yuʾʕud, ʾuʕād*
sitting	*ʾāʕid*
sitting room	*ṣalōn, -āt*
	ʾōḍit gulūs
	ʾōḍit ʾuʕād
situation	*ḫāl, aḫwāl*
	ẓarf, ẓurūf
six	*sitta*
sixth	*sādis*
skin	*gild*
-- (fruit)	*ʾišr*
skirt	*žīb, -āt*

slaughter s/th	*dabaḫ, yidbaḫ ḫ, dabḫ*
sleep (v.)	*nām, yinām, nōm*
sleep (n.)	*nōm*
slow	*baṭīᵓ, buṭāᵓ*
	miᵓaxxaṛ (watch)
-- down!	*ɛala mahlak!*
slowly	*bi‿ṛṛāḫa*
sly	*laᵓīm, luᵓama*
small	*ṣuġayyaṛ*
smaller ~ smallest	*aṣġaṛ*
smart	*šāṭir, šaṭrīn ~ šuṭṭāṛ*
smell s/th	*šamm, yišimm ḫ, šamm*
smoking	*tadxīn*
snow	*talg*
so	*fa; baᵓa*
so and so	*kaza‿w kaza*
soap	*ṣabūn* (c.)
socks: pair of --	*šaṛāb, -āt*
sofa	*kanaba, -āt*
soft	*ṭari, ṭariyya, ṭurāy*
softly	*bi‿ṛṛāḫa*
	bi‿šwēš
soil	*ᵓarḍ, ᵓarāḍi*
sold	*mitbāɛ*
soldier	*ɛaskari, ɛasākir*
solve s/th	*ḫall, yiḫill ḫ, ḫall*
some	*baɛḍ; kām*
	šuwayya
-- water	*šuwayyit ṃayya*
somebody	*ḫadd*
something	*ḫāga, -āt*
	šēᵓ, ašyāᵓ
sometimes	*awᵓāt, saɛāt*
	ᵓaḫyānan
somewhat	*šuwayya*
son	*ibn, abnāᵓ*
sorry	*ᵓāsif!*
	la muᵓaxza!
sorry for s/o	*zaɛlān ɛala w*
sort	*nōɛ, anwāɛ*
	nawɛiyya, -āt
	ṣanf, aṣnāf
soup	*šurba*
source	*maṛgaɛ, maṛāgiɛ*
	maṣdaṛ, maṣādir
south	*ganūb*
southern	*ganūbi*
spare time	*waᵓtᵊ farāġ*
speak to s/o	*kallim, yikallim w*
-- (intr.)	*ikkallim, yikkallim*
stop --ing	*sikit, yuskut, sukūt*

specialization	*taxaṣṣuṣ*
specialist	*axiṣṣāᵓi*
speech	*xiṭāb, -āt*
	xuṭba, xuṭab
speed	*surɛa, -āt*
spend (time)	*ᵓaḍa, yiᵓḍi ḫ*
	ᵓaḍḍa, yiᵓaḍḍi ḫ
	maḍḍa, yimaḍḍi ḫ
-- the night	*bāt, yibāt, biyāt*
spoil: be --ed	*xisir, yixsaṛ*
sponge	*isfing* (c.)
spring	*rabīɛ*
square	*midān, mayadīn*
stable (adj.)	*mustaqirr*
	sābit
stairs	*sillim, salālim*
stamp	*ṭābiɛ, ṭawābiɛ barīd*
stand up	*ᵓām, yiᵓūm, ᵓiyām; wiᵓif, yuᵓaf, wuᵓūf*
start (n.)	*bidāya, -āt*
start (intr.)	*ibtada, yibtidi*
make a -- to s/th	*ibtada, yibtidi ḫ ~fi ḫ*
state	*dawla, duwal*
station	*maḫaṭṭa, -āt*
statue	*timsāl, tamasīl*
stay (v.)	*ᵓaɛad, yuᵓɛud, ᵓuɛād; fiḍil, yifḍal*
-- up late	*sihir, yishar, sahaṛ*
staying	*muqīm*
steady	*mustaqirr*
steal s/th	*saraᵓ, yisraᵓ ḫ, sirᵓa*
steel	*ṣulb*
step	*xaṭwa, xaṭawāt*
still	*lissa, ma-zāl*
stockings (a pair)	*šaṛāb, -āt*
stomach	*baṭn* (f.), *buṭūn*
stop doing s/th	*baṭṭal, yibaṭṭal ḫ*
	balāš ...
-- here!	*ɛandak hina!*
come to a --	*wiᵓif, yuᵓaf, wuᵓūf*
storm	*zawbaɛa, zawābiɛ*
story	*ḫikāya, -āt*
	qiṣṣa, qiṣaṣ
straight on	*duġri; ɛala ṭūl*
strange	*ġarīb, aġṛāb*
street	*šāriɛ, šawāriɛ*
street corner	*naṣya, nawāṣi*
on the --	*ɛa‿naṣya*
strip s/th	*ᵓalaɛ, yiᵓlaɛ ḫ, ᵓalɛ*

stroll (v.)	*itfassaḫ, yitfassaḫ, fusḫa*
	itmašša, yitmašša
student (f.)	*ṭālíba, -āt*
student (m.)	*ṭālib, ṭullāb ~ ṭalaba*
study	*diṛāsa, -āt*
study s/th	*zākir, yizākir ḫ*
	daras, yidris ḫ, dars
studybook	*maṛgaɛ, maṛāgiɛ*
stuff s/th with s/th	*ḫaša, yiḫši ḫ ḫ*
stuffed	*maḫši*
subject	*mawḍūɛ, -āt ~ mawaḍīɛ*
-- (study)	*mādda, mawādd*
substance	*mādda, mawādd*
Sudan	*isSudān*
Sudanese	*sudāni*
Suez Canal	*qanāt isSuwēs*
sufficient	*kifāya* (inv.)
	mikaffi
sufficient: to be -- for s/o	*kaffa, yikaffi w*
sugar	*sukkaṛ* (c.)
suit	*badla, bidal*
suit s/o	*nāsib, yināsib w*
suitable for s/th	*ṣāliḫ li ḫ*
suitcase	*šanṭa, šunaṭ*
suited	*munāsib*
summer	*ṣēf*
summer (adj.)	*ṣēfi*
sun	*šams* (f.)
supply s/o with s/th	*mawwin, yimawwin w bi ḫ*
sure	*mitᵓakkid*
surprize s/o	*fāgiᵓ, yifāgiᵓ w*
be --ed at s/th	*istaġṛab, yistaġṛab min ḫ*
swab s/th	*masaḫ, yimsaḫ ḫ, masḫ*
sweat (n.)	*ɛaraᵓ*
sweat (v.)	*ɛiriᵓ, yiɛraᵓ, ɛaṛaᵓ*
sweater	*bulōfar, -āt*
sweet	*ḫilw*
Swiss	*suwisri*
switch on s/th	*wallaɛ, yiwallaɛ ḫ*
Switzerland	*Suwisra*
system	*niẓām, nuẓum*

t

table	*taṛabēẓa, -āt*
tact	*zōᵓ*
take s/th	*xad, yāxud ḫ*
-- s/th out	*ṭallaɛ, yiṭallaɛ ḫ*
-- s/o s/wh	*waṣṣal, yiwaṣṣal w ḫ*
-- off s/th	*ᵓalaɛ, yiᵓlaɛ ḫ, ᵓalɛ*
talk to s/o	*kallim, yikallim w*
-- (intr.)	*ikkallim, yikkallim*
talk (n.)	*kalām*
tall	*ṭawīl, ṭuwāl*
taller ~ tallest	*aṭwal*
tap	*ḫanafiyya, -āt*
tarbush (hat)	*ṭarbūš, ṭarabīš*
taste s/th	*dāᵓ, yidūᵓ ḫ*
taste (n.)	*ṭaɛm*
tastier ~ tastiest	*alazz*
tasty	*lazīz, luzāz*
tax	*ḍarība, ḍarāyib*
taxi	*taks, -iyāt ~ tukúsa*
-- meter	*ɛaddād, -āt*
tea	*šāy*
teach s/th to s/o	*ɛallim, yiɛallim w ḫ*
teacher	*mudarris, -īn*
tear s/th	*ᵓaṭaɛ, yiᵓṭaɛ ḫ, ᵓaṭɛ*
be torn	*itᵓaṭaɛ, yitᵓiṭiɛ*
tease s/o	*ɛākis, yiɛākis w*
teasing	*miɛaksa*
telephone	*tilifōn, -āt*
telephone call	*mukalma, -āt*
television	*tilivizyōn, -āt*
tell s/o s/th	*ᵓāl, yiᵓūl ḫ li w*
	ḫaka, yiḫki ḫ li w
temperature	*ḫaṛāṛa*
-- (grade)	*daṛagit ilḫaṛāṛa*
temple	*maɛbad, maɛābid*
ten	*ɛašaṛa*
tenth	*ɛāšir*
terrible	*faẓīɛ, fuẓāɛ*
testify	*šahad, yišhad, šahāda*
testimony	*šahāda*
text	*naṣṣ, nuṣūṣ*
than	*min; ɛan*
thank s/o	*šakaṛ, yuškur w, šukr*
thanks	*šukr*
thank you	*mitšakkir*
	mutašakkir
	šukṛan
that	*inn*
-- (dem.)	*da* (m.), *di* (f.)
-- is to say	*yaɛni*
theft	*sirᵓa*

theme	*mawḍūʿ, -āt ~ mawaḍīʿ*
then	*fa; baʿdēn; baʾa*
there	*hināk*
-- is ~ are	*fī(h)*
-- is (he, etc)	*áho, ahé, ahúm*
these	*dōl*
they	*humma*
thick	*tixīn, tuxān*
thickness	*tuxn*
thief	*ḥarāmi, -yya*
	liṣṣ, luṣūṣ
thin	*rufayyaʿ*
thing	*ḥāga, -āt*
	šēʾ, ašyāʾ
think of s/o ~ s/th	*fakkar, yifakkar fi w ~ ḥ*
thinking (n.)	*tafkīr*
third	*tālit*
	tilt (1/3)
thirsty	*ʿaṭšān*
be --	*ʿiṭiš, yiʿṭaš, ʿaṭaš*
thirty	*talatīn*
this (dem.)	*da* (m.), *di* (f.)
those	*dōl*
thought	*bāl; fikr*
thousand	*ʾalf, alāf*
three	*talāta*
throw (away) s/th	*rama, yirmi ḥ, ramy*
be --n away	*itrama, yitrimi*
ticket	*tazkara, tazākir*
tie	*karafatta, -āt*
till	*liġāyit, liḥadd*
time	*waʾt, awʾāt*
at the same --	*bi‿lmarra*
several --s	*kaza marra*
tip (money)	*baʾšīš*
tired	*taʿbān; hamdān*
tires	*kawitš*
title (book)	*ʿinwān, ʿanawīn*
today	*innaharda*
together	*sawa*
tomatoes	*ʾūṭa* (c.f.)
	ṭamāṭim (c.f.)
tomorrow	*bukra*
tooth	*sinna, sinān ~ asnān*
tour	*gawla, -āt*
tourism	*siyāḥa*
tourist	*sāʾiḥ, suwwāḥ*
towel	*fūṭa, fuwaṭ*
tower	*burg, abrāg*
town	*balad* (f.), *bilād*
traffic	*murūr*

train	*ʾaṭr, ʾuṭurāt ~ ʾuṭúra*
train s/o	*darrab, yidarrab w*
-- (intr.)	*iddarrab*
training (n.)	*tadrīb*
	tamrīn, -āt
trample s/th	*dās, yidūs ʿala ḥ*
transfer (n.)	*taḥwīla, -āt*
transfer s/o ~ s/th	*naʾal, yinʾil w ~ ḥ, naʾl*
be --ed	*itnaʾal, yitniʾil*
travel	*sāfir, yisāfir*
traveling	*misāfir*
tray	*ṣaniyya, ṣawāni*
treaty	*ittifāʾ, -āt*
trees	*šagar* (c.), *ašgār*
trousers (a pair)	*banṭalōn, -āt*
true	*ṣaḥīḥ*
truly	*ṣaḥīḥ; ḥaʾīʾi*
truth	*ḥaʾīʾa*
try (to do) s/th	*ḥāwil, yiḥāwil ḥ*
Turk	*turki, tarakwa*
Turkey	*Turkiya*
Turkish	*turki*
turn (intr.)	*dār, yidūr, dawarān*
-- s/th around	*dawwar, yidawwar ḥ*
-- (direction)	*xašš, yixušš ḥ*
	ḥawwid, yiḥawwid ḥ
-- off s/th	*ṭafa, yiṭfi ḥ, ṭafy*
be --ed upside down	*itʾalab, yitʾilib*
twenty	*ʿišrīn*
two	*itnēn*
type	*nawʿiyya, -āt*

u

uglier ~ ugliest	*awḥaš*
ugly	*wiḥiš*
unbearable	*šēʾ lā yuṭāq*
unbelievable	*miš maʿʾūl*
uncle	*xāl, xilān* (mater.)
	ʿamm, aʿmām ~ ʿimām (paternal)
under	*taḥt*
undershirt	*fanilla, -āt*
understand s/th	*fihim, yifham ḥ, fahm*
understood	*mafhūm*
unfortunately	*li‿lʾasaf*
university	*gamʿa, gāmiʿāt*

untie s/th	*fakk, yifukk ḫ, fakk*
until	*liġāyit; liḫadd*
upbringing	*tarbiya ~ tarbiyya*
uproar	*hēṣa*
be in an --	*wiᵓif, yuᵓaf ɛala rigl*
USA	*ᵓAmrīka* *ilWilayāt ilMuttáḫida*
usage	*istiɛmāl; istixdām*
use s/th	*istaɛmil, yistaɛmil ḫ*
be --ed to s/o ~ s/th	*mitɛawwid ɛala w ~ ḫ*
use (n.)	*istiɛmāl, istixdām* *fayda, fawāyid*
useful	*mufīd*
be --	*nafaɛ ~nifiɛ, yinfaɛ, nafɛ*

v

valley	*wādi, widyān*
vegetables	*xuḍār* (c.), *xuḍrawāt*
veranda	*veranda, -āt*
very	*ᵓawi, giddan, xāliṣ*
village	*qarya, quṛa* *balad* (f.), *bilād*
visa	*vīza, -āt*
visit	*ziyāṛa, -āt*
visit s/o ~ s/th	*zāṛ, yizūr w ~ ḫ, ziyāṛa*
vocative particle	*ya*

w

wages	*ᵓugṛa*
wait for s/o ~ s/th	*istanna, yistanna w ~ ḫ* *intaẓar, yintiẓir w ~ ḫ*
waiter	*sufṛagi, -yya*
waiting	*mistanni; muntaẓir*
waiting (n.)	*intiẓār*
wake up	*ṣiḫi, yiṣḫa, ṣaḫayān*
walk (v.)	*miši, yimši, mašy*
wall	*ḫēṭa, ḫiṭān*
want s/o ~ s/th	*ɛāz, yiɛūz w ~ ḫ*
wanting	*ɛāwiz ~ ɛāyiz*
war	*ḫaṛb* (f.), *ḫurūb*
warm	*dāfi; suxn; ḫaṛṛ* (weather)
warmth	*ḫaṛṛ*
wash s/th	*ġasal, yiġsil ḫ, ġasīl*
be --ed	*itġasal, yitġisil*
washer: leather --	*gilda, -āt*
washing (n.)	*ġasīl*
watch s/o ~ s/th	*itfaṛṛag, yitfaṛṛag ɛala w ~ ḫ*
watch (n.)	*sāɛa, -āt*
water	*ṃayya*
mineral --	*ṃayya maɛdaniyya*
watermelons	*baṭṭīx* (c.)
wave to s/o	*šāwir, yišāwir li w*
way	*ṭarīᵓa, ṭuruᵓ*
in that --	*kida*
we	*iḫna*
wear s/th	*libis, yilbis ḫ, libs*
weather	*gaww*
the -- is oppressive	*iddinya katma*
wedding	*faṛaḫ, afṛāḫ*
week	*ᵓusbūɛ, ᵓasabīɛ*
weigh s/th	*wazan, yiwzin ḫ, wazn*
weight (n.)	*wazn*
welcome s/o ~ s/th	*ṛaḫḫab, yiṛaḫḫab bi w ~ ḫ*
welcome	*ᵓahlan wa sahlan!*
weld s/th	*laḫam, yilḫim ḫ, liḫām*
west	*ġarb*
western	*ġarbi*
wet	*mablūl*
what?	*ᵓē?*
--were you saying?	*afandim?*
wheel	*ɛagala, -āt*
when?	*imta?*
-- (conj.)	*lamma*
where?	*fēn?*
-- from?	*minēn?*
-- to?	*ɛala fēn?*
which ...?	*ᵓayy ...?*
-- (rel.pr.)	*illi*
-- one(s)?	*anhū, anhī, anhūm?*
whine (v.)	*zann, yizinn, zann*
white	*abyaḍ, bēḍa, bīḍ*
who?	*mīn?*
-- (rel.pr.)	*illi*
whole	*kull*

why?	*lē?*
wide	*wāsiʿ*
wider ~ widest	*awsaʿ*
width	*ʿarḍ*
wife	*zōga, zawgāt*
-- of ...	*miṛāt ...*
wind	*hawa; rīḥ, riyāḥ*
window	*šibbāk ~ šubbāk, šababīk*
wine	*nibīt*
winter	*šita*
wipe off s/th	*masaḥ, yimsaḥ ḥ, masḥ*
wish: as you --	*ʿala kēfak* *zayyᵊ ma‿tḥibb*
with	*bi; maʿa*
without	*min ġēr*
woman	*sitt, -āt*
wonder: I -- ...	*ya-taṛa ...?*
wood	*xašab*
wooden	*xašab*
wool	*ṣūf* (c.), *aṣwāf*
woollen	*ṣūf*
word	*kilma, kalimāt*
work (v.)	*ištaġal, yištaġal*
work (n.)	*šuġl, ašġāl*
world	*dinya ~ dunya* *ʿālam, ʿawālim*
worn: be -- out	*ittākil, yittākil*
worn out	*mittākil*
worse ~ worst	*awḥaš*
worth: be -- s/th	*sāwa, yisāwi ḥ*
wrap s/th	*laff, yiliff ḥ, laff*
be --ped	*itlaff, yitlaff*
write s/th	*katab, yiktib ḥ, kitāba*
be written	*inkatab, yinkitib* *itkatab, yitkitib*
writer	*kātib, kuttāb*
wrong	*ġalaṭ* (inv.)

y

year	*sana, sinīn ~ sanawāt*
yellow	*aṣfaṛ, ṣafra, ṣufr*
yes	*aywa* *naʿam*
yesterday	*imbāriḥ*
you	*inta* (m.), *inti* (f.), *intu* (pl.)
-- (polite)	*ḥaḍritak; siyadtak*
young	*ṣuġayyaṛ (fi‿ssinn)*
-- man	*šābb, šubbān*
-- woman	*šābba, -āt*
younger ~ youngest	*aṣġaṛ*
youth	*šabāb*

z

Zamalek	*izZamālik*
zero	*ṣifr, aṣfāṛ ~ iṣfāṛ*
zoo	*ginent‿ilḥayawanāt*

KEY TO THE EXERCISES

LESSON I

I.	*bintak*	*ibnak*	*giddak*	*¿ammak*	*ummak*	*uxtak*
	bintu	*ibnu*	*giddu*	*¿ammu*	*ummu*	*uxtu*
	bintaha	*ibnaha*	*giddaha*	*¿ammaha*	*ummaha*	*uxtaha*
	bintik	*ibnik*	*giddik*	*¿ammik*	*ummik*	*uxtik*
	binti	*ibni*	*giddi*	*¿ammi*	*ummi*	*uxti*
II.	*bintu*	*ibnu*	*giddu*	*¿ammu*	*ummu*	*uxtu*
	bintaha	*ibnaha*	*giddaha*	*¿ammaha*	*ummaha*	*uxtaha*
	bintak	*ibnak*	*giddak*	*¿ammak*	*ummak*	*uxtak*
	bintik	*ibnik*	*giddik*	*¿ammik*	*ummik*	*uxtik*
	binti	*ibni*	*giddi*	*¿ammi*	*ummi*	*uxti*

III. 1. *lā, da miš giddi.* 2. *aywa, di ᵓummu.* 3. *lā, di miš uxtaha.* 4. *aywa, di binti.* 5. *lā, da miš ibnaha.* 6. *aywa, di ᵓummak ~ ᵓummik.*

IV. 1. *lā, di miš uxti ᵓana, di uxtak inta!* 2. *lā, da miš ibni ᵓana, da‿bnak inta ~ ibnik inti!* 3. *lā, da miš ¿ammi ᵓana, da ¿ammak inta ~ ¿ammik inti!* 4. *lā, di miš ummi ᵓana, di ᵓummak inta ~ ᵓummik inti!* 5. *lā, da miš giddi ᵓana, da giddak inta!* 6. *lā, da miš ismi ᵓana, da‿smak inta ~ ismik inti!*

V. 1. *lā, di bintaha.* 2. *lā, di ᵓummaha.* 3. *lā, da‿bnaha.* 4. *lā, di sittaha.*

VI. 1. *ya‿Mḫammad, ibnak fēn?* 2. *ya Samya, ummik fēn?* 3. *ya Fawzi, giddak fēn?* 4. *ya Maha, ibnik fēn?* 5. *ya ¿Ali, ¿ammak fēn?* 6. *ya Ḫasan, uxtak fēn?* 7. *ya Muna, bintik fēn?* 8. *ya ¿Abdu, sittak fēn?*

VII. 1. *Ḫasan, ¿ammu f‿Iskindiriyya.* 2. *Maḫmūd, ummu fi‿gGīza.* 3. *Aḫmad, ¿ammu fi-Luᵓṣur.* 4. *ana, ¿ammi‿f-ᵓAswān.* 5. *Maha, bintaha fi-Bur Sa¿īd.* 6. *Samya, ibnaha fi‿sSuwēs.* 7. *Mirvat, uxtaha fi‿lFayyūm.* 8. *Aḫmad, bintu fi Sīwa.*

VIII. 1. *Samya muhandisa kamān.* 2. *uxti mudarrisa kamān.* 3. *Samya ṭāliba kamān.* 4. *uxti mawgūda kamān.* 5. *binti ṭāliba kamān.* 6. *ummi mudarrisa kamān*

IX. 1. *huwwa mis mawgūd, wi ᵓuxtu kamān miš mawgūda.* 2. *hiyya miš mudarrisa, wi bintaha kamān miš mudarrisa.* 3. *ana miš muhandisa, wi ᵓibni kamān miš muhandis.* 4. *Samya miš mawgūda, wi ¿ammaha kamān miš mawgūd.* 5. *inti miš ṭālíba, wi Ḫasan kamān miš ṭālib.* 6. *inta miš mudarris, wi hiyya kamān miš mudarrisa.*

LESSON II

I.

gidduku	*ummuku*	*uxtuku*	*ibnuku*	*ɛammuku*	*bintuku*
giddi	*ummi*	*uxti*	*ibni*	*ɛammi*	*binti*
giddu	*ummu*	*uxtu*	*ibnu*	*ɛammu*	*bintu*
giddina	*ummina*	*uxtina*	*ibnina*	*ɛammina*	*bintina*
giddik	*ummik*	*uxtik*	*ibnik*	*ɛammik*	*bintik*
gidduhum	*ummuhum*	*uxtuhum*	*ibnuhum*	*ɛammuhum*	*bintuhum*
giddak	*ummak*	*uxtak*	*ibnak*	*ɛammak*	*bintak*

II. 1. *lā, di miš ummina, lākin ummuhum.* 2. *lā, da miš ibnina, lākin ibnuhum.* 3. *lā, da miš giddina, lākin gidduhum.* 4. *lā, di miš uxtina, lākin uxtuhum.* 5. *lā, da miš ismina, lākin ismuhum.* 6. *lā, da miš ɛammina, lākin ɛammuhum.*

III. 1. *di miš uxtina, di bintina.* 2. *di miš ummina, di ˀuxtina.* 3. *da miš ɛammina, da giddina.* 4. *da miš ibnina, da ɛammina.* 5. *di miš bintina, di ˀuxtina.*

IV. 1. *di min inNimsa, yaɛni hiyya nimsawiyya.* 2. *di min Faṛansa, yaɛni hiyya faṛansawiyya.* 3. *da min ˀIṭalya, yaɛni huwwa ˀiṭāli ~ ṭalyāni.* 4. *di min ˀAmrīka, yaɛni hiyya ˀamrikiyya ~ ˀamrikaniyya.* 5. *da min Ingiltira, yaɛni huwwa‿ngilīzi.* 6. *di min ˀAlmanya, yaɛni hiyya ˀalmaniyya.* 7. *da min Maṣr, yaɛni huwwa maṣri.* 8. *di min ilYunān, yaɛni hiyya yunaniyya.*

V. 1. *dōl min Maṣr, yaɛni humma maṣriyyīn.* 2. *dōl min Lubnān, yaɛni humma lubnaniyyīn.* 3. *dōl min ˀIṭalya, yaɛni humma ˀiṭaliyyīn ~ ṭalayna.* 4. *dōl min Surya, yaɛni humma suriyyīn.* 5. *dōl min Faṛansa, yaɛni humma faṛansawiyyīn.* 6. *dōl min ˀAmrīka, yaɛni humma ˀamrikiyyīn ~ ˀamrikān.* 7. *dōl min Ingiltira, yaɛni humma ˀingilīz.* 8. *dōl min ˀAlmanya, yaɛni humma ˀalmān.* 9. *dōl min Rusya, yaɛni humma rūs.*

VI. 1. *huwwa yunāni, wi hiyya kamān yunaniyya.* 2. *ana ˀalmāni, w‿inti kamān ˀalmaniyya.* 3. *ana ˀamrīki, w‿inti kamān ˀamrikiyya ~ ˀamrikaniyya.* 4. *di nimsawiyya, wi da kamān nimsāwi.* 5. *di suriyya, wi da kamān sūri.* 6. *hiyya faṛansawiyya, wi huwwa kamān faṛansāwi.* 7. *huwwa mudarris, wi hiyya kamān mudarrisa.* 8. *inti ṭalíba, w‿inta kamān ṭālib.* 9. *ana muhandis, w‿inti kamān muhandisa.*

VII. 1. *ana min Hulanda‿w bakkallim hulandi.* 2. *ana min Faṛansa‿w bakkallim faṛansāwi.* 3. *ana min ilYunān wi bakkallim yunāni.* 4. *ana min ˀAmrīka‿w bakkallim ˀamrikāni ~ ingilīzi.* 5. *ana min ˀIṭalya‿w bakkallim ṭalyāni ~ ˀiṭāli.* 6. *ana min inNimsa‿w bakkallim nimsāwi ~ ˀalmāni.* 7. *ana min Suwisra‿w bakkallim suwisri ~ ˀiṭāli ~ faṛansāwi ~ ˀalmāni.*

VIII. 1. *iḥna‿ngilīz.* 2. *humma‿kwayyisīn fi‿lɛaṛabi.* 3. *intu maṣriyyīn.* 4. *dōl faṛansawiyyīn.* 5. *humma muhandisīn.* 6. *iḥna ˀamrikān ~ ˀamrikiyyīn.* 7. *intu ṭālibāt?* 8. *humma miš mawgudīn.* 9. *iḥna lubnaniyyīn.* 10. *dōl nimsawiyyīn.*

IX. 1. *Sāmi‿w Samya maṣriyyīn.* 2. *Jane wi Mike kuwayyisīn fi‿lɛaṛabi.* 3. *John wi Kate ˀamrikāniyyīn.* 4. *Mirvat wi Samya miš ˀagānib.* 5. *Sāmi‿w Mark mudarrisīn.* 6. *Samya‿w Janet ṭālibāt.* 7. *Mirvat wi Michael muhandisīn.* 8. *Janet wi Samya miš mawgudīn.* 9. *John wi Jane ˀingilīz.* 10. *Ann wi Kevin usturaliyyīn*

X. 1. *ana lubnāni, miš maṣri.* 2. *uxti muhandisa, miš mudarrisa.* 3. *humma ʾalmān, miš suwisriyyīn.* 4. *da rūsi, miš hulandi.* 5. *ummina lubnaniyya, miš maṣriyya.* 6. *dōl ṭalaba, miš mudarrisīn.* 7. *John wi Jane ʾamrikān ~ ʾamrikiyyīn, miš faṛansawiyyīn.* 8. *Mary wi Jane mudarrisāt, miš muhandisāt.*

LESSON III

I.

waṛāk	*axūk*	*bintak*	*ḅaḅāk*	*abūk*
waṛā	*axū*	*bintu*	*ḅaḅā*	*abū*
waṛāki	*axūki*	*bintik*	*ḅabāki*	*abūki*
waṛāna	*axūna*	*bintina*	*ḅaḅāna*	*abūna*
waṛāya	*axūya*	*binti*	*ḅaḅāya*	*abūya*
waṛāhum	*axūhum*	*bintuhum*	*ḅaḅāhum*	*abūhum*
waṛāku	*axūku*	*bintuku*	*ḅaḅāku*	*abūku*

II. 1. *da ʾabūha, miš axūha.* 2. *da ʾaxūya, miš ɛammi.* 3. *da ʾaxūki, miš ɛammik.* 4. *da ḅāḅāya, miš giddi.* 5. *di bintaha, miš uxtaha.* 6. *da giddu, miš abū(h).* 7. *da ɛammaha, miš abūha.* 8. *ḅāḅāki fēn, ya Samya?*

III. 1. *ahó.* 2. *ahó.* 3. *ahé.* 4. *ahé.* 5. *ahó.* 6. *ahé.* 7. *ahúm.* 8. *ahúm.* 9. *ahé.* 10. *ahúm.*

IV.

baɛdᵊ bukṛa	*ana gayyᵊ ḥālan*	*bi-kullᵊ‿srūr*	*intu saknīn fēn?*
bintᵊ waḥda	*bēt wāḥid*	*gambᵊ Maḥmūd*	*ma-ɛandakšᵊ‿flūs*
kitāb wāḥid	*ɛammᵊ ɛali*	*ma ɛandakšᵊ waʾt*	*zayyᵊ baɛdu*

V. 1. *ana taɛbān šuwayya.* 2. *da miš kitīr ʾawi.* 3. *da ʾaḥsan bi-ktīr.* 4. *dōl kuwayyisīn ʾawi.* 5. *inti taɛbāna‿šwayya.* 6. *di sahla ʾawi.* 7. *hiyya ɛayyāna giddan.* 8. *humma lissa fi‿ssinima.*

VI. 1. *ilbintᵊ di‿smaha ʾē?* 2. *iṭṭiflᵊ da‿smu ʾē?* 3. *iṭṭālib da‿smu ʾē?* 4. *innās dōl ismuhum ʾē?* 5. *izẓābiṭ da‿smu ʾē?* 6. *issittᵊ di ‿smaha ʾē?* 7. *iṭṭāliba di ‿smaha ʾē?* 8. *iṭṭalaba dōl ismuhum ʾē?*

VII. 1. *ilwaraʾ da makānu fēn?* 2. *ilfūṭa di makanha fēn?* 3. *iṭṭaʾṭūʾa di makanha fēn?* 4. *ilkutub di makanha fēn?* 5. *illamḅa di makanha fēn?* 6. *iliʾlām di makanha fēn?* 7. *ilḥagāt di makanha fēn?* 8. *issiggāda di makanha fēn?* 9. *ilkursi da makānu fēn?*

VIII. 1. *šīl iṣṣūra di, ya Ḥasan!* 2. *šīl ilfūṭa di, ya Ḥasan!* 3. *šīl ikkitāb da, ya Ḥasan!* 4. *šīl iššanṭa di, ya Ḥasan!* 5. *šīl ikkuṛṛāsa di, ya Ḥasan!* 6. *šīl ittaṛabēẓa di, ya Ḥasan!* 7. *šīl iṣṣabūn da, ya Ḥasan!* 8. *šīl izzēt da, ya Ḥasan!*

IX. 1. *da ʾaḥsan bi-ktīr.* 2. *ilmustašfa di‿kwayyisa giddan.* 3. *ana waxda bardᵊ‿ šwayya.* 4. *iṭṭālibāt gayyīn ḥālan.* 5. *ya-taṛa, hiyya lissa fi‿lmustašfa?* 6. *ilmukalma di ɛašānak!* 7. *da ~ huwwa ʾaḥsan šuwayya.* 8. *da‿ktīr ʾawi ~ giddan ~ xāliṣ.* 9. *ilbintᵊ di‿smaha ʾē?* 10. *ɛAli fi‿ssinima.* 11. *huwwa gayyᵊ ḥālan ~ dilwaʾti.* 12. *bukṛa tibʾi ~ tibʾa ʾaḥsan!* 13. *Sāmi gayyᵊ baɛdᵊ bukṛa.* 14. *faṣlukum fēn?* 15. *giddukum, ismu ʾē?*

LESSON IV

I.

mudárris	*mudarrísa*	*ṭálaba*	*ibnáha*	*báladu*
baládha	*báladik*	*siggāda*	*máṛṛa*	*maṛṛitēn*
šawāriɛ	*šawariɛna*	*waraʾāt*	*wáraʾ*	*ísmi*
ismáha	*šāriɛ*	*šaríɛna*	*máṭɛam*	*šibbāk*
daʾāyiʾ	*ɛarfīn*	*ɛārif*	*muhándis*	*muhandisīn*
muhandísa	*ɛaṛabiyyíti*	*šánṭa*	*šanṭíti*	*xidmítak*

II. 1. *aywa, dōl nimsawiyyīn.* 2. *aywa, humma lubnaniyyīn.* 3. *aywa, iḥna ʾamrikān ~ ʾamrikiyyīn.* 4. *aywa, iḥna suriyyīn.* 5. *aywa, dōl sudaniyyīn.* 6. *aywa, dōl yunaniyyīn.* 7. *aywa, dōl faṛansawiyyīn.* 8. *aywa, humma ʾiṭaliyyīn ~ ṭalayna.* 9. *aywa, iḥna maġarba.* 10. *aywa, dōl rūs.*

III. 1. *izzayyak ya Sāmi?* 2. *izzayyuku ya banāt?* 3. *izzayyik ya Maha?* 4. *izzayyuku ya ʾawlād?* 5. *izzayyak ya ḅāḅa?* 6. *izzayyik ya Samya?* 7. *izzayyak ya Sayyid?* 8. *izzayyak ya Ḥasan?* 9. *izzayyik ya Mirvat?* 10. *izzayyuku ya ʾaṭfāl?*

IV. 1. *bintik fēn ya Maha?* 2. *ɛammik fēn ya bint?* 3. *giddak fēn ya Sāmi?* 4. *ummuku fēn ya banāt?* 5. *ḅaḅāku fēn ya ʾawlād?* 6. *abūki fēn ya Salwa?* 7. *uxtak fēn ya Maḥmūd?* 8. *awlādik fēn ya Mirvat?*

V. 1. *ʾulli, uxtak Samya, izzayyaha?* 2. *ʾulli, ḅāḅa‿w ṃāṃa, izzayyuhum?* 3. *ʾulli, bintak Mirvat, izzayyaha?* 4. *ʾulli, ɛAyda, izzayyaha?* 5. *ʾulli, ibnak, izzayyu?* 6. *ʾulli, awlādak, izzayyuhum?* 7. *ʾulli, ɛammak Aḥmad, izzayyu?* 8. *ʾulli, iṭṭalaba, izzayyuhum?*

VI. 1. *huwwa miš wāxid bard, lākin hiyya waxda bard.* 2. *huwwa miš mitṛabbi‿f-Ṭanṭa, lākin hiyya mitṛabiyya‿f-Ṭanṭa.* 3. *Ḥasan miš šāṭir, lākin Samīḥa šaṭra.* 4. *ana miš ɛārif, lākin hiyya ɛarfa.* 5. *huwwa miš ɛāwiz, lākin hiyya ɛawza.* 6. *iggāmiɛ miš ʾuṛayyib, lākin ikkinīsa‿ʾṛayyiba.* 7. *iṭṭālib miš wiḥiš, lākin ilmadrasa wiḥša.* 8. *abūya miš misāfir, lākin ummi‿msafra.* 9. *Aḥmad miš mawgūd, lākin uxtu mawgūda.* 10. *innādi miš biɛīd, lākin ilmaḥaṭṭa‿bɛīda.*

VII. 1. *Aḥmad miš misāfir, lākin Sāmi‿w Maha‿msafrīn.* 2. *huwwa miš laṭīf lākin Sāmi‿w Maha luṭāf.* 3. *ana miš šāṭir, lākin Sāmi‿w Maha šaṭrīn.* 4. *huwwa miš ṭawīl, lākin Sāmi‿w Maha ṭuwāl.* 5. *inta miš ġani, lākin Sāmi‿w Maha ġunāy ~ ʾaġniya.* 6. *inti miš kibīra, lākin Sāmi‿w Maha‿kbāṛ.* 7. *inta miš ɛārif, lākin Sāmi‿w Maha ɛarfīn.* 8. *huwwa miš ɛāwiz, lākin humma ɛawzīn.* 9. *inti miš faʾīra, lākin humma fuʾaṛa.* 10. *iṭṭālib da miš gidīd, lākin intu ṭalaba‿gdād.*

VIII. 1. *innādi ʾuṣād ilmaṭɛam.* 2. *iššanṭa taḥt ikkursi.* 3. *ikkitāb ɛala‿ttaṛabēza.* 4. *ilʾalam fi‿ššanṭa.* 5. *ilbint^e ɛand ummaha.* 6. *iggāmiɛ gamb ilmustašfa. ilʾawwal.* 7. *iššaʾʾa ɛala‿nnaṣya.* 8. *iddōr ittāni fōʾ iddōr*

IX.

gawāmiɛ, gāmiɛ	*lumaḍ, lamḅa*	*kararīs, kuṛṛāsa*	*maḥaṭṭāt, maḥaṭṭa*
kubāṛ, kibīr	*alwān, lōn*	*madāris, madrasa*	*gudād, gidīd*
kutub, kitāb	*maṭāɛim, maṭɛam*	*ṣuwar, ṣūra*	*gumāl, gamīl*
banāt, bint	*šuṭṭār, šāṭir*	*biyūt, bēt*	*šawāriɛ, šāriɛ*
bilād, balad	*nawāṣi, naṣya*	*aṭfāl, ṭifl*	*iʾlām, ʾalam*
šunaṭ, šanṭa	*fuʾaṛa, faʾīr*	*abwāb, bāb*	
gudūd, gidd	*kanāyis, kinīsa*	*asmāʾ, ism*	

X. 1. *ilmuhandisīn miš mawgudīn.* 2. *ilmustašfayāt kuwayyisa.* 3. *ilṭṭalaba luṭāf giddan.* 4. *iggawāmiɛ biɛīda ɛan hina.* 5. *ilmaṭāɛim fatḫa.* 6. *ilbanāt gumāl.* 7. *ilbanāt dōl mawludīn fi‿gGīza.* 8. *ilʾaṭfāl gaɛanīn.* 9. *ilbiyūt kibīra.* 10. *ittaṛabeẓāt ṣuġayyara.*

XI. 1. *iḫna gaɛanīn ʾawi.* 2. *dōl miš kitīr ʾawi.* 3. *humma yimkin fi‿nnādi.* 4. *ilmadrasa‿ʾṭayyiba min hina.* 5. *ilbalad di‿bɛīda xāliṣ.* 6. *humma mawludīn wi mitṛabbiyyīn hina.* 7. *iggāmiɛ waṛa‿lmadrasa ɛala ṭūl* ~ *ilmadrasa waṛa‿ggāmiɛ ɛala ṭūl.* 8. *iṣṣuwar di miš wiḫša.* 9. *ilmaṭɛam da ġāli ʾawi.* 10. *Ṭanṭa balad rīfi gamīla.* 11. *law samaḫti, ilmaḫaṭṭa fēn?* 12. *iššāriɛ da‿smu ʾē?*

XII. 1. *ilbanāt ḫilwīn.* 2. *iṭṭālibāt fi‿nnādi.* 3. *ilfiṭār miš gāhiz.* 4. *inta mawlūd* ~ *inti mawlūda fēn bi‿ẓẓabṭ?* 5. *ilmaṭɛam ɛa‿nnaṣya.* 6. *binti‿w bintak miš mawgudīn innahaṛda.* 7. *ilmaṭɛam da ʾaḫsan šuwayya.* 8. *ana ʾaṣlan min Iskindiriyya.* 9. *ilmukalma di miš ɛašānak* ~ *ɛašānik.* 10. *iggawāmiɛ di miš biɛīda ɛan innādi.* 11. *ya-taṛa‿lmadāris biɛīda ɛan hina?* 12. *ilmaṭāɛim di miš baṭṭāla.* 13. *huww‿ Aḫmad* ~ *ya-taṛ‿Aḫmad lissa fi‿lmustašfa?* 14. *iḫna ɛawzīn ilmafatīḫ di!* 15. *dilwaʾti issāɛa talāta* ~ *issāɛa talāta dilwaʾti.* 16. *issagagīd di ġalya ʾawi.* 17. *Rašīd balad rīfi gamīla.* 18. *Ḫasan wi Samya awlād* ~ *aṭfāl kuwayyisīn.* 19. *ya-taṛa bētak* ~ *bētik* ~ *betkum fēn?* 20. *Salma, ḅaḅāha* ~ *abūha miš mudarris.*

LESSON V

I. 1. *ɛandi bintᵊ waḫda bass.* 2. *ɛandaha kalbᵊ wāḫid bass.* 3. *ɛandu šaʾʾa waḫda bass.* 4. *maɛāya ʾalam wāḫid bass.* 5. *maɛāya kuṛṛāsa waḫda bass.* 6. *ɛandina‿ktāb wāḫid bass.* 7. *ɛandina villa waḫda bass.* 8. *maɛāha ṣūra waḫda bass.*

II. 1. *lā, ma-ɛandīš banāt.* 2. *lā, ma-ɛanduhumš ixwāt.* 3. *lā, ma-ɛandūš ɛimām.* 4. *lā, ma-ɛanduhumšᵊ kutub.* 5. *lā, ma-ɛandināš abb.* 6. *lā, ma-ɛandīš ʾilíma.* 7. *lā, ma-ɛandīš ɛaṛabiyya.* 8. *lā, ma-ɛandīš filūs.*

III. 1. *ɛandi walad wāḫid bass.* 2. *ɛandina ɛaṛabiyya waḫda bass.* 3. *ɛandaha šaʾʾa waḫda bass.* 4. *līna uxt waḫda bass.* 5. *ɛandi wallāɛa waḫda bass.* 6. *ɛandu bintᵊ waḫda bass.* 7. *liyya ʾaxxᵊ wāḫid bass.* 8. *ilbēt lī(h) bāb wāḫid bass.* 9. *maɛāya ʾalam wāḫid bass.* 10. *maɛāna šanṭa waḫda bass.* 11. *ɛandina bēt wāḫid bass.*

IV. 1. *maɛāk wallāɛa?* 2. *maɛāki‿flūs?* 3. *maɛāhum ɛaṛabiyya?* 4. *maɛāku sagāyir?* 5. *maɛāna fakka?* 6. *maɛā kām ginē(h)?* 7. *maɛāha šanṭa?*

V. 1. *laʾ, ma-ɛandināš.* 2. *laʾ, miš ɛandaha.* 3. *laʾ, ma-lhāš.* 4. *laʾ, ma-lnāš.* 5. *laʾ, ma-ɛanduhumš.* 6. *laʾ, miš maɛāya.* 7. *laʾ, ma-ɛandīš.*

VI. 1. *ɛandaha ɛaṛabiyya, lākin ilɛaṛabiyya miš maɛāha.* 2. *ɛandi wallāɛa, lākin ilwallāɛa miš maɛāya.* 3. *ɛandina‿flūs, lākin ilfilūs miš maɛāna.* 4. *ɛanduhum sagāyir, lākin issagāyir miš maɛāhum.* 5. *ɛandu kabrīt, lākin ikkabrīt miš maɛā.*

VII. 1. *ma-mɛayīš kabrīt, yimkin Samya‿mɛāha.* 2. *ma-mɛayīš kabrīt, yimkin iṭṭalaba‿mɛāhum.* 3. *ma-mɛayīš kabrīt, yimkin inta‿mɛāk.* 4. *ma-mɛayīš kabrīt, yimkin Maḫmūd maɛā(h).* 5. *ma-mɛayīš kabrīt, yimkin inti‿mɛāki.*

6. *ma-mɛayīš kabrīt, yimkin intu‿mɛāku.* 7. *ma-mɛahumš^{ə} kabrīt, yimkin iḥna‿mɛāna.* 8. *ma-mɛahūš kabrīt, yimkin ana‿mɛāya.*

VIII. 1. *ilmukalma di lu(h) huwwa.* 2. *ilmukalma di liyya‿na.* 3. *ilmukalma di līna‿ḥna.* 4. *ilmukalma di līku‿ntu.* 5. *ilmukalma di līha hiyya.* 6. *ilmukalma di līki‿nti.* 7. *ilmukalma di līhum humma.*

IX. 1. *itnēn w‿aṛbaɛa yibʔu sitta.* 2. *iṭnāšar nāʔiṣ tisɛa yisāwi talāta.* 3. *tamanya nāʔiṣ wāḥid yisāwi sabɛa.* 4. *xamsa‿w sitta yibʔu‿ḥdāšaṛ.* 5. *ɛašaṛa w‿itnēn yibʔu ‿tnāšaṛ* 6. *ḥidāšar nāʔiṣ aṛbaɛa yibʔu sabɛa.*

X. 1. *aṛbaɛa ʔahwa, min faḍlak!* 2. *xamsa šāy, min faḍlak!* 3. *wāḥid ʔahwa, min faḍlak!* 4. *itnēn kōka, min faḍlak!* 5. *sabɛa ʔahwa turki, min faḍlak!* 6. *ɛašaṛa šāy, min faḍlak!* 7. *sitta buṛtuʔān, min faḍlak!* 8. *aṛbaɛa lamūn, min faḍlak!* 9. *tisɛa bibsi, min faḍlak!* 10. *talāta niskafē, min faḍlak!* 11. *wāḥid bīra, min faḍlak!* 12. *itnāšaṛ ʔahwa, min faḍlak!*

XI. 1. *xamsa nāʔiṣ talāta yibʔu‿tnēn, yaɛni liyya ɛandak itnēn ginēh.* 2. *sabɛa nāʔiṣ aṛbaɛa yibʔu talāta, yaɛni liyya ɛandak talāta‿gnēh.* 3. *tisɛa nāʔiṣ tamanya yibʔa wāḥid, yaɛni liyya ɛandak ginēh.* 4. *talāta nāʔiṣ wāḥid yibʔu‿tnēn, yaɛni liyya ɛandak itnēn ginēh.* 5. *ɛašaṛa nāʔiṣ xamsa yibʔu xamsa, yaɛni liyya ɛandak xamsa‿gnēh.*

XII. 1. *ma-kanš^{ə} mawgūd imbāriḥ.* 2. *Ḥasan kān ɛandu maɛād imbāriḥ.* 3. *ma-kanitš^{ə} fi‿lmadrasa‿mbāriḥ.* 4. *kunt^{ə} baštaġal fi‿lmaṣnaɛ zamān.* 5. *Samya kānit miggawwiza zamān.* 6. *kunna fi‿lmustašfa‿mbāriḥ.* 7. *kunt^{ə} waxda bard imbāriḥ.* 8. *ma-kanūš lissa ɛarfīn imbāriḥ.* 9. *kunt^{ə} fi‿nnādi‿mbāriḥ.* 10. *iṭṭalaba ma-kanūš mawgudīn imbāriḥ.*

XIII. 1. *lā, ma-kanš^{ə} mudarrisi.* 2. *lā, ma-kanš^{ə} ɛandaha waʔt.* 3. *lā, ma-kanūš maɛāna.* 4. *lā, ma-kanš^{ə} ġāli.* 5. *lā, ma-kuntiš fi-ʔAlmanya.* 6. *lā, ma-kunnāš waxdīn bard.* 7. *lā, ma-kunnāš taɛbanīn.* 8. *lā, ma-kunnāš ~ ma-kuntūš ɛarfīn.* 9. *lā, ma-kanitš^{ə} miggawwiza.* 10. *lā, ma-kunnāš fi‿lbēt.*

XIV.

ṣurtak	*ʔoḍtak*	*xidmitak*	*wallaɛtak*	*šanṭitak*
ṣurtu	*ʔoḍtu*	*xidmitu*	*wallaɛtu*	*šanṭitu*
ṣuritna	*ʔoḍitna*	*xidmitna*	*wallaɛitna*	*šanṭitna*
ṣurithum	*ʔoḍithum*	*xidmithum*	*wallaɛithum*	*šanṭithum*
ṣurtik	*ʔoḍtik*	*xidmitik*	*wallaɛtik*	*šanṭitik*
ṣurti	*ʔoḍti*	*xidmiti*	*wallaɛti*	*šanṭiti*
ṣuritha	*ʔoḍitha*	*xidmitha*	*wallaɛitha*	*šanṭitha*

XV. 1. *dōl banāt Salwa.* 2. *da bēt Salwa.* 3. *di šanṭit Salwa.* 4. *di wallāɛit Salwa.* 5. *da gidd^{ə} Salwa.* 6. *da ʔabu Salwa.* 7. *di ʔumm^{ə} Salwa.* 8. *di sāɛit Salwa.* 9. *di mudarrisit Salwa.* 10. *da mudarris Salwa.*

XVI. 1. *di sāɛit Samya.* 2. *di‿gnēnit Ḥasan.* 3. *da maṣnaɛhum.* 4. *dōl awlād Ḥasan.* 5. *di šaʔʔit aṣḥābi.* 6. *da maṭɛam Sāmi.* 7. *di bintina.* 8. *di ʔuxt^{ə} Samīr.* 9. *di ʔuṭṭit Ṭariʔ.* 10. *di giddit Mirvat.*

XVII. 1. *ɛandi bint^{ə} waḥda bass.* 2. *ma-mɛahūš wallāɛa.* 3. *ilʔawlād miš maɛāna.* 4. *ma-ɛandināš ɛaṛabiyya.* 5. *talāta kōka min faḍlak!* 6. *wāḥid ʔahwa min faḍlak!* 7. *ya-taṛa‿mɛāk ʔalam ruṣāṣ?* 8. *yimkin Ḥasan maɛā(h) sagāyir?* 9. *yimkin Samya ma-ɛandahāš waʔt?* 10. *ma-mɛayīš fakka.* 11. *maḥaṭṭit ilʔutubīs fēn, ya-taṛa?* 12. *awlād mīn dōl, ya-taṛa?* 13. *ilwalad da‿smu ʔē?* 14. *ilbanāt lissa‿ṣġayyarīn wi miš miggawwizīn.* 15. *hiyya kānit mudarrisa wi huwwa kān mudarris fi-madrasa sanawi.* 16. *baštaġal dilwaʔti‿f madrasa* *f‿Iskindiriyya.* 17. *kunᵊ zamān ṭabbāx ɛandᵊ wāḥid ingilīzi.* 18. *baštaġal muhandis fi-maṣnaɛ.* 19. *awlād Maḥmūd fi-madrasa faṛansāwi.* 20. *nimrit tilifonha kām min faḍlak?* 21. *fi‿mḥaṭṭit banzīn ɛa‿nnaṣya.*

LESSON VI

I.

nāzil	*nazla*	*nazlīn*	*miṛawwaḥ*	*miṛawwaḥa*	*miṛawwaḥīn*
ɛārif	*ɛarfa*	*ɛarfīn*	*gayy*	*gayya*	*gayyīn*
šāyif	*šayfa*	*šayfīn*	*wāxid*	*waxda*	*waxdīn*
nāyim	*nayma*	*naymīn*	*ɛāwiz*	*ɛawza*	*ɛawzīn*
misāfir	*misafra*	*misafrīn*	*fākir*	*fakra*	*fakrīn*

II. 1. *ana miš ɛārif ilbēt, lākin hiyya ɛarfa ilbēt.* 2. *ana miš ɛāwiz ʾahwa, lākin humma ɛawzīn ʾahwa.* 3. *iḥna ṛayḥīn iggāmiɛ, lākin hiyya miš ṛayḥa‿ggāmiɛ.* 4. *inta miš sāmiɛ ḥāga, lākin hiyya samɛa ḥāga.* 5. *huwwa miš šāyif ḥāga, lākin hiyya šayfa ḥāga.* 6. *ana sakna fi‿dDuʾʾi, w‿inta sākin fēn?* 7. *Sāmi ṛāyiḥ innādi, w‿inti ṛayḥa fēn?* 8. *Ḥasan gayyᵊ bukṛa, wi Maha gayya ʾimta?* 9. *ilwalad nāyim, wi‿lbintᵊ nayma kamān.* 10. *inti fakra‿kwayyis, lākin ana li‿lʾasaf miš fākir ~ fakra.* 11. *hiyya‿msafra innahaṛda, wi‿ḥna‿msafrīn bukṛa.*

III. 1. *talāta‿w ɛašaṛa yibʾu talattāšaṛ.* 2. *xamsa‿w sabɛa yibʾu‿tnāšaṛ.* 3. *itnēn wi tisaɛṭāšar yibʾu wāḥid wi ɛišrīn.* 4. *tisɛa‿w tisɛa yibʾu tamantāšaṛ.* 5. *sitta‿w xamsa yibʾu‿ḥdāšaṛ.* 6. *ɛašaṛa‿w sabɛa yibʾu sabaɛtāšaṛ.* 7. *sabɛa‿w sabɛa yibʾu ʾaṛbaɛtāšaṛ.* 8. *xamsa wi‿ḥdāšaṛ yibʾu sittāšaṛ.* 9. *aṛbaɛa‿w tisɛa yibʾu talattāšaṛ.* 10. *tamanya‿w talāta yibʾu‿ḥdāšaṛ.* 11. *ɛašaṛa‿w tisɛa yibʾu tisaɛtāšaṛ.*

IV. 1. 14 + 7 *yibʾu wāḥid wi ɛišrīn.* 2. 57 +12 *yibʾu tisɛa‿w sittīn.* 3. 17 + 21 *yibʾu tamanya‿w talatīn.* 4. 15 + 13 *yibʾu tamanya‿w ɛišrīn.* 5. 62 + 22 *yibʾu aṛbaɛa‿w tamanīn.* 6. 47 + 15 *yibʾu itnēn wi sittīn.* 7. 8 + 37 *yibʾu xamsa w‿arbiɛīn.* 8. 19 + 22 *yibʾu wāḥid w‿arbiɛīn.* 9. 35 + 37 *yibʾu itnēn wi sabɛīn.* 10. 12 + 19 *yibʾu wāḥid wi talatīn.* 11. 44 + 33 *yibʾu sabɛa‿w sabɛīn.* 12. 27 + 34 *yibʾu wāḥid wi sittīn*

V.

xamsa	*xamastāšaṛ*	*xamsīn*	*xumsumiyya*	*xamas t-alāf*
tisɛa	*tisaɛtāšaṛ*	*tisɛī*	*tusɛumiyya*	*tisaɛ t-alāf*
talāta	*talatāšaṛ*	*talatīn*	*tultumiyya*	*talat t-alāf*
aṛbaɛa	*aṛbaɛṭāšaṛ*	*arbiɛīn*	*rubɛumiyya*	*aṛbaɛ t-alāf*
wāḥid	*ḥidāšaṛ*	*ɛašaṛa*	*miyya*	*ʾalf*
sitta	*sittāšaṛ*	*sittīn*	*suttumiyya*	*sitt -alāf*
itnēn	*itnāšaṛ*	*ɛišrīn*	*mitēn*	*ʾalfēn*
sabɛa	*sabaɛtāšaṛ*	*sabɛīn*	*subɛumiyya*	*sabaɛ t-alāf*
tamanya	*tamantāšaṛ*	*tamanīn*	*tumnumiyya*	*taman t-alāf*

VI. 1. *xamas maṛṛāt wi kamān ɛašaṛa yibʾu xamastāšaṛ maṛṛa.* 2. *bintēn wi kamān ɛašaṛa yibʾu itnāšaṛ bint.* 3. *šanṭa waḥda‿w kamān ɛašaṛa yibʾu ḥidāšaṛ šanṭa.* 4. *xamas šuʾaʾ wi kamān ɛašaṛa yibʾu xamastāšaṛ šaʾʾa.* 5. *aṛbaɛ madāris wi kamān ɛašaṛa yibʾu aṛbaɛtāšaṛ madrasa.* 6. *talat gawāmiɛ wi kamān ɛašaṛa yibʾu talattāšaṛ gāmiɛ.* 7. *sabaɛ aṭfāl wi kamān ɛašaṛa yibʾu sabaɛtāšaṛ ṭifl.* 8. *tisaɛ saɛāt wi kamān ɛašaṛa yibʾu tisaɛtāšaṛ sāɛa.* 9. *sittᵊ kanāyis wi kamān ɛašaṛa yibʾu sittāšaṛ kinīsa.* 10. *talat šababīk wi kamān ɛašaṛa yibʾu talattāšaṛ šibbāk.* 11. *sabaɛ ṭalaba‿w kamān ɛašaṛa yibʾu sabaɛtāšaṛ ṭālib.* 12. *tisaɛ sagāyir wi kamān ɛašaṛa yibʾu tisaɛtāšaṛ sigāṛa.*

13. *aṛbaɛ t-iyyām wi kamān ɛašaṛa yibʔu aṛbaɛtāšaṛ yōm.* 14. *taman ɛimaṛāt wi kamān ɛašaṛa yibʔu tamantāšaṛ ɛimāṛa.* 15. *talat ɛāʔilāt wi kamān ɛašaṛa yibʔu talattāšaṛ ɛēla ~ ɛāʔila.* 16. *xamas t-ibwāb wi kamān ɛašaṛa yibʔu xamastāšaṛ bāb.*

VII.

ɛišrīn ṭāliba	*talata‿w talatīn ṣaniyya*	*tisaɛ sagāyir*
aṛbaɛtāšaṛ muwaẓẓaf	*itnāšaṛ maṛṛa*	*xamastāšaṛ šaʔʔa*
ɛašaṛ madāris	*xamas kalimāt*	*ḫidāšaṛ maṣnaɛ*
sabaɛ t-iyyām	*aṛbaɛ t-ibwāb*	*sittᵊ ḫafalāt*
talat ɛanawīn	*sabɛa‿w tisɛīn šibbāk*	*aṛbaɛa‿w ɛišrīn bint*
		talattāšaṛ sāʔiḫ

VIII. 1. *baʔāli xamas t-iyyām fi-Maṣr.* 2. *baʔāli ʔaṛbaɛ asabīɛ fi-Maṣr.* 3. *baʔāli‿tnāšaṛ sana‿f-Maṣr.* 4. *baʔāli xamas t-ušhur ~ šuhūr fi-Maṣr.* 5. *baʔāli sabaɛtāšaṛ šahrᵊ‿f-Maṣr.* 6. *baʔāli talat saɛāt fi-Maṣr.* 7. *baʔāli xamastāšaṛ yōm fi-Maṣr.*

IX. 1. *ya-taṛa baʔālik ʔaddᵊ ʔē waxda bard?* 2. *ya-taṛa baʔalha ʔaddᵊ ʔē‿f-Maṣr?* 3. *ya-taṛa baʔalku ʔaddᵊ ʔē f-Aswān?* 4. *ya-taṛa baʔalku ʔaddᵊ ʔē miggawwizīn?* 5. *ya-taṛa baʔalhum ʔaddᵊ ʔē mistanniyyīn?* 6. *ya-taṛa baʔālak ʔaddᵊ ʔē mašġūl?* 7. *ya-taṛa baʔalha ʔaddᵊ ʔē‿msafra?* 8. *ya-taṛa baʔālu ʔaddᵊ ʔē sākin hina* 9. *ya-taṛa baʔalhum ʔaddᵊ ʔē fi‿lmadrasa?*

X. 1. *since* 2. *in ~ after* 3. *after* 4. *before* 5. *ago* 6. *after* 7. *since* 8. *ago* 9. *in* 10. *before* 11. *in*

XI. 1. *il basbōṛ da‿btāɛ axūya.* 2. *ilvilla di‿btāɛit Farūʔ.* 3. *ilɛaṛabiyya di‿btāɛit Maha.* 4. *iššunaṭ di‿btaɛt‿issuwwāḫ.* 5. *ilwallāɛa di‿btāɛit Ḫasan.* 6. *ilhidūm di‿btāɛit Samya.* 7. *ilhidiyya di‿btāɛit uxti.*

XII. 1. *ilhadāya di‿btāɛit Ḫasan.* 2. *ikkitāb da‿btāɛ ilmudīr.* 3. *ikkalbᵊ da‿btāɛ ilbulīs.* 4. *ilbanāt dōl bitūɛ Samya.* 5. *ilwallāɛa di‿btāɛit ilmudarris.* 6. *ilmudarrisīn dōl bitūɛ ilfaṛansāwi.* 7. *ilmaktab da‿btāɛ issikirtēra.* 8. *issuwwāḫ dōl bitūɛ maktab inNīl.* 9. *ilɛaṛabiyyāt di‿btāɛit maṣnaɛ issukkaṛ.*

XIII. 1. *iššanṭa‿btaɛti.* 2. *iššawāriɛ bitaɛitha.* 3. *ilbanāt bituɛhum.* 4. *igginēna‿btaɛitha.* 5. *ikkitāb bitāɛik.* 6. *ilḫafla‿btaɛitna.* 7. *ilbēt bitaɛkum.* 8. *issāɛa‿btaɛtu.* 9. *iṭṭalaba‿btuɛna*

XIV. 1. *lā, di miš bitaɛti, lākin bitaɛtu huwwa.* 2. *lā, di miš bitaɛitna lākin bitaɛithum humma.* 3. *lā, di miš bitaɛti lākin bitaɛitha hiyya.* 4. *lā, di miš bitaɛtu lākin bitaɛitha hiyya.* 5. *lā, di miš bitaɛti lākin bitaɛithum humma.* 6. *lā, da miš bitāɛi lākin bitāɛu huwwa.* 7. *lā, dōl miš bituɛna ~ bituɛkum lākin bituɛhum humma.* 8. *lā, di miš bitaɛitha lākin bitaɛtu huwwa.* 9. *lā, di miš bitaɛitna lākin bitaɛitha hiyya.* 10. *lā, di miš bitaɛti lākin bitaɛithum humma.*

XV. 1. *ilbasbōṛ bitāɛak fēn?* 2. *innādi‿btaɛna fi‿lMuhandisīn.* 3. *ilmudarrisīn bituɛna miš mawgudīn.* 4. *iššāriɛ bitaɛku fī(h) maṭɛam.* 5. *iššaʔʔa‿btaɛithum kibīra ʔawi.* 6. *igginēna‿btaɛtik gamb innādi.* 7. *iṭṭalaba‿btuɛna gayyīn bukṛa.* 8. *ilbēt bitāɛi gamīl giddan.*

XVI. 1. *aywa, ilɛaṛabiyya di‿btaɛitha hiyya.* 2. *aywa, ilʔawlād dōl bituɛhum humma.* 3. *aywa, igginēna di‿btaɛti ʔana.* 4. *aywa, iššaʔʔa di‿btaɛtu huwwa.* 5. *aywa, ilbēt da‿btaɛhum humma.* 6. *aywa, issāɛa di‿btaɛti ʔana.* 7. *aywa,* *ilkitāb da‿btaꜥha hiyya.* 8. *aywa, innimra di‿btaꜥitna iḫna.* 9. *aywa, ilmaḫaṭṭa di‿btaꜥti ʾana.*

XVII. 1. *Maha kānit ṛayḫa‿lMuhandisīn imbāriḫ.* 2. *inti kunti sakna hina zamān?* 3. *dōl kānu gayyīn minēn?* 4. *hiyya kānit ꜥawza ʾē?* 5. *intu ma-kuntūš ꜥarfīn ḫāga.* 6. *humma gayyīn hina bukṛa bi‿llēl.* 7. *issāꜥa kām dilwaʾti?* 8. *hiyya ma-kanitšᵊ šayfa ḫāga.* 9. *ʾāsif, ana ma-kuntiš fāḍi‿mbāriḫ iṣṣubḫ.* 10. *ilḫafla‿btāꜥit imbāriḫ kānit laṭīfa.* 11. *kān maꜥāya talat šunaṭ.*

XVIII. 1. *Ḫasan gayy issāꜥa talāta.* 2. *kuntᵊ nāyim ~nayma imbāriḫ baꜥd iḍḍuhr.* 3. *iṭṭalaba ṛayḫīn (ꜥala) fēn?* 4. *Maha sakna fēn ya-taṛa?* 5. *ya-taṛa‿nti šayfa ~ inta šāyif ḫāga?* 6. *ilġada miš gāhiz.* 7. *iḫna ṛayḫīn innādi‿ssāꜥa tisꜥa.* 8. *taꜥāla hina bukṛa!* 9. *ana miš fāḍi dilwaʾti.* 10. *li‿lʾasaf bukṛa ma-ꜥandīš waʾt.* 11. *ya-taṛa tiꜥraf šāriꜥ ʾAṣr inNīl?* 12. *ya-taṛa taslīm iššunaṭ fēn?* 13. *ilvīza‿btāꜥit ḫaḍritak ~ ḫaḍritik fēn?* 14. *Ḫasan ꜥandu talat banāt.* 15. *ilmukalma di ma-kanitšᵊ ꜥašānak ~ līk.* 16. *ḫaḍritak gayyᵊ‿syāḫa walla šuġl?* 17. *baʾāli talat t-iyyām fi-Maṣr.* 18. *miṛāti kānit misafra.* 19. *baʾālik ʾaddᵊ ʾē sakna ~ꜥayša fi-ʾAmsterdam.* 20. *muwaẓẓaf iggamārik fēn?* 21. *Nadya ya fi‿lmadrassa ya fi‿lbēt dilwaʾti.*

LESSON VII

I. 1. *arkab ilʾutubīs?* 2. *aʾfil ilbāb?* 3. *aftaḫ iššibbāk?* 4. *astanna liġāyit imta?* 5. *aꜥmil ʾahwa?* 6. *arūḫ fēn?* 7. *āxud ḫāga saʾꜥa?* 8. *axuššᵊ dilwaʾti?* 9. *afūt ꜥalēk issāꜥa kām?* 10. *anzil fi-Midān itTaḫrīr?* 11. *awaṣṣalak šāriꜥ ʾAṣr inNīl?* 12. *aꜥaddi ꜥala Midān itTaḫrīr?*

II. 1. *Mark lāzim yirkab ilʾutubīs.* 2. *Mark lāzim yāxud taks.* 3. *Mark lāzim yisʾal ilꜥaskari.* 4. *Mark lāzim yimši‿lġāyit ilmidān.* 5. *Mark lāzim yinzil fi-Midān itTaḫrīr.* 6. *Mark lāzim yirūḫ šāriꜥ Ṭalꜥat Ḫarb*

III. 1. *Fawziyya lāzim tiḫuṭṭ ikkarāsi fi‿lbalakōna.* 2. *Fawziyya lāzim tiꜥmil ilʾahwa.* 3. *Fawziyya lāzim tirūḫ issūʾ.* 4. *Fawziyya lāzim tiʾfil iššababīk.* 5. *Fawziyya lāzim tistanna‿šwayya.* 6. *Fawziyya lāzim tinaḍḍaf ittaṛabēẓa.* 7. *Fawziyya lāzim tiftaḫ ilbāb.*

IV. 1. *Fawziyya‿w Ḫusniyya lāzim yiḫuṭṭu‿kkarāsi fi‿lbalakōna.* 2. *Fawziyya‿w Ḫusniyya lāzim yiꜥmilu‿lʾahwa.* 3. *Fawziyya‿w Ḫusniyya lāzim yirūḫu‿ssūʾ.* 4. *Fawziyya‿w Ḫusniyya lāzim yiʾfilu‿ššababīk.* 5. *Fawziyya‿w Ḫusniyya lāzim yistannu‿šwayya.* 6. *Fawziyya‿w Ḫusniyya lāzim yinaḍḍafu‿ttaṛabēẓa.* 7. *Fawziyya‿w Ḫusniyya lāzim yiftaḫu‿lbāb.*

V. 1. *iftaḫi‿lbāb! iftaḫu‿lbāb!* 2. *iʾfili‿ššibbāk! iʾfilu‿ššibbāk!* 3. *iꜥmili‿ššāy! iꜥmilu‿ššāy!* 4. *istarayyaḫi! istarayyaḫu!* 5. *itfaḍḍali! itfaḍḍalu!* 6. *naḍḍafi‿kkursi! naḍḍafu‿kkursi!* 7. *irkabi‿ttaks! irkabu‿ttaks!* 8. *isʾali‿lbawwāb! isʾalu‿lbawwāb!* 9. *inzili‿ssūʾ! inzilu ‿ssūʾ!* 10. *xušši‿ymīn! xuššu‿ymīn!*

VI. 1. *aywa, iʾfil ilbāb ya Ḫasan!* 2. *aywa, iftaḫi‿ššibbāk ya Maha!* 3. *aywa, istarayyaḫi hina, ya Samya!* 4. *aywa, istannu hina ya ʾawlād!* 5. *aywa, iꜥmil šāy ya Ḫasan!* 6. *itfaḍḍal ya Ḫasan, isʾal!* 7. *itfaḍḍali ya Samya, inzili!* 8. *itfaḍḍal ya Ḫasan, xud ilʾalam!* 9. *itfaḍḍalu ya banāt, imšu!* 10. *aywa, iʾri‿lkitāb min faḍlik!* 11. *ṭabꜥan, xuššu!* 12. *ṭabꜥan, itfaḍḍal ꜥaddi!*

VII. 1. *miš ꜥāwiz anzil.* 2. *miš ꜥawza‿nzil.* 3. *miš ꜥawzīn ninzil.* 4. *miš ꜥāwiz ašṛab.* 5. *miš ꜥāwiz arkab.* 6. *miš ꜥawza‿starayyaḫ.* 7. *miš ꜥawzīn niftaḫ.*

8. *miš ɛawzīn nākul.* 9. *miš ɛawza ʔākul.* 10. *miš ɛawzīn nistanna.* 11. *miš ɛāwiz arūḫ.* 12. *miš ɛawzīn nāxud.*

VIII. 1. *lā ya Ḫasan, ma-timšīš!* 2. *lā ya Ḫasan, ma-tiftaḫš!* 3. *lā ya Ḫasan, ma-txuššiš!* 4. *lā ya Ḫasan, ma-tɛaddīš!* 5. *lā ya Ḫasan, ma-tisʔalš!* 6. *lā ya Ḫasan, ma-tištirīš!* 7. *lā ya Samya, ma-tinzilīš!* 8. *lā ya Samya, ma-truḫīš!* 9. *lā ya Samya, ma-taxdīš!* 10. *lā ya Samya, ma-taklīš!* 11. *lā ya Samya, ma-tistannīš!*

IX. 1. *ṭabɛan, lāzim tinzil ya Ḫasan!* 2. *ṭabɛan, lāzim tišṛab ya Fawzi!* 3. *ṭabɛan, lāzim tisʔali ya Fawziyya!* 4. *ṭabɛan, lāzim tirūḫ ya‿bni!* 5. *ṭabɛan, lāzim tistannu ya banāt!* 6. *ṭabɛan, lāzim timšu ya ʔawlād!* 7. *ṭabɛan, lāzim tirkabu ya ʔaṭfāl!* 8. *ṭabɛan, lāzim taklu ya banāt!* 9. *ṭabɛan, lāzim taxdi taksᵊ ya binti!* 10. *ṭabɛan, lāzim tiftaḫi ya Samya!* 11. *ṭabɛan, lāzim tinaḍḍafi ya Fawziyya!* 12. *ṭabɛan, lāzim tixuššᵊ ya Ḫasan!*

X. 1. *miš ɛāwiz arkab, lāzim yirkabu humma!* 2. *miš ɛāwiz astarayyaḫ, lāzim yistarayyaḫu humma!* 3. *miš ɛawza astanna, lāzim yistannu humma!* 4. *miš ɛāwiz asʔal, lāzim yisʔalu humma!* 5. *miš ɛawza‿mši, lāzim yimšu humma!* 6. *miš ɛāwiz anaḍḍaf, lāzim yinaḍḍafu humma!* 7. *miš ɛawzīn ništaġal, lāzim yištaġalu humma!* 8. *miš ɛawza‿nzil, lāzim yinzilu humma!*

XI. 1. *ya-taṛa ʔarkab walla ma-rkabš ilʔutubīs da?* 2. *ya-taṛa nistanna walla ma-nistannāš ḅāḅa?* 3. *ya-taṛa taxdu walla ma-taxdūš taks?* 4. *ya-taṛa tišṛabi walla ma-tišṛabīš illaban da?* 5. *ya-taṛa ʔaɛmil walla ma-ɛmilš ilʔahwa?* 6. *ya-taṛa ʔaxuššᵊ walla ma-xuššiš šimāl?* 7. *ya-taṛa‿ngīb walla ma-ngibš ilʔawlād maɛāna?* 8. *ya-taṛa nākul walla ma-nakulš issamak da?* 9. *ya-taṛa ʔaddi walla ma-ddīš Sāmi‿kkutub?* 10. *ya-taṛa ʔakallim walla ma‿kallimš ilmudīr?* 11. *ya-taṛa ništiri walla ma-ništirīš ilɛaṛabiyya di?* 12. *ya-taṛa‿twaṣṣalu walla ma‿twaṣṣalūš Randa‿lbēt?* 13. *ya-taṛa‿nbīɛ walla ma-nbiɛš iššaʔʔa?* 14. *ya-taṛa‿nrūḫ walla ma-nruḫš ilḫafla?* 15. *ya-taṛa ʔafukkᵊ walla ma-fukkiš ilmīt ginēh dōl?*

XII. 1. *inti ɛawza ʔahwa turki?* 2. *ɛawzīn nizūr ilmaṣāniɛ iggidīda.* 3. *Maṣrᵊ fīha maṭāɛim rixīṣa kitīr.* 4. *issagāyir ilingilīzi di‿btāɛit mīn?* 5. *baḫibb iššawāriɛ ilhadya.* 6. *fēn iṭṭalaba‿ggudād?* 7. *āxud walla ma-xudš iššaʔʔa ‿lġalya di ?* 8. *huwwa miggawwiz waḫda ġaniyya xāliṣ.* 9. *Samya ṭālíba zakiyya giddan.* 10. *fī suwwāḫ kitīr ʔawi‿f-Maṣr.* 11. *miš ɛāwiz ilhadāya‿lġalya di.* 12. *iššanṭa‿kkibīra di‿btaɛti ʔana!* 13. *innās ilfuʔaṛa ma-ɛanduhumšᵊ‿flūs.* 14. *ilʔawlād iṣṣuġayyarīn lāzim yināmu badri.* 15. *mumkin tiddīni nimritak iggidīda?* 16. *inta šāyif ilɛimāṛa‿kkibīra di?* 17. *Samya ma-ɛandahāš waʔt, hiyya miš faḍya dilwaʔti.*

XIII. 1. *ɛAzīza miš ɛawza tistanna.* 2. *Kawsaṛ miš lāzim timši.* 3. *asʔal mīn?* 4. *iɛmili ʔahwa min faḍlik ya Samīra!* 5. *miš lāzim tistanna.* 6. *iṭṭālibāt lāzim yistannu‿šwayya.* 7. *ya-taṛa‿nnādi‿bɛīd ɛan hina?* 8. *aɛmil ʔē?* 9. *arūḫ ~ awṣal hināk izzāy?* 10. *iʔfili‿ššibbāk min faḍlik ya Fawziyya!* 11. *miš ɛawzīn nistanna.* 12. *iḫna mistaɛgilīn šuwayya.* 13. *ḫuṭṭ ittarabēẓa fi‿lbalakōna min faḍlak ya‿Mḫammad!* 14. *lāzim timši‿lġāyit maḫaṭṭit ilbanzīn iggidīda.* 15. *isʔal ~ isʔali ilbawwāb ilʔawwil!* 16. *lāzim tinzil ɛand iggāmiɛ ilʔadīm.* 17. *ɛawza tišṛabi‿sgāṛa ya Samya?* 18. *astanna‿lġāyit issāɛa kām?* 19. *ma-taxdīš ittaksᵊ da ya Samīra!* 20. *ma-tgīš ʔabl iḍḍuhrᵊ ~ issāɛa‿tnāšaṛ ya Ḫasan!* 21. *ma-tɛaddīš ɛala Midān itTaḫrīr innaharda ya Samya!* 22. *ma-tistannāš ~ tistannīš ligāyit bukṛa!* 23. *li‿lʔasaf ana miš fāḍi ~ faḍya dilwaʔti.* 24. *iddinya zaḫma ʔawi‿nnaharda.* 25. *waṣṣali Samīra‿lbēt min faḍlik!*

LESSON VIII

I. 1. *Ḥasan ᵓāɛid fi‿ṣṣaff issābiɛ.* 2. *Samya sakna fi‿ddōr ilxāmis.* 3. *sana ᵓūla ṣaɛbᵊ ᵓawi.* 4. *iṣṣaff ittāsiɛ miš maḥgūz.* 5. *Madīḥa sakna fi‿ddōr ilḥidāšar.* 6. *lāzim yiṭlaɛu li‿ddōr ittāmin?* 7. *sīb iššāriɛ ilᵓawwal wi‿ttāni wi xuššᵊ fi‿ššāriɛ ittālit!* 8. *issawṛa‿f-Maṣrᵊ kānit fi‿lqarn ilɛišrīn.* 9. *ɛUmaṛ fi-sana talta fi‿ggamɛa.* 10. *miš ɛāwiz yirūḥ wi yirgaɛ maṛṛa tanya*

II. 1. *ɛAmrᵊ sākin fi-tāmin dōr.* 2. *ilᵓasansēr wāᵓif fi-sādis dōr.* 3. *ṛābiɛ wi xāmis ṣaffᵊ maḥguzīn li‿lmudīr.* 4. *ɛāšir darsᵊ ṣaɛbᵊ ᵓawi.* 5. *di tāsiɛ maṛṛa ᵓaɛazzil fīha.* 6. *ya‿sṭa, xuššᵊ min faḍlak fi-ṛābiɛ šāriɛ yimīn.* 7. *di tālit šaᵓᵓa‿šufha‿nnahaṛda.* 8. *Samīḥa daxla tāni‿ɛmāṛa ɛa‿lyimīn.* 9. *di ᵓawwil ḥāga yiɛmilha‿nnahaṛda.* 10. *ṣaḥbiti ɛAzza ᵓaɛda‿f-sābiɛ ṣaff.*

III. 1. *ɛalē huwwa.* 2. *ɛalayya‿na.* 3. *ɛalēki‿nti.* 4. *ɛalēhum humma.* 5. *ɛalēha hiyya ɛalēna‿ḥna.* 6. *ɛalēku‿ntu.*

IV. 1. *aywa, intu bāyin ɛalēku fiɛlan ɛayyanīn.* 2. *aywa, huwwa bāyin ɛalē(h) fiɛlan taɛbān.* 3. *aywa, hiyya bāyin ɛalēha fiɛlan miš mabsūṭa.* 4. *aywa, di bāyin ɛalēha fiɛlan taɛbāna.* 5. *aywa dōl bāyin ɛalēhum fiɛlan kuwayyisīn.* 6. *aywa‿lfaršᵊ bāyin ɛalē(h) fiɛlan gidīd lang.* 7. *aywa‿lᵓaṣansēr bāyin ɛalē(h) fiɛlan ɛaṭlān.*

V. 1. *iḥna ṛayḥīn ninām.* 2. *ana ṛāyiḥ aštiri sagāyir.* 3. *ana ṛayḥa‿tmašša‿šwayya.* 4. *iḥna ṛayḥīn nišūf iššaᵓᵓa‿ggidīda.* 5. *ṛayḥīn yitɛaššu fi‿lmaṭɛam.* 6. *ana ṛayḥa‿zūr uxti.*

VI.

miš kitāb wāḥid, kitabēn!	-	*miš bēt wāḥid, betēn!*
miš sāɛa waḥda, saɛtēn!	-	*miš šaᵓᵓa waḥda, šaᵓᵓitēn!*
miš ḥāga waḥda, ḥagtēn!	-	*miš ṣūra waḥda, ṣurtēn!*
miš ɛaṛabiyya waḥda, ɛaṛabiyyitēn!	-	*miš dōr wāḥid, dorēn!*
miš ᵓōḍa waḥda, ᵓoḍtēn!	-	*miš dulāb wāḥid, dulabēn!*
miš ḅaᵓara waḥda, ḅaᵓartēn!	-	*miš šanṭa waḥda, šanṭitēn!*
miš kursi wāḥid, kursiyyēn!	-	*miš hidiyya waḥda, hidiyyitēn!*
miš ṣāla waḥda, ṣaltēn!	-	*miš ɛimāṛa waḥda, ɛimartēn!*

VII. 1. *aywa, idfaɛu.* 2. *aywa, iᵓfilu.* 3. *aywa, iftaḥu.* 4. *aywa, iṣṛabu.* 5. *aywa, kulha.* 6. *aywa, naḍḍafu.* 7. *aywa, isᵓalu.* 8. *aywa, xudu.*

VIII. 1. *aywa, irkabu.* 2. *aywa, ḥuṭṭu.* 3. *aywa, iᵓfilha.* 4. *aywa, išṛabha.* 5. *aywa, iftaḥha.* 6. *aywa, naḍḍafha.* 7. *aywa, isᵓalha.* 8. *aywa, waṣṣalha.*

IX. 1. *ilbalakōna di, lāzim anaḍḍafha?* 2. *ikkursi wi‿ttaṛabēẓa dōl, lāzim anaḍḍafhum?* 3. *ᵓoḍt‿innōm di, lāzim anaḍḍafha?* 4. *ilbēt da, lāzim anaḍḍafu?* 5. *iššababīk di, lāzim anaḍḍafha?* 6. *iššawāriɛ di, lāzim anaḍḍafha?* 7. *ilmaṭbax wi‿lḥammām dōl, lāzim anaḍḍafhum?* 8. *ilᵓuwaḍ di, lāzim anaḍḍafha?*

X. 1. *ilmaṭbax wi‿lḥammām, lāzim tinaḍḍafīhum, ya Ḥusniyya!* 2. *ikkursi, lāzim tinaḍḍafī(h), ya Ḥusniyya!* 3. *ᵓoḍt‿innōm, lāzim tinaḍḍafīha, ya Ḥusniyya!* 4. *iššaᵓᵓa, lāzim tinaḍḍafīha, ya Ḥusniyya!* 5. *iššababīk, lāzim tinaḍḍafīha, ya Ḥusniyya!* 6. *iddawalīb wi‿rrufūf, lāzim tinaḍḍafīhum, ya Ḥusniyya!* 7. *ilmaṭbax, lāzim tinaḍḍafī(h), ya Ḥusniyya!* 8. *ilᵓuwaḍ, lāzim tinaḍḍafīha, ya Ḥusniyya!*

XI. 1. *ana ɛarifhum, lākin humma miš ɛarfinni.* 2. *hiyya fakrāni, lākin huwwa miš fakirni.* 3. *iḥna ɛarfīnak, lākin inta miš ɛarifna.* 4. *intu šayfinni, lākin ana miš šayifku ~ šayfāku.* 5. *ana ɛarfākum, lākin intu miš ɛarfinni.* 6. *inta fakirha, lākin hiyya miš fakrāk.* 7. *huwwa ɛarfak, lākin inta miš ɛarfu.* 8. *hiyya samɛāki, lākin inti miš samɛāha.* 9. *ana šayfik, lākin inti miš šayfāni.* 10. *humma samɛinha, lākin hiyya miš samɛāhum.*

XII. *kān fī fi‿lktāb bitāɛi ṣūra‿l-wāḥid ṛāgil ġarīb ʔawi:*

wiššu kān abyaḍ.	-	*šaɛṛu kān aṣfar.*
ɛenē kānit ɛasali.	-	*widānu kānit ḥamṛa.*
ʔidē kānit samṛa.	-	*manaxīru kānit ruṃādi.*
gallabiyyitu kānit xaḍra.	-	*ṭarbūšu kān azraʔ.*
ilfanilla‿btaɛtu kānit burtuʔāni.	-	*ilbulōfaṛ bitāɛu kān zatūni.*
ʔamīṣu kān kuḥli.	-	*iggazma‿btaɛtu kānit bēḍa.*
ilkaṛafatta‿btaɛtu kānit bunni.	-	*ižžakitta‿btaɛtu kānit xaḍra.*
innaḍḍāra‿btaɛtu kānit sōda.		

XIII. 1. *ana miš ɛawza‿lbulōfaṛ ilʔaṣfar da, iddīni‿lbulōfaṛ ilʔaxḍar.* 2. *ana miš ɛāwiz ikkuṛṛāsa‿lḥamra di, iddīni‿kkuṛṛāsa‿ṣṣafra.* 3. *ana miš ɛawza‿ ššanṭa‿lbēḍa di, iddīni‿ššanṭa‿lbunni.* 4. *iḥna miš ɛayzīn issiggāda‿zzarʔa di, iḥna ɛawzīn issiggāda‿lḥamṛa.* 5. *ana miš ɛāwiz ittaṛabēẓa‿ssōda di, ana ɛāwiz ittaṛabēẓa‿lkuḥli.* 6. *iḥna miš ɛawzīn ilʔalam ilʔaḥmaṛ da, hāt ilʔalam ilʔazraʔ.* 7. *ana miš ɛawza‿lward ilʔaṣfar da, iddīni‿lward ilʔaḥmaṛ.*

XIV. 1. *iḥna saknīn fi-ṛābiɛ dōr.* 2. *iššaʔʔa‿ggidīda ma-fihāš takyīf.* 3. *iggawwᵊ kān aḥsan šuwayya‿mbāriḥ.* 4. *ilʔawlād ɛawzīn yirūḥu‿ynāmu ɛala ṭūl.* 5. *ilʔaṣansēr ɛaṭlān wi lāzim yitṣallaḥ.* 6. *iddinya kānit ḥaṛṛᵊ ʔawi fi‿ṣṣēf.* 7. *kān fī nās kitīr fi‿lḥafla‿mbāriḥ.* 8. *ya Nabīl, mumkin tidfaɛ ilḥisāb innahaṛda!* 9. *ižžakitta‿ssōda di‿btāɛit mīn?* 10. *iššunaṭ izzarʔa di‿btaɛti ʔana.*

XV. 1. *bēti ~ ilbēt bitāɛi‿ṣġayyar.* 2. *ana kuntᵊ sākin zamān fi‿skindiriyya.* 3. *ḅaḅāya ṛāyiḥ yidfaɛ ilʔigāṛ.* 4. *ṃaṃtak fēn?* 5. *iṣṣūra‿btaɛtak ~ ṣurtak iggidīda ḥilwa ʔawi.* 6. *ilbēt ma-kanšᵊ fī(h) takyīf ~ ma-kanšᵊ fī takyīf fi‿lbēt.* 7. *ilɛimāṛa ma-fihāš ʔaṣansēr.* 8. *ɛAmrᵊ ɛarifni‿kwayyis ʔawi.* 9. *fī fustanēn ṭuwāl fi‿lvitrīna.* 10. *kānit miʔaggaṛa šaʔʔa‿ṣġayyara.* 11. *Samya ṛayḥa tištiri ɛēš.* 12. *šaʔʔiti fi‿ddōr ilxāmis.* 13. *iddinya kānit ḥaṛṛᵊ ʔawi‿mbāriḥ.* 14. *Ḥasan ɛandu banṭalonēn, wāḥid aḥmaṛ wi wāḥid axḍar.* 15. *mumkin tiʔfil ittakyīf min faḍlak?* 16. *humma mistanniyyīn aṣḥabhum.* 17. *kuntᵊ ɛāwiz ~ ɛawza šanṭitēn sūd min faḍlak! ~ faḍlik!* 18. *ilʔilíma‿ṣṣafra ɛašānak.* 19. *mumkin ya nākul fi‿lbēt ya nitɛašša fi‿lmaṭɛam.*

LESSON IX

I. 1. *kām ṭālib bi‿ẓẓabṭ?* 2. *kām kitāb bi‿ẓẓabṭ?* 3. *kām sāʔiḥ bi‿ẓẓabṭ?* 4. *kām ɛaskari bi‿ẓẓabṭ?* 5. *kām istimāṛa bi‿ẓẓabṭ?* 6. *kām damġa bi‿ẓẓabṭ?* 7. *kām ʔōḍa bi‿ẓẓabṭ?* 8. *kām šaʔʔa bi‿ẓẓabṭ?*

II. 1. *ana‿lli saʔalt.* 2. *ana‿lli‿ṭliɛt.* 3. *ana‿lli‿nzilt.* 4. *ana‿lli ɛazzilt.* 5. *ana‿lli safirt.* 6. *ana‿lli‿ɛrift.* 7. *ana‿lli‿rgiɛt.* 8. *ana‿lli kalt*

III. 1. *ana‿lli futt.* 2. *ana‿lli ʔult.* 3. *ana‿lli šuft.* 4. *ana‿lli nimt.* 5. *ana‿lli ʔum* 6. *ana‿lli xuft.* 7. *ana‿lli gibt.* 8. *ana‿lli biɛt.*

IV. 1. *ana‿lli malēt.* 2. *ana‿lli laʔēt.* 3. *ana‿lli‿nsīt.* 4. *ana‿lli‿mšīt.* 5. *ana‿lli ɛaddēt.* 6. *ana‿lli ṣallēt.* 7. *ana‿lli ṭaffēt.*

V. 1. *ana‿lli xaffēt.* 2. *ana‿lli fakkēt.* 3. *ana‿lli xaššēt.* 4. *ana‿lli ḫaṭṭēt.* 5. *ana‿lli laffēt.* 6. *ana‿lli ṛaddēt.*

VI. 1. *laʾ, hiyya‿lli fataḫit.* 2. *laʾ, hiyya‿lli saʾalit.* 3. *laʾ, hiyya‿lli širbit.* 4. *laʾ, hiyya‿lli safrit.* 5. *laʾ, hiyya‿lli naḍḍafit.* 6. *laʾ, hiyya‿lli ṭabaxit.* 7. *laʾ, hiyya‿lli ḫawlit.* 8. *laʾ, hiyya‿lli ɛazzilit.* 9. *laʾ, hiyya‿lli nizlit.*

VII. 1. *laʾ, humma‿lli bāɛu.* 2. *laʾ, humma‿lli ʾāmu.* 3. *laʾ, humma‿lli ʾālu* 4. *laʾ, humma‿lli nāmu.* 5. *laʾ, humma‿lli xāfu.* 6. *laʾ, humma‿lli gābu.* 7. *laʾ, humma‿lli šāfu.*

VIII. 1. *laʾ, humma‿lli malu.* 2. *laʾ, humma‿lli laʾu.* 3. *laʾ, humma‿lli ṣallu.* 4. *laʾ, humma‿lli naʾʾu.* 5. *laʾ, humma‿lli nisyu.* 6. *laʾ, humma‿lli ɛaddu.* 7. *laʾ, humma‿lli mišyu.*

IX. 1. *xalāṣ ṭallaɛtaha.* 2. *xalāṣ dafaɛtu.* 3. *xalāṣ ɛamaltaha.* 4. *xalāṣ fataḫtaha* 5. *xalāṣ ḫaṭṭētu.* 6. *xalāṣ ʾafaltu.* 7. *xalāṣ baɛattaha.* 8. *xalāṣ ḫaṭṭetha.* 9. *xalāṣ sibtaha.* 10. *xalāṣ nazziltu.* 11. *xalāṣ waṣṣaltaha.*

X. 1. *ištaṛūha. min zamān.* 2. *gaddidūha min zamān.* 3. *malūha min zamān.* 4. *maḍūha min zamān.* 5. *katabūha min zamān.* 6. *xadūha min zamān.* 7. *ɛamalūha min zamān.* 8. *ʾaggaṛūha min zamān.* 9. *xadūha min zamān.* 10. *xallaṣūha min zamān.*

XI. 1. *ʾultilha tisʾal issikirtēra wi saʾalitha fiɛlan.* 2. *ʾultilu yištiri‿listimāṛa wi‿ štarāha fiɛlan.* 3. *ʾultilha timḍi taḫt ittarīx wi maḍit fiɛlan.* 4. *ʾultilhum yigību‿ddamġa wi gabūha fiɛlan.* 5. *ʾultilha tibɛat axūha wi baɛatitu fiɛlan.* 6. *ʾultilhum yidxulu‿w daxalu fiɛlan.* 7. *ʾultilha‿tɛaddi ɛa‿kkubri wi ɛaddit ɛalē(h) fiɛlan.* 8. *ʾultilu‿ysīb iggamɛa wi sabha fiɛlan.* 9. *ʾultilha tinsa‿ṛṛāgil da wi nisyitu fiɛlan.* 10. *ʾultilu yidfaɛ ilḫisāb wi dafaɛu fiɛlan.* 11. *ʾultilhum yixallaṣu‿ššuġl wi xallaṣū(h) fiɛlan.* 12. *ʾultilha tiftaḫ ilɛiyāda wi fataḫitha fiɛlan.*

XII. 1. *ṛāḫit li‿lɛaskari wi saʾalitu.* 2. *xadit iggawāb wi ʾaritu.* 3. *ṭallaɛit ilmuftāḫ wi‿dditu li‿lbawwāb.* 4. *katabit iggawāb wi ramitu fi‿ssandūʾ.* 5. *ṛāḫit li‿ ššibbāk wi ʾafalitu.* 6. *naḍḍafit ilxuḍār wi ġasalitu.* 7. *xadit issamak kullu wi kalitu.* 8. *šāfit Ḫasan maṛṛa waḫda bass, wi ḫabbitu ɛala ṭūl.*

XIII. 1. *ilʾiqāma‿btaɛitha ɛayza tagdīd.* 2. *ḫawwid šimāl fi šāriɛ Lubnān!* 3. *ya Munīr, isʾal ilɛaskari‿lli ɛa‿lbāb!* 4. *ana šāyif mabna‿kbīr ʾawi.* 5. *ma-tinsāš tigīb maɛāk ṣuwar basbōṛ!* 6. *warrīni‿lbasbōṛ bitāɛak min faḍlak!* 7. *taɛāli hina bukṛa ya madām.* 8. *naʾṣīn ittarīx wi‿lʾimḍa.* 9. *xuššu min ilbāb illi ɛa‿lyimīn.* 10. *abūya kān muwaẓẓaf ḫukūma.* 11. *ɛAli nizil issūʾ ɛašān yištiri ɛēš.*

XIV. 1. *kunna ɛawzīn nirūḫ ginent‿ilḫayawanāt.* 2. *xaznit ~ ilxazna‿btāɛit ilMugammaɛ kānit ʾafla.* 3. *sūʾ issamak miš biɛīd ɛan hina.* 4. *ilgirān illi fōʾ hadyīn.* 5. *sābit Maṣrᵊ‿w ṛāḫit tištaġal sanatēn fi Lubnān.* 6. *kunti fēn imbāriḫ bi‿llēl ya Randa?* 7. *lāzim aštaġal ɛašān aɛīš.* 8. *rūḫi‿štiri‿tnēn damġa!* 9. *ma‿tsibš basbōṛak ~ ilbasbōṛ bitāɛak fi‿lbēt!* 10. *warrīni basbōṛak wi‿ʾiqamtak! ~ ilbasbōṛ bitāɛak wi‿lʾiqāma‿btaɛtak!* 11. *mumkin ḫaḍritak timla / ḫaḍritik timli‿listimāṛa?* 12. *basbōṛak ~ ilbasbōṛ bitāɛak ɛāwiz tagdīd.* 13. *ʾiqamti ~ ilʾiqāma‿btaɛti ɛawza tagdīd.* 14. *ma-šuftikīš fi‿lmadrasa‿mbāriḫ.* 15. *kuntᵊ ɛāwiz ~ ɛawza ʾatɛallim ilɛaṛabi wi ɛašān kida‿lgamɛa baɛatitni Maṣr.* 16. *bāɛu ilɛaṛabiyya‿btaɛithum ~ ɛaṛabiyyithum ilʾadīma wi‿štaru ɛaṛabiyya‿gdīda.* 17. *ana mawlūd ~ mawlūda fi-balad ṣuġayyara f‿lWilayāt ilMuttaḫida.*

XV. *itwaladt^ə‿f Amsterdam sanat ʔalf^ə tusɛumiyya tisɛa‿w sittīn. ɛandi ʔaxx aṣġar minni‿b sana‿w uxt akbaṛ minni‿b sanatēn. ḅaḅāya‿byištaġal muhandis fi-šarika ʔagnabiyya‿w ṃaṃti mudarrisa‿f madrasa‿btidāʔi. ana dilwaʔti badris ilɛaṛabi‿f-gamɛit Amsterdam wi baštaġal fi-maṭɛam ṣuġayyar bi‿llēl. lamma‿xallaṣ iddiṛāsa di ɛawza‿štaġal fi‿ṣṣaḫāfa‿w aktib ɛan iššarq ilʔawsaṭ.*

LESSON X

I. 1. *aywa, ḫarūḫ innahaṛda.* 2. *aywa, ḫaštirīha ɛala ṭūl.* 3. *aywa, ḫanām badri‿nnahaṛda.* 4. *aywa, ḫanakulha‿nnahaṛda.* 5. *aywa, ḫaɛmilha dilwaʔti.* 6. *aywa, ḫanšūfu‿nnahaṛda.* 7. *aywa, ḫalbisha‿nnahaṛda.* 8. *aywa, ḫāgi‿nnahaṛda.* 9. *aywa, ḫanaḍḍafha dilwaʔti.* 10. *aywa, ḫanisʔalu baɛd iddars.*

II. 1. *ma-txafš, miš ḫansā(h).* 2. *ma-txafš, miš ḫansāhum.* 3. *ma-txafš, miš ḫaxuššaha.* 4. *ma-txafš, miš ḫalbisha.* 5. *ma-txafš, miš ḫašṛabha.* 6. *ma-txafš, miš ḫanʔaggaṛha.* 7. *ma-txafš, miš ḫaštirīha.* 8. *ma-txafš, miš ḫamḍīha.* 9. *ma-txafš, miš ḫabiɛha.* 10. *ma-txafš, miš ḫansāhum.* 11. *ma-txafš, miš ḫaklu.*

III. 1. *ana ḫaftaḫhūlik.* 2. *ana ḫaʔṛahūlak.* 3. *ana ḫaštirihālak.* 4. *ana ḫagibhūlak ~ik.* 5. *ana ḫaɛmilhalkum.* 6. *ana ḫanaḍḍafhālak ~ ik.* 7. *ana ḫaktibhālik.* 8. *ana ḫamlahalkum.* 9. *ana ḫaftaḫhulkum.* 10. *ana ḫabɛathālak ~ik.* 11. *ana ḫafukkahalkum.*

IV. 1. *huwwa‿lli katabhūli.* 2. *hiyya‿lli ṭallaɛithāli.* 3. *huwwa‿lli ḫaḍḍarhūli.* 4. *hiyya‿lli naḍḍafithāli.* 5. *humma‿lli gabuhūli.* 6. *iḫna‿lli malenahalhum.* 7. *humma‿lli ḫakuhāli.* 8. *hiyya‿lli ɛamalithalna.* 9. *iḫna‿lli ṣallaḫnā (li-nafsina).* 10. *hiyya‿lli baɛatithalna ~ baɛatithalkum.* 11. *huwwa‿lli fakkuhumli.*

V. 1. *ṭabɛan, kull^ə balad fīha nās.* 2. *ṭabɛan, kull^ə ʔōḍa fīha takyīf.* 3. *ṭabɛan, kull^ə bēt fī(h) dušš.* 4. *ṭabɛan, kull^ə šaʔʔa fīha farš.* 5. *ṭabɛan, kull^ə mustašfa fīha duktūr.* 6. *ṭabɛan, kull^ə balad fīha madrasa.* 7. *ṭabɛan, kull^ə šāriɛ fī(h) maṭɛam.* 8. *ṭabɛan, iḫna binsāfir kull^ə sana.* 9. *ṭabɛan, kull^ə‿gnēna fīha ward.* 10. *ṭabɛan, kull^ə maktaba fīha kutub.* 11. *ṭabɛan, kull^ə šaʔʔa fīha tilifōn.* 12. *ṭabɛan, binrūḫ iššuġl^ə kull^ə ʔusbūɛ.*

VI. 1. *ilmaṭāɛim kullaha fatḫa.* 2. *ilmudarrisīn kulluhum mawgudīn.* 3. *ilʔuwaḍ kullaha faḍya.* 4. *ilɛimāṛa kullaha‿nḍīfa.* 5. *kull^ə ḫāga gahza.* 6. *iṭṭalaba kulluhum šaṭrīn.* 7. *iššuʔaʔ kullaha mafrūša.* 8. *kull^ə sana w‿inti ṭayyiba!* 9. *ilmuwaẓẓafīn kulluhum taɛbanīn.* 10. *issaɛāt kullaha maẓbūṭa.*

VII. "the whole (of)"; "all"; "every"

1. ❑ ❑ ✔	5. ❑ ✔ ❑	9. ❑ ❑ ✔	13. ❑ ❑ ✔
2. ❑ ✔ ❑	6. ✔ ❑ ❑	10. ✔ ❑ ❑	
3. ❑ ✔ ❑	7. ❑ ✔ ❑	11. ❑ ✔ ❑	
4. ✔ ❑ ❑	8. ❑ ❑ ✔	12. ❑ ✔ ❑	

VIII. 1. *miš mumkin, kull ilmadāris fīha mudirīn.* 2. *miš mumkin, kull ilbiyūt fīha ṃayya.* 3. *miš mumkin, kull ilmudarrisīn luṭāf.* 4. *miš mumkin, kull iṭṭalaba‿kwayyisīn.* 5. *miš mumkin, kull ilkutub mawgūda.* 6. *miš mumkin, kull ilmudarrisīn fi-ʔagāza.* 7. *miš mumkin, kull iššuʔaʔ kibīra.* 8. *miš mumkin, kull ilmustašfayāt fīha ʔaṣansērāt.*

IX. 1. *innādi ˀurayyib, lākin ilbēt ˀaˀṛab.* 2. *ilbulōfaṛ tiˀīl, lākin ižžakitta ˀatˀal.* 3. *ilbēt da ġāli, lākin ilbēt bitāɛak aġla.* 4. *ilbintᵊ di ḥilwa, lākin uxtaha ˀaḥla.* 5. *ilbintᵊ ṭawīla‿w axūha ˀaṭwal minha.* 6. *iṭṭālib šāṭir, lākin iṭṭālíba ˀašṭar.* 7. *ilɛēš muhimm, lākin ilṃayya ˀahamm.* 8. *Ḥasan mitɛallim, lākin Maḥmūd mitɛallim aktaṛ ~ aḥsan minnu.* 9. *bēti ɛāli, lākin bēt Muna ˀaɛla.* 10. *Ḥasan mitnarfis, lākin Faṭma mitnarfisa ˀaktaṛ.* 11. *iššanṭa di ṣaḥīḥ xafīfa, lākin šanṭiti ˀaxaffᵊ minha.* 12. *Ramaḍān karīm! - Aḷḷāhu ˀakṛam.*

X. 1. *ilfakha di b‿ɛašaṛa‿gnēh wi‿lxuḍār bi-sabɛa‿gnēh, yaɛni‿lfakha ˀaġla min ilxuḍār bi-talāta‿gnēh.* 2. *ilBurg irtifāɛu tamanīn mitrᵊ wi‿lMuˀaṭṭam irtifāɛu 200 mitr, yaɛni‿lMuˀaṭṭam ˀaɛla min ilBurgᵊ‿b-miyya‿w ɛišrīn mitr.* 3. *Faṭma ṭulha 169 santi‿w Samya ṭulha 165 santi, yaɛni Faṭma ˀaṭwal min Samya‿b-arḅaɛa santi.* 4. *Fatḥi waznu 70 kīlu‿w Fawziyya waznaha 50 kīlu, yaɛni Fatḥi ˀatˀal min Fawziyya‿b-ɛišrīn kīlu.* 5. *bēn Maṣrᵊ‿w Ṭanṭa mīt kīlumitrᵊ‿w bēn Maṣrᵊ w‿Iskindiriyya 230 kīlumitr, yaɛni‿skindiriyya ˀabɛad min Ṭanṭa‿b-miyya‿w talatīn kīlumitr.* 6. *ilˀaṭrᵊ‿byiɛmil mīt kīlu fi‿ssāɛa wi‿lɛaṛabiyya‿btiɛmil tamanīn kīlu fi‿ssāɛa, yaɛni‿lˀaṭr asṛaɛ min ilɛaṛabiyya‿b-ɛišrīn kīlu fi‿ssāɛa.*

XI. 1. *da ˀaḥdas mudēl ɛandina.* 2. *di ˀaḥla ṣūra ɛandina.* 3. *di ˀarxaṣ sāɛa ɛandina.* 4. *da ˀaˀṛab bēt min ilbalad.* 5. *da ˀaxaffᵊ‿blōfaṛ ɛandina.* 6. *da ˀaṭwal banṭalōn fi‿lmaḥall.* 7. *da ˀashal tamrīn fi‿kkitāb.* 8. *da ˀaˀallᵊ wāgib!*

XII. 1. *iggazma di‿ṣġayyara ɛalayya, hāt gazma ˀakbaṛ šuwayya.* 2. *issiggāda di wiḥša, hāt siggāda ˀaḥla minha.* 3. *ššanṭa di‿tˀīla ɛalayya, ɛawza šanṭa ˀaxaffᵊ‿šwayya.* 4. *ittamrīn da sahl, iddīna tamrīn aṣɛab šuwayya.* 5. *ilfustān da ṭawīl ɛalayya, šufli fustān aˀṣar šuwayya.* 6. *ilˀamīṣ da‿ˀṣayyaṛ ˀawi, šufli ˀamīṣ aṭwal šuwayya.* 7. *innaḍḍāra di‿kbīra ˀawi, ɛawza naḍḍāra ˀaṣġar šuwayya.* 8. *iššaˀˀa di ġalya ˀawi, ɛāwiz šaˀˀa ˀarxaṣ šuwayya.*

XIII. 1. *ilfilūs ṣaḥīḥ šēˀ muhimm, lākin ahammᵊ šēˀ huwwa‿ṣṣiḥḥa.* 2. *ilmudēl da ṣaḥīḥ ḥadīs, lākin aḥdas mudēl lissa ma-nzilš issūˀ.* 3. *ilmudarris da‿ kwayyis, lākin Sāmi ˀaḥsan mudarris fi‿lmadrasa.* 4. *iggahlᵊ ṣaḥīḥ ḥāga wiḥša, lākin awḥaš ḥāga hiyya‿lˀihmāl.* 5. *ilfustān da šīk, lākin ašyak fustān huwwa‿btāɛ Faṭma.*6. *ilxuḍār rixīṣ ˀawi hina, lākin arxaṣ xuḍār ḥatlaˀī‿f-sūˀ ilɛAtaba.* 7. *ilfakha ġalya‿šwayya hina, lākin aġla fakha ḥatlaˀīha fi‿lMaɛādi.* 8. *Ḥasan fiɛlan ṭālib zaki, lākin azka ṭālib huwwa Sāmi.* 9. *ilˀaklᵊ da lazīz, lākin alazzᵊ ˀaklᵊ‿btāɛ ṃaṃti.* 10. *madrasti‿kwayyisa, lākin aḥsan madrasa mawgūda fi‿gGīza.*

XIV. 1. *di miš ḥilwa‿w bass, di ˀaḥla ḥāga šuftaha.* 2. *di miš ḥadīsa‿w bass, di ˀaḥdas ḥāga šuftaha.* 3. *di miš xafīfa‿w bass, di ˀaxaffᵊ ḥāga šuftaha.* 4. *di miš laṭīfa‿w bass, di ˀalṭaf ḥāga šuftaha.* 5. *di miš muhimma‿w bass, di ˀahammᵊ ḥāga šuftaha.* 6. *di miš ɛalya w‿bass, di ˀaɛla ḥāga šuftaha.* 7. *di miš šīk wi bass, di ˀašyak ḥāga šuftaha.* 8. *di miš kuwayyisa‿w bass, di ˀaḥsan ḥāga šuftaha.* 9. *di miš sarīɛa‿w bass, di ˀasṛaɛ ḥāga šuftaha.* 10. *di miš ġalya‿w bass, di ˀaġla ḥāga šuftaha.*

XV. 1. *ɛAli sawwāˀ kuwayyis giddan, da min aḥsan issawwaˀīn illi fi‿lbalad.* 2. *ilɛaṛabiyya di sarīɛa giddan, di min asṛaɛ ilɛaṛabiyyāt illi fi‿ggarāž.* 3. *Faṭma ṭālíba zakiyya ˀawi, di fiɛlan min azka‿ṭṭālibāt illi fi‿lfaṣl.* 4. *Sanāˀ bintᵊ laṭīfa giddan, di min alṭaf ilbanāt illi‿ɛrifnāhum.* 5. *Ḥasan ṛāgil karīm giddan, da min akṛam irriggāla‿lli‿f-baladna.* 6. *ilbalad di gamīla giddan, di min agmāl ilbilād illi šufnāha.* 7. *innuṣūṣ di muhimma giddan, di min ahamm innuṣūṣ illi fi‿kkitāb* 8. *ilmaḥallᵊ da ġāli giddan, da min aġla‿ lmaḥallāt illi fi‿lQāhira.*

XVI. 1. miš ¿ārif aˀullaha ˀē. 2. miš ¿arfīn niḫkilhum ˀē. 3. miš ¿ārif axudluhum ˀē. 4. miš ¿ārif addīlu ˀē. 5. miš ¿arfīn niˀulluhum ˀē. 6. miš ¿arfa‿ktiblu ˀē. 7. miš ¿arfīn niddilha ~ niddīha ˀē. 8. miš ¿arfīn nib¿atlu ˀē. 9. miš ¿arfa‿giblaha ˀē. 10. miš ¿arfa‿¿millu ˀē.

XVII. 1. aywa, min faḍlak i¿milli šāy. 2. aywa, min faḍlak iktiblaha gawāb. 3. aywa, min faḍlak iftaḫlina. 4. aywa, min faḍlak iˀfilli‿lbāb! 5. aywa, min faḍlak naḍḍafli‿ššibbāk. 6. aywa, min faḍlak fukkili. 7. aywa, min faḍlak iˀṛalna‿ktāb. 8. aywa, min faḍlak i¿millina ˀahwa. 9. aywa, min faḍlak ib¿atli‿lˀawlād. 10. aywa, min faḍlak gaddidli‿lˀiqāma.

XVIII. 1. lā, da‿ktīr ˀawi ¿alēna. 2. lā, di ġalya ˀawi ¿alēna. 3. lā, da‿kbīr ˀawi ¿alayya. 4. lā, da‿ˀṣayyar ˀawi ¿alayya. 5. lā, di‿ṣġayyara ˀawi ¿alēna. 6. lā, di ṭawīla ˀawi ¿alayya. 7. lā, di‿kbīra ˀawi ¿alēna. 8. lā, di‿tˀīla ˀawi ¿alayya. 9. lā, da sahl^{ə} ˀawi ¿alēna. 10. lā, di‿ṣġayyara ˀawi ¿alayya.

XIX. 1. iššanṭa‿btā¿it idduktūr lonha ˀiswid. 2. mūsim iššita ˀuṣayyar ˀawi‿f-Maṣr. ~ iššita mūsim ˀuṣayyar ˀawi‿f-Maṣr. 3. iḫna ¿arfīn muhandis kuwayyis. 4. Ramaḍān aḫla šahr^{ə} ¿and ilmuslimīn. 5. ya-taṛa‿ntu miš miwafˀīn? 6. di ḫāga basīṭa ˀawi! 7. ilgāmi¿ a¿la mabna fi‿lbalad. 8. ilbintēn dōl ḫilwīn ˀawi. 9. iḫna‿bništaġal ṭūl innahāṛ. 10. Ḫasan misāfir Iskindiriyya bukṛa. ~ bukṛa Iskindiriyya. 11. il¿aṛabiyyāt ilˀamrikāni ġalya xāliṣ. 12. igginēna‿bta¿ti fīha naxlitēn ¿alyīn. 13. iṭṭalaba‿ggudād biyištaġalu‿kwayyis. 14. ilbalad kullaha ḫayawiyya‿w našāṭ. 15. miṛātu kānit miḫaḍḍara‿lfiṭār.

XX. 1. fi‿ṣṣēf binilbis hidūm ṣēfi xafīfa. ~ binilbis hidūm ṣēfi xafīfa fi‿ṣṣēf. 2. ilwāḫid biyiḫtāg li-blōfaṛ fi‿ššita. 3. iddinya bitbaṛṛad bi‿llēl. 4. innās kullaha‿btitmašša fi‿gganāyin liġāyit wišš iṣṣubḫ. 5. yimkin ˀasanṣēr il¿imāṛa ¿aṭlān. 6. gidditi ma-bitšufš^{ə}‿kwayyis bi‿nnaḍḍāra di. 7. bitiktib ˀē? 8. ma-kuntiš ¿ārif aktib ˀē. 9. ḫanrūḫ ~ iḫna ṛayḫīn Sīna bi‿lˀutubīs ilˀusbū¿ iggayy. 10. Ḫasan ¿andu ˀasṛa¿ ¿aṛabiyya fi‿lbalad. 11. (ahé) di‿l¿ṛabiyyāt ilˀamrikāni. 12. ilˀutubīs dayman biyiwṣal issā¿a‿tnāšaṛ. 13. binrūḫ ilmadrasa kull^{ə} yōm. 14. ¿Ali‿byāxud dušš^{ə} kull^{ə} yōm iṣṣubḫ. 15. (huwwa) gayy^{ə} yāxud ˀigāṛ ilbēt. 16. ġasalit wiššaha wi‿ snanha. 17. fī nās kitīr bitrūḫ ilBaḫr^{ə}‿lAḫmaṛ fi‿ššita. 18. baladi ˀagmal balad fi‿l¿ālam. 19. ḫankūn kullina mawgudīn fi‿nnādi bukṛa.

LESSON XI

I. 1. ma-tsāfir bukṛa. 2. ma-tišṛab ḫāga saˀ¿a. 3. ma-tirkab taks. 4. ma-tākul ba¿dēn. 5. ma-tinzilu bukṛa. 6. ma-tisˀalu‿ssikirtēra. 7. ma-tˀaggarūha ba¿dēn. 8. ma-tiktibilha kart

II. 1. miš ˀadra‿ˀūm badri. 2. miš ¿arfīn ninām bi‿llēl. 3. miš ˀādir aštaġal hina. 4. miš ˀādir ākul ḫāga. 5. miš ˀadra‿šṛab ḫāga. 6. miš ¿ārif aṣallaḫ ilmutūr. 7. miš ¿arfīn nixallaṣ šuġlina. 8. miš ˀādir astanna‿ktīr. 9. miš ¿arfa‿mla‿listimāṛa‿bta¿ti. 10. miš ˀādir agīb ṣaḫbi‿m¿āya. 11. miš ¿arfīn niˀṛa‿l¿aṛabi.

III. 1. ana gayy asˀal siyadtak suˀāl. 2. huwwa gayy^{ə}‿yšūf ittakyīf. 3. intu gayyīn taxdu‿lˀugṛa‿bta¿itkum. 4. hiyya gayya tidfa¿ ilˀigāṛ bitā¿ iššaˀˀa. 5. iḫna gayyīn ništaġal ma¿ākum. 6. ana gayya‿ṣallaḫ ilḫanafiyya. 7. humma gayyīn yigaddidu‿lˀiqāma. 8. inta gayy^{ə} tištiri damġa. 9. inti gayya timḍi‿listimāṛa. 10. humma gayyīn yizurūk fi-bētak.

IV.

1a + 5b	2a + 6b	3a + 7b
4a + 8b	5a + 10b	6a + 11b
7a + 12b	8a + 4b	9a + 3b
10a + 9b	11a + 1b	12a + 2b

V. 1. *ma-trūḫi li‿dduktūr yišūf ʿandik ʾē!* 2. *ma-trūḫu li‿dduktūr yišūf ʿandaku ʾē!* 3. *ma-trūḫ li‿dduktūr yišūf ʿandaha ʾē!* 4. *ma-yrūḫu li‿dduktūr yišūf ʿanduhum ʾē!* 5. *ma-yrūḫ li‿dduktūr yišūf ʿandu ʾē!* 6. *ma-nrūḫ li‿dduktūr yišūf ʿandina ʾē!* 7. *ma-rūḫ li‿dduktūr yišūf ʿandi ʾē!*

VI. 1. *ā, ilʾawrāʾ itʾaddimit xalāṣ!* 2. *ā, ilḫanafiyya‿tfakkit xalāṣ!* 3. *ā, iggilda‿trakkibit xalāṣ!* 4. *ā, ilʿaṛabiyya‿tġasalit xalāṣ!* 5. *ā, ilʾahwa‿tʿamalit xalāṣ!* 6. *ā, ilḫisāb iddafaʿ xalāṣ!*

VII. 1. *ittakyīf miš lāzim yitṣallaḫ!* 2. *ilmaṭbax miš lāzim yitnaḍḍaf!* 3. *iggilda miš lāzim titġayyaṛ!* 4. *ilḫanafiyya miš lāzim titfakk!* 5. *ilʿaṛabiyya miš mumkin titbāʿ!* 6. *Salwa miš mumkin titnisi!* 7. *ilʿaṛabiyya miš lāzim titġisil!* 8. *ilṃayya di miš mumkin titširib!* 9. *iššibbāk miš mumkin yitfitiḫ!* 10. *inti miš mumkin titnisi!* 11. *ilḫisāb da miš lāzim yiddifiʿ!* 12. *da miš mumkin yitʾifil!* 13. *da miš mumkin yittākil!* 14. *ilbāb da miš mumkin yitʾifil!* 15. *ikkarāsi miš lāzim titšāl!* 16. *ilbēt miš lāzim yitbāʿ!* 17. *inta miš mumkin titnarfis!* 18. *ilbasbōṛ miš lāzim yitgaddid!* 19. *ilmuškila miš mumkin titḫall!* 20. *ikkalām da miš mumkin yitʾāl!*

VIII. 1. *ʿawzīn yirgaʿu‿ssāʿa‿tnēn.* 2. *niḫibbᵊ nišṛab ṃayya.* 3. *ʿawzīn nimḍi hina.* 4. *ilmafrūḍ nisʾal ilʿaskari.* 5. *ilmafrūḍ niʿaddi min hina.* 6. *ʿawzīn nixuššᵊ‿šmāl.* 7. *ilmafrūḍ nimla‿listimāṛa.* 8. *ilmafrūḍ nāxud ilʾutubīs.* 9. *niḫibbᵊ‿nṛawwaḫ dilwaʾti.* 10. *ḍarūri niwṣal bukṛa‿ṣṣubḫ.*

IX. 1. *ilʿaskari ḫayʾullak timḍi fēn.* 2. *ilʿaskari ḫayʾullak tištiri damġa‿mnēn.* 3. *ilʿaskari ḫayʾullak tidxul fēn.* 4. *ilʿaskari ḫayʾullak tisʾal mīn.* 5. *ilʿaskari ḫayʾullak timla ʾē.* 6. *ilʿaskari ḫayʾullak tiktib ʾē.* 7. *ilʿaskari ḫayʾullak tirūḫ fēn.* 8. *ilʿaskari ḫayʾullak tiʾūl ʾē.* 9. *ilʿaskari ḫayʾullak tāxud ʾē.* 10. *ilʿaskari ḫayʾullak tiʿmil ʾē.*

X. 1. *lāzim ašṛab ilmayya di?* 2. *ḍarūri ninzil hina.* 3. *tiʾdaṛu‿tġayyaṛu‿lfilūs di?* 4. *tiḫibbᵊ‿twarrīna‿lbalad?* 5. *nifsi‿štaġal ṭabbāx.* 6. *tiḫibbi tisʾali suʾāl?* 7. *nifsina ništiri ʿaṛabiyya.* 8. *lāzim aggawwiz Randa.* 9. *lāzim asīb iggamʿa.* 10. *nifsi ʾaʿīš fi-Maṣr.*

XI. 1. *iššamsᵊ lissa ma-ṭilʿitš.* 2. *baṭni‿btiwgaʿni* 3. *ilmarkib di‿rkibnāha‿mbāriḫ.* 4. *inti šayfa‿lmabna‿lʿāli da?* 5. *iṛṛāgil da ʾīdu ṭawīla.* 6. *ilḫarbᵊ lissa ma-xilṣitš.* 7. *issittᵊ di manaxirha‿kbīra ʾawi.* 8. *ilʾarḍᵊ mablūla.* 9. *ʿēni ʿalēk barda.* 10. *ikkilma di laha maʿna tāni.* 11. *riglu maksūṛa.*

XII. 1. *fi‿ššita‿ddinya bitlayyil badri.* 2. *kullᵊ yōm iṣṣubḫᵊ‿bnākul fūl midammis.* 3. *ana miš fākir tarīx innahaṛda ʾē.* 4. *ya-taṛa bukṛa ḫaykūn kām fi‿ššahṛ?* 5. *ilḫanafiyya di miš lāzim titṣallaḫ.* 6. *Miryam ṛāḫit ilMaġrib ʿašān titʿallim ilʿaṛabi.* 7. *itmaššēna fi‿lbalad liġāyit wišš iṣṣubḫ.* 8. *ya-taṛa iggawwᵊ ḫaykūn kuwayyis bukṛa?* 9. *issittᵊ baʾit zibūna ʿand issabbāk.*

XIII. 1. *ilʿaṛabiyya lāzim titġisil.* 2. *ilʾawlād miš ʿawzīn yirūḫu‿ynāmu.* 3. *itʾabilna fi‿lmaḫaṭṭa‿mbāriḫ.* 4. *fī mustašfa‿f kullᵊ balad kibīra.* 5. *kullina mistanniyyīnak ~ mistanniyyīnik.* 6. *uxti‿kkibīra‿btištaġal fi‿lmaṣnaʿ da.* 7. *ilḫamdu li‿llāh ʿaṛabiyyitna‿lʾadīma‿tbāʿit.* 8. *ḫaktiblaha ʿašān tīgi‿tšūf iššaʾʾa ~ titfaṛṛag ʿala ššaʾʾa.* 9. *ana mistannīha bukṛa‿ṣṣubḫ issāʿa ʿašaṛa.* 10. *ilbintᵊ di miš mumkin titnisi.* 11. *ilʿaddād iggidīd xaṣrān wi lāzim yitṣallaḫ.* 12. *baḫibb arūḫ issinima.* 13. *nifsuku‿trūḫu‿mʿāna‿*

lḫafla? ~ tiḫibbu‿trūḫu‿mᶓāna‿lḫafla 14. *iššawāṭiᵓ (bitkūn) niḍīfa‿w hadya fi‿lxarīf.* 15. *fī nās kitīr bitḫibbᵊ‿trūḫ Sīna fi‿ṣṣēf.* 16. *ana gayy ~ gayya aᵓullak ~ aᵓullik ḫāga muhimma.* 17. *šāfit fi‿lmaḫallᵊ fustān gamīl wi‿štaritu.* 18. *itᶓarrafit ᶓala‿tnēn ṭalaba maṣriyyīn fi‿ggamᶓa.*

LESSON XII

I. 1. *ᵓafalt ilbāb lē? da‿na lissa fatḫu ~ fatḫā min šuwayya!* 2. *Aḫmad rāḫ fēn? da‿na lissa šayfu ~ šayfā min šuwayya!* 3. *amḍi tāni lē? miš ana lissa māḍi ~ maḍya ᵓuddamak!* 4. *illaḫma‿mtalliga, ana lissa‿mṭallaᶓha ~ mṭallaᶓāha min ilfirīzir.* 5. *ikkubbayāt di‿nḍīfa, ana lissa ġasilha ~ ġaslāha ‿nnaharda.* 6. *ilkutub fēn? da‿na lissa šarīha ~ šaryāha ‿nnaharda‿ṣṣubḫ!* 7. *ana ma-šuftahāš, di lissa ragᶓa mi‿lxārig.* 8. *ana miš gaᶓāna, ana lissa wakla min šuwayya.* 9. *balāš ᵓahwa min faḍlik, ana lissa šārib ~ šarba šāy!* 10. *li‿lᵓasaf, Samya miš mawgūda, di lissa xarga min xamas daᵓāyiᵓ!*

II. 1. *Muḫammad biyrūḫ ilmadrasa kullᵊ yōm.* 2. *ana šāmim ~ šamma ~ šammēt rīḫa ġarība.* 3. *hiyya‿msafra ~ ḫatsāfir innaharḍa bi‿llēl.* 4. *ana šāyif ~ šayfa kuwayyis bi‿nnaḍḍāra‿ggidīda.* 5. *ᶓala fēn in šāᵓ Allā? - ana nāzil ~ nazla‿lbalad.* 6. *iḫna dayman binsāfir Iskindiriyya fi‿ṣṣēf.* 7. *ilkalbᵊ biyšimm aḫsan min ilᵓinsān.* 8. *ana ḫāsis ~ ḫassa bi-ᵓalam fi-baṭni.* 9. *inta ḫatuᵓᶓud hina? - lā, ana rāyiḫ li‿dduktūr baᶓdᵊ‿šwayya.* 10. *kullᵊ yōm issāᶓa ᶓašara ᵓAḫmad biyinzil issūᵓ.* 11. *ya-tara inti šayfa mīn illi‿hnāk da?* 12. *dayman lamma bašrab mayya saᵓᶓa baḫissᵊ‿b-ᵓalam fi-snāni.*

III. 1. *ilbawwāb ġasal ilᶓarabiyya, yaᶓni‿lᶓarabiyya dilwaᵓti maġsūla wi‿nḍīfa.* 2. *iṭṭabbāx ᵓala‿ssamak wi dilwaᵓti‿ssamak maᵓli‿w gāhiz li‿lᵓakl.* 3. *Aḫmad itkasarit riglu‿w dilwaᵓti riglu maksūra‿w miggabbisa.* 4. *šawēna‿llaḫma‿w dilwaᵓti‿llaḫma mašwiyya‿w gahza.* 5. *ilbāb itᵓafal min sāᶓa‿w dilwaᵓti ḫatlaᵓī(h) maᵓfūl.* 6. *ilbulīs manaᶓ ilmurūr, yaᶓni‿lmurūr dilwaᵓti mamnūᶓ.* 7. *Aḫmad itwalad fi Ṭanṭa, yaᶓni huwwa mawlūd wi mitṛabbi fi‿rrīf.* 8. *issabbāk fakk ilḫanafiyya‿w sabha mafkūka‿w rawwaḫ.* 9. *ḫagazt imbāriḫ ᵓōḍa fi‿lfunduᵓ, yaᶓni dilwaᵓti‿lᵓōḍa maḫgūza xalāṣ.* 10. *Ḫasan xaṭab Randa, yaᶓni dilwaᵓti Randa maxṭūba rasmi.* 11. *Ḫasan ṭafa‿llamba, yaᶓni‿llamba dilwaᵓti maṭfiyya‿w ma-fīš nūr.* 12. *ilmayya lāzim tiġli, ma-tišrabūš ġēr mayya maġliyya!* 13. *ilmudīr maḍa‿lᵓawrāᵓ, yaᶓni‿lᵓawrāᵓ dilwaᵓti mamḍiyya‿w gahza.* 14. *Samīr iggawwiz Samya, yaᶓni humma dilwaᵓti miggawwizīn.*

IV. 1. *lā, huwwa bass illi miši.* 2. *lā, huwwa bass illi sāfir.* 3. *lā, huwwa bass illi nisi.* 4. *lā, huwwa bass illi ᶓazzil.* 5. *lā, huwwa bass illi maḍa.* 6. *lā, huwwa bass illi rawwaḫ.* 7. *lā, huwwa bass illi‿tnaᵓal.* 8. *lā, huwwa bass illi‿ddāyiᵓ.* 9. *lā, huwwa bass illi rikib ilᵓaṭr.* 10. *lā, huwwa bass illi simiᶓ ilkalām.*

V. 1. *gibt iṭṭamāṭim min ilfakahāni‿lli‿f-šāriᶓ Ḫasan Ṣabri.* 2. *ištarēt issagāyir min ikkušk illi ᵓuddām issinima.* 3. *ištarēt ilbadla min ilbutīk illi gambina ᶓala ṭūl.*4. *saᵓalt ilᶓaskari‿lli wāᵓif ᵓuddām ilbāb.* 5. *laᵓēt ilmafatīḫ ᶓala‿ttarabēẓa‿lli‿f-ᵓoḍt‿innōm.* 6. *xuššu min ilbāb illi ᶓa‿lyimīn!* 7. *ṣallaḫ ilḫanafiyya‿lli bitnaᵓᵓaṭ mayya!* 8. *ᶓawza‿tfarrag ᶓala‿lfustān illi fi‿lfitrīna.* 9. *ᶓawzīn iggawāb illi wiṣil innaharḍa‿ṣṣubḫ.* 10. *ᶓawz‿āxud iṣṣūra‿lli fīha ṣaḫbiti.*

VI. 1. *mīn irrāgil illi‿ggawwizitu?* 2. *fēn ilḫagāt illi gibtīha min issūᵓ?* 3. *áho da‿lmaḫall illi‿tfarragna ᶓalē(h) imbāriḫ.* 4.*fēn ilmafatīḫ illi xadtaha minni mbāriḫ?* 5. *mīn irrāgil illi kuntᵊ bitkallimu?* 6. *ma-laᵓētš ikkitāb illi kunti*

ʿawzā(h). 7. *warrīni_ṣṣuwar illi ʿamaltīha_f-Maṣr!* 9. *ittallāga_lli inta ṣallaḥtaha ahé!* 10. *ilmatʿam illi_tʿaššēna fī(h) imbāriḥ kuwayyis giddan.* 11. *lāzim nirgaʿ ilmaḥall illi daxalnā(h) min šuwayya.*

VII. 1. *ḥāxud ilfustān illi tamanu mitēn ginē(h).* 2. *iḥna ʿawzīn ilmuftāḥ illi xadtu min Ḥasan.* 3. *ḥāxud ilbadla_lli lonha bunni.* 4. *inta šāyif iṛṛāgil illi šaklu wiḥiš?* 5. *ʿawzīn ilġurfa_lli balakonitha ʿa_nNīl.* 6. *fēn ilfilūs illi ġayyaṛtaha mi_lbank?* 7. *aho da_lkātib illi ʾarēt kitābu fi_lʾagāza.* 8. *ittaṣalt^{ə} bi_ssitt illi kunna ʾabilnāha fi_lmaḥaṭṭa.*

VIII. 1. *badawwaṛ ʿala ṭālib ismu Ḥasan.* 2. *badawwaṛ ʿala ṭabbāx yiʿṛaf yuṭbux kuwayyis.* 3. *badawwaṛ ʿala badla_lbisha fi_lḥafla.* 4. *badawwaṛ ʿala ṭamāṭim tinfaʿ li_ssalaṭa.* 5. *badawwaṛ ʿala ṭālība_smaha Mirvat.* 6. *laʾēt šaʾʾa ʾaggaṛtaha ʿala ṭūl.* 7. *laʾēt kitāb ištarētu ʿala ṭūl.* 8. *ʾaʿadt^{ə} sanatēn fi-Maṣr itʿallimt^{ə} fīhum ilʿaṛabi.* 9. *ya-taṛa fī film^{ə}_kwayyis nitfaṛṛag ʿalē fi_ttilivizyōn?* 10. *ya-taṛa fī ʾutubīs naxdu min hina?*

IX. 1. *šuft imbāriḥ film^{ə} ʿagabni xāliṣ.* 2. *ana miḥtāga_l-šaġġāla šaṭra tiʿṛaf tuṭbux.* 3. *da ʾawwil maḥall^{ə} daxalnā_f-Xān ilXalīli.* 4. *kān fī hina ṛāgil saʾal ʿalēk* 5. *laʾēt funduʾ laṭīf nizilt^{ə} fī .* 6. *fī_hnāk ʿaskari murūr mumkin nisʾalu .* 7. *ʿandi walad tāni ʿumru_tnāšaṛ sana.* 8. *ʿanduhum bint^{ə} tanya ʿumṛaha ʿašaṛ sinīn.* 9. *ʿāwiz ašūf badla tanya lonha ʾaḥla_šwayya.* 10. *ḥanlāʾi ʾinšāʾ Aḷḷāh maḥall^{ə} tāni ʿandu buḍāʿa ʾarxaṣ.*

X. 1. *kunt^{ə} ʿāwiz aštiri ṭawābiʿ barīd.* 2. *kunt^{ə} ʿāwiz aʾullak ḥāga.* 3. *kunt^{ə} ʿāwiz agaddid ilʾiqāma_btaʿti.* 4. *kunt^{ə} ʿāwiz asʾal suʾāl.* 5. *kunt^{ə} ʿāwiz āxud ilbasbōṛ bitāʿi.* 6. *kunt^{ə} ʿāwiz aḥgiz makān kuwayyis* 7. *kunt^{ə} ʿāwiz atfaṛṛag ʿa_lkutub.* 8. *kunt^{ə} ʿāwiz adfaʿ ilʾigāṛ* 9. *kunt^{ə} ʿāwiz adris fi_ ggamʿa* 10. *kunt^{ə} ʿāwiz asāfir Maṣr?*

XI. 1. *kunna ḥaništaġal, lākin ġayyaṛna fikrina.* 2. *kunt^{ə} ḥaggawwiz, lākin ġayyaṛt^{ə} fikri.* 3. *kunt^{ə} ḥaḥgiz makān, lākin ġayyaṛt^{ə} fikri.* 4. *kunt^{ə} ḥabīʿ ilbēt, lākin ġayyaṛt^{ə} fikri.* 5. *kunna ḥaninzil issūʾ, lākin ġayyaṛna fikrina.* 6. *kunt^{ə} ḥarūḥ Luʾsur, lākin ġayyaṛt^{ə} fikri.* 7. *kunt^{ə} ḥargaʿ badri, lākin ġayyaṛt^{ə} fikri.* 8. *kunna ḥanitniʾil lākin ġayyaṛna fikrina.* 9. *kunt^{ə} ḥaʾʿud hina, lākin ġayyaṛt^{ə} fikri.* 10. *kunt^{ə} ḥabʿat ilʾawlād lākin ġayyaṛt^{ə} fikri.*

XII.

1a + 10b	2a + 5b	3a + 9b	4a + 3b
5a + 4b	6a + 8b	7a + 6b	8a + 1b
9a + 2b	10a + 7b		

XIII. *kunt^{ə} ḥaʾʿud yomēn fi Maṣr.* – *kunt^{ə} ḥaʾʿud talat t-iyyām fi Maṣr.* – *kunt^{ə} ḥaʾʿud sabaʿ sinīn fi Maṣr.* – *kunt^{ə} ḥaʾʿud ʿišrīn yōm fi Maṣr.* – *kunt^{ə} ḥaʾʿud sanatēn fi Maṣr.* – *kunt^{ə} ḥaʾʿud xamastāšaṛ šahr fi Maṣr.* – *kunt^{ə} ḥaʾʿud xamas t-ušhur ~ šuhūr fi Maṣr.* – *kunt^{ə} ḥaʾʿud tisaʿ ʾasabīʿ fi Maṣr.* – *kunt^{ə} ḥaʾʿud ḥidāšaṛ ʾusbūʿ fi Maṣr.* – *kunt^{ə} ḥaʾʿud sitt^{ə}_snīn fi Maṣr.* – *kunt^{ə} ḥaʾʿud sabaʿtāšaṛ yōm fi Maṣr.* – *kunt^{ə} ḥaʾʿud ʿašaṛ t-ušhur ~ šuhūr fi Maṣr.* – *kunt^{ə} ḥaʾʿud aṛbaʿ saʿāt fi Maṣr.*

XIV. 1. *ilbēt illi kān ʿandina fi_gGīza kān ṣuġayyar.* 2. *baʾalna dilwaʾti šahrēn saknīn f_Iskindiriyya.* 3. *ahó da_lbēt illi ʿawzīn ništirī(h).* 4. *ilfiṭāṛ ḥaykūn gāhiz issāʿa sabʿa.* 5. *mumkin nāxud ʾutubīs tāni.* 6. *kānu ḥaymūtu mi_ lḥaṛṛ.* 7. *issitt^{ə} kānit labsa fustān aḥmaṛ ṭawīl.* 8. *iṭṭalaba kānu lissa hina min sāʿa.* 9. *miš lāzim tīgu ʾabl issāʿa tamanya.* 10. *mumkin ḥaḍritak tīgi_f ʾayy^{ə} waʾt.* 11. *inta šāyif iṛṛāgil illi lābis bulōfaṛ axḍar, ahó da_lbawwāb.* 12. *ya-taṛa, fī hina bank aġayyaṛ fi_flūs?* 13. *ya-taṛa, alāʾi ʿandak istimāṛa_ w damġa?* 14. *kunti ʿawza_lfustān illi fi_lfitrīna?* 15. *ḥāxud ilʾōda_lli fi_ddōr ittālit.* 16. *ana gayy ~ gayya ašūf ~ atfaṛṛag ʿala iššaʾʾa_lʾawwil.*

17. *ilmudīr miḥtāg li‿skirtēra‿kwayyisa.* 18. *nimrit ˀōḍit ḥaḍritak tultumiyya xamsa‿w ɛišrīn.* 19. *kānit ɛawza tiktib gawāb lākin ġayyaṛit fikraha.* 20. *lamma‿wṣilt kān ilmuwaẓẓaf ṛawwaḥ.*

LESSON XIII

I. 1. *lā, (šāfu) nafs ilɛaṛabiyya.* 2. *lā, da nafs issabab.* 3. *lā, da nafs ilmaṛad.* 4. *lā, (ˀaggartᵊ)nafs iššaˀˀa.* 5. *lā, (ḥāxud) nafs ilˀutubīs.* 6. *lā, (ḥayīgi)‿f-nafs ilyōm.* 7. *lā, (ḥanrūḥ) nafs ilḥafla.* 8. *lā, (ˀalli) nafs ilkalām.* 9. *lā, (iššaˀˀa‿btaɛti)‿f-nafs ilɛimāṛa.* 10. *lā, (ḥanām) fi-nafs ilˀōḍa*

II. 1. *aywa, ana‿b-nafsi.* 2. *aywa, iḥna‿b-nafsina.* 3. *aywa, huwwa‿b-nafsu.* 4. *aywa, hiyya‿b-nafsaha.* 5. *aywa, humma‿b-nafsuhum.* 6. *aywa, intu‿b-nafsuku.* 7. *aywa, ana‿b-nafsi.*

III. 1. *ḥassᵊ‿b-ˀalam w‿huwwa‿byitɛašša.* 2. *šuftaha w‿ana batfassaḥ fi‿nnādi.* 3. *šufnā xārig wi‿ḥna ˀaɛdīn fi‿lbalakōna.* 4. *kunna binfakkaṛ fīha w‿ḥna fi‿ggamɛa.* 5. *fātu ɛala Asyūṭ wi humma ṛayḥīn Aswān.* 6. *w‿ana ṛayḥa‿ssūˀ, ˀabiltuhum fi‿ssikka.* 7. *saˀalu ɛala ḥaḍritak wi‿nta miš mawgūd.* 8. *ɛamaltu ˀē w‿ana‿msafra?* 9. *wi‿ḥna‿bnišṛab iššāy, gōzi ḥakāli kullᵊ šēˀ.* 10. *w‿ana baḥaḍḍar ilfiṭāṛ, laˀēt innᵊ ma-fīš šāy fi‿lbēt.*

IV. 1. *daxal maktabu‿w huwwa zaɛlān.* 2. *ˀallaha kida‿w humma‿byitmaššu.* 3. *sallimtᵊ ɛalē(h) w‿ana farḥāna.* 4. *xaṛagna w‿mɛāna ɛišrīn ginē(h).* 5. *ṛāḥu Maṣrᵊ ‿w humma lissa‿ṣġayyaṛīn.* 6. *simiɛnāha‿w hiyya bitkallim Ḥasan.* 7. *šufnāhum wi humma‿byitmaššu ɛa‿kkurnīš.* 8. *inḍarab bi‿rruṣāṣ wi huwwa rākib ilɛaṛabiyya‿btaɛtu.* 9. *ˀaṛa‿ggurnāḷ wi huwwa ˀāɛid fi‿lbalakōna.* 10. *ištara‿lɛaṛabiyya di‿w huwwa‿f-ˀUṛubba.*

V.

1a + 3b	2a + 4b	3a + 6b	4a +5b
5a + 8b	6a + 7b	7a + 2b	8a +1b

VI. 1. *min imbāriḥ wi huwwa ɛandu suxuniyya.* 2. *min sanatēn w‿ana baštaġal sawwāˀ.* 3. *min šahrᵊ Māris w‿ana‿f-Maṣr.* 4. *min imbāriḥ iṣṣubḥᵊ w‿ana ɛandi ṣudāɛ.* 5. *min sāɛa‿w nuṣṣᵊ w‿ana mistanniyyāki.* 6. *min issāɛa tamanya‿w humma biyitfaṛṛagu ɛa‿ttilivizyōn.* 7. *min talat t-iyyām wi ṃāṃa fi‿lmustašfa.* 8. *min mudda ṭawīla w‿ana baḥāwil atɛallim ilɛaṛabi.* 9. *min talat šuhūr wi humma biyiddaṛṛabu fi‿lxārig.* 10. *min ɛašaṛ sinīn wi‿ḥna saknīn fi‿zZaˀazīˀ.*

VII. 1. *Jane gat Maṣrᵊ min sanatēn.* 2. *ilˀutubīs lissa ma-gāš.* 3. *bukṛa ḥaddīlak ilˀigāṛ.* 4. *iddīni‿lmuftāḥ ya madām!* 5. *taɛāli hina min faḍlik!* 6. *iḍḍiyūf gum imbāriḥ.* 7. *ya-taṛa humma gum walla lissa ma- gūš?* 8. *iddēti Ḥasan ilmuftāḥ lē, ya Maha?* 9. *idditu‿lmuftāḥ wi mišyit.* 10. *ana gayya ḥālan!* 11. *gēti badri kida lē, ya Samya?* 12. *mumkin tiddīni fikra ɛan ilmawḍūɛ da?*

VIII. 1. *laˀ, ma-fhimnāš wala kilma.* 2. *laˀ, ma-ɛandīš ˀayyᵊ fikra.* 3. *laˀ, miš ḥassa‿b-ˀayyᵊ ˀalam.* 4. *laˀ, ma-fīš wala tuffāḥa.* 5. *laˀ, ma-mɛayīš wala‿sgāṛa.* 6. *laˀ, ma-ɛandīš wala badla.* 7. *laˀ, ma-fihāš wala šibbāk.* 8. *laˀ, ma-mɛayīš ˀayyᵊ tazākir.*9. *laˀ, ma-fīš wala šaˀˀa faḍya.* 10. *laˀ, ma-ɛandināš ˀayyᵊ‿drūs.* 11. *laˀ, ma-fīš wala mutusikl.* 12. *laˀ, ma-ḥasalitšᵊ ˀayyᵊ gaṛāyim.*

IX. 1. *ṭabɛan, iddā(h) ilˀigāṛ.* 2. *ṭabɛan, idditu‿lmuftāḥ.* 3. *ṭabɛan, ḥawarrīha‿lbalad.*4. *ṭabɛan, warrāhum Xān ilXalīli.* 5. *ṭabɛan,* *salliftu‿lkitāb bitāɛi ~ ktābi.* 6. *ṭabɛan, fahhimtu‿lmawḍūɛ.* 7. *ṭabɛan, nawiltu‿lmalḫ.* 8. *ṭabɛan, ḫasallifu‿lmīt ginē(h).* 9. *ṭabɛan, ɛallimnāhum illuġa‿lɛaṛabiyya.* 10. *ṭabɛan, sallimnā(h) mafatīḫ ilmaktab.* 11. *ṭabɛan, warrethum ilmaktaba.* 12. *ṭabɛan, iddenā(h) ilfilūs.*

X. 1. *ṛawwaḫu‿mbāriḫ bi‿llēl mitʾaxxaṛ šuwayya.* 2. *fataḫit ittilivizyōn ɛašān tišūf našrit ilʾaxbāṛ.* 3. *itfaṛṛagna ɛala nafs ilfilmᵊ fi‿ttilivizyōn imbāriḫ.* 4. *iddīni‿lmuftāḫ bitāɛ ilɛaṛabiyya law samaḫt!* 5. *ya Maḫmūd fūt ɛalēna wi‿nta ṛāyiḫ iššuġl!* 6. *ḍarabū(h) bi‿rruṣāṣ wi huwwa rākib ilɛaṛabiyya.* 7. *kān ɛandi nafs ilʾalam min šahr.* 8. *lāzim tiɛmil ɛamaliyyit izzayda‿f aʾṛab waʾt.* 9. *yimkin nisāfir Aswān baɛdᵊ bukṛa.* 10. *ibni wiʾiɛ wi‿tkasarit riglu.*

XI. 1. *kān ɛāwiz yirūḫ yigīb ilʾawlād bi-nafsu.* 2.*issawwāʾ, ma-gaṛalūš ḫāga‿lḫamdu li‿llāh.* 3.*iḫna ɛawzīn nitfaṛṛag ɛa‿ttilivizyōn dilwaʾti!* 4. *ma-fīš wala bintᵊ ~ bintᵊ waḫda fi‿lfaṣl.* 5. *min iṣṣubḫᵊ‿w (ana) ɛandi ṣudāɛ.* 6. *ana ḫāsis bi-ʾalam šidīd fi-riglayya.* 7.*abūya ~ ḅaḅāya māt w‿ana fi‿lxārig.* 8. *kān maɛāya talatīn ginē(h).* 9. *ištara kitabēn w‿ddāhum li-Layla.* 10. *ilfilūs, ḫaġayyaṛha‿lʾusbūɛ iggayy. ~ ḫaġayyaṛ ilfilūs ilʾusbūɛ iggayy.* 11. *iṭṭiflᵊ kān ɛandu suxuniyya.* 12. *ilbulōfaṛ da, miš ḫaštirihūlik ya Samya! ~ miš ḫaštirīlik ilbulōfaṛ da ya Samya!* 13. *maɛadna, ma-tinsahūš ya Ḫasan!* 14. *kunti fēn ya Maha? ma-šuftikīš min zamān!* 15. *lāzim ašūf našrit ilʾaxbāṛ kullᵊ yōm.* 16. *ilbulīs kān biydawwaṛ ɛalē fi-kullᵊ makān lākin ma-laʾahūš.* 17. *kānu ʾaɛdīn fi‿lbēt wi‿ddinya bitmaṭṭar baṛṛa.* 18. *Ṭāriʾ ma-kansᵊ lu(h) nifsᵊ fi‿lʾakl.* 19. *ilbulīs gih yisʾal ɛan ~ ɛala Aḫmad wi Ṭāriʾ.* 20. *daxalit wi‿f ʾidha‿ktāb.*

LESSON XIV

I. 1. *lā, fī waraʾa waḫda kamān.* 2. *lā, fī burtuʾāna waḫda kamān.* 3. *lā, fī baṣala ~ baṣalāya waḫda kamān.* 4. *lā, fī baṭaṭsāya waḫda kamān.* 5. *lā, fī moza ~ mozāya waḫda kamān.* 6. *lā, fī ʾuṭāya waḫda kamān.* 7. *lā, fī samaka waḫda kamān.* 8. *lā, fī lamūna waḫda kamān.* 9. *lā, fī bēḍa ~ beḍāya waḫda kamān.*

II. 1. *lā, kaltᵊ mōza waḫda bass.* 2. *lā, kaltᵊ mangāya waḫda bass.* 3. *lā, kaltᵊ burtuʾāna waḫda bass.* 4. *lā, kaltᵊ bēḍa waḫda bass.* 5. *lā, kaltᵊ ṭamaṭmāya waḫda bass.* 6. *lā, xadtᵊ lamūna waḫda bass.* 7. *lā, xadtᵊ warda waḫda bass.* 8. *lā, kaltᵊ baṭaṭsāya waḫda bass.* 9. *lā, xadtᵊ waraʾa waḫda bass.*

III. 1. *xamas lamunāt wi kamān sitta yibʾu ḫidāšaṛ lamūna.* 2. *aṛbaɛ naxlāt wi kamān tamanya yibʾu‿tnāšaṛ naxla.* 3. *sabaɛ baʾaṛāt wi kamān baʾaṛa yibʾu taman baʾaṛāt.* 4. *sittᵊ samakāt wi kamān sabɛa yibʾu talattāšaṛ samaka.* 5. *taman šagaṛāt wi kamān sabɛa yibʾu xamastāšaṛ šagaṛa.* 6. *sittᵊ beḍāt wi kamān tisɛa yibʾu xamastāšaṛ bēḍa.* 7. *aṛbaɛ baṣalāt wi kamān baṣaltēn yibʾu sittᵊ baṣalāt.*

IV. 1. *yaɛni kām lamūna bi‿ẓẓabṭ?* 2. *yaɛni kām baʾaṛa bi‿ẓẓabṭ?* 3. *yaɛni kām samaka bi‿ẓẓabṭ?* 4. *yaɛni kām mōza bi‿ẓẓabṭ?* 5. *yaɛni kām šagaṛa bi‿ẓẓabṭ?* 6. *yaɛni kām warda bi‿ẓẓabṭ?* 7.*yaɛni kām burtuʾāna bi‿ẓẓabṭ?* 8. *yaɛni kām bēḍa bi‿ẓẓabṭ?*

V. 1. *lā, ma-fīš aktaṛ min šagartēn talāta.* 2. *lā, ma-fīš aktaṛ min samaktēn talāta.* 3. *lā, ma-fīš aktaṛ min baṣaltēn talāta.* 4. *lā, ma-fīš aktaṛ min mangitēn talāta.* 5. *lā, ma-fīš aktaṛ min baʾaṛtēn talāta.* 6. *lā, ma-fīš aktaṛ min baṭaṭsitēn talāta.* 7. *lā, ma-fīš aktaṛ min beḍtēn talāta.* 8. *lā, ma-fīš aktaṛ min lamuntēn talāta.*

VI. 1. *balāš manga baʾa!* 2. *balāš ʾūṭa baʾa!* 3. *balāš baṭāṭis baʾa!* 4. *balāš mōz baʾa!* 5. *balāš lamūn baʾa!* 6. *balāš wardᵊ baʾa!* 7. *balāš samak baʾa!* 8. *balāš ṭamāṭim baʾa!*

VII. 1. *baħibb ilward.* 2. *baṭṭixa waħda‿kfāya ʾawi.* 3. *iddīni kamān šuwayyit ṛuzz!* 4. *ilburtuʾān ġāli‿lyomēn dōl.* 5. *iddīni xamas beḍāt min faḍlak!* 6. *ma-fīš aktaṛ min iṣṣabūn hina.* 7. *ana ɛawza talat baṣalāt.* 8. *iddīni kām ʾuṭāya law samaħt!* 9. *ma-fīš ġēr moztēn itnēn.* 10. *maɛāk kām samaka, ya‿btāɛ issamak?* 11. *ɛawzīn šuwayyit waraʾ min faḍlak.* 12. *ɛišrīn warda‿kfāya ʾawi.* 13. *ma-baħibbiš ilbaṭāṭis, baṭaṭsāya waħda‿kfāya ʾawi.* 14. *da fallāħ faʾīr, ɛandu baʾaṛa waħda bass.*

VIII. 1. *ilmōz lōnu ʾaṣfar, yaɛni‿lmōza di ṣafra barḍu.* 2. *iṭṭamāṭim lonha ʾaħmaṛ, yaɛni‿ṭṭamaṭmāya di ħamṛa barḍu.* 3. *ilbaṭṭīx lōnu ʾaħmaṛ, yaɛni‿lbaṭṭīxa di ħamṛa barḍu.* 4. *ilwaraʾ da lōnu ʾabyaḍ, yaɛni‿lwaraʾa di bēḍa barḍu.* 5. *ilbēḍ da lōnu ʾabyaḍ, yaɛni‿lbēḍa di bēḍa barḍu.* 6. *ilbaʾaṛ lōnu ʾiswid, yaɛni‿lbaʾaṛa di sōda barḍu.* 7. *issamak da lōnu ʾazraʾ, yaɛni‿ssamaka di zarʾa barḍu.* 8. *ilmanga lonha burtuʾāni, yaɛni‿lmangāya di burtuʾāni barḍu.*

IX. 1. *laʾ, iddinya ma-kanitšᵊ zaħma ɛa‿kkurnīš.* 2. *laʾ, ma-šufnāš ilɛasākir illi waʾfīn ɛa‿lbāb.* 3. *laʾ, humma miš waxdīn balhum.* 4. *laʾ, Samya ma-bitšufšᵊ‿kwayyis.* 5. *laʾ, iħna ʾaṣlan miš min hina.* 6. *laʾ, ilwafdᵊ miš ħayɛaddi min iššāriɛ da.* 7. *dōl, la ~ miš ẓubbāṭ wala ɛasākir.* 8. *laʾ, humma miš masʾulīn ɛan ilmašruɛāt di.* 9. *ma-fīš la ɛīd ~ la fī ɛīd wala mūlid innahaṛda.* 10. *ikkitāb da la‿kwayyis wala wiħiš.* 11. *di, la‿mṛātu wala bintu.* 12. *laʾ, ilmudarris miš ħayišṛaħ iddarsᵊ da kamān maṛṛa.* 13. *laʾ, iħna miš samɛīn ʾayy aṣwat ġarība. ~ iṣṣōṭ ilġarīb da.* 14. *laʾ, ma-fīš la ʾaklᵊ wala šurbᵊ fi‿lħafla.*

X. 1. *la ɛawza mōz wala manga.* 2. *la gibt ilbaṣal wala‿ṭṭamāṭim.* 3. *la‿mɛāya ʾalam wala waraʾa.* 4. *la ɛawzīn kabrīt wala wallāɛa.* 5. *la ħayīgi bukṛa wala baɛdu.* 6. *la ɛandina zēt wala sukkaṛ.* 7. *Samīr la‿tnaʾal wala ɛazzil.* 8. *da, la Ħasan wala Samīr.* 9. *la tinzil wala‿trūħ issūʾ.* 10. *la‿ddētu‿lmuftāħ wala‿ rruxṣa.* 11. *la laʾetha ɛand ilfakahāni wala ɛand ilxuḍari.* 12. *ilfustān la wāsiɛ wala dayyaʾ ɛalayya.*

XI.

1a + 3	2a + 5	3a + 6	4a + 7
5a + 4	6a + 8	7a + 1	8a + 2

XII. 1. *laʾ, nisīt agibha.* 2. *laʾ, lākin ħawlit tidfaɛu.* 3. *laʾ, nisīna nimlāha.* 4. *laʾ, lākin ħawilna nittiṣil bī(h).* 5. *laʾ, nisīt aɛallim ɛalēha.* 6. *laʾ, lākin ħawilt aħkihalhum.* 7. *laʾ, nisīna nitfaṛṛag ɛalē(h).* 8. *laʾ, lākin ħawilt aɛmilu.* 9. *laʾ, nisīna‿nɛaddi ɛalēhum.* 10. *laʾ, lākin ħawilt afhamu.*

XIII. 1. *sibha‿trūħ ilxārig li-waħdaha!* 2. *xallīna niɛmil iššuġlᵊ‿w ṛawwaħ inta!* 3. *sibni ʾaʾūl ill‿ana ɛawzu!* 4. *xallīhum yiktibu‿ggawabāt kullaha!* 5. *ma-tsibhāš tištiri‿lħagāt ilwiħša di!* 6. *xallīni aštaġal bi-hudūʾ!* 7. *ma-txallinīš azɛal minnak!* 8. *xallīha‿tgīb ikkutub maɛāha!* 9. *ma-tsibhūš yuxrug li-waħdu bi‿llēl!* 10. *sibtaha‿tfattaħ wi‿tʾaffil fi‿ššababīk zayyᵊ ma hiyya ɛawza.*

XIV. 1. *bāyin ɛalēku taɛbanīn šuwayya.* 2. *kān ɛandaha ṣudāɛ imbāriħ.* 3. *mumkin ħaḍritak tifukkili mīt ginē(h)?* 4. *ilħāga kullaha ġilyit kida lē?* 5. *kīlu‿lʾūṭa tamanu tisɛīn ʾirš.* 6. *xaragt atfassaħ šuwayya innahada‿ṣṣubħ.* 7. *baɛdᵊ ma wiṣil ilwafdᵊ ṛāħ ʾAṣrᵊ ɛAbdīn ɛala ṭūl.* 8. *kānu ɛawzīn yištiru nafs ilɛaṛabiyya.* 9. *ma-banamšᵊ xāliṣ bi‿llēl.* 10. *baštaġal hina baʾāli sabaɛ sinīn.* 11. *bāyin ɛalēk fiɛlan ɛayyān.* 12. *iddinya kānit ~ kānit iddinya zaħma ʾawi ɛala‿kkurnēš.* 13. *yaretna ma-safirna‿mbāriħ!* 14. *kānu ɛawzīn yiʾaggaṛu* šaᵓᵓa mafrūša. 15. iṛṛāgil da ɛumrina ma-šufnā(h). 16. mumkin nīgi‿nšūf ilfaršᵊ bukṛa? 17. ana muntaẓir ḫaḍritik bukṛa‿ssāɛa sabɛa. 18. waḷḷāhi ma‿na ṛāyiḫ ilḫafla!

XV. 1. sābu‿bnuhum yisāfir li-waḫdu. 2. Maṣrᵊ ma‿lhāš ɛilaqāt iqtiṣādiyya maɛa baladkum. 3. ilbaṭāṭis ġilyit ᵓawi‿lyomēn dōl. 4. illi wāxid bardᵊ miš lāzim yirūḫ iššuġl ~ yištaġal. 5. iṛṛaᵓīs gi(h) Asyūṭ bi-munasbit ilᵓaɛyād. 6. xallīni aɛmillak fingān ᵓahwa! 7. ya‿Mḫammad, ma-tinsāš tidfaɛ ilḫisāb! 8. ma-fīš ġēr tuffaḫa waḫda fi‿ttallāga. 9. nisīt aᵓullak ḫāga muhimma. 10. kān fī zaḫma zayyᵊ ma‿tkūn ḫāga ḫaṣalit. 11. ɛumri ma-šuftᵊ ḫāga zayyᵊ di! 12. yaretni ma-ruḫt ilḫafla‿mbāriḫ! 13. ma-txallinīš azɛal minnak! 14. ilmabāḫis bitdawwaṛ fi‿lbalad ɛala‿lgamaɛāt ilmutaṭarrifa. 15. ma-ɛandināš maṭār fi-baladna la‿kbīr wala‿ṣġayyar. 16. yaretni ma‿štarēt ilbēt ilᵓadīm da! 17. ilwazīr la ᵓābil ilwafd ilᵓiṭāli wala‿lwafd ilingilīzi. 18. ana la biɛtᵊ bēti wala‿štarēt bēt gidīd.

LESSON XV

I. 1. iza kuntᵊ ɛāwiz baṭṭīxa‿kwayyisa, lāzim tibɛat Hāni‿ssūᵓ! 2. iza kānit Maṣrᵊ ɛawza‿tṣaddar ilxuḍrawāt, lāzim tiḫassin nawɛiyyit ilᵓintāg. 3. iza kuntᵊ‿tḫibbᵊ‿tfāṣil, lāzim tikūn šāṭir! 4. iza kuntᵊ ḫāsis bi-ᵓalam fi-baṭnak, xalli‿dduktūr yikšif ɛalēk! 5. iza kān ɛandak iltihāb fi‿zzayda, lāzim tiɛmil ɛamaliyya ɛala ṭūl! 6. iza ma-kuntiš lāᵓi ṭamāṭim fi‿ssūᵓ, rūḫ izZamālik! 7. iza kānit Maha ɛawza tinzil issūᵓ, lāzim tāxud taks. 8. iza‿nzilt issūᵓ badri, ḫatlāᵓi xuḍār ṭāza! 9. iza kuntu ɛawzīn tigaddidu‿lᵓiqāma, lāzim tirūḫu‿lMugammaɛ! 10. iza ḫabbēt tišūf našrit ilᵓaxbāṛ, lāzim tiftaḫ ittilivizyōn dilwaᵓti!

II. 1. law kunti nadahti‿lmunādi ma-kanitš ilɛaṛabiyya‿tsaraᵓit. 2. law ma-kuntūš sibtu‿ššanṭa maftūḫa ma-kanitš ilɛaṛabiyya‿tsaraᵓit. 3. law kuntᵊ sibtaha fi‿ggaṛāž ma-kanitš ilɛaṛabiyya‿tsaraᵓit. 4. law kunti rakantīha‿f-mawᵓaf tāni ma-kanitš ilɛaṛabiyya‿tsaraᵓit. 5. law kuntu‿ddētu‿lmunādi‿lmuftāḫ ma-kanitš ilɛaṛabiyya‿tsaraᵓit. 6. law kuntᵊ ᵓafalt ilbāb bi‿lmuftāḫ ma-kanitš ilɛaṛabiyya‿tsaraᵓit. 7. law ma-kuntiš rakantaha ɛa‿nnaṣya ma-kanitš ilɛaṛabiyya‿tsaraᵓit. 8. law ma-kanš iggaṛāž maftūḫ ma-kanitš ilɛaṛabiyya‿tsaraᵓit. 9. law ma-kuntiš rigiɛtᵊ mitᵓaxxaṛ ma-kanitš ilɛaṛabiyya‿tsaraᵓit. 10. law kuntᵊ šilt ilbaṭṭariyya ma-kanitš ilɛaṛabiyya‿tsaraᵓit.

III. 1. law kān ɛandi‿flūs kunt ištarēt ɛaṛabiyya‿gdīda. 2. law kān iggawwᵊ ḫilw, kunna safirna‿skindiriyya. 3. law kān Willy biyikkallim ilɛaṛabi‿kwayyis, ma-kanšᵊ ḫaṣal sūᵓ tafāhum. 4. law ma-kanšᵊ fī munādi, ma-kuntiš rakant ilɛaṛabiyya hina. 5. law kānit ilmaktaba fatḫa‿nnahaṛda, kuntᵊ ġayyaṛt ilkutub. 6. law kān ɛandi waᵓt, kuntᵊ gēt maɛāk. 7. law ma-kanšᵊ fī mitru, ma-kunnāš ᵓidirna‿nrūḫ ilMaɛādi. 8. law ma-kanšᵊ fī mawᵓaf ɛaṛabiyyāt, ma-kuntiš nizilt ilbalad bi‿lɛaṛabiyya. 9. law ma-kanšᵊ fī šuġl, kuntᵊ ᵓaɛadtᵊ fi‿lbēt innahaṛda. 10. law ma-kuntīš ittaṣalti biyya, kuntᵊ‿nsīt ilmaɛād bitaɛna.

IV. 1. wāḍiḫ inn ilᵓutubīs lissa ma-gāš. 2. ġarība ᵓinnaha kānit li-waḫdaha. 3. ḍarūri‿tfaṛṛagna ɛala kullᵊ ḫāga. 4. ɛagība ᵓinnᵊ kull ilᵓuwaḍ maḫgūza. 5. ṣaḫīḫ innuku ḫatsafru‿mɛāna? 6. bāyin (inn) ilmaḫallāt fatḫa bi‿llēl. 7. lāzim yimsiku kull ilmugrimīn. 8. yiẓhar (inn) Faṭma ma-gatš innahaṛda. 9. mamnūɛ tīgi min ġēr taṣrīḫ. 10. ma‿yṣaḫḫiš tirgaɛu min issafaṛ min ġēr hadāya.

V. 1. *ṃāṃa ʕawzāna nuʔʕud dilwaʔti.* 2. *abūha kān ʕawizha tiggawwiz.* 3. *Samya kānit ʕawzāni ʔāxud ilfilūs di‿mʕāya.* 4. *ana kuntᵊ fakrāki ṣaḫbit ilbēt.* 5. *iftakaṛtak ma-bitḫibbiš iššukulāṭa.* 6. *ana ʕāwiz ilʕaṛabiyya titġisil.* 7. *kānu fakrinni miš mawgūd.* 8. *ilmudīr ʕawizni ʔāxud ʔagāza.* 9. *ḅāḅa‿w ṃāṃa ʕawzinni ʔarūḫ ilmadrasa.* 10. *iḫna ʕawzīnik tiṭbuxi dilwaʔti.*

VI.

(il)kīs (il)waraʔ	*(il)sāʕa (id)dahab*
(il)ʔalam (ir)ruṣāṣ	*(il)badla (iṣ)ṣūf*
(iṭ)ṭarīʔ (il)ʔasfalt	*(il)iswira (il)faḍḍa*
(il)mandīl (il)ḫarīr	*(is)sikka (il)ḫadīd*
(iž)žakitta (il)gild	*(it)timsāl (il)ʔalabastaṛ*
(ig)gazma (il)kawitš	*(iṣ)ṣaniyya (in)naḫās*
(il)ʔamīṣ (il)ʔuṭn	*(il)bilūza (in)naylon*

VII. 1. *huwwa da ʔalabastaṛ? ana kuntᵊ ʕāwiz timsāl ʔalabastaṛ! ʔāsif, ittamasīl ilʔalabastaṛ xilṣit!* 2. *huwwa da ṣūf? ana kuntᵊ ʕāwiz bulōfaṛ ṣūf! ʔāsif, ilbulofaṛāt iṣṣūf xilṣit!* 3. *huwwa da ḫarīr? ana kuntᵊ ʕāwiz mandīl ḫarīr! ʔāsif, ilmanadīl ilḫarīr xilṣit!* 4. *huwwa da dahab? ana kuntᵊ ʕāwiz sāʕa dahab! ʔāsif, issaʕāt iddahab itbāʕit!* 5. *huwwa da ʔuṭn? ana kuntᵊ ʕawza‿blūza ʔuṭn! ʔasfa, ilbiluzāt ilʔuṭnᵊ xilṣit!* 6. *huwwa da‿nḫās? iḫna kunna ʕawzīn ṣaniyya‿nḫās! ʔāsif, iṣṣawāni‿nnaḫās kullaha‿tbāʕit!* 7. *huwwa da gild? ana kuntᵊ ʕawza šanṭa gildᵊ ṭabīʕi! ʔāsif, iššunaṭ iggildᵊ xilṣit!* 8. *huwwa da ʔuṭn? ana kuntᵊ ʕawza ʔamīṣ ʔuṭn!ʔasfa, ilʔumṣān ilʔuṭnᵊ xilṣit!*

VIII. 1. *baṭṭal ḍiḫkᵊ ʕa‿nnās!* 2. *balāš ġasīl ilʕaṛabiyya!* 3. *balāš ṭabīx innahaṛda!* 4. *baṭṭal ʔuʕād ʕa‿lʔahāwi!* 5. *balāš sahaṛ illēla!* 6. *baṭṭal ʔakl illuḫūm!* 7. *balāš taʔxīr kullᵊ yōm!* 8. *balāš tanḍīf ilʔuwaḍ innahaṛda!* 9. *balāš fiṣāl fi‿ssūʔ!* 10. *balāš istiʕmāl iddawa da!* 11. *balāš taṣlīḫ ilḫanafiyya!* 12. *balāš dardaša fi‿lfaṣl!*

IX. 1. *wi baʕdᵊ šurb ilʔahwa ḫatiʕmilu ʔē?* 2. *wi baʕdᵊ ġasīl ilʕaṛabiyya ḫatiʕmil ʔē?* 3. *wi baʕdᵊ šawy illaḫma ḫatiʕmilu ʔē?* 4. *wi baʕd ilʔaklᵊ ḫatiʕmilu ʔē?* 5. *wi baʕdᵊ‿zyārit aṣḫabkum ḫatiʕmilu ʔē?* 6. *wi baʕdᵊ taġyīr ilfilūs ḫatiʕmil ʔē?* 7. *wi baʕdᵊ taḫḍīr ilfiṭār ḫatiʕmil ʔē?* 8. *wi baʕdᵊ muʔablit ilwafd ḫatiʕmilu ʔē?* 9. *wi baʕdᵊ dafʕ ilʔigāṛ ḫatiʕmil ʔē?* 10. *wi baʕdᵊ taṣlīḫ ittalāga ḫatiʕmil ʔē?* 11. *wi baʕd ilmuzakra ḫatiʕmil ʔē?*

X. 1. *ilbadla di tamanha kām?* 2. *banṭalōnak iggidīd lōnu ʔē?* 3. *ṣaḫbitik Fawziyya šaklaha ʔē?* 4. *ya Ḫasan, bitḫibbᵊ Samīḫa ʔaddᵊ ʔē?* 5. *ʕarīs Samya ʕumru kām sana?* 6. *iššaʔʔa‿lggidīda ʔigaṛha kām?* 7. *burg ilQāhira ʕuluwwu kām mitr?* 8. *Hiba ṭulha ʔaddᵊ ʔē?* 9. *min hina li‿lbalad ilmasāfa ʔaddᵊ ʔē?* 10. *iṭṭalaba ʕandukum ʕadadhum kām?*

XI. 1. *kuntᵊ ʕāwiz asʔal iza kān Ḫasan mawgūd walla laʔ.* 2. *kuntᵊ ʕāwiz asʔal iza kānit ilʔūṭa gamda walla laʔ.* 3. *kuntᵊ ʕāwiz asʔal iza kān fī ʕanduku baṣal walla laʔ.* 4. *kuntᵊ ʕāwiz asʔal iza kān ilmudīr mawgūd walla laʔ.* 5. *kuntᵊ ʕāwiz asʔal ilmanga ḫilwa walla laʔ.* 7. *kuntᵊ ʕāwiz asʔal iza kunna mumkin ninzil hina walla laʔ.* 8. *kuntᵊ ʕāwiz asʔal iza kuntᵊ tiʔdaṛ tiġsilli‿lʕaṛabiyya walla laʔ.* 9. *kuntᵊ ʕāwiz asʔal iza kān ilʔaṭrᵊ waṣal walla laʔ.*

XII. 1. *iza kunti ʕawza‿tsafri bukṛa, lāzim tiʔūmi min innōm badri.* 2. *iza kuntu ʕawzīn tištiru bēt gidīd, lāzim tibīʕu ilbēt ilʔadīm ilʔawwil.* 3. *iza kuntᵊ ʕāwiz tiʔṛa kutub gidīda, mumkin tirūḫ ilmaktaba.* 4. *iza kuntu ʕaṭšanīn, mumkin tišṛabu ḫāga saʔʕa.* 5. *iza kān Ḫasan ʕāwiz yisāfir bukṛa, lāzim yiḫgiz tazkaṛa fi‿lʔaṭr.* 6. *iza kānit Samya ʕawza tuxrug bi‿llēl, lāzim tilbis bulōvar ṣūf.*

7. *iza kānit Maṣrᵊ ɛawza‿tzawwid iddaxl, lāzim tiḥassin nawɛiyyit ilʾintāg.* 8. *iza kān Samīr ɛāwiz yiɛṛaf ilḥaʾīʾa, lāzim yisʾal Maha.* 9. *iza kunna ɛawzīn niwṣal badri, lāzim nirkab taks.* 10. *iza kānit Karīma ɛawza‿tsāfir, lāzim tuṭlub vīza .*

XIII. 1. *law ma-kunnāš faḍyīn innahaṛda, ma-kunnāš ruḥna‿ssinima.* 2. *law ma-kanšᵊ ḥaṣal ḥādis, ma-kanūš ittaṣalu bi‿lbulīs.* 3. *law kānit iddinya zaḥma‿nnahaṛda, ma-kuntiš itmaššēt ɛa‿lkurnīš.* 4. *law ma-kuntīš ḥassa‿b-ʾalam fi-baṭnik, ma-kuntīš ruḥti li-dduktūr.* 5. *law ma-kuntiš taɛbān ʾawi, kuntᵊ ruḥt iššuġl.* 6. *law ma-kanšᵊ ɛanduku ʾagāza, ma-kuntūš safirtu‿lBaḥr ilʾAḥmaṛ.* 7. *law ma-kunnāš fataḥna‿ttilivizyōn, ma-kunnāš itfaṛṛagna ɛala našrit ilʾaxbāṛ.* 8. *law ma-kānš ilwafdᵊ ɛadda min hina, ma-kunnāš itfaṛṛagna ɛalē(h).* 9. *law kān liyya nifsᵊ fi‿lʾakl, kuntᵊ ʾaɛadtᵊ ɛa‿ssufṛa.* 10. *law kān ɛandu ɛaṛabiyya, kunna rūḥna Sīna.* 11. *law kān ɛandina waʾtᵊ, kunna ruḥna‿lḥafla.* 12. *law kān Aḥmad ḥāgiz makān fi‿lmaṭɛam , kān laʾa ṭarabēza faḍya.* 13. *law ma-kanšᵊ maɛād ilġada ʾaṛṛab, ma-kunnāš ṛawwaḥna.* 14. *law ma-kunnāš binḥibb iṣṣaḥra, ma-kunnāš ištaṛakna fi‿rriḥla.*

XIV. 1. *baʾāli xamas sinīn baštaġal mudarris fi‿sSaɛudiyya.* 2. *kān aḥsan law kuntu gētu badri‿šwayya.* 3. *iza kunti‿tḥibbi‿tšūfi‿lmudīr, lāzim tistanni‿šwayya.* 4. *ḥāxud iššaʾʾa di, iza kān ʾigaṛha maɛʾūl.* 5. *lolāk ma-kunnāš ɛirifna niɛmil ʾē.* 6. *law kān ɛandina muḥaḍrāt, kunna ruḥna‿lkulliyya.* 7. *aẓunn inn isSadd ilɛāli muhimmᵊ bi‿nnisba‿l-Maṣr.* 8. *Fawziyya‿štarit imbāriḥ gazma‿w šanṭa gildᵊ ḥilwīn.* 9. *issufun bitmurrᵊ min qanāt isSuwēs baɛdᵊ dafɛ irrusūm.*

XV. 1. *iddēt ilbawwāb muftāḥ iššaʾʾa.* 2. *ma-tiddihulhum!* 3. *ɛāwiz awarrīhum ~ afarraghum ilmaktaba.* 4. *imta ḥatraggaɛli‿lfilūs illi salliftahālak?* 5. *la‿mɛāya‿lbasbōṛ bitāɛi wala‿rruxṣa‿btaɛti.* 6. *šaṛaḥlina mawḍūɛ kān gidīd ɛalēna.* 7. *la‿štara‿lxuḍār wala ṭabaxu.* 8. *law kān ɛandi waʾtᵊ kuntᵊ zurtukum ~ zurtak ~ zurtik.* 9. *kānit iddinya ḥaṛṛᵊ giddan w‿iḥna‿f-Aswān.* 10. *la‿na‿ɛṛafha wala hiyya tiɛṛafni. ~ la‿na‿ɛarifha ~ ɛarfāha wala hiyya ɛarfani.* 11. *lamma yirgaɛ Samīr min ilKuwēt ḥayiggawwiz Hiba.* 12. *ilʾumṣān ilʾuṭn aḥsan ḥāga fi‿lḥaṛṛᵊ da.* 13. *iza kān ilʾaṣansēr ɛaṭlān lāzim niṭlaɛ issalālim ɛala riglēna.* 14. *law ma-kanitšᵊ Maṣrᵊ banit fanādiʾ arxaṣ ma-kanūš issuwwāḥ gum.* 15. *law kānit ilɛaṛabiyya‿tṣallaḥit ma-kanš ilḥādis ḥaṣal.*

LESSON XVI

I. 1. *irkab ʾayyᵊ ʾutubīs min ilʾutubisāt!* 2. *ilbis ʾayyᵊ badla min ilbidal!* 3. *xudu ʾayyᵊ dawa min ilʾadwiya!* 4. *irkabu ʾayyᵊ ɛaṛabiyya min ilɛaṛabiyyāt!* 5. *iftaḥ ʾayyᵊ baku min ilbakuwāt! ~ ilbawāki!* 6. *xuššᵊ ʾayyᵊ ṣaydaliyya min iṣṣaydaliyyāt!* 7. *isʾal ʾayyᵊ ɛaskari min ilɛasākir!* 8. *ʾaggaru ʾayyᵊ šaʾʾa min iššuʾaʾ!* 9. *nām fi ʾayyᵊ ʾōḍa min ilʾuwaḍ!* 10. *rūḥ ʾayyᵊ madrasa min ilmadāris!*

II. 1. *iḥna miš ɛarfīn nāxud ʾanhu ʾutubīs.* 2. *ya-taṛa, ʾanhi ɛaṛabiyya ʾarxaṣ?* 3. *ɛawzīn titkallimu maɛa ʾanhu ~ ʾanhi ṭalaba?* 4. *ḥatirkabu ʾanhu ʾaṭr?* 5. *ya Sāmi, nifsak tišūf ʾanhu film?* 6. *intu‿xtartu‿lmaṭɛam ʾanhū?* 7. *ḥatrūḥ ginent‿ilḥayawanāt maɛa ʾanhu ~ ʾanhi ʾawlād?* 8. *Ḥasan miš ɛārif lāzim yištaġal fi ʾanhi madrasa.* 9. *ɛawzīn tištiru ʾanhi taṛabēẓa?* 10. *ʾarētu ʾanhi kutub?*

III. 1. *ɛAli sākin gambᵊ Maḥmūd yaɛni humma litnēn saknīn gambᵊ baɛḍ.* 2. *Samya gat maɛa Samīra yaɛni humma litnēn gum maɛa baɛḍ.* 3. *Aḥmad* *kān biyitɛašša maɛa Maḥmūd yaɛni humma litnēn kānu‿byitɛaššu maɛa baɛḍ. 4. Samīr ʔābil Muḥammad ɛa‿ssalālim yaɛni humma litnēn ʔablu baɛḍ ɛa‿ssalālim. 5. ana ḥašūfak baɛd^{ə} bukṛa yaɛni‿ḥna litnēn ḥanšūf baɛḍ baɛd^{ə} bukṛa. 6. Fikri‿ biyfahhim ɛAli wi ɛAli‿biyfahhim Fikri yaɛni humma‿litnēn biyfahhimu baɛḍ. 7. Maḥmūd ṛāḥ ilMugammaɛ, wi Sayyid ṛāḥ maɛā(h) yaɛni humma litnēn ṛāḥu maɛa baɛḍ. 8. Sayyid biyidris wi Badr^{ə}‿byidris maɛā(h) yaɛni humma‿litnēn biyidrisu maɛa baɛḍ. 9. Maha xadit ɛala Sanāʔ wi Sanāʔ xadit ɛala Maha yaɛni humma‿litnēn xadu ɛala baɛḍ. 10. ilfustān da zayy ilfustān da yaɛni humma litnēn zayy^{ə} baɛḍ. 11. huwwa ɛagabha w‿hiyya ɛagabitu yaɛni humma litnēn ɛagabu baɛḍ. 12. imbāriḥ kalna samak wi ʔawwil imbāriḥ kamān yaɛni yomēn waṛa baɛḍ^{ə} samak.*

IV. 1. *iššanṭa di, ana miš šayfa šanṭa ġerha.* 2. *ilmaḥallāt di, ana miš ɛarfa maḥallāt ġerha.* 3. *da‿bni wi di binti, ma-ɛandīš awlād ġerhum.* 4. *yiẓhar gēna badri ʔawi, ma-fīš ġerna fi‿lmaktab.* 5. *ana ʔuxtu‿lwaḥīda, wi ma-lūš ġēri.* 6. *intu samɛinni, lākin ma-ḥaddiš ġerkum samiɛni.* 7. *ana ɛāwiz aštiri‿lkutub di bass, miš ɛāwiz aštiri kutub ġerha.* 8. *inta ṣadīqi‿lwaḥīd, ma-līš ṣadīq ġērak.* 9. *issikirtēra di‿kwayyisa, miš ɛawzīn sikirtēra ġerha.* 10. *ahum dōl iṭṭalaba‿btuɛna, ma-ɛandināš ṭalaba ġerhum.* 11. *ittilivizyōn da miš ḥilw^{ə} lākin ma-ɛandināš tilivizyon ġēru.* 12. *inti ʔuxti‿w ḥabibti‿w ma-līš ġērik fi‿ddunya.* 13. *ilʔummiyya hiyya sabab ilmašākil di, ma-fīš ġerha.* 14. *maɛād ilfaṛaḥ itḥaddid, miš binfakkaṛ fi maɛād ġēru.* 15. *faḍillina šahrēn bass, ma-fīš ġerhum.*

V. 1. *ma-ɛandīš ġēr xamsa‿gnē(h).* 2. *ma-šuftūš illa maṛṛa waḥda.* 3. *ma-ɛagabnīš ġēr ilbulōvar da.* 4. *ma-ɛanduhumš ġēr ilmudēl da.* 5. *ma-bnaxudš^{ə} ʔagāza ġēr fi‿ṣṣēf.* 6. *miš ɛawzīn ġēr salamtak.* 7. *ma-rkabš illa taks^{ə} fāḍi.* 8. *ilḥagāt di miš mawgūda ġēr ɛandina.* 9. *ilmaṭar ma-byinzilš ɛandina ʔilla fi‿ššita.* 10. *ma-ʔaɛadš^{ə}‿f-Maṣr illa sanatēn.* 11. *miš ḥakūn fi-Maṣr illa yomēn.* 12. *ma-baktibš illa bi‿lʔalam ilḥibr.*

VI. 1. *lamma daxalt ilḥammām laʔēt ilmayya maʔṭūɛa.* 2. *lamma‿btadēt aḥaḍḍar ilfiṭār, gaṛas ilbāb ḍarab.* 3. *lamma ḥabbēt aɛmil fingān ʔahwa, ma-laʔets^{ə} bunn^{ə} fi‿lbēt.* 4. *lamma ʔaɛadt afṭar, ibtada gaṛas ittilifōn yirinn.* 5. *lamma ruḥt^{ə} maktab iggawazāt kān ilmuẓẓaf ġāyib.* 6. *lamma ḥabbēt awallaɛ innūr ma-kanš^{ə} fī kahṛaba.* 7. *lamma xaṛagt^{ə} mi‿lbēt kānit iddinya bitmaṭṭar.* 8. *lamma‿rkibt ilʔaṭr^{ə} ma-laʔetš^{ə} fī ʔamākin faḍya.* 9. *lamma zurtaha fi‿lmustašfa kānit uxti ɛamla ɛamaliyya.* 10. *lamma‿nzilt issūʔ laʔēt ilmaḥallāt bitiʔfil.*

VII. *baɛd^{ə} ma‿ṣḥa‿ṣṣubḥ barūḥ ilḥammām – baɛd^{ə} ma‿rūḥ ilḥammām bāxud dušš – baɛd^{ə} m‿āxud dušš^{ə} baġsil sināni – baɛd^{ə} ma‿ġsil sināni babtidi albis hidūmi – baɛd^{ə} ma‿lbis hidūmi baḥaḍḍar ilfiṭār – baɛd^{ə} ma‿ḥaḍḍar ilfiṭār bafṭar – baɛd^{ə} ma‿fṭar barūḥ iššuġl – baɛd^{ə} ma‿rūḥ iššuġl^{ə} bašṛab šāy – baɛd^{ə} ma‿šṛab šāy baʔṛa‿ggurnāl – baɛd^{ə} m‿aʔṛa‿ggurnāl baktib šuwayyit gawabāt*

VIII. *baɛd^{ə} ma‿ṣḥīt iṣṣubḥ^{ə} ruḥt ilḥammām – baɛd^{ə} ma‿ruḥt ilḥammām xadt^{ə} dušš – baɛd^{ə} ma‿xadt dušš ġasalt^{ə}‿snāni – baɛd^{ə} ma‿ġasalt^{ə}‿snāni ibtadēt albis hidūmi – baɛd^{ə} ma‿lbist^{ə}‿hdūmi ḥaḍḍart ilfiṭār – baɛd^{ə} ma‿ḥaḍḍart ilfiṭār fiṭirt –baɛd^{ə} ma‿fṭirt ruḥt iššuġl –baɛd^{ə} ma‿ruḥt iššuġl širibt^{ə} šāy –baɛd^{ə} ma‿šṛibt šāy ʔarēt iggurnāl –baɛd^{ə} ma‿ʔarēt iggurnāl katabt iggawabāt*

IX. 1. *awwil ma‿ṣḥīt min innōm ḥassēt bi-ṣudāɛ šidīd.* 2. *dawwaṛt^{ə} ɛala‿sbirīna ʔaxudha ɛašān yixiff iṣṣudāɛ šuwayya, lākin ma-kanš^{ə} fī wala‿sbirināya fi‿lbēt.* 3. *baɛd^{ə} ma xadt^{ə} dušš, ḥassēt inni ʔaḥsan bi-ktīr.* 4. *fiṭirt^{ə} wi‿nzilt^{ə}*

mi‿lbēt. rikibt ilꜥaṛabiyya‿btaꜥti‿w lamma ḥabbēt aftaḥ ilkuntakt laʾēt ilbaṭariyya faḍya. 5. kullᵊ ma‿šaġġal ilmutūr yirūḥ wāʾif ꜥala ṭūl. 6. ṭalabtᵊ mi‿lbawwāb yizuʾʾili‿lꜥaṛabiyya‿lḥaddᵊ ma ʾāmit wi‿lḥamdu lillāh. 7. ꜥand ilkubri‿lꜥilwi ibtada ilmutūr yisxan, fa-daxaltᵊ‿šmāl maꜥa ʾinnᵊ da kān mamnūꜥ. 8. wi badal ma‿ꜥaddiꜥala‿tTaḥrīr futtᵊ ꜥala Gardin Siti. 9. lamma‿wṣiltᵊ ʾaxīṛan šuġli kānit issāꜥa tisꜥa. 10. yaꜥni min sāꜥit ma‿nziltᵊ min ilbēt liġāyit ma‿wṣilt ilmaktab kān fāt aktaṛ min sāꜥa‿w nuṣṣ.

X. 1. xallaṣ iššuġlᵊ ʾablᵊ ma‿tṛawwaḥ! 2. xud dušš ʾablᵊ ma‿tḥaddaṛ ilfiṭār! 3. itġadda ʾablᵊ ma‿tnām! 4. ilbis hidūmak ʾablᵊ ma tiꜥmil iššāy! 5. ifṭar ʾablᵊ ma‿trūḥ iššuġl! 6. ʾiʾṛa‿ggurnāl ʾablᵊ ma titfaṛṛag ꜥa‿ttilivizyōn! 7. iġsil sinānak ʾablᵊ ma tāxud dušš! 8. itꜥašša ʾablᵊ ma tirgaꜥ ilbēt! 9. ḥaḍḍar ilġada ʾablᵊ ma tinzil issūʾ! 10. waṣṣal Suꜥād ʾablᵊ ma‿tṛawwaḥ! 11. rūḥ li‿lmudīr ʾablᵊ ma‿tiktib iggawabāt! 12. iꜥmil ṣuwar ʾablᵊ ma‿tgīb ilistimāṛa!

XI. 1. ʾawwil ma wiṣil ilʾutubīs rikibna ꜥala ṭūl. 2. maꜥa ʾinni kuntᵊ taꜥbān, ruḥt atmašša ꜥa‿kkurnēš. 3. zayyᵊ ma‿nta ꜥārif, ilmurūr‿f Maṣr ṣaꜥb. 4. biyigru‿b-surꜥa zayyᵊ ma‿ykūnu mistaꜥgilīn. 5. ya Ḥasan, gahhiz ilfiṭār ʾablᵊ ma tinzil issūʾ!6. min yōm ma‿ggawwizu‿w humma saknīn fi‿gGīza. 7. imši‿lġāyit ma tiwṣal li-ʾāxir‿iššāriꜥ! 8. min sāꜥit ma wiṣil ma-baṭṭalšᵊ kalām. 9. ʾawwil ma šafni gih yisallim ꜥalayya. 10. kullᵊ ma‿sʾalu‿ssuʾāl da wiššu yiḥmarr.

XII. 1. maꜥa ʾinnᵊ kān ꜥandi ṣudāꜥ ibtadēt aštaġal. 2. lamma yirgaꜥ Samīr mi‿lKuwēt ḥayiggawwiz Samya. 3. kānit iddinya ḥarrᵊ ʾawi lamma kunna ~ wi‿ḥna‿f Aṣwān. 4. marr ilwafdᵊ ʾablᵊ ma‿wṣal midān itTaḥrīr. 5. (tiḥibb) tišrab ʾē? –miš muhimmᵊ ya šāy ya ʾahwa. 6. ittaꜥlīm aṣbaḥ igbāri ꜥala gamīꜥ ilmuwaṭinīn. 7. Samya miš ꜥawza tiggawwiz liʾannaha lissa‿ṣġayyara. 8. baꜥdᵊ ma‿xallaṣ diṛasti fi‿lmadrasa ḥaxušš iggamꜥa. 9. fiḍlit ilbint mistanniyya‿lġāyit ma nadahha‿lʾustāz. ~ liġāyit ma‿lʾustāz ʾallaha tudxul. 10. ya Faṭma, gībi‿lfanagīn maꜥāki! - anhi fanagīn?11. ya Samīr, lāzim tixallaṣ šuġlak ʾablᵊ ma‿ṣḥābak yīgu! 12. kullᵊ ma yīgi yiḥki‿ḥkayāt ġarība. 13. ilʾaṭrᵊ ma-byuʾafšᵊ ġēr fi‿lmaḥaṭṭāt ikkibīra. 14. miš ꜥāyiz asāfir illa law safirtᵊ ~ gēt mꜥāya. 15. Mirvat wi Hāla baṣṣu‿l baꜥdᵊ min ġēr ma yitkallimu ~ min ġēr kalam. 16. ma-biykallimšᵊ ġēr innās illi‿byiꜥṛafhum kuwayyis. 17. lāzim nidris sabaꜥ mawād fi‿ggamꜥa‿ssanādi. 18. wiṣil ittaṭawwur iliqtiṣādi li-mustawa ꜥāli. 19. ꜥagabitu min ʾawwil ~ min sāꜥit ~ min yōm ma šafha. 20. ma-ḥaddiš ġērak gayy innahaṛda.

INDEX